The Moment of Existence

ROBERT CRAFT

The Moment
of Existence

☙

Music, Literature, and the Arts
1990–1995

Vanderbilt University Press • *Nashville and London*

This publication is made from recycled paper and meets the minimum requirements of American National Standard for Information Sciences—Permanence of Paper for Printed Library Materials.

∞

The author and Vanderbilt University Press wish to thank the following publishers for permission to include those pieces originally published, in part or in whole, in their journals.

Chicago Tribune: "Against Interpretation," "Rosen's Romantics."

New York Review of Books: "Uncle Whiz," "His Ewe Lamb," "Words for Music Perhaps," "Huxley in Hollywood," "Dangerous for Ordinary People," "Great Dane," "Austria's Negative Poet Laureate," "Bali B'hai," "Paul Bowles's Pipe Dreams," "Who Savoureth Musicke," "Women Musicians of Venice and the Red Priest," "'A Certain Sigr Mozzart,'" "Love in a Cold Climate," "Furtwängler's Compromise."

Times Literary Supplement: "Dictionary of Divas."

Washington Post Book World: "T. S. Eliot's Cambridge Lectures," "Isaiah Berlin's Philosophical Bestiary," "At Play in the Fields of the Mind," "Con Molto Spirito," "Martha Graham and the Poetry of Motion," "Tycoons at the Musical Top," "'A Certain Sigr Mozzart,'" "Diaghilev," "Massine Centenary."

Library of Congress Cataloging-in-Publication Data

Craft, Robert.
The Moment of existence : music, literature, and the arts 1990–1995 / by Robert Craft.
p.   cm.
Includes bibliographical references and index.
ISBN 0-8265-1276-3 (cl : alk. paper)
1. Arts. I. Title.
NX65.C75 1996   95-52713
700' .9'049--dc20   CIP

Published by Vanderbilt University Press
Printed in the United States of America

With Love to Alva

Contents

The Arts

Preface

"Song is praise of the creator; it completely expresses the moment of existence," or so Johann Wilhelm Ritter, the philosopher and physicist (he discovered ultraviolet rays), wrote in 1810. In the pages that follow I try to identify moments of existence, of creative afflatus, in music, poetry and fiction, and the visual arts. The rest is context—biography, explanation, rhetoric, analysis.

We live momently, from one to the next. But Ritter's "moment" has shrunk to Robert Graves's "momentariness." His exhortation, "Take your delight in momentariness," is a built-in message of this book.

With few exceptions the writings collected here are topical, their subjects well-advertised events and publications of the first half of the 1990s. To some extent their topicality and unity in time holds them together. The essays are addressed to general readers with a special interest in music and literature. (I do not mention the "visual arts" here for the reason that the two essays on them are primarily concerned with kinds of *writing* about art, by Updike, Ashbery, and Robert Hughes, in the first instance, and by assorted authorities on Italian Renaissance painting in the second.)

The most extensive literary pieces explore two Continental European authors who became widely known in English during the early part of the decade: Jens Peter Jacobsen, the Danish poet, novelist, and translator of Darwin; and Thomas Bernhard, the Austrian novelist and playwright who died prematurely in 1989. Bernhard's savage irony is often hilarious, and laughter, as Hobbes said, is "sudden joy," but on every count Bernhard is one of the representative and most innovative writers of our age. English readers have been able to savor the gentler irony and the many other delectable qualities of Jacobsen only recently, thanks to an excellent translation of his novel *Niels Lyhne*. Joyce regarded him as one of the great writers of the latter half of the nineteenth century.

Of the two American authors to whom I have accorded the most space, Paul Bowles was a best-selling novelist and short-story writer at the end of the 1940s, after which he virtually disappeared until recognized in the nineties as a founding father of the drugs-and-violence culture. My essay on his work may have contributed marginally to the rediscovery of his fiction, but perhaps more to kindling the curiosity in his music that eventuated in the festival devoted to it in New York in September 1995. The real impetus behind the Bowles boom, however, was the R-rated film of his novel *The Sheltering Sky*, rather than the novel itself or any writing by or about its author. Like Bowles, Colin McPhee, the other American (Canadian-born) writer discussed here at some length, was a composer first (and last), but, unlike him, was and is better known for his music than his writing; I believe, nevertheless, and McPhee himself ultimately realized, that his verbal talent was his more natural and greater gift. His redis-covered, reprinted, and herein re-reviewed book is a minor masterpiece.

I cannot classify by country the only major writer examined close-up, W. H. Auden, for the reason that he is both English and American, and at the same time neither. (T. S. Eliot, when questioned as to which of these categories he belonged, replied wryly that "whichever Wystan Auden is, I am the other.") My three Auden pieces responded to important first publications dating from the early 1990s; the revival of popular interest in his work came slightly later and, as in Bowles's case, thanks to a film, *Four Weddings and a Funeral.* I begin the book with Auden because I find his *Table Talk* (and splutterings) both brilliant and funny—the latter often unintentionally—for which reason my review consists largely of quotations; *Table Talk* was relegated to the under-the-counter cate-gory on publication, henceforth spoken of only in whispers, and it is still cer-tain to raise the superciliaries of even the broadest minded. I can claim a smidgen of personal involvement in some of the subject matter of the third Auden article.

The late Philip Larkin titled his essays *Required Writings*, meaning by it that he wrote only at the request of editors and for a price. In contrast, the choices of subjects in the present collection were my own, though space constraints in some cases prescribed the length. In this sense, as well as others, the book rep-resents my primary interests and tastes. Some of these are in the visual arts; a companion volume to this one, *About Must, and About Must Go*, a chronicle of my travels during the composition of these essays, reveals that much of my time abroad is spent in museums. In our specialized age, a diversity of interests—music, dance, painting, poetry, fiction, political philosophy (the essay on Isaiah Berlin)—may be suspect, but my criticism will have to and, I think, can stand on its own.

The principal event in music during the early nineties was the world-wide celebration of two centuries of Mozart. Since I am old enough to have partici-pated as a performer in the bicentennial of his birth, my essay on the one mark-ing his death may seem to dwell on the cruel brevity of his life. My reviews of the principal Mozart books published in the quinquenniade are supplemented by my first-person account of the festivities in New York and in Vienna. The result is the longest, but factually perhaps the most interesting, of the arts essays.

The short guide to five works by Schoenberg is designed for readers with an interest in his music but no handle on its technical aspects, still less with the argot employed to describe them. The three short lectures on Stravinsky, one of them written for and read at Vanderbilt University's Blair School of Music in November 1994, range from biography to music history; all three are published here for the first time. Most readers will remark on their own that my two twentieth-century composers occupy the same pre-eminent positions at the end of the period as they did near the beginning of it, and that no composer of comparable stature has come within sight. Influence and imitation notwithstanding, *Pierrot Lunaire* and *The Rite of Spring* have lost none of their spell; indeed, the better we know them the more their dimensions expand. But the book does not ignore more recent developments. The final item includes a thumbnail analysis of two of the most notable as well as radically dissimilar composers of the period, Elliott Carter and Philip Glass.

The art of ballet receives less space than I would have liked, partly because of editors' restrictions, partly because I know less about it. All the same, one of the events of the half-decade, the death of Martha Graham, is discussed here, together with a roughshod resumé of her achievements. The biography of Massine and the book on Diaghilev present the great impresario in a new, much larger light, both as artistic genius and magisterial entrepreneur. A contribution to background knowledge of the ballet *Agon* comprises the latter part of my discourse on one of the idiosyncrasies of Stravinsky's composing method.

The two essays on the visual arts are no less representative of the period, however limited my spectrum. The first of them exposes, if only incidentally, the deplorable supersession of the critic over the maker (and, *mutatis mutandis,* of the performer over the composer) in the present-day world of art. The second, which cost me more labor in reading, in struggling with Italian dictionaries and texts, and in footwork—standing in line in Arezzo and at the Istituto Restauro in Rome, and climbing hills in the rain at Monterchi to see the restored and newly presented (disastrously in both cases) *Madonna del Parto*—celebrates the 500th anniversary of one of the greatest painters.

I hope that some of these essays survive long enough to provide a measure for the different perspectives at the turn of the new and unimaginable millennium. For myself, I look longingly two millennia backward to the five-year purification ritual of ancient Rome.

I wish to acknowledge gratefully the work of the editors of the reviews that first published many of these pieces, especially Barbara Epstein of the *New York Review of Books*, Michael Dirda and Dennis Drabelle of *Book World* (the *Washington Post*), and Larry Kart of the *Chicago Tribune*. I am indebted to my sister, Phyllis Crawford, for numerous suggested improvements. I would also like to thank those at Vanderbilt University Press, especially the editor, Bard Young, and Vanderbilt's talented designer, Gary Gore, who helped to make of these many pieces the one book.

R. C. 10/8/95

I
❧ Literature

Uncle Whiz

ystan Auden's obiter dicta, as heard and transcribed by Alan Ansen, [1] are funny, brilliant, outrageous. Anyone who knew the poet—in my own case very slightly compared to Ansen—must agree that the voice rings as true as the often preposterous pronouncements, whose authenticity is verified not only by the exclusion principle that no one else could have made them up, but also by the word-of-mouth survival of some of them in Auden lore.

Alan Ansen met WHA in 1946, while the poet was lecturing at the New School for Social Research, and subsequently became his secretary. At age twenty-four, Ansen seems to have had a prodigious knowledge of ancient and modern languages and literatures, as well as near-verbatim recall. Though about half of the entries are printed in dialogue form, the others as monologues, the young philologist is intrusive only on questions of scansion ("In 'heavy like us' you could save the alliteration by syncopating the *ke* and positing the *k* as the fourth alliterating letter"), and he credits his own most recondite contributions only indirectly, through Auden's responses: "Oh, did Hobbes do a translation of Thucydides?"; "You're right, Landor's epigrams do represent a further use of Greek models."

The stream-of-consciousness sequence of subjects appears to have been preserved. But Auden's "baltering torrent" (Joyce's "irruent") better describes both the jumble of ideas later to be processed into essays and poems, and the reader's sense of a lonely man's exuberance in finding a receptive listener: Auden sounds "high" most of the time, hyperventilated by his own wit and intelligence. A typical entry (May 17, 1947; the other thirty are dated between November 1946 and April 1948) jumps from Rimbaud to Churchill, the rutting season of tom cats ("they have a rugged time of it trying to service so many ladies"), a projected guide to England, book reviewing, and the artist Paul Cadmus. But the startling juxtapositions and droll non sequiturs help to establish

---

[1] *The Table Talk of W. H. Auden,* by Alan Ansen, edited by Nicholas Jenkins. Introduction by Richard Howard. New York: Sea Cliff, 1990.

the reader's sense of being in the poet's company. In addition to bits of background—occasion and location, the contents and condition of Auden's apartment, the kinds and quantities of drinks consumed—Ansen provides a sprinkling of parenthetical stage directions ("smiling mysteriously," "to the cat," "to me," "looking it up in the *OED* and finding he was right") and clues to enigmatic references: "If you want special knowledge, there's just one place to get it from. (*Presumably himself.*)"

The discussions alight most frequently on literary, sexual, political (antidisestablishmentarian), and religious matters ("I'm coming to doubt whether [Dante] really was a Christian"), leavened with gossip ("Did you see that Mary McCarthy has joined the anti-Homintern?"), snippets of autobiography ("My mother used to get ill every time I came home, which gives you some idea of the relation between us"), and observations on American and European differences of decorum ("For an Englishman coming over here to teach, the rudeness of the students is quite shocking"; "Chester [Kallman] thinks that when I expect him to get a cab for us it's because I'm me, when it isn't at all. It's simply what an older person expects from a younger one"). A high proportion of Auden's conceits takes the form of fiats and caveats beginning "All," "Everyone," "No one," "The only": "The only way to spend New Year's Eve is either quietly with friends or in a brothel"; "Americans ought to live in Europe."

As anticipated, the Auden of 1947 seems not to have been a pioneering feminist—"Women should be quiet. When people [!] are talking, they ought to retire to the kitchen"—or indeed a man of "progressive" views in other respects. "I am a convinced monarchist," the newly-sworn U.S. citizen announces. "Why doesn't the United States take over the monarchy and unite with England?... At least you could use it as a summer resort instead of Maine." Contradictions of a sort arise, as when he disapproves of "the American practice of allowing one partner to a homosexual act to remain passive—it's so undemocratic," and at the same time defends the supposedly "European" view that "the lower classes simply ought to go to bed when asked."

The American presidents, Lincoln excepted, and Taft, because "he was so fat," do not make a favorable impression. "Jefferson, I think, must have been a great bore," and "One wonders whether Roosevelt developed paralysis in order to become President.... No one really good can get to occupy the position he did." To be taken more seriously are the comments on American social distinctions: Americans who like Samuel Johnson tend to be "nasty types of Anglophiles who think they have to be rude and are usually Republicans"; "the important thing in America is not to have money but to have had it."

Table Talk suggests that Auden's famous Francophobia became more rabid with World War II: at the beginning of it the French "lie down like a doormat, and afterward they're meanly vindictive … using German prisoners of war as slave labor." Kallman, the Italo- and Germanophile, operatically speaking, seems to have fueled the prejudice. Even so, Auden's real trouble with the French is "their terrible Cartesianism. To them, you agree or you don't agree. And that's perfectly logical. But it doesn't find any place for the irrational element which is always present." Baudelaire "was absolutely right when he talked about *'l'esprit de Voltaire.'*" (What Baudelaire actually said was *"Je m'ennui en France, surtout parce que tout le monde ressemble à Voltaire."*) But Auden's shocker on the subject, clearly intended as such, occurs in his introduction to the *Viking Portable Greek Reader*: "The Crucifixion was actually performed by the Romans, or, to make it contemporary, by the French." One pictures him trying this out on Kallman, for whose amusement he probably concocted it in the first place.

French literature, despite Pascal's "wonderfully malicious *Provincial Letters*," Balzac, "a great writer on money," the "extraordinarily clever" Cocteau and the "very intelligent" Valéry, also leaves much to be desired. "I don't like Montaigne at all." (But the *New Year Letter* dedication borrows an epigraph from him.) La Rochefoucauld "simply says what one has always known." (Yes, but without him some of us would not have known that we knew.) Flaubert's pre-*Bouvard et Pécuchet* novels "are so dull." Verlaine "wasn't so good." Gide is "really commonplace"; imagine "getting off with this Arab boy [and] stopping to say, *'Que le sable était beau.'*" Even Racine "isn't quite so fine as people say," while Mark Twain [!], bad as he was ("I've read two books … and I don't want to read any more"), is "at least better than Corneille."

Auden's best bon mot about music is apparently unintentional: the *Kyrie* in the B-minor Mass is "marvelous for the first two [78 RPM] sides, and then you realize he's going on with the thing to the bitter end." But then, Bach is a mere "Alpha" composer, in comparison to "the Alpha plus" Mozart. In any case, Auden's musical interests, as indicated here, are virtually confined to opera, even though "the characters always manage to fall in love with unsuitable people." *Tristan and Isolde* should not be "done" by "hetties" but by "lizzies." "They eat each other up, try to replace the world. Isolde is the English Mistress, Tristan the Hockey Mistress…. Neither extreme, Tristan or Don Giovanni"—the Don being "a certain type of male homosexual"—is "compatible with heterosexual love." Auden abominates Brahms—"Whenever I hear a peculiarly obnoxious combination of sounds, I spot it as Brahms and I'm right every time"—but likes Liszt: "The opening of the *Totentanz* is so good. (*Sang* it.) But why does MGM hire people to write music for them? Liszt has done it so well already."

Auden's thoughts about Greek literature, expressed shortly before he began to compile his anthology, should be read more closely than anything else in the book, together with the passages on English prosody, too specialized for discussion here. The most remarkable feature of Greek civilization is not, as we might have expected, the inquiring, skeptical intelligence and the unities of abstract and concrete thought and feeling, but "the use of hypothesis in every subject." What most puzzles is "their failure to see the importance of freedom of choice," and their apparent indifference to the question of existence. What *did* the Greeks believe? "I'm not talking about the Roman period when it was generally held that the gods were allegorical personifications, but when people were serious about following the ritual. And yet they didn't seem to care whether their deities existed or not...." The anthology essay bypasses the difficulty: "The kind of god who is both self-sufficient and content to remain so could not interest us enough to raise the question of his existence." But another crucial question remains unanswered: "I don't see how Plato reconciled the Demiurge of the *Timaeus* with the vision of Er at the end of *The Republic* with its system of rewards and punishments. How far did he believe in either of them?"

The published Greek anthology lacks the variety and scope of the outline as exposed in *Table Talk*, which includes the thirteenth chapter of *Corinthians* and the *Romans*. Thucydides, not Aristotle, is Plato's "real rival." Auden may have downgraded Aristotle partly because "I don't think [he] really liked poetry. I think he had a wife who liked to go to the theater and came home raving about the latest play." Unlike Aristotle and Plato—"a man of genius who's always wrong"—Thucydides "did not deify the state but regarded it as a convenience." Part of Auden's exalted opinion of the Atomists ("the people I really like") seems to derive, *a rovescio*, from their influence on Thucydides.

Some of Auden's Petrine judgments on poetry are familiar: "Blake's longer poems won't do"; with exceptions, Browning's lyrics are "atrocious"; "*Twelfth Night* is really a very nasty play.... Oh yes, it's well written all right"; "I'd leave *Coriolanus* to the French"; *Antony and Cleopatra* is "much better poetry" than *The Tempest*: "It has to be; they've nothing else to live on." Pope is "the real test of liking English poetry.... *The Rape of the Lock* is the most perfect poem in English.... Some of his lines are wonderful—'Bare the mean Heart that lurks beneath a Star.'" And *The Prelude* is "a marvelous work.... My landscapes aren't really the same as Wordsworth's. Mine ... come from books first."

Auden mentions Eliot more frequently than any other poet, but largely to distance himself: the difference between us is that "he thinks ... society can be made into something good." But other differences surface as well: "I certainly disagree with Milton's beliefs as much as Eliot does, but that doesn't put me off the poetry ... his unfavorable estimate prompted me to read Milton and find out how good he was." (Elsewhere Auden illustrates the four stresses of the basic English line with "In *hideous ruin* and *combustion down*.") Still, "Eliot does realize his danger of falling into a Manichaean condemnation of the flesh per se. But our poetry is the product of our feelings. There's an awfully revealing anecdote about Eliot. A woman who was seated next to him at table said, 'Isn't the party wonderful?' He said, 'Yes, if you see the essential horror of it all.'"

Auden's sex talk is largely directed toward Kallman, the absent philanderer: "Sexual fidelity is more important in a homosexual relationship than in any other [where] there are a variety of ties. But here, fidelity is the only bond." And with a papal gesture he divides the world into oral and anal. "Americans are violently oral," this practitioner of buccal coition says. "Even the American passion for laxatives can be explained as an oral manifestation. They want to get rid of any unpleasantness taken in through the mouth.... America is a very queer country." Ultimately he decides that "it's wrong to be queer," mainly because "all homosexual acts are acts of envy." (Not elucidated.) Perhaps with this in mind he resolves to "lead the life of a monk this summer, an absolute monk. Oh, one may drop in on a party for half an hour and eye it coldly with one's lorgnette."

* * *

Auden is the focal figure in the first part of Harold Norse's autobiography.[2] They were introduced by Kallman who, without Auden's "stupendous gift" in sharing honors as librettist of *The Rake's Progress*, would have remained "an obscure minor poet writing inpenetrable verse in metrical feet of clay." But would Auden have undertaken a full-length libretto without the help of his opera-mad companion? Ansen, who typed the first manuscript version of the opera, does not say.

As Auden's secretary at an earlier period than Ansen, Norse must also have had opportunities to record talk, but chose instead to dramatize his quarry, most extensively in an icky tale of attempted seduction (Auden hovered "over me ... stark naked ... behaving like a klutz"), and in a version of an argument in a subway between Auden and Kallman as to which one, in their psychological role-enacting, was the other's father or mother; perhaps the acclaimed portrayal of the young Auden in *Once in a While the Odd Thing Happens*, the London stage version of the beginning of the Benjamin Britten-Peter Pears love affair, could mean that "*Wystan and Chester*" will soon follow *Tom and Viv*, *Harold and Vita*. But Norse's accounts of Auden's irascible moods and of his upper middle-class snobbery are accurate.

[2] *Memoirs of a Bastard Angel*, by Harold Norse. New York. W. Morrow, 1989.

The first volume of *Auden Studies*[3] publishes six of the poet's love lyrics written in student German; eleven letters to Stephen Spender; six letters (from the forthcoming complete correspondence) to Professor (*The Greeks and the Irrational*) and Mrs. E. R. Dodds, friends of Auden from about 1928; the "Writing" essay of 1932, for the first time as originally written, complete and unedited; and a number of critical pieces. The letters to Spender show that Auden's critical faculties were highly developed at twenty-three, along with his didactic and dogmatic tendencies: "All poetry in our time is comic. There are two modes...."

A few years later Auden defines himself to Spender as "a parabolic writer," as distinguished from "a realist like Christopher" Isherwood, and identifies his "dominant faculties" as "intellect and intuition," his subordinate ones as "feeling and sensation." In the last letter included here, self-analysis sometimes sounds like self-accusation, as when, through the discovery of weaknesses in "X.'s" (Kallman's) character, Auden, now forty-four, realizes that "what I had imagined was affection and good-will on my part was really a devouring passion for possession." But Auden's toughness on himself was always one of his most admirable qualities.

The critical essays explore terra incognita, enough of it to indicate that much more remains. John Bridgen writes on the influence of Frank McEachran, one of the early teen-ager's teachers. John Fuller reflects on Flaubert as Auden's model—except when he was dismissing *"le mot juste"* as exhibitionistic—of the artist in relation to society. Katherine Bucknell's notes on the "Writing" essay examine the considerable influence of Gerald Heard, the BBC sage and, later, in California and Arizona, the prophet, drug culturalist, mystery writer (H. F. Heard), and guru to, among others, Frank Lloyd Wright and the *Time-Life* Luces.

Dissenting from both Freud and Malinowski, Heard maintained that hunger is the strongest instinct in the primal group, and that group life, based on food and companionship, was more stable than, and did not evolve from, family life, which in fact was the root of social revolution. However this may be, the Heard mythology was a liberating one for the budding poet who had accepted the dispute between father and son as the origin of culture, and attributed his sexual and psychological ills to relationships in his own family. (I can testify that as late as the 1960s, meals in Heard's Pacific Palisades home preserved something of his idea of the liturgical character of primal group life, from hand-holding to the share-alike distribution of food—seeds, grains, nuts, raw vegetables, fruit.)

---

[3] *The Map of All My Youth: Early Works, Friends and Influences. Auden Studies I,* edited by Katherine Bucknell and Nicholas Jenkins. New York: Oxford University Press, 1990.

* * *

"I think that poetry is fundamentally frivolity," Auden says in *Table Talk*. "I do it because I like it. The only serious thing is loving God and"—what a true philadelphian he was!—"your neighbor." This deordination of the poet is the subject of Lucy McDiarmid's *Auden's Apologies For Poetry*."[4] The poetics of the later Auden, she writes, is "a poetics of apology and self-deprecation, a radical undermining of poetry itself. Every major poem and every major essay became a *retractio*, a statement of art's frivolity, vanity, and guilt." The later, "baggy-pants" Auden, as she calls him, reduces poetry to the status of a game played with words, a game that has little to do with "the real feelings of WHA." These real feelings "get into the poem only when Auden insists on poetry's inability to talk about them." The poem ending with the lines " ... love, or truth in any serious sense, / Like orthodoxy is a reticence," must end where it does, since to say more would be unreticent.

Whereas the young Auden had "attributed great powers to art," going so far as to hope that it could "teach man to unlearn hatred and learn love," and that poetry should "move our emotions or excite our intellect," the older Auden became obsessed with delimiting these powers, establishing the ontological boundaries that poetry cannot cross. Unlike *The Tempest*, which is "full of dissolving borders," the "actors that melt into thin air, the morning that 'steals upon the night / melting the darkness,'" Auden's later poems are "full of absolute borders."

What, besides the emigration to New York, the affair with Kallman, the War, and the return to religion (reading theology, attending church) led up to the 1939 manifesto that "poetry cannot make anything happen"? McDiarmid's answer is the shift from space to time, from the travels of the 1930s to the realization that writing begins with the sense of separateness in time (*Another Time* and *For the Time Being*), and the literate mode from the oral, which Auden had seemed to believe could effect spiritual change in the listener. We write because we "feel alone," he said, "cut off from each other." Books "are like people, and make the same demands on us to understand and like them."

Above all, poetry cannot induce the requital of love, Auden's real-life longing "to be loved alone," as he wrote in "September 1939." In *Table Talk*, the remark that Shakespeare left *The Tempest* "in a mess" means *not* in a lustrum of love and forgiveness, but in disingenuousness and theatrical trumpery; "what a lot a little music can do," he says, in *The Sea and the Mirror*. McDiarmid convincingly

---

[4] Princeton, N.J.: Princeton University Press, 1990.

argues that love in Auden's "later poetics [is] a literary subject but never an emotion...."

In a well-known homiletic on the nature of human egoism, Auden remarks that humility is easier for a poet or novelist to acquire than for a critic, since the creative writer's subject matter is "life in general," the critic's mere authors, human individuals. To say that "life is more important than anything I can say about it" is easier than to say, "Mr. A.'s work is more important than anything I can say about it." But in an age of the usurpation of creation by criticism, is the critic's subject matter really limited to authors, and does the critic think of his or her work in relation to degrees of "importance"?

Auden continued to publish his performances in poetry—claiming no more for them than that they *were* performances—out of pride in his art, whether or not this was more than pride in his mastery of means: "Every poet thinks of himself as a craftsman, a maker of verbal objects: what he hopes for is that critics will notice the technical means by which he secures his effects." But he acknowledges this small sin against humility in his great invocation, "At the Grave of Henry James": "Pray for me, and for all writers, / living or dead [...] because there is no end / To the vanity of our calling...."

His Ewe Lamb

Thekla Clark[1] describes herself as "a giddy young woman ... no intellectual," and "aggressively heterosexual," not the ideal qualifications for the subject, one would have thought, quite wrongly. Her portraits of both Auden and Kallman are truer and, in a seemingly offhand manner, as penetrating as any of those by their other memoirist friends. Adding to her non-aptitudes, Mrs. Clark claims to be unmusical, yet she perfectly catches the nuances and intonations of Wystan's and Chester's voices, simply, as their friends would have to attest, by quoting them believably.

The first third of the narrative takes place in Ischia in the early 1950s, the remainder in Kirchstetten between 1960 and Auden's death in 1973. After the author's marriage to John Clark, her house in Florence provided Wystan and Chester respite from Lower Austria as well as, more often than not, from each other. The Italian years were comparatively idyllic for the two poets, and a time of "suspended innocence" for the twenty-four-year-old woman from Oklahoma. The Austrian period began auspiciously; Wystan was happy at last to have his own home, and Vienna, only a short drive away, was one of the world's great opera centers. But separations were frequent and Wystan, during the months that he stayed in New York, grew increasingly lonely. Soon Chester met and became infatuated with Yannis Boras, a twenty-one-year-old Greek who would become his lover for the next five years, until his untimely death in an automobile accident. Mrs. Clark suggests, plausibly, that the failure of the opera, *Elegy for Young Lovers*, whose libretto was largely Chester's work, precipitated his eventual move to Athens, and hence away from hostile reviewers in London and New York. Chester, looking for another Yannis, was seldom thereafter without a young Greek companion.

Mrs. Clark publishes excerpts from a handful of Wystan's letters to her, one of them containing the first version of his poem "For Friends Only," and many more of them from Chester, who in this book emerges for the first time as a per-

---

[1] *Wystan and Chester: A Personal Memoir of W. H. Auden and Chester Kallman*, by Thekla Clark, Introduction by James Fenton. London and New York: Faber & Faber, 1995.

son with dimensions of his own apart from his partnership with Auden. Chester's early communications from Kirchstetten are upbeat and divertingly campy. The later ones from there, and more so those from Athens, expose a disturbed state of mind, even, when he begins to refer to Boras as a saint and himself as his "voice on earth," a psychotic one. Once when she was delinquent in writing to Chester, this always remiss correspondent told her, "one begins to brood that one has left an *offesa* behind.... I'm just an amateur paranoid, but I have my little twitches." One of his communications from Athens ends: "And so I'm incoherent.... I'll bore you further when I see you." He "knew he was being criticized," Mrs. Clark remarks, "judged both for himself and for what some considered his effect on Wystan." Many thought that Chester, "as the lesser talent, should sacrifice himself to the greater," and should feel content "to be the power behind the throne." Clearly Chester felt that he was the focus of an odium, partly as a result of his having lost his "Lana Turner looks." By this time "dependence on drink and casual sex (the more degrading the better) were no longer reversible," but at an unspecified earlier date he had already begun to drink ouzo at breakfast and was never, ever, entirely sober.

As Chester's life disintegrated, Thekla Clark became an intermediary between him and Wystan, who did not even know how to reach Chester in Athens. "Naughty Chester has, of course, not written ...," one of Wystan's letters begins, and a later letter, "I entirely agree with your feelings about Chester's mental condition. Incidentally, if you know his new Athens address, please send it. Am in despair because all appeals ... have been fruitless...." Chester, she writes, "gradually slipped away from us all."

Chester "could never accept the person he was, so could never become the person he should be," and "needed wishes and fantasies to soften the self-despair." How, Mrs. Clark asks, could Chester, who "agonized over sleights" real and imagined, "ever have forgiven his father," who constantly put him down in public? Here it must be said that no Auden biographer has shown Chester as much sympathy as Thekla Clark, or given him as much hospitality, which, despite her disclaimers, cannot always have been that much fun. He once lived alone with the Clarks in their Florence home for as long as two months, and at other times stayed there with one or another of his Greek friends: the book includes a droll photo of Chester against the Tuscan background gazing admiringly upon a splendidly kilted and tasseled Evzone Royal Guardsman.

Neither Wystan nor Chester could "recognize each other's vulnerability. Each thought the other could take it, and sometimes they went too far." But the combatants were not evenly matched. "As a devout Christian, [Wystan] was satisfied to let 'Miss God' pardon him. Chester as a romantic atheist couldn't."

Even in the early years "Chester would say things like 'writing in Wystan's shadow.'" Mrs. Clark quickly understood that the two were happiest when collaborating on librettos. "Chester felt that the partnership was equal, or nearly so, and Wystan delighted in Chester's serenity." This last phrase identifies the most important ingredient in the collaboration.

Mrs. Clark delineates some of the opposites in the partners' characters and tastes. When telling a story, Chester was a performer, exercising his considerable thespian talent, whereas Wystan was a dismal raconteur. Moreover, Wystan's letters were short and "rather dull," while Chester wrote "long, revealing, honest, and enormously amusing ones." Wystan was attracted by some women, but Chester was not. Wystan believed that homosexuality was wrong, while Chester regarded it as "beautiful and morally right." Wystan "wanted a certain blond beauty in his lovers," but Chester's tastes "ran to beetle brows."

Wystan and Chester contributes richly to Auden mythology. Mrs. Clark says that in the course of her "long and detailed gynecological discussions" with Wystan, he confessed to being jealous of her womb, and on one occasion observed to her that "you are so fortunate to have all your reproductive organs inside you ... not these ridiculous things I find attached to me as an afterthought." That he saw himself as at least partly female is evident from another story. In April 1968, momentarily losing control of his car, he swerved into a telegraph pole, fracturing his right shoulder. Seeing what was coming, he said, "No, no! He couldn't, not to His ewe lamb."

On her second visit to Ischia, Thekla brought her four-year-old daughter, Lisa, with her. One night when Thekla was entertaining guests, "Lisa kept coming into the room in her nightie, until Wystan said, 'My dear, you are not wanted now,' and she did not return." The next day, as a reward, Wystan removed his dentures for her. Later, reading a fairy tale to her from Andrew Lang's collection, Wystan told her that it should be believed because it was "based on ritual and myth," but "Lisa agreed to believe it only if Wystan would take his teeth out again."

The book's best anecdote, however, is in Wystan's remark, after a sticky visit to Bernard Berenson at "I Tatti," his villa near Florence: "How perfect everything was. I longed to slip a satin pillow with 'Souvenir of Atlantic City' into the place."

Auden disapproved of any show of affection in public, including T. S. Eliot's hand-holding and mooning over his young wife. When Mrs. Clark defended Eliot, Auden ruled, in his *dixit* W.H.A. manner, that "happiness, like grief, should be private," with which, later in the book, an unintimidated Mrs. Clark disagrees: "Some grief can be shared." The story she tells of Auden's Ischia houseboy, Giocondo, exemplifies the absent-mindedness with which Auden sometimes managed his business affairs. He sent a check for expenses to this factotum but mistakenly added a zero too many. Discovering his error, he sent a second one for the correct amount, instructing him to destroy the first. Instead, Giocondo tried to cash both of them, but the account lacked sufficient funds to cover the ten-times-larger sum. When the banker understood what had happened, Giocondo tried to cover his attempted theft by saying—"viciously," Mrs. Clark writes—that the larger check was for "services rendered."

Auden's motive in moving to America, the author believes, was the hope that it "would bring out the best in him." Two years after the move, he met Chester, who was "not only beauty ... he was America." Wystan was never an American, she rightly maintains. He never adjusted to American behavior, or to the rapidity of change in American life, and "when he dreamed of 'home' the landscape was British and the food always nursery." But he did grow to love New York. Mrs. Clark is a sharp critic of certain American types herself, among them an "exhaustingly *au courant*" young couple who attended one of her Florentine parties, and an academic-minded boyfriend, "with that think-tank look ... dressed with studied casualness" and exuding "pure essence of California." When he asked Wystan if he had ever done anything that would send him to hell, the eschatological poet's memorable reply was, "I should leave that to higher authorities."

The book is not without a few errors and oversights. Mrs. Clark neglects to say that Chester sometimes stammered (as Edmund Wilson noted in his diary on meeting him in New York in December 1959). As for mistakes of fact, Carlos Chávez (not Carlo Chavéz) composed the music for Kallman's *The Tuscan Women*. Finally, I would like to have read even a word of Mrs. Clark's on Auden's reaction to Stravinsky's death, since he learned of it in her Florentine home and cabled the widow from there. Auden was the composer's last longtime friend to see him alive.

Words for Music Perhaps

Most opera libretti have only a marginal existence apart from the music they inspire. Monteverdi's Striggio; Lully's Quinault; Cavalli's Faustini; Gluck's Calzabigi; Mozart's Metastasio (if not his Da Ponte); Bellini's Romani; Rossini's Foppa and Sterbini; Verdi's Piave, Somma, and Ghislanzoni; Puccini's Illica and Giacoso are known almost exclusively through their composer-collaborators. If their libretti are read at all, it is as cribs, before, between the acts of, and while listening to operas, not as examples of a literary genre. Yet some of the exceptions are major: the young Voltaire and Rameau; Boito and Verdi; the composer-librettists Berg and Wagner: by way of *The Wasteland*, the Steersman's song in *Tristan* is perhaps the best-known German verse in the English-speaking world. In the twentieth century, Hugo von Hofmannsthal and Wystan Hugh Auden are the only writers of high achievement outside the opera house to have attained distinction in it as well.

Edward Mendelson's compendious and invaluable edition of libretti written by W. H. Auden, and Auden and Chester Kallman,[1] necessarily revises our perspectives of the poet, since heretofore his libretti have been the least understood part of his work, his career in music-related *bricolage*, which was a substantial one, the least known: the songs contributed to other people's plays; the translations from Goldoni, Da Ponte, Brecht; the unused show-biz lyrics (for, too good for, *Man of La Mancha*); the commentaries for documentary films; the adaptations of fiction for radio plays (*Pride and Prejudice*, D. H. Lawrence's "The Rocking Horse Winner"); the failed partnerships, notably with Brecht on Webster's *Duchess of Malfi*.

Collaborating with Henry Purcell on *King Arthur*, John Dryden complained of having to "cramp" his verses, but he accepted the constriction because "operas are principally designed for the ear and the eye.... My art ought to be subservient to his"—to which Mozart added, a century later, "Poetry absolutely has

---

[1] *W. H. Auden and Chester Kallman: Libretti and Other Dramatic Writings by W. H. Auden (1939–1973). The Complete Works of W. H. Auden: Vol. IV*, edited by Edward Mendelson. Princeton, N.J.: Princeton University Press, 1993.

to be the obedient daughter of music." At an opposite extreme, Pierre Corneille insisted that the true poet's inspiration "is powerless when it depends for utterance on the capricious tunes of a musical dreamer; when it must take its laws from his strange whims ... when rhymes must be adapted to every musical inflection." Rhyming verse, we should bear in mind, is the norm in seventeenth-century French poetic drama, as blank verse is in English, Dryden himself being the qualified exception: the dialogue in his early rhyming-couplet plays is widely thought to be more "natural" than the dialogue in his later blank-verse plays, of which *All for Love* is the most popular.

At the time of *The Rake's Progress*, begun in 1947 and completed in 1951, Auden and Kallman adopted Dryden's position, although soon afterward they moved toward Corneille's side, stating that the choice of subject, the construction of the plot, and the creation of the characters must be the librettist's prerogatives. The composer might be allowed to make cuts, but the "book" should be printed intact and as written. These conditions governed the librettists' later collaborations with Hans Werner Henze, most importantly on *The Bassarids*, their 1966 adaptation of Euripides' *The Bacchae*. In that opera, however, Henze's music obscures the rhythms of the strictly-metered lines and buries many of the words. In any event, clearly the music of the *Bassarids* was remote from anything the librettists had expected: Kallman had subtitled one number a Cabaletta, as if Henze, a young Schoenberg-school modernist might be itching to compose a pastiche of Donizetti.

The comments that follow will be directed chiefly to *The Rake's Progress*, for the reasons that it is the only one of the six Auden-Kallman operas to have entered the repertory, and the only one in which Auden's genius as poet and versifier perfectly suits the symmetries and balances of the composer's style. Perhaps I should declare a private reason, too: as a young man I was involved with the opera to the extent that Stravinsky would ask me to read aloud, over and over and at varying speeds, the lines of whichever aria, recitative, or ensemble he was about to set to music. He would then memorize them, a line or a couplet at a time, repeating them while walking about the house or when seated in his wife's car en route to a restaurant, movie, or doctor's appointment. Much of the vocabulary was unfamiliar to him, but he soon learned it and began to use it in conversation, charging me once with "dilatoriness," which sounded very odd from him. In setting words, he began by writing rhythms in musical notation above them, note-stems with beams indicating time-values, adding melodic or intervallic ideas as they occurred to him.

* * *

Auden's first and only unpartnered libretto, *Paul Bunyan*, was unavailable between the premiere of this "operetta for children" at Columbia University, May 1941, and 1976, three years after the poet's death, at which time Benjamin Britten, who had withdrawn the music from performance after the tepid New York reception, revised it. This version is now published in vocal score, and can be heard in a recording.[2] In at least one opinion, the music will not win the composer new admirers, and it must be admitted that the libretto shows weaknesses as well in, for example, the disproportionate amount of the narrative taken up with the lumberjacks' food (a "Cooks' Duet," a nine-stanza "Food Chorus") and the grousing thereon ("But I can't secrete saliva / At the thought of a screw-driver").

Still, the verse is accomplished and conveys Auden's high spirits during his travels in the American West with Chester Kallman in the summer of 1939. Auden described the operetta's rhymes as "Gilbertian," an odd model for the work that marks his exploration of outpost America ("In Arkansas / Where instead of Father they say Paw"), but the following stanza, Broadway refrain and New York "r" pronunciation apart, evokes Cole Porter as much as it does the great Savoyard:

> I would paint St. Sebastian the Martyr
> Or dig up the temples of Crete
> Or compose a D-major sonata
> But I guess that a guy gotta eat.

Paul Bunyan incorporates period-Americanisms: "Atta boy," "Scram," "Don't be a sap," Johnny is from "out in the sticks," and, charmingly, the trees think "how swell to be a chair." *Bunyan* also reveals the Auden of 1939 as still politically and socially committed. How perfect the targeting, the wit and skill of

> From a Pressure Group that says I am the Constitution,
> From those who say Patriotism and mean Persecution.
> From a Tolerance that is really inertia and disillusion....

When Bunyan, the giant, orders a jacket,

> The New England mills
> For months had no more unemployment ills.

Auden, too, showed considerable feeling for the ecology:

---

[2] London: Faber Music, 1988. Virgin Classics, CD VCD 7907 102.

The woods are cut down, and the young are grown old ...
No longer the logger shall hear in the Fall
The pine and the spruce and the sycamore call.

Mendelson publishes alternate versions and discarded fragments of early
drafts, among them some that seem superior to, or as good as, the verses ultimately used. Whatever else, the beginning of the original Prologue,

To begin with
Paul Bunyan is an American myth
A myth is a collective dream
Where all our nights and lives
Are not as lonely as they seem,
For each one adds a bit
And shares in it

is more direct than

Since the birth
Of the earth
Time has gone
On and on

which occurs later in the earlier text, and the varying line-lengths are more engaging. Only rarely, in any version, does the strain of finding the meaningful as
well as the musical ending show through.

Bunyan also contains passages that are genuinely memorable:

Some think they're strong, some think they're smart
Like butterflies they're pulled apart
America can break your heart.

Auden's infatuation with Chester Kallman antedates *Bunyan*, and the poet's
next theatrical-musical concoction—the music was a compilation of recorded
excerpts from Beethoven, Berlioz, Wagner, Tchaikovsky, and others—celebrates his companion's twenty-second birthday. *The Queen's Masque*, as Auden titled the scuzzy skit, written while Auden was contributing a column to
Commonweal under the pseudonym Didymus (double, pair, twosome), was performed on that occasion (January 7, 1943) in a private house in Ann Arbor—
Auden was then teaching at Swarthmore—where Kallman was a student of
English at the University of Michigan. The two longest speeches, in imperfect
German and French, are assigned to ghosts. The levity recalls a remote era:

La reine de belles fesses,
Anastase, m'a fait
Beaucoup, beaucoup de promesses

Au lit là-bas;
Pour Anastase j'ai perdu mon âme,
Elle m'a tué.
J'ai léché le cul de Madame....

Since Auden showed no particularly strong interest in opera before he met Chester Kallman, his conversion to its "high style" must be attributed to the young man's passion for it.[3] We suppose, but do not know for certain, that Auden had invited him to become his co-librettist before flying to California in November 1947 to draft the scenario of *The Rake's Progress* with Stravinsky, who had had the idea to base an opera on Hogarth's series of engravings when he saw an exhibition of them at the Chicago Art Institute in May 1947. In any case, the first emendation to the plot outline that was sent to the composer two days after the poet's return to New York may well have been Kallman's. The change switched the source of Tom Rakewell's sudden wealth from an inheritance bequeathed by a deceased father to one from a deceased but unknown uncle, thereby avoiding the pall of grief that would have confused the mood of the first scene. Kallman himself said that Rakewell's three wishes—for money, for happiness, and for a miracle that would make the fantastic machine, which is supposed to turn stones into bread, actually work—were among his contributions to the opera's plot. He must have been responsible as well for the designations of musical numbers, if only because Auden would have thought that such subtitles as "fugal chorus" and "voices in canon" trespassed on the composer's territory.

Perhaps, too, it was Kallman who noticed that the Faustian pact between Rakewell and Nick Shadow was missing from the draft of Act I sent to Stravinsky on January 16, 1948.[4] Nor was it sent with Act II on January 26, but only

---

[3] "I came rather late in life to an interest in operatic music; then, thanks above all to the enthusiasm and erudition of my friend and collaborator, Chester Kallman ... I became a real opera fan." *La Biennale di Venezia* (magazine), October 1951.

[4] Mendelson reports that when Auden sent the typescript of Act I to Stravinsky, the composer "was privately annoyed to learn that his opera had a co-librettist who was unknown to him." More exactly, Stravinsky was upset that Auden did not see fit to mention the question of a collaborator and instead presented him with a fait accompli: Kallman's and Auden's names share equal billing on the typescript's title page. One consequence of the triangulation was that it invalidated

two weeks later with Act III. The brevity with which the transaction between the two is concluded suggests that it was a late insert to remedy an oversight: the pact is not part of the original scenario. But the clarity and directness of the wording indicate that Auden wrote it: "Tell me, good Shadow, since born and bred in indigence, I am unacquainted with such matters, what wages you are accustomed to receive."

The contrast between his and Kallman's styles is never more striking than in Kallman's convoluted continuation of the scene, when Rakewell reasons that "all London shall be at her [his betrothed's] feet, for all London shall be mine, and what is mine must of needs at least adore what I must with all my being worship." It should be said, too, that the pact itself is dramatically incredible: Rakewell employs Shadow, whom he has never seen before and of whom he knows nothing, as his manservant, for a price to be disclosed "a year and a day hence."

Mendelson's sources in seeking to determine which librettist wrote what are the original Stravinsky-Auden draft of the scenario (November 1947), the authors' first and second typescripts of the full text (January–March 1948), and their surviving notebooks, work sheets, correspondence, interviews, and published commentaries about the opera. His intention is to establish "authorial" texts, free of apocryphal changes, by publishing each one as it was first sent to the composer. But in the case of the *Rake* he modifies this aim by allowing the inclusion of "revisions made by the librettists when preparing the second typescript"; "changes and additions made by the librettists while Stravinsky was composing the opera"; and "further changes made shortly after the premiere in 1951."[5]

These provisos, however, are not consistently observed. The text published here includes lines that had been superseded by the authors long before the premiere (Baba's "I am not in the habit of stepping from sedan chairs un-

the contract with the music publisher, and Stravinsky's attorney, Aaron Sapiro, advised him to protest. Later, seeing the complete libretto, Sapiro urged him not to compose the opera on grounds that he would be involving himself in a sexual hoax.

[5] Apropos the first performance, Mendelson remarks that "the weeks of rehearsal"—actually six days in Milan and five in Venice—"were frustrating ... mostly because of inequitable arrangements for the composer and the librettists.... Stravinsky lived in luxury while Auden and Kallman were installed in a brothel, later in scarcely better quarters...." In truth no "arrangements" had been made for anybody. Stravinsky had reserved rooms, and the librettists, who landed in the brothel innocently unawares and by accident, had not. In Venice, Stravinsky found accommodations for them in his by no means luxurious hotel.

aided," became " ... stepping from *my* sedan *chair* unaided" as early as 1949) and soon after (as when Auden adopted the revision "To shut my ears [as against eyes] to prude and preacher," and even used it in a broadcast talk). Auden's 1949 rewrite of a crucial part of the sedan chair scene is a major revision and improvement.

* * *

Thomas Campion's songs and those in Shakespeare's plays are words for music, words to be sung with or without the accompaniment of instruments. They do not express ideas, and are as simple in thought as possible—unlike, for example, those lyric's of Donne's which, if sung, would lose their sense. The opening scene of the *Rake* follows Shakespeare's and Campion's principle of simplicity and pure verbal music:

> The woods are green and bird and beast at play
> For all things keep this festival of May.

The setting evoked is Edenic, and the hero and heroine, Tom Rakewell and Anne Trulove, are portrayed as truly in love. Anne's father joins them, adding a slightly ominous undertone. Alone with Rakewell, Trulove *père* offers him a position in a counting house. Rakewell declines it, Trulove reproves him and exits, whereupon Rakewell, alone, referring to him as an "old fool," reveals himself as a despicable opportunist without the slightest respect for Anne:

> Why should I labor
> For what in the end
> She will give me for nothing
> If she be my friend?

This hypocritical aspect of the hero is repeated and underscored at the halfway point in the opera. In this scene, Anne has come to London to find Tom, and they sing a love duet. But he has already betrayed her by marrying the freakish Baba the Turk, to whom he identifies Anne as "only a milkmaid, pet, to whom I was in debt," thus making a mockery of the profound feelings he has just avowed. The music tells us that these feelings are true, however, and the music stays with us. The final scenes of the opera also confirm the verity of the love between Anne and Tom, and, as a result, the two earlier exposures of the hero as double-dealing and weak perplex the audience.

Auden wrote the first part of the opening scene, Kallman the second. To compare the two is to deny Auden's claim that "two librettists are not two people but a corporate personality." (He later conceded that "any given passage must be written by one of them," and explained that the corporate personality "decides what will or will not do.") But here the duumivirate hybrid artist does not exist. Auden's lines,

> Till I die, then, of fever,
> Or by lightning am struck,
> Let me live by my wits
> And trust to my luck

are remote from Kallman's completion of the scene, an obstacle course of stuttering ("Anne. And ... "), yodeling ("You, who"), stilted language ("O clement love"), obscure metaphor and tangled trope ("Attorneys crouched like gardeners to pay / Bowers of paper only seals repair ... / A crop that wax and pen must cultivate"), and ambiguity: Shadow, Rakewell's Mephisto and the "projection of his self-destructive force," as Auden characterized him, sings the words, "Indeed, let all who will make their joy here of your glad tidings"; but the audience understands "hear."

Mother Goose's[6] London whorehouse, the setting of scene 2, is the first stop in Tom's education, *"Le Plaisir,"* in Auden's scheme of the "progress" of the Rake. The text is pure Auden, and it launches the *Rake* anew with some of the most felicitous verse in all opera. Having composed a fast-tempo chorus in which the whores and their clients sing of their wish to keep the aubade at bay, Stravinsky asked Auden for an additional stanza. In the one he provided—the *first* quatrain below: Stravinsky had already set the one with the arresting last line—staccato consonants and simple rhymes, abetted by syncopation in the music, confer the utmost clarity on every syllable:

> Soon dawn will glitter outside the shutter
> And small birds twitter; but what of that?
> So long as we're able and wine's on the table
> Who cares what the troubling day is at?

> While food has flavor and limbs are shapely
> And hearts beat bravely to fiddle or drum
> Our proper employment is reckless enjoyment
> For too soon the noiseless night will come.

---

[6] "Goose" was Elizabethan slang for Southwark whore. Auden probably borrowed the term "roaring boys," for the male clients in Mother Goose's establishment, from Thomas Dekker's play *The Roaring Girl* (1608).

Half a minute further into the opera, Auden adroitly contrasts this with a trans-fixing slow-tempo lyric, greatly enhanced in its musical setting by the remote-ness of the tonality:

> Love, too frequently betrayed
> For some plausible desire
> Or the world's enchanted fire,
> Still thy traitor in his sleep
> Resumes the vow he did not keep,
> Weeping, weeping,
> He kneels before thy wounded shade.

The brief third scene, by Kallman, in which Anne resolves to go to Tom in London, is straightforward, "operatic," and only slightly blemished by repeti-tions ("love" nine times). But it is flawed by a letdown last line:

> O should I see
> My love in need
> It shall not matter
> what he may be.

In February 1949, a year and a half before the premiere, Auden emended this fi-nale to

> Time cannot alter
> My loving heart,
> My ever loving heart

in order to provide an open-sounding vowel and cut-off consonant for a final high note; but the authorial text published here retains Kallman's original.

Kallman also wrote the opening scene of Act II, in which Rakewell, weary and alone in his London house, sings of his disenchantment with life in the city. In spite of cliché ("wrinkled as a raisin") and a precious image ("let Folly purr"), it is a marked improvement over his work in the first act. With the entrance of Shadow in response to Rakewell's "I wish I were happy," the pen passes to Auden, who is now faced with the insuperable problem of making dramatic sense out of the next step in his scheme of Rakewell's progress, *"L'Acte gratuite."*

Shadow unfurls a broadsheet likeness of Baba the Turk, a bearded lady and circus artiste, the librettists' substitution for and improvement on Hogarth's merely rich Ugly Duchess. "Do you desire her?" he asks. "Like the gout or the falling sickness." "Then marry her," Shadow says, going on to explain that hap-piness is obtainable only through freedom from Passion and Reason, those "twin tyrants of appetite and conscience." (How happiness can result from being shackled to an intolerable mate is not explained.)

Rakewell, for some mysterious reason, agrees to the "joke," as Auden called the episode, ignoring the pain that it will bring to Baba and Anne. But the audience cannot believe Shadow's argument nor adjust to the jolt and the burlesque into which the opera then sinks, to rise again only in the final scenes. As for Stravinsky, he suffered composer's block on reaching this crucial point and wrote nothing for two weeks.

To forestall criticism of Baba at the Metropolitan Opera premiere (February 14, 1953), Auden (or Kallman, or both, or someone else) included, in a synopsis of the plot contributed to the program book, the explanation that "since Tom is neither attracted to Baba nor obligated to her, he can therefore prove his freedom and obtain happiness by the completely unemotional and irrational act of marrying her." But do irrational and emotionally indifferent acts hurtful to innocent others bring happiness to those who commit them? Addressing the criticism again for a 1958 BBC Television broadcast of the last five scenes of the opera (i.e., after the wedding to Baba has taken place), Auden wrote a Prologue, to be spoken by Shadow, that further compounds the difficulty: "Look on this portrait of strange womankind," Shadow says here (in the opera he describes Baba as a "Gorgon"), and

> Marry her, Tom! Be happy and rejoice,
> Knowing you know no motive for your choice.
>
> . . . .
>
> Perhaps you ask, dear viewers, how this man
> Could think of marriage and not think of Anne
>   … but pride
> Soon won his guilty conscience to my side.

The viewer does indeed ask why Tom does not think of Anne. But whereas vanity is a feature of Tom's personality at the start of the opera, it is not much in evidence by this time. Elsewhere Auden diagnoses Rakewell as a "manic-depressive," noting that this "allowed for musical contrasts or moods," for whom (as with the rest of us) "the anticipation of experience is always exciting and its realization always disappointing."

In the next scene, the marriage has already taken place. Anne sees Tom in the street in front of his London house, and as Baba, hidden in her sedan chair, waits impatiently, they sing a duet. Stravinsky objected that Baba's natterings as she peers between the curtains were too long and destroyed the mood of the scene. (In truth, he wanted them cut entirely, and in his first draft omits them.)

Kallman being in Italy at the time, Auden wrote new ones, offering two versions of differing lengths. He deleted Kallman's "it could hardly be thought that wedded bliss entailed *such* manner of attention," and, for his partner's 135 or so words of prose, substituted seventy or so of his own in strongly accented rhyming lines carefully calculated to be heard above the orchestra and the other two voices.

Later he went on to compose yet a fourth version of Baba's grumblings, retaining some of Kallman's original, including the unfortunate "Hussy ... if I am found immured here, dead, I swear...." This final version is inferior to the previous two, which, combined and further cut by Stravinsky, became a permanent part of the opera in the autumn of 1949. The present text in the present volume is that of the fourth and last version.

It is likely that Auden reshaped and polished some of Kallman's lines. Certainly nothing in *The Tuscan Players*, the libretto for Carlos Chávez that Kallman wrote without Auden, or any of Kallman's own poetry, remotely approaches the wit of many lines from the *Rake* definitely attributed to him, as with, for example, "America, He fled / Spontaneous combustion caught him hurrying / He's dead." But in the event that Kallman's genius in imitating Auden had developed phenomenally during the three months of the pair's work on the *Rake*, how are we to account for the disappearance of this acquired talent when he wrote the poems collected in *Storm at Castelfranco* published eight years later?

In a retrospective essay published with the 1964 recording of the *Rake*, Kallman revealed that Auden had obliged him to "shrink" a long dialogue to four lines, and to throw out and rewrite the whole of the auction scene. Auden had also "mercilessly trimmed" Kallman's recitative telling the story of Rakewell's inheritance; Dryden had advocated short, unrhymed lines for recitatives, longer lines for the "songish parts," and Stravinsky, of the same mind, set the narrative as an arioso.

Auden wrote that the librettist "supplies the words, the characters and the plot," and of these "the words are the least important." This is not true of the *Rake*. The plot is creaky, even by operatic standards ("Opera plots allow that sort of marvelous and surprising conduct which is rejected in other plays," Dryden observed). In his notes for the 1964 recording, Kallman recognized that the scene in which Tom dreams of a machine that will turn stones into bread and thus put an end to poverty is "impossibly difficult to put across," not, presumably, because of the absurdity of the apparatus, but because credulity on such a scale is unimaginable, even for Tom Rakewell. Auden defended the scene as showing Rakewell "further removed from reality," but here he forgets that Tom becomes insane as a result of Shadow's curse, not gradually, in response to events.

The characters, in any case, are dimensionless, devoid of anything remotely like a psychological make-up. "Anne is a soprano. Period," Kallman's essay acknowledges. So, too, her father is no more than a morose voice, while Rakewell, far from being a Hogarthian toss-pot, is "almost entirely passive." In a lecture at the 1968 Salzburg Festival, Auden asserted, and Corneille would have concurred, that "the more willful a character the better, the more passive a character the worse." When Tom wins the card game, Auden attributes the defeat to Shadow's "over-confidence" and, in the opera, to his procrastination ("My own delay cost me my prey"), thus imbuing a supernatural being, capable of turning time backward, with a human weakness. It is Shadow who is the opera's willful character.

This leaves Baba, who, in the previous scene, in befriending Anne and warning her to beware of Shadow, becomes the only endearing member of the menage, a considerate person who does not linger over her wounds but determines to go back to the stage and bravely forward with her life.

Yet the opera survives in Auden's words and in the music they inspired. The melody of Anne's lullaby and its flute-duet accompaniment perfectly match the childlike simplicity and gentleness of

> Lion, lamb and deer,
> Untouched by greed or fear
> About the woods are straying:
>> And quietly now
>> The blossoming bough
> Sway, sway, sway
> Above the fair unclouded brow.[7]

Stravinsky's word-setting from the early to the ultimate scenes of the opera is a study in ever-increasing naturalness. Here, in the Graveyard and Bedlam episodes, words and music fuse and complement each other, accent and meter, vocable and vocal register, are in agreement. The composer feels the right speeds for polysyllables (that "dilatoriness"); and he imagines the sounds, piping viola harmonics and high, rasping oboe, to evoke the atmosphere of Bedlam,

> Madmen's words are all untrue,
> She will never come to you,

---

[7] See the perceptive discussion of this and the other two stanzas of the Lullaby in *The Hidden Law, The Poetry of W. H. Auden*, by Anthony Hecht. Cambridge: Harvard University Press, 1993.

the orchestration, pizzicato with low, crisp trumpet notes, that makes the consonants sparkle,

> Banker, beggar, whore and wit
> In a common darkness sit.

To some extent the greater flow and continuity in the last act than in the first two can be attributed to the absence of background-filling recitatives, and to thematic and stylistic linkages from scene to scene—the variations on the Ballad Tune in all three scenes, and the melismas that stylize Rakewell's fear in the Graveyard scene and the still more florid ones ("a swan-like music") as he dies. But above all, Act III has musical and dramatic power, in the quiet, hollow unison of the chorus's "Madman, no one has been here," no less than in the throbbing orchestral climax that accompanies Shadow's descent to Hell. Months before he had read the libretto itself, Stravinsky was inspired by the two final scenes. Without words to set, but impatient to compose, he wrote the haunting string-quartet Prelude to the Graveyard scene on December 11, 1947, three weeks after the scenario had been drafted, and three years before he composed the actual scene (November 1950).

The ending of the opera in Bedlam, where mad Tom, who thinks he is Adonis, embraces Anne, whom he imagines as Venus, inspired Auden no less profoundly:

> In a foolish dream, in a gloomy labyrinth
> I hunted shadows, disdaining thy true love;
> . . . .
> Rejoice, belovèd: in these fields of Elysium
> Space cannot alter, nor time our love abate;
> Here has no words for absence or estrangement
> Nor now a notion of almost or too late.

How regrettable it is that the two great artists did not find another subject to bring them together again.

* * *

On The Way, the next Auden-Kallman operatic project (1949), did not fulfill the claim of its title, despite an 11,000-word scenario. The subject, the Muse's relations with Rossini, Mendelssohn, and Berlioz, is complicated and dramatically unpromising. In New York, in December 1951, Stravinsky, Auden, and Kallman planned a one-act opera, but the libretto, *Delia, A Masque of Night*, completed three months later, was stiflingly literary, with Tudor-period language ("I trow," "I wiss," "the sun scorcheth"—try singing "scorcheth"), inverted word order ("I did not under lock my husband keep"), and an arch pedantry (Hic, haec, hoc / The fiddle and the stock / Horum, quorum, high cockalorum / Should *amor ferinus, etc.*).

The Auden-Kallman *Magic Flute* is a contemporary example of *"prima la musica e poi le parole,"* in that the librettists have fitted new verses to music and not merely translated the German text into English. In the process, Auden became fascinated with the story ("a proper treatment of its material would have made it one of the greatest libretti ever written") and preoccupied with the trials by fire and water that the hero and heroine of the opera, Tamino and Pamina, undergo. "The Proof,"[8] one of his best poems, and not only technically, is based on the theme:

> When rites and melodies begin
> To alter modes and times
>
> . . . .
>
> What promises, what discipline,
> If any, will Love keep?
> So roared Fire on their right:
> But Tamino and Pamina
> Walked past its rage.

The new version of Mozart's opera presents several hurdles, the highest of which is the transposition of the order of seven of the twelve numbers in Act II with the intention of eliminating confusions and inconsistencies in the plot, which, as everyone knows, reverses roles bewilderingly, turning Tamino's savior in the first scene into its villainess, the initial villain into the good, wise Priest.

Since the music is not continuous, each musical number being separated by spoken dialogue, the collaborators contend that Mozart's plan of tonalities may be disregarded; "ears," they say, do not retain tonalities during spoken dialogue, a by-no-means waterproof generalization. More important, the change in order, while making the story smoother, overlooks the sequencing of voices, and musical tempos and moods. Thus the Auden-Kallman version places two trios back to back and, to the detriment of contrast and pacing, two very slow and solemn movements. Still worse, Pamina's sorrowful minor-key aria, *"Ach, ich fühl's,"* is followed by an ensemble, which is not only in the related major of the same key, but in which, also, her voice is the first to be heard—in music that

---

[8] See the analysis in Hecht (414–416).

for no evident reason signals a more hopeful mood.

According to Auden, Chester Kallman wrote as much as 75 percent of the libretto of Henze's three-act-opera of *Elegy for Young Lovers*, as compared to something nearer 50 percent of *The Bassarids* (1966). For this reason, in part, the later opera has a greater claim on our attention; the other part is that *The Bassarids*,[9] an "Opera Seria with Intermezzo in one act based on 'The Bacchae' of Euripides," is the more interesting and successful work. That success is due, in large measure, to the closeness with which the librettists follow Euripides' drama of violence prevailing over enlightenment and reason. They also follow Gilbert Murray's interpretation of the crucial scene at the center of the play, and of the opera, in which King Pentheus of Thebes, who has vowed to extirpate the cult of Dionysus as dangerously subversive to the stability of Boeotia,

> Dionysus
> Is but a name
> For the nameless Nothing
> That hates the Light,

engages in a long dialogue with "The Stranger," whom he does not recognize as the maleficent god himself in disguise. At the end of the scene, Pentheus surrenders to Dionysus, as he does in Euripides, but Auden-Kallman add sexual overtones to Murray's Nibelungen-like hypothesis that the god has cast a spell over Pentheus. "You are beautiful," Pentheus exclaims. Although the Bassarids have asked Dionysus to "smite our lawless oppressor / Pentheus.... Slay this wicked man," Pentheus is determined to witness the Dionysian rites, in spite of the danger, and at night ascends Mount Kithairon to do so. He is discovered and torn to pieces by the Bassarids and Maenads. His mother, one of the latter and a Dionysian herself, mistakes her son's severed and disfigured head for the head of a lion, returns with it to Thebes and holds it up to the people as proof of the power of Dionysus in them. Her father, Cadmus, horrified by the savagery of the murder and by his daughter's intoxicated trance-like state, gradually makes her understand what she has done. Dionysus exiles both of them.

Henze's music is rich in atmospherics and scene-setting, as in the fanfare at the beginning of the opera. He can also compose compelling traditional operatic pieces within his broadly symphonic structure, such as Dionysus's barcarole

---

[9] Only a short time before the premiere, Henze wrote to the librettists asking "what the fuck the 'Bassarids' means." Auden answered that it referred "to male as well as female followers of Dionysus." Earlier, when Henze had proposed another title, Auden informed him that "... slightly puzzling titles cultivate public curiosity."

describing his voyage to Naxos. On the debit side, the opera loses impetus in some of the recitative-dialogues. But at best, in the eruptive passages that evoke the frenzy of Dionysians and the brutality and ferocity of their murder of Pentheus, the score is powerfully effective.

If the music renders some of the verse unintelligible, the composer could reply that some of it is scarcely intelligible in the first place. A line such as "Fields newly awake lifted our / Light steps as a green quickening / At a tip touch overtook all / Unawareness" seems like deliberate obfuscation, and the same can be said of the rash of inverted word orders throughout the opera: "You believe she was justly slain, / Semele, by the Thunderer for her lie?" No wonder the composer cut so much of the libretto, eliminating half of the chorus, "Now night opens wide," reducing Tiresius's "dissertation" from twenty-one to two and a half lines—the latter with encouragement from a performance direction to deliver it with "a speed that borders on incomprehensibility."

Auden loved to step out of his plays, operas, and longer poems, and, in the tradition of Greek and Latin comedy speak to the audience directly, to draw the moral and to distance art from life: thus "Caliban to the Audience" in *The Sea and the Mirror*, the Narrator in *For the Time Being*, and the prologues, metalogues, epilogues in the plays and operas. Even in the middle of *The Rake's Progress* Shadow shares asides across the footlights, and at the end of the opera, a quintet of its characters detain the audience for the lesson with words borrowed from the end of *Don Giovanni*: "Good people" ("*buona gente*"). In *The Bassarids* this direct address is contained in the Intermezzo, "The Judgment of Calliope," the opera's rhymed centerpiece, a "miniature satyr play," the poet wrote, "which represents what Pentheus *thinks*."

But no matter, since the text exists only in this book. It is cut in the otherwise excellent English-language recording of the opera and deleted in the new (1992) edition of the full score, which also excludes it from the title;[10] Auden would have died of apoplexy. The loss is especially regrettable for at least four reasons: its inclusion relieves the "sober air of religious disaster that envelops the rest," as the librettists claimed; it helpfully elucidates the mythological background (Pentheus as descendent of a serpent's tooth); it portrays Pentheus as epicene, thus providing a sexual subtext; and, most important, for those of us who love Auden, it fulfills his wish for an ode that would address the audience directly.

[10] Koch-Schwann Musica Mundi CD 314 006 K 3 [DDD]

The great poet-librettist must also speak to us directly here. He has the last word: "A verbal art like poetry is reflective; it stops to think," whereas "Music is immediate, it goes on to become." And, "The singer may be playing the role of the deserted bride who is about to kill herself, but we feel quite certain as we listen that not only we but she is having a wonderful time." And, finally, "No good opera plot can be sensible, for people do not sing when they are feeling sensible."

Huxley in Hollywood

David Dunaway[1] begins with a tabloid tale. Maria, Aldous Huxley's first wife, was a lesbian who invited "women Aldous might like" to tea, "then booked the restaurant and, in some cases, the motel." No instances are cited. He tells us, further, that when an attractive female was introduced, Maria regarded her with as much predatory interest as did Aldous; but no evidence of an adulterous liaison by either of them is forthcoming. "Maria had arranged a sexy encounter" for her husband, Dunaway goes on, and, true to the author's hit-and-run manner, he provides neither any specifics about it nor even any indication that it in fact took place.

Dunaway's nearest approach to substantiation is the diary confession of Grace Hubble, wife of the astronomer Edwin Hubble (the Hubble space telescope), of an attraction to Huxley that he may or may not have sought to exploit. Interpreting his tête-à-tête remark to her that not enough adultery took place in America as an intimation that they might help to rectify the lack, she was frightened off. Nevertheless, women were attracted to Aldous Huxley because of his fame as an author, his distinguished appearance, his intelligence and gentleness, the witty way in which he imparted bits—often sexually spiced—of his immense knowledge, his inheritance of "the two cultures" from grandfather Thomas Henry Huxley[2] and mother's uncle Matthew Arnold, and, by no means least, because women wanted to take care of the visually handi-

---

[1] *Huxley in Hollywood*, by David King Dunaway. New York: Harper & Row, 1989.

[2] One of Aldous Huxley's best essays, particularly in its analyses of styles of scientific description, is his 1932 memorial lecture on T. H. Huxley as a writer. *Evolution and Ethics*, now republished with the original Prolegomena (*T. H. Huxley's Evolution and Ethics, with New Essays on Its Victorian and Sociobiological Contexts*, by James Paradis and George C. Williams, Princeton, N.J.: Princeton University Press, 1989) is more pertinent than ever, quite beyond its verbal precision and elegance. The introduction by Professor Paradis of the Massachusetts Institute of Technology establishes the enduring validity of T. H. Huxley's synthesis of Victorian scientific thought, as well as his "challenge to eighteenth-century assumptions about the harmony of nature." Stony Brook's Professor Williams, the eminent evolutionary biologist, regards *Evolution and Ethics* as both a precursor of contemporary sociobiology and a precocious perception that the "cosmic process" by which we have come this far "is not able to continue a viable world." T. H. Huxley's thesis that "humans are alienated in a cos-

capped writer. Surrounded by adoring and in some cases willing females, he needed no procuress.

Dunaway puts together an imaginary lesbian community of Tallulah, Greta, Marlene, Anita (Loos), Elsie (De Wolfe, Lady Mendl), Mercedes (De Acosta), Salka Viertel, and Maria. Not all tomboyish females with Sapphic propensities are practicing lovers of their own sex, however, and I think that Anita Loos, identified on page 86 with the "Old Girl network," was not. Nor, as far as I know, was Maria Huxley, at least between the mid-1940s and her early death in 1955. Certainly she may have been three decades earlier at Garsington, Lady Ottoline Morrell's wartime refuge for pacifist intellectuals, at which time Maria strongly discouraged Huxley's courtship and long postponed marrying him. But "Lady Utterly Immoral," as both Maria and Aldous used to refer to her, seems to have had at least as many promiscuous involvements with men as with women.

Turning from female to male homosexuality in Hollywood, Dunaway digresses—inappositely in view of Huxley's well-known intolerance—on the sexual career of Christopher Isherwood, whom he places at MGM in the mid-1930s instead of the mid-1950s,[3] and grotesquely mis-describes as having "the mind of a de Sade in the body of a football player."

The chapters on Huxley's English background recount the traumas of his adolescence: brother Trevenen's suicide, his mother's premature death from cancer, and the keratitis punctata streptococcus that left him totally blind at first, and then with a small fraction of sight in one eye. The trajectory of the smart novels, *Crome Yellow* (1921) up to *Point Counter Point* (1928) and *Eyeless in Gaza* (1936), is also traced. But the subject of the book's title begins with the American hegira of 1937, the lecture tour with Gerald Heard proselytizing for pacifism, a cause that tainted Huxley politically for the remainder of his life.

Huxley thought of himself, correctly so far as he goes, as an "essayist, dis-

---

mos that has no special reference to their needs," and that "moral societies are of necessity in conflict with the natural conditions of their existence" is his grandson's point of departure. After more than a century, *Evolution and Ethics* can still enlighten. And we can still say, as this first and greatest Darwinian did—borrowing a passage from Proverbs and another from Hosea in the Book whose fundamentalism he did more than anyone to destroy—that "it is true now, as ever it was, that the people perish for lack of knowledge."

[3] Among Dunaway's numerous errors of simple fact are a reference to T. H. Huxley (1825–1895) as still living in 1910, to Aldous and the twenty-two-year-older Bertrand Russell as teenagers together, to the classmate who became Lord Justice as David, instead of Charles, Harman, and to J. B. S. Haldane, Aldous's coeval, as his "former teacher" (this was another Haldane).

guised from time to time as a novelist." But the transparency of the disguises and consequent failure of many of his novels did not affect his high opinion of the form:

> Dostoevsky is six times as profound as Kierkegaard, because he writes fiction. In Kierkegaard you have this Abstract Man going on and on— ... it's nothing compared with the really profound Fictional Man, who has always to keep ... ideas alive in a concrete form. In fiction you have ... the expression of the general in the particular. And this, it seems to me, is the exciting thing—both in life and in art.[4]

Huxley's inability to create fictional people of any dimension, even when basing a character on D. H. Lawrence, whom he knew well, and the discursiveness that sinks his final novels—to unreadable depths in *Island*, his artistic nadir—are in sorry contrast to the critical judgment that he displays in, for example, the letters to Hermann Broch concerning his *Death of Virgil*:

> I hope you will not think me unjust in what I have written regarding the two sections—near the beginning and at the end—where the lyrical-philosophical material is used for many pages without contrasting passage of narrative. My own feeling is that quantity destroys quality and that though intrinsically, the sentences of which these sections are composed are rich with beauty and meaning, the very number of them—because of their intensity and their stylistic strangeness—imposes a strain upon the reader's mind and makes him, in the long run, incapable of reacting adequately to them. What Edgar Allan Poe said about the permissible length of the lyric is sound psychology.[5]

Huxley the prophet, on the other hand, wins high scores for marksmanship. Already in 1946 he had predicted remote-control rockets capable of hit-

---

[4] *The Writer's Chapbook: A Compendium of Fact, Opinion, Wit, and Advice from the 20th Century's Preeminent Writers*, edited by George Plimpton. New York: Viking, 1990.

[5] Huxley also questions the book's historical basis: "I kept wondering, as I read the admirable conversations between Virgil and his friends, whether Plotius, Varius and Augustus—successful and self-satisfied members of the ruling class of an imperial nation as they were—would have found Virgil's viewpoint as odd and as incomprehensible as, for the purpose of art, you represent them as doing. They were all well educated men and must have known about, even if they did not approve of, the Orphic mysteries, Pythagoreanism and even Hermeticism, whose origins, according to authorities such as Flinders Petrie, go back to a century and a half before Virgil's birth." See *Letters of Aldous Huxley*, edited by Grover Smith. New York: Harper & Row, 1969.

ting targets five thousand miles away. His jeremiads on overpopulation and world hunger, on the devastation and squandering of the earth—deserts spreading, forests dwindling—ending in eco-catastrophe and an uninhabitable planet, seem to be coming true well ahead of his schedule. He was ahead, too, on such subjects as genetic engineering and the increasing use of mind-altering drugs. True, much of this literature is heavily rhetorical, and in the years of *Time Must Have a Stop, The Perennial Philosophy,* and *Ape and Essence,* his prose is weighted with horrible locutions such as "Suchness," "Isness," "Not-Self," "Mind-at-Large," "Pure Being," the divine "Ground," "Ultimate Reality."

But Dunaway's writing is worse. No temptation to exaggerate is resisted. In India, in 1925 (the trip Huxley took in 1960 is not mentioned), the not-yet-well-known future author of *Point Counter Point* was greeted by "hundreds of thousands." Kenneth Clark "ranked this purblind writer among the great art critics of his time." "The years went by on the Lawrence ranch near Taos." (The Lawrences left Taos for Mexico after only a few months and spent little time there later.) And Dunaway wholeheartedly agrees with the fatuous claim that Hollywood during Huxley's period was "as crowded with artists as Renaissance Florence."

Many of Dunaway's descriptions of people are inaccurate. Edwin Hubble was not as tall as Huxley (6′5″), and Peggy Kiskadden was not "tall" at all (5′2″?). Frieda Lawrence was not "sweet," but tough and loud, with a chain-smoker's rasp, and her boast that she could make "a second Lawrence" out of her barely literate third husband, Angelo Ravagli (the model for Lady Chatterley's lover), does not merit repetition. Nor is the portrait of Huxley himself always in focus. Southern Californians did not stare at him because they were "amused" by his "high baritone," but, rather, if they overheard his very soft voice at all, by his English accent. His height attracted attention, too, and the magnifying glass that he used even when not reading. Huxley's eyesight was so poor, Dunaway says, that he had "to hold a flower close enough to kiss to see its dainty heart." Its dainty sex organs, surely.

Dunaway confuses Kingsley Amis with Kingsley Martin, Christopher Fry with Christopher Wood, George Heard with Gerald Heard (p. 101), D. H. Lawrence's cow Susan with somebody else's cow Sally. On page 269 he has Salka Viertel "amicably divorcing Bertold Brecht," though they were never married. More important, he has overlooked potentially rich sources, among them George Cukor, mentioned only in passing but arguably closer to Huxley than anyone else in the cinema world; Yolanda, the proprietress of a restaurant in Hollywood's Farmers Market frequented by the Huxleys (and by Cary Grant), and an intimate to whom Aldous confided a letter describing Maria's death; Lesley Blanch, a good friend during a crucial period in the 1950s; and Michael Barrie, Gerald Heard's companion of many years, whose information would have been more reliable than that of some brief acquaintances ingenuously quoted.

About two thirds of the way through, Dunaway notes that Huxley "spoke and wrote French with complete fluency." Actually French had always been the Huxley household language; Belgian-born Maria Nys felt more at home in it and in the French-speaking world, and correspondingly less at home in America, than her husband. Dunaway neglects to say that Huxley was scarcely less fluent in Italian, which he spoke not only with both wives, but also in lectures in Italy. He knew Spanish as well, and in his sixties taught himself Portuguese in order to read the *Lusiad*. In addition to the languages of his classical education, he knew some Pali and Sanskrit.

Dunaway reviews the facts concerning the puzzle of Huxley's failure, or unwillingness, to acknowledge that between 1952 and 1955 his wife was dying of cancer, but without proposing a convincing explanation. Though aware that the disease had entered the lymph nodes shortly after her mastectomy, Huxley seems not to have realized, in spite of her swollen arm, complaints of back pains, and radiation treatment, that it had metastasized. In January 1955, while she was in a Los Angeles hospital and less than a month before her death, he referred to her "recurrent and very painful lumbago," in a letter otherwise devoted to a description of his second mescaline session. Writing at the end of the month, he changed the diagnosis to a "vaguely arthritic condition." This might appear as a simple wish to keep his secret from others, but when her doctors told him the truth, on February 5, a week before she died, he went into shock— to which I can testify, having been with Gerald Heard when Huxley broke the news to him.

Huxley in Hollywood presents alarming evidence for the early onset of paranoia in isolationist America. Only weeks after the arrival of this dangerous literary figure in New York, in May 1937, the FBI began to keep a file on him. By 1950 his name turns up in, of all places, an investigation of espionage, and it appears regularly thereafter in connection with questions of national security. A Congressional committee report, May 23, 1951, actually classifies him as "a Communist fellow-traveler." Two years later, a Federal judge denied him United States citizenship because he insisted that his refusal to bear arms— aged fifty-nine and legally blind—was not based on religious beliefs but on "philosophical conviction"; the judge had instructed him that the law recognizes religion as the only acceptable reason for pacifism. Aldous Huxley died a British subject. Queen Elizabeth had offered him a knighthood, but he refused it.

T. S. Eliot's Cambridge Lectures

Thirty Years after his death, T. S. Eliot is still in the ascendant, if the paean by the present poet laureate, Ted Hughes, *A Dancer to God: Tributes to T. S. Eliot*, is an indicator. True, the plays have not held the stage—which "does not mean they are any fun to read," as the younger Amis quipped—-the religious sociology is not for today's *bien-pensant* reader, and the once seminal literary criticism, after long academic siege, has been retired into literature itself. One wonders what Eliot, who took pride in the low circulation (250 copies) of his review, the *Criterion*, would have thought of the worldwide popularity of *Cats*, based on verses that attest the supremacy of his wit but were addressed privately to friends and never included in the *Collected Poems*.

At the same time, Eliot himself has been subjected to attempts at character assassination, partly because he and his brother-in-law, who was in awe of him, had his first wife committed to an insane asylum for life, apparently without having obtained a professional certification. However that may be, the prurient curiosity about his blighted marriage exploited in the play "Tom and Viv" is currently enjoying wider scope in a feature film that shows "Eliot" running around the apartment looking for his trousers and "Vivien," who has thrown them out the window, removing bedsheets bloodied from her almost constant menstrual flow. No less absurd, Vivien's grandniece has claimed a new role for her as her husband's co-author—"having written parts of T. S. Eliot's finest poems," a London *Observer* headline read—though only ten contributions to the *Criterion*, including some lines excised by Pound from the original *Waste Land*, have been identified as hers. It must be admitted, however, that the reaction and hullabaloo are understandable in view of the fortress built around Eliot by his publisher during the last seventy years, his own sphinx-like attitude toward his biography, and the Eliot Estate's sometimes arbitrary exercise of control over his writings.

Ronald Schuchard's elegant commentary to *The Varieties of Metaphysical Poetry*, Eliot's 1926 Clark Lectures at Cambridge and the abbreviation of them as the Turnbull Lectures, delivered by him at Johns Hopkins in January 1933, throw some glaring light on his feelings toward Vivien. Scott Fitzgerald, the poet's fellow guest at the Turnbull estate in Towson, Md., told Edmund Wilson that Eliot seemed "very broken and sad and shrunk inside." Schuchard reveals that on March 14 Eliot wrote to Ottoline Morrell informing her that he had asked for a Deed of Separation from Vivien: "For my part, I should prefer never to see her again; for hers I do not believe that it can be good for any woman to live with a man to whom she is morally, in the larger sense, unpleasant, as well as physically indifferent." The ostensible expression of concern for her welfare apart, the syntax makes the last phrase say the opposite of what he so obviously means: that *he* finds *her* physically repugnant.

In general, Eliot's lectures are less finely concentrated than his essays. The two series of talks dating from the same tour that brought him to Baltimore, *After Strange Gods* and *The Use of Poetry and The Use of Criticism*, may be his weakest books. The first was unreprintable even at the time (1934) because of its reactionary political views and blatant anti-Semitism, while the second, as Ezra Pound informed readers of the *New English Weekly* (June 1934), should not have been published in the first place. Eliot responded in the same periodical, "wholeheartedly" agreeing with "*il miglior fabbro*"—"an unsatisfactory attempt to say something worth saying"—but tearing into the manner of his criticism and ending with a parody of Pound's backwoods prose: "I am going to set round the chimbly and have a chaw terbacker with Miss Meadows and the gals, and then I am going away for a 4night where that old rabbit can't reach me with his letters"—[signed] "Your outraged POSSUM."

The Clark Lectures, in contrast, are already too concentrated, in spite of their wide range of allusions to, for a sampling, the music dramas and influence of Wagner, the Spanish mystics as psychologists, the German heretics (the school of Eckhardt), the French poets, Baudelaire, Laforgue, Corbière, Verlaine, Mallarmé, Rimbaud, without whom Eliot doubts whether "I should have been able to write poetry at all", and even, "in their peculiar mode of escape from life," the surrealists. What the reader doubts is that even the most sophisticated audience—and Eliot's included such luminaries as A. E. Housman, Sir J. G. (*The Golden Bough*) Frazer, G. E. Moore, A. N. Whitehead, I. A. Richards, and Herbert Read—would grasp many of the allusions in Eliot's arguments. Indeed, without Schuchard's guidance some passages are scarcely coherent. He identifies (and corrects) quotations, provides translations for most of those in Latin, Italian, and French, footnotes references to Eliot's other writings relating to the same things, and cross-references between the British and the Baltimore texts. His interpretations of meanings, his account of the background, the origins, the composition and reception of the lectures, and the history of the manuscript, are indispensable to the reader's comprehension of them. Heretofore the Clark

Lectures have been available to only a few scholars, none of whom conveyed the richness of the contents and the new areas of Eliot's "cranial lodging" that they open up.

As in all of Eliot's criticism, the theoretical parts are less engaging than the close-up analyses of individual poets, in this case Donne—"Lectures on Donne" is Eliot's description of the talks in his 1931 essay "Donne in Our Time"—Crashaw, and Cowley. The lectures extend and amplify Eliot's more caustic ("Keats and Shelley died, and Tennyson and Browning ruminated") early essay (1921) on the "Metaphysical Poets," a description borrowed from Johnson, who is the source, as well, of the most vivid definition of this particular species of poetry in which "heterogeneous ideas are yoked by violence together." The "force of this impeachment," Eliot remarks, "lies in the failure of the conjunction, the fact that often the ideas are yoked but not united."

Eliot turns to Johnson again in the lectures for help in clarifying the meaning "metaphysical." He elaborates on his own that "the tincture of human emotions by philosophy ... is essential to metaphysical poetry" and that metaphysical poetry is not likely to issue from the "political cosmologies of the immediate future," or "from a philosophy which lays under cultivation only the more social emotions and virtues." The metaphysical poet must be subjective, he goes on, reminding us that "it is not for nothing that the *Divine Comedy* is related in the first person." This metaphysical subjectivism must be distinguished from Milton's "self-dramatizing " kind: "Milton ... expresses his feelings towards the word through a dramatic figure," whereas "the metaphysical poet deals with his feelings directly.... One is the attitude of the theater, the other that of the confessional."

The largely negative 1931 essay, "Donne in Our Time," should be read as a corrective to the lectures and a gauge of the change in Eliot after he was received into the Church of England (June 1927). "Donne's poetry is a concern of the present and recent past rather than of the future," he now decides. Furthermore, Donne is "not even an absolutely first-rate devotional poet," and his sermons, which are less original than his satires, "will disappear as suddenly as they have appeared." Donne's "scoffing at the fickleness of women ... comes to me with none of the terrible sincerity of Swift's vituperation of the human race." (In the lectures, Swift is "the colossal.") Donne had a legal, rather than a theological or philosophical, mind, and might today "have been a very great company lawyer."

The lectures devote less space to Crashaw, and still less to Cowley, whom Eliot characterizes as a "pathetic little celibate epicurean, paraphrasing Horace on the virtues of a country life," and providing "an analogy to Saint-Evremond and the French freethinkers." Only a few months after writing this, Eliot took a vow of celibacy himself, an ostentatious action, one would think, for an inaction that might well have remained private.

Eliot quickly withdrew his only essay on Crashaw, a loss if only for one observation on the poem "The Tear" (of the Blessed Virgin):

> Faire Drop, why quak'st thou so?
> 'Cause thou streight must lay thy Head
> In the Dust? O no;
> The Dust shall never bee thy Bed
> A pillow for thee will I bring
> Stuft with Downe of Angels wing.

"There is no warrant for bringing a pillow (and what a pillow!) for the *head* of a *tear*," Eliot wryly noted.

One of the lectures examines some lines from the same poem,

> What bright soft thing is this?
> A moist spark it is,
> A watry Diamond,

and concludes that "'soft thing' is good, for a tear, 'moist spark' is still better, and 'the water of a diamond' is an excellent pass of pate" (this last phrase describing Trinculo's display of wit in *The Tempest*). One of Eliot's own most excellent passes of pate occurs near the beginning of the third Clark lecture: "The human mind, when it comes to a terminus, hastens to look up the next train for almost anywhere."

Dangerous for Ordinary People

The celebrityhood of Victoria Sackville-West and Harold Nicolson, "Vita and Harold" in the British television series, falls well below that of Di and Charles but is richer in both prurient and intellectual interest than that of the younger combatants. The present selection of the correspondence[1] has been condemned for its snobbery. But not to worry: most of it is too far away to be hurtful, and much of it can be enjoyed as unconsciously comic.

Not many readers are likely to take issue with Nigel Nicolson's judgment that his father was a "better"—he might have added a more forbearing and sympathetic—"letter-writer" than his mother. Nor will many wish to challenge his in any case unverifiable assertion that this very odd couple, if less and less so by the hour, who were unfaithful to each other by mutual consent with people of their own sex, achieved "a relationship richer and more enduring than most." He does not explain that the endurance was partly the result of the parallel, partly of the circumstance that the couple did not live together much of the time. Though at age eighteen she had certainly been the lover of Rosamund Grosvenor, late in life she told her husband that she had been ignorant of same-sex love before marriage. After it she renounced the other kind and denounced the marital "system" as "wrong" and "claustrophobic," while conceding that "very, very intelligent people like us ... are able to rise superior."

Vita is more frank about her affairs than Harold about his. He admits to loathing "women in general," but remains buttoned up about consummations with, among others, the "amazingly beautiful," if regrettably "bedint" (the Sackville shibboleth for middle-class) Patrick Hepburn. Vita, her son writes, was "born to be a lesbian lover," adding that "her only problem was to free herself of one love affair in order to begin the next." The callousness of this amorous *modus vivendi* is exposed in a line from one of her poems: "We take a heart and leave our own intact." In a letter attempting to rationalize her love-life by compartmentalizing it, she hides behind a sexual duality that, if it ever

[1] Vita and Harold: *The Letters of Vita Sackville-West and Harold Nicolson,* edited by Nigel Nicolson. New York: Putnam's, 1992.

existed, was remarkably lopsided:

> If you were in love with another woman, or I with another man, we should
> both of us be finding a natural sexual fulfillment which would inevitably
> rob our own relationship of something. As it is, the liaisons which you and
> I contract are something perfectly apart from the more natural and normal
> attitudes we have toward each other, and therefore don't interfere. But it
> would be dangerous for ordinary people....

As the letters testify, her "natural sexual fulfillment" was with women, for
which reason she abrogated all conjugal relations with her husband after the
birth of their children.

Nigel Nicolson tells us that his mother could be "merciless" as well as "reck-
less and cruel." While diverting herself on the Riviera with her lover, Violet
Trefusis, her usually acquiescent spouse accuses her of being "more selfish than
Agrippina in her worst moments." The letters confirm this possibility, as when,
during World War II, she deplores the requisitioning of the woods near her castle at Sissinghurst by a detachment of soldiers: "I shall never love the lake or the
wood again in the same way ... a thing of beauty, now tarnished forever." The
thought that the base intruders were training to protect lives, including hers, at
the risk of their own, does not occur to her.

Virginia Woolf figures as prominently in the correspondence as Violet, the
most transgressive among Vita's earlier paramours. Vita recalled her affair with
Violet as a "madness," perhaps remembering their elopement to Monte Carlo,
where she appeared dressed as a soldier named Julian, her hair covered with a
bandage; only two weeks after the 1918 Armistice and in a country with millions of soldiers mutilated or dead, this could not have been seen as in the best
of taste.

Virginia "rumpled my hair," while "I sat on the floor" by firelight, Vita
bluntly informs Harold, yet she pretends to be "scared to death of arousing
physical feelings in her because of the madness"—she is "*so* sane, when not
mad"—and he answers by warning of the "mess" that would ensue if an affair
were to trigger a new attack of insanity. Further on in the same letter, Vita discloses that she has "gone to bed with her (twice)," and in a later one tauntingly
reminds him that "I did sleep with her." Nigel Nicolson characterizes *Orlando*,
Virginia Woolf's mock-biography of his mother, as the "longest and most
charming love letter in literature." By the time it was published (1928), Vita's
fluxuous flirtations had swerved in the direction of Hilda Matheson, the BBC's
director of talks, and of Mary, wife of the poet Roy Campbell, a notorious liaison concealed from Harold, but revealed by Campbell in a scabrous satire.

Not surprisingly, Vita's best books are biographies of women, but the best of these, oddly—both she and Harold were anti-"Christophagist" (the wafer) and anti-resurrectionist—are of Saints Teresa of Avila, Teresa of Lisieux, and, currently a best-selling paperback, *Joan of Arc.* Vita's attraction to female forms and textures is evident even in her horticultural writings. She loves the *Cuisse de Nymphe,* as well as a rosebush that "tapers toward the top like the waist of a Victorian beauty," and a magnolia which has "all the softness and smoothness of youthful flesh."

"Harold's attitude to Americans was ambivalent," his son asserts; "He could not justly be called a snob." But the correspondence indicates that his attitude was unambivalently negative, as perforce it could only be in view of what the rest of the book tells us about him. When he writes that "there simply does not exist [in the U.S.] the sort of person whom we like," the observation may or may not be true, but he, doubtless, is being truthful.

The ambivalence is Nigel's invention, intended to make the letters more palatable to transatlantic book-buyers, but achieving the opposite by adding that on a second visit to this "exciting country" Harold met such acceptable Americans as the Morrows and the Lindberghs, the banker Thomas Lamont, Archibald MacLeish, and "the whole Roosevelt clan" at Oyster Bay. "I do not feel you would care for Long Island in the very least," Harold wrote, and, "I think it was a good thing your ancestors disposed of their possessions in this continent." Long Island, all of it, had been granted to a Sackville by Charles I in 1637.

Nigel Nicolson blames his father's unflattering reactions to the United States during the initial trip on the atmosphere of the 1933 Depression, the midwinter climate, and a lecture tour itinerary that took him to "some of the most unappetizing American cities." Harold wrote from Cincinnati that "you and I are very gifted and charming [but not] in the sort of way these people suppose." The exception was Charleston, South Carolina, where the "voices are as soft as the feet of the negro women selling narcissus in the street. It is the most unAmerican thing I have met." Furthermore, Charlestonians "talk of the Americans almost as enemies.... They still long for secession under the British crown."

What sort of person did Vita and Harold like? His sort should be able to "wear a top hat without feeling foolish," and, if someone referred to "Pinero's plays," would not need to ask, "Who's Pinero?" (*Pinero!!*) He relishes the company of statesmen, "Winston" and other august people, but not De Gaulle (though "he is less horrible with his hat off"). And the titled: "I rather liked" King Paul of Greece, "an old pansy really"; the Duchess of York "talked to me so intelligently about *Some People*.... [I]t is an absolute tragedy that she should be a royalty"; talking to her later, as the Queen Mum, widow of George VI (himself "just a snipe from the great Windsor marshes"), Harold "had to leave in the middle to go wee wee, but she took it well." He does not care for Edward VIII, and "Willy" Maugham tells him: "I knew Mrs. Simpson when she was *a* Mrs. Simpson, not-*t-t-the* Mrs. Simpson." Maugham, Harold notes, has "an old-fashioned courtesy," but is "rather bedint about it."

As a young woman Vita enjoyed parties, not those "scrimmages at the Ritz" for rich riff-raff but a proper ball at Sunderland House with "powdered footmen announcing duchesses.... I do like fit things. I do, I do." She looks forward to another ball the following week in which she will go as La Grande Mademoi-selle, wearing velvet clothes, a riding dress with high boots, and carrying a whip, and she asks him to look for her in this get-up in "the illustrated papers." Still a dedicated party-goer a decade later, in the 1920s, but less of a *precieuse ridicule*, she attends three in a day on one occasion, going from a reception by "those frauds the Sitwells" to a small gathering at Clive Bell's with Virginia Woolf and Maynard Keynes, then, after midnight, to an "immense party" at Ar-gyll House. In the 1930s she turns down invitations from Buckingham Palace and slightly less exalted addresses with the excuse that she no longer has any-thing to wear.

The Nicolsons lived in their possessions, she more deeply than he in that Knole, the vast Renaissance castle in which she grew up (sleeping in Cranmer's bedroom) and for which she yearned all her life, was her Sackville inheritance. Elizabethan drama might be said to have begun there, Thomas Sackville having been one of the authors of *Gorboduc*. Two centuries later Alexander Pope wrote the epitaph for the tomb of Charles Sackville, sixth earl of Dorset. One of the book's most amusing episodes develops from the higher elevation of her lineage to his: when Harold is knighted for his George V biography, Vita is appalled at the prospect of being addressed as "Lady Nicolson." During her first pregnancy, Vita instructs her husband in how to distribute her baubles should she not sur-vive the accouchement: "my emerald chain, my string of pearls"; "my other tiara, the one with the leaf pattern in emeralds and diamonds"; "my diamond crystal watch"; "the seven big diamonds, the emerald ornament ... and one or two of my rings...."

But the Nicolsons' proudest possession are the gardens of Vita's more mod-est second castle, Sissinghurst, now, like Knole, the property of the National Trust. He is more snobbish than she about the flowers that should and should not be cultivated there: "Rhododendrons are to us like large stock-brokers whom we do not want to invite to dinner"; "I don't feel that azaleas are very

Sissinghurst…. They are Ascot, Sunningdale sort of plants"; "Anything with the suggestion of suburbia should be excluded," and "Shrubbery is a great problem if one is to avoid the suburban"; "I quite see that those big pale yellow things … would look very well [but] they must be faint pallid yellow—nothing that shouts or raises its voice."

Both writers award themselves top marks on their culture, but the evidence of artistic appreciation in the letters is exiguous. Ballet, in the Diaghilev era, is mentioned only once, and while Harold is "really wild about Cézanne" at one time, and at another dislikes Ingres more than any other great artist, the names of painters occur only in passing. Vita visits Rodin, "a commonplace little French bourgeois" with "the Légion d'Honneur in his buttonhole," but confides to her diary, not to her husband, that the bedint sculptor had tried to seduce her—as he apparently did every woman who ventured into his atelier.

Both Nicolsons were unmusical. Vita describes an escape from the laureate Robert Bridges' twee tinkling away at Handel on his clavichord. And Harold describes his discovery, in Mozart, not of the superfetation of ideas but merely that one thing leads to another. (He actually wrote elsewhere that "musical people possess fantasy but no constructive imagination.") Arriving late "at the Aberconway party," he sits outside the door of a room in which the Quartet K. 464 is being performed: "On and on they went. Mozart is just like Bunny [a neighbor of theirs]. He says, 'Well I must be going now,' and then thinks of something else to say, and goes on and on till I could have struck the door with angry fists." One of Harold's letters reveals that he contemplated writing a biography of Ludwig II, a subject perfectly suited to his talents and temperament, except that Wagner meant nothing to him.

As repeated here, many of the Nicolsons' literary judgments are dubious, while their critical principles presuppose sanctuaries for those who belong to "a definite class, by birth"; thus Edmund Wilson's adverse article, "Through the Embassy Window: Harold Nicolson," falls "into a common error of critics … to demand that a writer shall be something he is not," and to expect "a gentle person of sensibility and culture to care for the rough and tumble." She recoils from "the dunghill despair of Eliot," and his "combinations drying in the sun." And he peeves about not having been able to "disinfect myself from the slime of *Lolita*." Both of them profess high opinions of Vita's poems, one of which inspires him to an allocution beginning "If there was ever a work of art about which I felt *certain*, it is this," after which, by way of demonstration, he cites the Kilmer-ish couplet "How delicate in spring they be / That mobled blossom and that wimpled tree." Robert Bridges also praises her poetry, or may have intended to, with "not a woman's writing at all—damn good."

The best passages in the correspondence are the cameo portraits—in G. B. Shaw's case, of his "white ashes," which Harold goes to see in a car "very rich and American ... central heating and so on." Sinclair Lewis is a "red-faced noisy young man who called me Harold from the start ... and drank and drank.... He said he was too tight to dress for a ball," and asked me "did he look tight, because Edith [Dorothy Thomson] minded." Joyce "told me that a man had taken Oolissays to the Vatican and had hid it in the shape of a prayer book and that it had been blessed in such disguise by the Pope." Minna Curtiss, with whom Harold stays in the Berkshires, tells him that Lindbergh was "no more than a mechanic" who, if he had not flown to Paris, "would now be in charge of a gasoline station on the outskirts of St. Louis." After spending considerable time with the "lone eagle," Harold finds him "shrewd and intelligent," if "quite uneducated," but wickedly quotes him in his native dialect on President Coolidge's medal presentation ceremony at the White House: "Just because I flew alone to Purris ... I had to go through the whole damned show over again in the yard, I mean the lawn...."

As one of his country's delegates to the Versailles Peace Conference, Harold Nicolson attended closed meetings between Lloyd George, Wilson, and Clemenceau, "three ignorant and irresponsible men cutting Asia Minor to bits as if they were dividing a cake ... the happiness of millions being decided in that way." But Nicolson's writings on diplomacy are unjustly neglected, and the chapter on "The Bosnian Crisis," 1909, in the biography of his father, Lord Carnock, is still enlightening on the background of the siege of Sarajevo, 1994.

Isaiah Berlin's
Philosophical Bestiary

Isaiah Berlin's *Conversations*,[1] like *The Hedgehog and the Fox*, the essay that established his American reputation forty years ago, reveals his continuing preoccupation with categorical opposites. In the new book, a "memoir in the form of a dialogue" with Iranian philosopher Ramin Jahanbegloo, the zoomorphic metaphor—hedgehogs (Marx, Dostoevsky) know one big thing, foxes (Goethe, Herzen) know many small things—becomes briefly ichthyomorphic, in a remark on the incompatibility of absolute liberty and absolute equality: The rich and powerful are pikes, the poor and meek are carps. An ingenious spin-off of this method of measurement is introduced, dividing nineteenth-century philosophers according to their probable sympathies during World War II: "Tocqueville might not have collaborated, but I don't think he would have joined the underground." But the main sorting out is of monists, who explain all phenomena by one unifying principle or as manipulation of a single substance, and pluralists, who explain all phenomena in terms of many principles or embodiments of various substances. "Every classification throws light on something," Sir Isaiah says.

The making of distinctions is the task of all philosophy, of course, but no one does it with the perspicuity and finesse of Isaiah Berlin. Comparing ideas of liberty, he reminds us that in Socrates' Athens anyone could bring charges against anyone else, and that the modern concept of liberty conferring a certain measure of privacy is rarely encountered in ancient thought. Comparing individual philosophers, he contrasts Spinoza, "a rigid determinist" with "no sense of change and evolution" and even "no sense of history," with Leibniz, an antideterminist with "a sense of the continuity of history and of the uniqueness of each moment."

Machiavelli is a crucial figure for Berlin in that he recognized the possibility of two opposed value systems, two kinds of social morality, the antique Roman, which he clearly preferred (*virtù*, stoicism, self-assertion), and the

---

[1] *Conversations With Isaiah Berlin*, by Isaiah Berlin and Ramin Jahanbegloo. New York: Scribner's, 1992.

Christian (humility, freedom from worldly ambition). As a dualist, in this sense, Machiavelli was the first "to break the monist tradition," and "once you have two equally valid possibilities you might have more." Machiavelli perceived that a powerful and efficient state cannot be built on the morality of the Gospels, and this undermining of the idea of a Christian state is at least as important historically as his advocacy of bad means to successful ends.

The *Conversations* includes some discussion of philosophers about whom Berlin has written little—Thomas Hobbes, for one, who was "more monist than anyone," and Benjamin Constant, "A thinker whom I greatly admire ... a genuine liberal." But the ideas that receive his closest scrutiny are the familiar ones of his earlier books, the ideas of Giovanni Battista Vico, "the first man who understood (and told us) what human culture is," and who "taught us to understand alien cultures," and of Johann Gottfried von Herder who goes beyond Vico in the pursuit of cultural empathy. Hegel, the target of Berlin's *Historical Inevitability*, is refuted yet again: "Once people say: We should do this or that, because history demands it [and] anything which gets in the way must be swept aside ... you tend to trample on human rights and values.... I do not believe in historical determinism ... history as an autobahn from which deviations cannot occur." In the Hegelian system, "all the footsteps point one way." But when Berlin boasts that "everything I have written has usually been attacked from both sides, from the Right and from the Left, with equal vehemence," one's impression persists that the stronger attacks came from the fellow-traveling Hegelian-Marxist Left.

Like Vico, and Edmund Burke, Berlin does not believe in a universal human nature, but he does believe in "universal human values," values that "a great many human beings in the vast majority of places and situations at almost all times do in fact hold in common." The apparent inconsistency may be attributed to his phobia against analogies between the life of a society and that of a biological organism, which have "led to irrational and brutal forms of nationalism and intolerance." All the same, Irenaus Eibl-Eibesfeldt's recent *The Biology of Human Behavior* is said—by E. H. Gombrich, among others—to demonstrate convincingly that certain human reactions are undeniably universal.

For many readers the most absorbing parts of the book will be the passages on Zionism, the "very civilized" origins of which, in the ideas of the nineteenth-century German socialist Moses Hess, have lately been derouted in "a nationalistic phase." Hess understood Herder's principle that "people can only create if they are independent and they can only be independent if they have a land of their own ... a homeland." Berlin tells us that he was a Zionist even as a schoolboy in Petrograd, having realized quite early in life that "Jews were a minority everywhere ... that there was no Jew in the world who was not, in some degree, socially uneasy," even if "genuinely integrated"—an impossibility, as the "deep assimilation" of the German Jews demonstrated.

Berlin feels "free" in Israel, he says, and "I don't particularly feel a Jew"; but "in England I do." One can only suppose that this saddening remark is related to his fear that "today's young ... seek absolutes," which "sooner or later ... ends in blood." He draws our attention to the failure of Saint-Simon, Marx, and Lenin to predict the rise of nationalism over the entire globe during the twentieth century, and to foresee that nationalism and religious fanaticism would become the most powerful political forces of our time. And he warns that at the end of "one of the worst centuries of human history ... there is a world shift to the Right. I wish it were not so. I am a liberal."

Among twentieth-century philosophers, Berlin admires G. E. Moore, "an acute and totally honest thinker [who] converted Bertrand Russell to the belief that what we see and hear and touch and smell and taste, must, in the end, be the basis of all we know of the external world." He finds Heidegger "unreadable," and "cannot understand a word of the philosophical writings of ... Adorno [and] Derrida": after the Second World War, German and French philosophers "abandoned prose intended to be generally understood." He remains personally sympathetic to Leo Strauss, while rejecting his beliefs, but zaps Hannah Arendt as an "egregious" lady who produces "no arguments, no evidence of serious philosophical or historical thought ... [and who] moves from one sentence to another without logical connection.... *The Human Condition* [seems to be] based on two ideas, both historically false.... I am not ready to swallow her idea about the banality of evil. It is false. The Nazis were not banal. Eichmann deeply believed in what he did, it was, he admitted, at the center of his being."

Asked about the usefulness of philosophy, Sir Isaiah says that it can "teach us to see through political rhetoric, bad arguments ... every kind of chicanery and disguise." Moreover, philosophers "clarify ideas; they analyze the words and concepts and ordinary terms in which you and I think." One of the aims of philosophy is "to understand the relationships of men, things, words to each other," and the aim of political theory should be to concern itself with the real "goals of social existence." In a book that tells us more about himself than ever before, Berlin avows that "Anglo-American philosophy and Kant formed me," and admits to being "hopelessly secular." The values of the Enlightenment, "what people like Voltaire, Helvétius, Holbach, Condorçet preached are deeply sympathetic to me. Maybe they were too narrow, and often wrong about the facts of human experience, but ... they liberated people from horrors, obscurantism, fanaticism.... [T]hey were against cruelty, they were against oppression...."

The five conversations are presented as if they followed in chronological order, but the text does not always bear this out. Thus Herder's *"Einfühlung"* appears twice in the first conversation (differently spelled), but is translated as "empathy" only in the last. Vissarion Belinsky is identified only at the fifth reference to him; and when Berlin says to his interviewer, "I don't know if you have seen my lecture on the Agnelli prize," he cannot have forgotten their supposedly earlier discussion of it. But, in the interests of greater cohesiveness and avoidance of repetition, passages on individual philosophers might have been collated and grouped together in the first place, rather than spread throughout the book. Occasionally, too, a statement might have been clarified by a minor edit: "The neglect of the ambiguity of the word 'in' when we speak of an image *in* the mirror, can lead to avoidable philosophical confusions." (Delete *avoidable*.)

The *Conversations* are free of technical jargon ("as" instead of "qua") and of what laymen think of as typical philosophical subject matter ("Why does the universe exist?"). The scope is broad, if not compendious, and while we are not surprised at the absence of the monist Kierkegaard, the pragmatist C. S. Peirce, the Marxist Antonio Gramsci, and the sociologists Emile Durkheim and Max Weber, we would have welcomed some comment on Ortega's concept of dehumanization—and more on the structure, the volutions, of Berlin's own metaphor of history moving in "spirals." For our enlightenment, too, Jahanbegloo might have posed a question about Vico's autobiography and the exemplification of the philosophical method in the life; and a question about ancient prototypes of historical inevitability, such as the notion, in the later writings of Polybius, of Tyche (Fortune) sending all of the world's affairs in one direction.

What one most regrets, is that Berlin's famous humor does not come through frequently enough. One example of it—the twinkle is in the qualifying clause—can be heard in his response to a question as to why Alexander Herzen turned his back on the Slavophils and toward the West. "In Russia people were at the whim of landowners or officials, beaten violently or sent to Siberia. In the West, by and large, they were not."

We can say of Isaiah Berlin as he says here of the late Andrei Sakharov: "Herzen's great liberal voice is heard again."

At Play in the
Fields of the Mind

"The American essay has been dormant for a long time," Cynthia Ozick remarks,[1] distinguishing the genre from the magazine article, "though its history is brilliant enough: Emerson to Edmund Wilson." But a recrudescence is underway: "The essay is waking up and turning muscular." This at any rate is true of Ozick's essays, which are also the most topical and contemporary (all from the 1980s) of the three collections considered here.

Robert Penn Warren's title[2] misleads: none of the contents is new; the most recent pieces date from 1977, and seven of the remaining eleven appeared in the early 1940s. The appreciation of Whittier (1946), moreover, has already been reprinted as the preface to a book of his poems. But no matter. The emeritus poet laureate's essays are larger in scale than Ozick's and William Maxwell's, and some of them, above all the acute reading of the *Rime of the Ancient Mariner*, have retained their status as classics despite the shelves of interim criticism. Warren can be read and reread for sheer pleasure. His paragraphs, and the essays as wholes, develop their ideas and arguments with a logical fluency, to borrow his distinction from the purely rhythmical Hemingway kind, "founded on the conjunction *and*," as elegant as it is solid.

Perhaps the finest essay on a fictional opus is "Conrad and *Nostromo*." Conrad's characters, the doyen tells us, do not share the delights of Shakespeare and Dickens in the "variety and richness of personality," but live in terms of "typical involvement with situation and theme." This has been recognized before, but it bears emphasizing for young readers who find themselves as much at sea in *Lord Jim* as the character of the title does quite literally.

After remarking on the remoteness of some connections between the "germ in real life" and its "imaginative fulfillment," Warren addresses the question of apparent discrepancies between Conrad's comments in prefaces and letters in relation to the "dark inwardness" of his world of fiction. The most evident of

[1] *Metaphor and Memory: Essays*, by Cynthia Ozick. New York: Knopf, distributed by Random House, 1989.

[2] *New and Selected Essays*, by Robert Penn Warren. New York: Random House, 1989.

these is in his professions of skepticism, "the attitude of the intelligence that would be self-sufficient," and his professions of faith. But surely Conrad's belief in "the human communion" is not contradicted by the "cold unconcern" of his artistic credo, the "attitude of perfect indifference, the part of creative power."

"E. B. White," William Maxwell says[3] in a review of the writer's letters, "set the prevailing tone of the [*New Yorker*], insofar as it had one." But Maxwell himself, during forty years as a fiction editor, must have contributed as much to the magazine's tonality and literary manners. In any case, *The Outermost Dream*, with its biographical, story-telling approach to criticism, the condensed retelling of the contents and the concluding twists, would have no effect on a stylistic concordance of the *New Yorker*. Two of Maxwell's reviews are of books by other staff-members, White and Louise Bogan (whose "chiselled opinions" offended some poets), and two more are devoted to such regulars as Frank O'Connor and Sylvia Townsend Warner (144 stories published there!), affable notices that further document the magazine's already copiously reported "behind-the-scenes" editorial life.

Despite his decided preference for British authors, Maxwell's most affecting essays are his skillful recounting of the diaries of two Russians from radically different societies. Andrei Amalrik's *Notes of a Revolutionary* is the chronicle of a decade spent in Soviet prisons, a decade of physical and mental torture, but also of guts and indomitable will. The "twist" is that he survived and reached the West in time to die at the age of forty-two in an automobile accident. Maxwell's title, "A Life," is perfect.

While Amalrik's story resembles an appalling number of others, Marie Vassiltchikov's is unique. Her father, Prince Illarion Vassiltchikov, moved his family to France during the Russian Revolution, and from there in the 1930s to the newly independent state of Lithuania, where he had once owned property. The Soviet invasion, shortly after the beginning of the Second World War, forced them to move again, this time to the country house in Germany of another aristocratic Russian refugee. Marie soon went to Berlin where she managed to find employment in a News Service, and to keep a surreptitious record of her experiences during the war.

The most curious aspect of *Berlin Diaries, 1940–1945* is its picture of a network of noblemen—Metternichs, Bismarcks, assorted Princes, Counts, and Barons from all over Europe—helping each other but leading remarkably detached lives, apparently not much incommoded by Hitler. Marie's most aston-

---

[3] *The Outermost Dream, Essays and Reviews*, by William Maxwell. New York: Knopf, 1989.

ishing entry tells of the death of one of her Galitzine aunts from the direct hit of a German bomb on a London bus, and the memorial service held in Berlin!

Burton Visotzky, professor at the Jewish Theological Seminary of America, told the *New York Times* that when he opposes Cynthia Ozick "I have this feeling of inner alarm." The present writer, though he knows little enough about midrashic studies, Professor Visotzky's subject, and has virtually nothing to oppose, understands the feeling. True, Ozick's strings of qualifiers are long, though on a close look both apt and indispensable ("not all juxtaposed adjectives are coordinate adjectives," she usefully reminds us), and while she may appear to be overly fond of paradoxes, they prove to be necessary starting points leading to rich rewards. Perhaps some of her images are not entirely successful. "Cascading" is a favorite word ("cascading novels" from Henry James's cornucopia, her mother's "cascading heart"), but it does not seem an altogether suitable one for a thick and sticky liquid ("cascading syrup").

Ozick is one of the most intelligent writers on the American scene, and she has the integrity to match. One of the few statements in her book that might be interpreted as disingenuous, albeit deliberately, is the speculation that its title essay may sound "more like a lecture in morals than the meditation on language it professes to be." No one knows better than Cynthia Ozick that at some point the two are the same.

Ozick tells us that she suffers from "word-besottedness," that one of her adolescent phantoms was of "rowing in the ablative absolute with *pius* Aeneas." Not surprisingly, her principal target is imprecision and other misuses of language. Her essay on the return to oral culture should be compulsory reading in English courses at all levels. "The degeneration of punctuation and word-by-word literacy" began about 1930, she says, and by 1980, with the reversion "via electronics, to the simple speaking face," it is all over "for mass literacy." The word processor, we are warned, wipes out "any *progressive* record of thought"— and in this connection she might have mentioned that in the case of Paul Celan, all twenty or so of his revisions, the average number, may be equally valid. Conversation also comes under attack, though most effectively in a quotation from Kafka: "Conversation takes the importance, the seriousness, the truth out of everything I think."

Of the studies of individual authors, Ozick is at her best on Sholem Aleichem. She begins with an illuminating characterization of the Yiddish language as "direct, spirited, and spiritually alert.... It is hard to be pretentious or elevated in Yiddish.... Yiddish is especially handy for ... familiarity, abuse, sentimentality ... and for putting people in their place.... Yiddish is a household tongue, and God, like other members of the family, is sweetly informal in it."

The essay includes a comparison of the Tevye stories in Yiddish with the distorting Americanization in *Fiddler on the Roof*.

Turning to Saul Bellow, Ozick manages to enumerate his "salubrious omissions" in a single mouthful:

> No preciousness, of the ventriloquist kind or any other; no carelessness either (formidably the opposite); no romantic aping of archaisms or nostalgias; no restraints born out of theories of form, or faddish tenets of experimentalism, or ideological crypticness; no neanderthal flatness in the name of cleanliness of prose; no gods of nihilism; no gods of subjectivity; no philosophy of parody.

Ozick enters into many of her essays with bits of family background (Russia to the Bronx), chunks from school years, and the struggle to succeed as a writer. Of her purely autobiographical pieces, the most appealing, easiest-going, is "Washington Square, 1946," but this opinion must be discounted, coming, as it does, from someone who seems to have been in many of the same places at approximately the same time, and who finds a large slice of his own life in her descriptions—which he mentions only to say first hand that she is an uncannily accurate observer.

Con Molto Spirito

"The world, when one is happy, is the place upon which one stands," Barbara Grizzuti Harrison exclaims in one of the many enraptured moments that heightened her nights and days in Milan, Bergamo, Venice, Florence, Rome, Naples, Sorrento, and the South in the early 1980s. This sophisticated, dextrous, contagiously exuberant, immediately and continuingly likable lady takes the reader on illuminating walks through both past and present-day Italy in a book[1] that, safe to predict, will be the companion of visitors there for years to come.

Mrs. Harrison's highly oxygenated first-person prose resembles, if anybody's, that of D. H. Lawrence in his explorations of some of the same territory. Unlike him, she draws on the wisdom of a host of predecessors—Dante to Vico, Goethe to Gaston Bachelard—sometimes differing with and even censuring them: Stendhal "considered a lie the proper embellishment of the truth." But she has a mind and an imagination of her own, and is by no means dependent on her pantheon of edifying witnesses.

Italian Days might be described as a diary transformed into a selective and personal guide. But this would be to leave out the joie de vivre and fun that pervade the book: On the Amalfitana road, "Giuseppina drives two miles an hour. Everybody hates us"; in Naples, Laura drives the wrong way down a one-way street: "Moses parting the Red Sea was nothing to it"; Antonella "thinks that New York must look like Dallas, and that Brooklyn, where I live, must consist of houses like J. R. Ewing's ranch." A feature of Mrs. Harrison's style is the running dialogue between her own and other people's observations, and her parenthetical afterthoughts: in Florence, part of the population is "strolling to watch the show (they are the show)"; in Rome, one feels "like a privileged child on the mend (we are all on the mend from our lives)"; and, "I don't know if this is true ... or, if it is true what it means, or if it is not true, what it means that they perceive it to be true."

---

[1] *Italian Days*, by Barbara Grizzuti Harrison. New York: Weidenfeld & Nicolson, 1989.

Even the most fleetly encounters with fellow tourists, friends and acquaintances, foreigners and inhabitants, are turned into delectable anecdotes. The setting and the other participants are sketched ("an oiled pompadour, a shiny mohair suit, three-toned ventilated shoes, unlit cigar in his mouth"), and the episode is brought to life through exchanges both spoken and—as in this scene where she and her friend Jane are attracted to a waiter—unspoken:

> I am falling in love ... my feelings (after the first course) are, however, still reversible: Perhaps he will say something stupid. (He doesn't.) Jane kicks me in the shins. We read each other's faces; hers is glowing. Oh, dear. She is falling in love with him, too. Out of respect for her feelings ... I rein my feelings in. I do not fall in love. Out of respect for my feelings, she reins her feelings in. He goes off with a third woman.

Apart from people and places and their relationships, Mrs. Harrison is preoccupied with the reaffirmation of her faith—a Roman Catholic baptism, "like a vaccination," eventually "takes"—and with the quest for family roots: she is the Brooklyn-born-and-bred daughter of first-generation immigrants from Abruzzo and Calabria, and her journey ends in these ancestral lands. In Rome, her primary subject is her faith—"there is something mean, stingy, about the failure to wish to believe"—and her chapter on the city is the heart, the soul and most of the body of the book; those on Milan ("no question of drowning in beauty; there is not enough to wade in"), Venice (comparatively skimpy), Florence, Naples, and the Mezzogiorno are less fervent.

While rejoicing at St. Peter's, "The visible heartbeat of Christ's Church on earth," she reacts against the sight of "the unhappy young, who sprawl and prowl" near Bernini's colonnades: "Life is never boring and it is particularly not boring in Rome." The Church inspires a dithyrambic tone, in one instance with a touch of Molly Bloom: "Nothing separates you from God but Yes. Mary is His Mother; she said Yes." She is sharply critical of a bigoted priest, of any kind of evangelizing, of the trifling with the Church by non-Catholics who tolerate it as good theater, and of all pietisms. When the Vatican bans Jean-Luc Godard's *Hail Mary*, she rushes to see it, then emerges with the verdict that the Pope "has made a silliness of a silliness." One of her brief hagiographies tells us that St. Paul was "bald, bearded, bowlegged, and pale.... Nothing to write home about!"

Mrs. Harrison is on firmer ground with painting than with music: *The Magic Flute*, at La Scala (or anywhere), cannot be dismissed as musical "confectionery." But with few exceptions the pictures on which she dwells, Carpaccio to Caravaggio, are religious; in Rome, Piranesi and the painters of architectural ruins, of *veduta* and landscape, Lorrain and Poussin, are not mentioned. Instead, looking at a portrait of a pregnant Mary ("so many Madonnas look sly and smug, and with their secret, who wouldn't?"), she wonders whether the Madonna had labor pains—and decides that Her delivery was like those of other women. So, too, she sets out to explain pictures of Mary "fondling" the infant Jesus' genitals, with the not altogether focused argument that "we come naked into the world, and so did the man / God who shared our human condition"; but she finds a point in Leo Steinberg's *The Sexuality of Christ in Renaissance Art and Modern Oblivion*: "'The Child's lower body concedes its humanity.'" Some of her evocations of color are quaint: "whore-red," "slutty yellow."

Reflecting on art is like eating "an exquisite meal," Mrs. Harrison writes, and the culinary arts, as detailed in her extensive notes on food and cooking, are among the book's highlights. She includes the complete menus of her more memorable lunches and dinners, filling three of her pages on Florence with an appetizing aside on food—which, she confesses, "exists for solace" and "often becomes an obsession when one lives alone." In stalls and markets, shop windows and restaurants, edibles of every kind are scrumptiously described. In church, feeling that the light is "honeyed" and "nourishing," she thinks "I could eat this light." Even at the excavation site of St. Peter's grave she is reminded of "the joy of the food that was the symbol of the invisible preserve of the dead." Her knowledge and palate experience of wines are apparently less developed, and in her report that a Sorrento white "tastes interestingly of sulfur," the adverb undermines confidence.

The book contains a sprinkling of factual errors (and some verbal ones: "cul-de-sacs"; "obdurable"), one of them the attribution to St. Augustine of Tertullian's "*Credo quia absurdum*," surprising from so vigilant a writer; another, the statement that Jews could become prime ministers in Italy—Lugzatti, for one, "as they could not in other European countries," is contradicted by Léon Blum. But this sounds like grousing.

Humanity, here and now, and whether or not in the image of a humanized God, is the pulsing center of *Italian Days*.

Great Dane

The Danish writer Jens Peter Jacobsen (1847–1885) is little known in America except among musical people and largely through Arnold Schoenberg's *Gurrelieder* (1900–1911), a German-language setting of Jacobsen's *Gurresange* ballad. Some of Jacobsen's shorter poems have also reached concert audiences in the form of songs by his compatriot Carl Nielsen and by Frederick Delius, whose last opera, *Fennimore and Gerda*, is an adaptation of the two main episodes of Jacobsen's novel *Niels Lyhne*.[1]

In contrast, Jacobsen's high European reputation is essentially literary. "*Niels Lyhne*," Freud wrote to Wilhelm Fliess in 1895, "has moved me more profoundly than any other reading of the last ten years; the last chapters I recognize as classic." Niels Lyhne (*sic*) Jensen, a Professor of Scandinavian literature in Aarhus, Denmark, and Jacobsen's most acute and comprehensive critic in English, comes close to explaining Jacobsen's attraction for Freud: "[Most] likely it is the deep tragic disillusionment of the novel that appealed to a man who did not regard happiness as inherent in the plan of creation while accepting that existence was hard to bear both for mankind and the individual."[2] Freud also must have been struck by the Oedipal relations between mother and son in Jacobsen's story, *Fru Fonss*. When the woman of the title tells her teenage son of her intention to remarry, he replies angrily:

> Have you any idea of the things you make me think of? My mother loved by a strange man, my mother desired in the arms of another and holding him as hers. Nice thought for a son.

Ibsen, who had known Jacobsen in Rome, had a high opinion of *Niels Lyhne*, echoes of which are heard in *Ghosts* and *Rosmersholm*. Strindberg based *Miss Julie*

---

[1] *Niels Lyhne*, by Jens Peter Jacobsen, newly translated from the Danish by Tiina Nunnally, Afterward by Eric O. Johannesson. Seattle: Fjord Press, 1990. Jacobsen had a strong influence on the American composer Charles Griffes, according to Maisel, his biographer.

[2] *Jens Peter Jacobsen*, by Niels Lyhne Jensen. Boston: Twayne, 1980.

on Jacobsen's novel *Marie Grubbe* and attempted to dramatize it. Hofmannsthal, Musil, Thomas Mann, and, above all, Joyce were admirers. Stefan Zweig described Jacobsen as "the poet of poets for a whole generation in Germany" and *Niels Lyhne* as its *Werther*, while Hermann Hesse thought of Jacobsen as "the completely modern writer." But it is Rilke who best expresses the deeper reasons for Jacobsen's fascination:

> There is nothing [in *Niels Lyhne*] that does not seem to have been understood, grasped, experienced, and fully known in the tremulous after-ring of memory.... [T]he least incident unfolds like a destiny, and fate itself is like a wonderful wide web in which each thread is guided by an infinitely tender hand.

The excellent new translation of *Niels Lyhne*, which makes Jacobsen's greatest fiction available in English for the first time since Hanna Astrup Larsen's 1919 translation (republished in New York in 1960), is accompanied by the publisher's note that Jacobsen "produced only a small body of work in his short lifetime." What seems more remarkable is that, chronically ill with tuberculosis from the age of twenty-two, and dead at thirty-seven, he should have produced so much. Moreover, the six-volume Danish collected edition contains writings that would have assured him a niche in the history of science if he had published nothing else.[3]

Born April 7, 1847 in Thisted, Jutland, the eldest of five children in a merchant-class family with no cultural horizons, Jacobsen entered the University of Copenhagen in 1868 as a biology student. The imaginative writer in him, as well as the biologist, is already evident in his first published work, an article, "Darwin's Theory" (1871), which appeared in a new periodical, *Nyt dansk Maanedsskrift*:

> What he had to say was that all life on earth was like a gigantic garment weaving itself, where the trend and color of each thread presuppose those of another, and as time passed the texture became richer and lovelier.

Jacobsen's social as well as biological Darwinism provoked discussion and dissension in Copenhagen. His replies, in which, Jensen tells us, he dealt with his opponents "in a sober and elegant fashion," demonstrated his command of the subject. On the strength of his article, Jacobsen was invited to translate *The*

---

[3] *Samlede Vaerker*, J. P. Jacobsen, edited by Frederik Nielsen. Copenhagen: Gyldendal, 1972–1974. A three-volume edition, published by Lademan, appeared in Copenhagen in 1984.

Origin of Species and *The Descent of Man* into Danish, a task he completed in 1874. Between 1870 and 1873 he published a series of popularizing pieces on the new biology, and his dissertation, a study of algae in Denmark, written in French, *Aperçus systématique et critique sur les Desmidiacées du Danemark*, was awarded a prestigious gold medal in 1873.

Meanwhile, Jacobsen was pursuing his literary interests, writing poems—a selection of them, *Hervert Sperring*, was rejected by every publisher to whom he sent it—and founding a literary society, Agathon. When he showed his poems to Georg Brandes, the leader of a new literary movement dedicated to radicalism in politics and Realism in literature, this otherwise discerning critic was also dismissive, though some of them are now among the classics of Danish poetry. Later, the Brandes brothers, Edvard and Georg, became Jacobsen's good friends.[4]

One of Jacobsen's early letters lists his reading before he was twenty: in English, Shakespeare, Byron, Tennyson; in German, all of Goethe, Schiller, Wieland, Heine, and the *Nibelungenlied*; in French, Sainte-Beuve and Taine; in Danish, Kierkegaard, Andersen, and the Bible; in Old Norse, Eddic and Skaldic, the Scandinavian mythologies; and, in whatever language, the *Kalevala*. Paul Kierkegaard, Søren's nephew and, as a disciple of Feuerbach, in revolt against him, was a close friend whose influence on Jacobsen's obsessive agnosticism is evident.

Flaubert was a later discovery. As a day-dreamer in conflict with reality, Marie Grubbe is a sister of Emma Bovary, the feckless, failed-lover Niels Lyhne a brother of Frédéric Moreau. But the voice of the author-narrator is a principal component in Jacobsen's fiction, unlike Flaubert's. Joyce, in characterizing George Moore as "struggling in the backwash of that tide which has advanced from Flaubert through Jakobsen [sic] to D'Annunzio,"[5] may have been the first to recognize the link to Flaubert. The link in the other direction is puzzling: Jacobsen's gentleness and refinement, his playful ironies—"when you have become the possessor of the whole truth ... wouldn't it be unforgivable if you kept

---

[4] *Breve fra J. P. Jacobsen*, edited and with a forward by Edvard Brandes. Copenhagen: Glydendal, 1899.

[5] *The Day of the Rabblement*, privately published in Dublin in 1901 and published in *Critical Writings* (of James Joyce), edited by Ellsworth Mason and Richard Ellmann. London: Faber & Faber, 1959. Joyce's own connection to Jacobsen seems not to have been explored. He could have read *Niels Lyhne* in the English translation, *Siren Voices*, published in 1896, with an introduction by Edmund Gosse, who had been alerted to Jacobsen by Georg Brandes during a stay in Copenhagen in 1874, or, conceivably, in Danish, in this period of his letter to Ibsen in Norwegian. Some hundred

it all to yourself"—and his comic kinship with Smollett, are at an opposite extreme from the sensibilities of D'Annunzio.

During a vacation in Florence, between his Darwin translations, Jacobsen suffered a pulmonary hemorrhage. Back home, tuberculosis, advanced and incurable, was diagnosed, though a medical report rejecting him from military service suggests that the disease had been detected four years earlier. He was given no more than two years to live. Yet he continued to write for six more, and lived, too feeble to work, five years beyond that.

In spite of the pain and inanition of illness, Jacobsen's world is neither confining nor moribund. From the beginning, however, it was pervaded by a preoccupation with death and disillusion with religion. In his first story, "Strangers," unpublished in his lifetime, a man and a woman, social misfits, stigmatized by their lowly births, meet at a country fair where their apparel and manner of dancing, so different from that of the others, are ridiculed. They marry and live, virtually ostracized, in the moorland, away from the peasant village to which they go from time to time to earn a pittance, she by dancing at various gatherings, he by accompanying her on the clarinet. Their lives are marked by tragedy and deprivation. When their only child dies, his mother blames God for the infant's sufferings. When she dies from a disease herself, her husband plays the music that they both loved over her corpse and, when discovered doing so by outraged villagers, is driven away. Both the theme of the story, the conflict of individual lives with convention, and the ironic narrative style are characteristic of Jacobsen's later work.

Jacobsen's first published fiction and his only long short story, *Mogens* (1872), was perceived as the work of an original and appealing talent. A youth of about twenty, of independent means, Mogens lives alone as a forest warden in a remote, sparsely populated part of Sealand, twelve miles from a town. In the woods one day, he is surprised by a young girl, Camilla, who comes upon him unexpectedly. She flees and hides in a thicket, but he catches a glimpse of her. A little later, when she accompanies her father, councilor of the district, on

---

Danish usages have been identified in *Finnegans Wake* (see Richard Wagner's "Danish at the Wake," *James Joyce Quarterly* 6, no. 2 (1968), not including references to Kierkegaard and *Either/Or*. An influence of *Niels Lyhne* has been remarked in *Portrait of the Artist*, and of *Fru Fonss* in *The Dead*. In 1905 Joyce read *Mogens*, Jacobsen's book of stories (*Fru Fonss* is one of them), in German. The *Mogens* collection would have attracted him for its psychological insights, sexual openness, atheism, and, above all, its technical innovations—in *The Plague in Bergamo* the rhetorical intensification by switching from preterite to present, reported speech to direct speech, and the simulation of sexual excitation in the use of polysyndeton.

a visit to the warden, the two young people recognize each other. Mogens takes his guests rowing on a neighboring lake, and the councilor invites him to visit them in turn. That night, preparing for bed and thinking about Mogens's talk, Camilla undresses "with affected slowness," while Mogens's thoughts ask him "how a human being could be so wonderfully beautiful."

As he approaches the councilor's house, Mogens glimpses a red shawl as it "disappears behind the balcony windows ... and the back of a still-moving empty rocking-chair." Embarrassed at having been caught out watching for him, Camilla appears in a "glaring blue shawl," and greets him with "a faint welcome." Mogens's visits become more and more frequent, and the pair becomes easier in each other's company. Eventually they decide to marry.

An abrupt change of mood at this point disturbs us even though we realize that the euphoria and sweetness of the early part of the novella can only be ephemeral. The councilor is called away, and Camilla goes to stay in their house in town. One night a fire breaks out in a nearby factory and quickly spreads to the councilor's house. Mogens, staying not far away and at the moment laughing over a passage in a novel by Smollett, runs to the scene, breaks in, and tries to save Camilla, but is in time only to see her burn to death. He goes wild with grief and is found days later lying in the forest.

After a long recovery from "brain fever," he begins to lead a dissolute life with a succession of loose women, one of whom he abandons in a brutal manner. "Everything was full of injustice and lies, the entire earth was a huge rotting lie," and "love was the hollowest of all things." He then meets Thora, after overhearing her sing during his nightly strolls past her house, and falls in love with her. They marry, but fearing a return of the person he was during his violent period, that "what had been surely still was there," he does not, perhaps cannot, immediately consummate the marriage. And when at last he does, Jacobsen's happy ending, his only one, seems as sentimental as a movie fadeout. Having been told almost nothing about Thora, we replace her with a vision of the deceased Camilla:

> They went out together into the freshness of the morning. The sunlight was jubilant above the earth, the dew sparkled, flowers that had awakened early gleamed, a lark sang high up beneath the sky, swallows flew swiftly through the air. He and she walked across the green field toward the hill with the ripening rye; they followed the footpath which led over there. She went ahead very slowly and looked back over her shoulder toward him, and they talked and laughed. The further they descended the hill, the more the grain intervened; soon they could no longer be seen.

The fairy-tale opening, with its account of the innocent love of Mogens and Camilla, its descriptions of landscapes and the feelings expressed for the moods of nature, are the most successful parts of the novella, and one passage, in which Jacobsen disassociates colors and forms as attributes of objects, has become celebrated, despite the early critic who said that the author's pen "has the impossible ambition to be a brush":

> Within the room all forms of colors had awakened, all lines and contours had come to life. Whatever was flat extended, whatever was bent curved, whatever was inclined slid, and whatever was broken refracted the more.... Reddish-brown tones flooded in flames across the surface of the mahogany table ... on the carpet all the colors broke and mingled in a joyous, shimmering confusion.

Against this, the vagueness about the backgrounds and personalities of the dramatis personae can be exasperating, while the botanical and arboricultural opinions, extraneous to the story and merely mouthed by the otherwise totally undeveloped councilor, are often irritating: "Gardens were nothing but nature spoiled.... There was no style in nature, providence has wisely made nature natural." Yet some of the perceptions of Danish life are witty and shrewd, as when Mogens complains to Camilla about her worldly friends:

> There isn't a thing between heaven and earth which they cannot dispose of in the turn of a hand. *This* is common, and *that* is noble.... Every one of them knows the same things and talks about the same things.... One of them in his passion says something which he doesn't mean, and then the other says the direct opposite which he doesn't mean either, and then the one attacks that which the other doesn't mean, and the other that which the first didn't mean.

Jacobsen began the full-length historical novel *Marie Grubbe* in 1872, worked on it only intermittently because of ill health, and completed it in 1876. It is based on the life of a noblewoman born in 1643, who married a bastard son of King Frederik III, divorced him for a social and financial inferior, was caught in *flagrante delicto* with a stable-boy, and spent the later years of her long life in poverty and degradation. Although H. C. Andersen and others had written about the historical Marie Grubbe, Jacobsen alone seems to have undertaken extensive research, not only in the original documents in the Royal Library in Copenhagen, but even, according to Niels Lyhne Jensen, spending "months on the streets of Copenhagen to study historical buildings under varying conditions of light." Unfortunately, the admired feature in the Danish original, the pastiche of seventeenth-century language in which it is written, is all but indigestible in the English rendering. T. E. Lawrence, who learned Danish in order to read *Marie Grubbe*, tried but failed to interest a London publisher in commissioning a better translation.

When the novel begins, Marie is fourteen, a lonely child living with her uncaring widowed father and his mistress. During the Dano-Swedish war of 1657–1658 she is taken to Copenhagen to live with her maternal aunt, through whom she meets, and at a distance falls in love with, the King's natural son. The royal bastard dies horribly of syphilis, leaving Marie devastated until her aunt introduces her into court society, where she makes the acquaintance of Ulrik Frederik Gyldenlove, the viceroy of Norway, whom she later marries. At first the match seems a brilliant one, but eventually Ulrik, restless and bored, goes abroad. Returning after fifteen months, he treats Marie with great insensitivity, and in an irrational fit of hatred and resentment, she tries to kill him with a table knife. He begins to fear her, turns to the company of whores, but still feels love for her, while hers for him vanishes: "I believe that your love is great and strong, but mine you have strangled with your own hands."

The marriage is dissolved, and Marie has an affair with her brother-in-law which ends in disenchantment. When her next lover dies in an accident, she goes home to her father for a time, then manages to attract a nobleman, who marries her. She wrecks this relationship by an involvement with a peasant twenty years younger than herself, who subjugates and humiliates her. Jacobsen sees her acceptance of this as a reflection of her own innermost desires: "In this self-abasement there was a strange, voluptuous pleasure ... for such was the manner in which the clay had been mixed and of which she was fashioned."

The headstrong, self-destructive Marie entirely dominates the novel. Desiring her brother-in-law as a lover after seeing his display of physical strength in a tavern brawl, and the stable boy after watching him struggle with his horses during a fire, she reminds us of a D. H. Lawrence heroine. *Marie Grubbe* is an astonishingly modern study of a woman driven and undone by her sexuality. This daring portrait was attacked by Danish reviewers, who, apparently for no reason other than to disguise their distaste, saw Marie as "lacking consistency." Jacobsen wrote to Georg Brandes, by this time a strong supporter of his work:

> Certain facets of people do not cohere. Why should a complex thing such as a spiritual side to man hang together, culled from so many places, molded and influenced in so many ways?

Marie herself, answering a question as to whether she believes in the resurrection of the flesh, says much the same thing:

How shall I arise? As the young innocent child I was when I first came out among the people, or as the honored and envied favorite of the King and the ornament of the court, or as the poor hopeless ferryman's Marie?

Niels Lyhne, Jacobsen's only other full-length novel, is a *Bildungsroman* set in the Denmark of the 1840s. Perhaps, like *Marie Grubbe*, which is similarly episodic, it is best described as a chain of stories, each with the same central character, tracing the growth of his disbelief and disillusion. Niels is the prototype of the ineffectual man, the unheroic hero who fails at virtually everything he attempts, from his early ambition to be a poet to his several defeats as a lover. But only when praying for his dying wife and, later, his dying son, and then temporarily, does he betray his disbelief. On his own deathbed, after he has been mortally wounded by a bullet in the Dano-Prussian war of 1864, he does not surrender to "the pact of bread and wine with the inscrutable God." As Jensen points out, the last words of the novel, "And then finally he died the death—the difficult death," are indebted to Kierkegaard's *Sickness Unto Death*:

> For to die means that is the end, but to die death means to experience what it is to die; and to have this experience for one moment is to have it forever.

The novel chronicles Niels's successive experiences with six women. The first is his infatuation, aged twelve, with his widowed aunt, the young and beautiful Edele, who inspires fantasies in him of a solo-sexualist kind. His tutor is also in love with her, and she briefly responds with a love that "surrounded him with an ephemeral aura of spirituality and loftiness—something that often happens with inferior temperaments." But his utterances irritate her; they had "something brashly absolute about [them], rather like a misplaced drum in a dolce concert." Niels secretly witnesses a scene in which Edele rather too preachingly rejects this groveling suitor ("We close our eyes to our real life, we will not hear the 'No' it pronounces in the face of our wishes"), and the boy is drawn to her all the more intensely.

Like other Jacobsen women, Edele is mortally consumptive. Niels's prayers for her are not heeded, of course, even though "addressed not to Jesus," who "was ... only the son of God, not God himself, and thus it was to God the Father that he had prayed."[6] God the Father, of course, "betrayed him in his bit-

---

[6] This sounds like the seventh-century doctrine of dyothiletism, distinguishing between the human and the divine natures in the incarnate Christ, but Jacobsen's atheism ignores theology.

ter need," and on the day Edele was buried, Niels "stomped his foot on the earth of the grave with contempt every time the pastor mentioned the Lord's name." How ridiculous, Niels thought, that the

> mighty Old Testament God, the one who was so fond of Adam and Eve ... barely has created life before He ... drowns His world in waters from His heaven, who thunders down laws that are too weighty for the people He has created, and who then in the days of Caesar Augustus develops sympathy for them and sends His son to death so that the law may be broken, even as it is obeyed.

While this will remind Baron Grimm's readers of his scorn for the God "who must sacrifice his son because he once allowed an apple to be eaten," the soliloquy seems overly precocious for a boy of twelve. The book's early critics contended that however strong his feelings, Edele's death is not likely to have made a lifelong atheist of him. But Jacobsen may have been thinking of Darwin, whose rejection of Christianity began with the death of his beloved daughter Annie.

Niels's next romantic adventure, as an older student, is with a femme fatale, Mrs. Boye, a member of a Bohemian circle in Copenhagen, who leads him on. Critics have objected that, even from a very forward woman, her arguments in favor of greater sexual explicitness and candor in literature would have been unthinkable in conversation with a younger man at the time (c. 1850), but one could reply that the two are alone and that the atmosphere, including the furniture—in particular a sexually suggestive rocking chair—is charged with seduction. Niels is called away to his father's deathbed, and when on his return she coolly informs him of her engagement to another man, he is deeply hurt. Jacobsen's portrait of Mrs. Boye is convincing and perfectly drawn: she is the coquette of any period.

Niels's dying mother, Bartholine, is the subject of the next episode, a parody of Rousseauean sentimentality, for which reason, no doubt, Jacobsen, who had lived for a time in Montreux, set it in the philosopher's native Clarens. Bartholine, who is reading *Héloïse*, drips wistfulness: "Niels, take me along in your thoughts, my son, when someday you take part in all that glory I will never, ever see."

The centerpiece of the novel is Niels's love for his nineteen-year-old cousin, Fennimore. During his annual summer visit to his Aunt Rosalie, Fennimore's mother, Niels takes along his artist friend, Erik, who has also been in love with and abandoned by Mrs. Boye. Both young men fall in love with Fennimore and are overcome by the eroticism that she exudes, above all when singing and letting herself

be taken by those notes ... breathing into them ... as though she were singing herself naked before him.... There was such a fresh, unconscious sensuality about her entire figure; even her walk whispered of her body, there was a nakedness about her movements.

Fennimore, who had imagined her cousin as "more firmly defined" than he is, marries Erik.

Three years later, Erik invites Niels, now "a little more bitter and a little less trusting," for a visit, and since Erik's letter indicates that something is seriously wrong, Niels accepts, resolving to show "that he had so completely forgotten that he didn't even remember there was anything to forget." He discovers that Erik is neglecting Fennimore for the company of a group of farmers, who ease the dullness of country life with "whatever excesses their none-too-lively imaginations come up with." Niels falls in love with Fennimore all over again and they are soon engaged in an adulterous affair.

When Erik is killed in an accident in Aalborg, Niels, unaware of the death, has set out for a rendezvous with Fennimore, who, meanwhile, receives the news. She is standing outside in the snow as he approaches, and at the sight of the black figure he slows his pace. "It's me, the whore Fennimore," she shouts out to him. When he suggests that they talk inside, her fury explodes: "Never will you set your cowardly, dishonest foot in this house again.... Can't you hear that I hate you ... your lies dragged me down into the dirt with you." The irony of the scene is delectable. Fennimore's responsibility for their affair is at least as great as Niels's, since, as a founding feminist, she had repeatedly expressed contempt for "males who worship the purity of females." Moreover, only minutes before the arrival of the fateful telegram, she is shown pacing the floor in anticipation, and worrying, "Dear God, maybe he isn't coming!"

Niels's next encounter is with Madame Odero, an opera prima donna no longer in her prime, whom he meets in a hotel in Riva on Lago di Garda. The episode is of little consequence, and when she jilts him he is not angry, but has instead "a little resigned smile for this new hostility of fate." The cholera scare that empties Riva's and other hotels in the region seems to have been borrowed, and given only a small change of locale, by the author of *Death in Venice*.[7]

Finally, Niels marries his very young cousin Gerda, whom he tries to con-

---

[7] In an interview in *Die Zeit*, Vienna, 1904, Mann acknowledged his debt to Jacobsen, also apparent in the death scenes in *Buddenbrooks*, and in the Niels Lyhne descendants Tonio Kroger and Hans Castorp.

vert to his agnosticism, teaching her that "the belief in a personal God who ... in another life punishes and rewards [is] ... a futile attempt to remove the thorn from the bleak arbitrariness of life." But on her deathbed, succumbing to pulmonary disease, she returns to her faith and begs him to send for the pastor. He does so, out of love for her, then kneels in prayer himself to a God in whose existence he does not believe. In a conversation recorded by Georg Brandes, Jacobsen conceded that "most people cannot manage to get through life without, every now and then, appealing to heaven for help.... In *Niels Lyhne* I wish to show how difficult it is for a man to be a free-thinker in a country like Denmark, with on one side the siren-voices of tradition and the memories of childhood, and on the other the censoriousness of society."

The scheme of *Niels Lyhne* is transparent, moving, step by Bunyan-like step, through the principal stages of Niels's disillusionment. "Belief in a ruling, judgmental God [is] the last great illusion of humanity," his friend Dr. Hjerrild remarks to Niels one Christmas Eve, "and when it is gone people will be wiser, but not happier.... Atheism will make greater demands on people than Christianity does." Niels concurs, acknowledging that neither the present generation nor the next two will be able to bear atheism, for "the innermost marrow" of most people "will still be steeped in tradition." But he looks forward to the time when heaven, "instead of a threatening, watchful eye ... will give life when everything must be contained in life and nothing is placed outside it ... what nobility would spread over humanity if people could leave their lives freely and meet their deaths without fear of death or hope of heaven."

"You cannot find the word 'happiness' in the New Testament; it is decidedly a pagan idea," Niels tells Gerda. The anti-Christian bias in *Niels Lyhne*, in view of the survival of the Lutheran Church in Denmark today as a quasi-state religion (to the extent that the salaries of the clergy and the cost of upkeeping church buildings are paid by the Government[8]) and the novel's religious skepticism seem remarkably aggressive. Yet *Niels Lyhne*, far from a tract, is verbal, narrative, and psychological art of a high order. And surely it will now be read more in spite of its scientific materialism and positivist platforms than because of them.

* * *

Rilke, recognizing that Jacobsen's essential gift was as a poet, regarded the best of his fiction as poetry:

---

[8] The chrism was last applied at the coronation of Christian VIII, in 1840, but today the monarch is proclaimed by the prime minister in front of the people, not crowned.

If I am to say from whom I have learned something about the nature of creative work, there are but two names I can mention: that of Jacobsen, the great, great, great poet, and that of Auguste Rodin.

The *Gurresange*, a poem of passion, loss, and despair, Jacobsen's most moving work, was written when he was twenty-one, before any of his prose, and published only after his death. It is based on the great legend of medieval Denmark, the love of King Valdemar the Great (1131–1182) for his mistress Tove, or, as the Valdemar in Jacobsen's poem (Valdemar the Fourth c1320–1375), calls her, Tovelille, little Tove. During Valdemar's absence, his jealous queen, Helvig, induces her lover Folkvard to kill Tove by locking her in her bath house and scalding her with steam. Valdemar, in his grief, incurs his own eternal damnation by placing the blame on God:

Lord, do you not blush with shame?
Killing a beggar's only lamb....

The castle at Gurre, on the lake at Gurreso, not far from Elsinore, was excavated in the nineteenth century (from 1835) and has recently been restored. It is first mentioned in court chronicles in 1364, when Pope Urban V sent a gift of relics to its chapel, and it is recorded that Valdemar the Fourth—the Valdemars ruled from the twelfth to the fourteenth centuries—died there in October 1375. In the Tove and Valdemar ballads (*Folkeviser*), first written down in the fifteenth century, upon which Jacobsen based his poem, Valdemar the Great—Jacobsen transposed people (Tove) and events (the manner of Tove's death) to the later King—discovers Tove living in a small castle on a Baltic island and falls in love with her. In the original, Helvig, holding a torch, which in Jacobsen's version corresponds to the "vengeance aflame in her heart," follows Folkvard as he locks the door of Tove's bath. Valdemar's vengeance on him is as grisly as Tove's scalding death: he is stuffed into a barrel bristling with nails and rolled about, which was the actual fate of a Danish criminal called Folkvard Lavmandsson. But Jacobsen eliminates the violence in both cases.

The first part of Jacobsen's poem is narrated by Valdemar and Tove in alternation, and, after her death, by the Voice of the Wood Dove ("Wood doves of Gurre! Woeful tidings I bear over the island sea"), the Voice of the Peasant, the Voices of Valdemar's men, the Voice of Claus the Fool, and the Voice of the Poet. This dramatization is Jacobsen's invention, as is the character of Claus, who is intended as, but fails to provide, comic relief.

Jacobsen's identification of Tove with a forest wood dove—*Taube*—exploits the alliterative relationship in their names; in Old Norse, Tove is Tofa and "gurre" the onomatopoeic word for the sound emitted by the dove. As the symbol of purity, fidelity, and happiness, the dove is contrasted with other birds—"Helvig's falcon it was that has slain Gurre's dove," and "howling hawks cry from the spire of the church over Tove's grave"—which are associated as well with times of night and day, the raven, the owl, the chanticleer. Like *Pelléas*, the *Gurresange* begins at twilight in a forest at the edge of the sea. It ends, following a night of love and horror, at sunrise.

After Tove's murder, Valdemar searches for her beyond her death and even beyond his own:

> My Tove is here, and Tove is there.
> Tove is far and Tove is near.
> Tove bound by magic to the lake and the wood.
> Tove, Tove, Valdemar yearns for you.

And he rediscovers her in Nature:

> With Tove's voice whispers the wood,
> Through Tove's eyes shines the lake....

The most memorable music in Schoenberg's mammoth cantata[9] was inspired by the "Song of the Wood Dove" and the "Voice of the Poet" in *The Summerwind's Wild Hunt* ("Sir Ganderfoot and Mother Goose"). The wind is compared to a horseman ("In the corn stalks hear the wind go by like a rider"), and some of the verse is Tennysonian: "White horses all over the lake are prancing / And through the meadow crickets are dancing." Perhaps the heroic attitudes, the medieval atmosphere, and the *fin-de-siècle* symbolism (though *Gurresange* was written in 1869) are greater in concept than in poetic realization, but one would have to know Danish to be able to say. Jacobsen's champions, including Niels Lyhne Jensen, regard it as the pinnacle of Danish poetry.

During a walk together, Camilla, the councilor's daughter, asks Mogens to

---

[9] Schoenberg's text was the Robert Franz Arnold translation for the complete works in German edited by Marie Herzfeld and published jointly in Florence and Leipzig in 1898, then in Vienna in 1899. The composer must have had a copy while it was still being drafted, to judge by the numerous minor and some major discrepancies between the score and the first published version. Schoenberg completed most of the composition in 1901, the orchestration a decade later. Jan Maegaard, the Danish musicologist and author of the most important study of the composer to date (*Praeludier til musik of Arnold Schonberg*, Copenhagen: Wilhelm Hansen, 1976), defends the German translation, but John Bergsagel reminds us that the metrical intricacies of Jacobsen's poetry are scarcely approximated in the translation.

pick some convolvuluses from a hedge for her. When he hands them to her, she says that she had not wanted so many, and lets them fall to the ground. Mogens gently reproves her: "Then I wish I had let them be." So, too, on the morning of Jacobsen's death, April 30, 1885, when his mother brought him the earliest spray of cherry blossom, he whispered to her, "What a pity to break it off for me."

Austria's Negative
Poet Laureate

After the boisterous reception of Thomas Bernhard's *Heldenplatz* (*Heroes' Square*) at the Vienna Burgtheater in November 1988, just three months before the author's death, President Kurt Waldheim denounced the play,[1] which denounces him as a "devious, lying philistine," as a "crude insult to the Austrian people." It tells the story of a Jewish professor who left Austria in 1938 when the Nazis annexed it, returned fifty years later, and, finding the attitude toward Jews unchanged ("Jew-hatred is the pure, absolute, unadulterated nature of the Austrian"), committed suicide. In the play, the professor's brother characterizes Austria as "a nation of six and a half million idiots living in a country that is rotting away, ... run by the political parties in an unholy alliance with the Catholic Church." The statement expresses one of Bernhard's major themes.

Following Bernhard's instructions, his death, of a heart attack ("No heart can put up with a nature like mine," one of his stand-in narrators says) at home in his farmhouse at Ohlsdorf (Gmunden) two days after his fifty-eighth birthday, was not announced until after he had been buried (in Vienna's Grinzing cemetery). The obituary in the London *Times* said that he is "thought by many of his compatriots to be one of the greatest writers of the century," while acknowledging that in his native land detractors are equally numerous. One can understand from the available translations why his novels and plays have aroused such strong reactions, for even though Bernhard is a stylist foremost, and much of his power lies in his use of German, his work has crossed language barriers with considerable success.[2]

A little more than half of it has been crossed into English: the autobiography, seven of his twenty or so plays, and a dozen of his sixteen books of fiction, not including the first and paradigmatic *Frost*. Since none of the poetry (collected in *Auf der Erde und in der Hölle*), short stories, cabaret sketches, film scripts, or criticism (his 1957 school paper on Artaud and Brecht) has appeared in trans-

---

[1] See Amos Elon's "Letter From Vienna," *New Yorker*, May 13, 1991. Bernhard was physically attacked on the fashionable Billrothstrasse in downtown Vienna "by an elegantly dressed man wielding a stick."

[2] Albeit with losses, such as the mockery of German compound nouns (*"Kaffeehausaufsuchkrankheit"*).

lation, monoglot, anglophone readers will not be able to grasp Bernhard's diversity. Still, enough of his work is now in English to enable them to appreciate that he is a writer of great originality and fascination.

Perhaps Bernhard's autobiography, *Gathering Evidence*, published originally in five separate volumes between 1975 and 1982, should be read after the novels, the artistic transmutations before their sources—although, as Bernhard told a *Le Monde* interviewer, *Evidence* is "not as it really was—there's no such thing as objectivity—but as I see it today." Indeed, he sometimes refers to himself in the book in the third person to distinguish "how I felt at the time and the way I think now." In this account of his first nineteen years the author inevitably looms like a doppelgänger next to his character. "I continually trick up myself, for I incessantly describe myself," he says in *Evidence*: "I do not write my own acts, but myself and my essence." For the moment, however, and until the dissertations begin to appear, he may best be introduced by some of the events of his early life as he himself presents them.

Bernhard was born February 10, 1931, in a convent in Holland, where his unwed mother had fled from an Austrian village when her pregnancy could no longer be concealed. After the accouchement, she found work as a domestic and placed the illegitimate infant in a nursery of sorts on a trawler in Rotterdam harbor. (Bernhard conflates this experience with that of the title character in his 1975 play *The President*: "Put in a hammock / on a fishing boat / with foster parents / in Rotterdam / His mother subjected him / to abject poverty / but only those people / who come up from the gutter / make it way up to the top.") Thomas's father, a farmer trained as a carpenter, married in Germany and was never heard from again: his German-born son, Dr. Peter Fabjan, eventually became one of Bernhard's physicians and the executor of his will. A photograph of his natural father given to Bernhard decades later by his paternal grandfather was "so like me that I had a fright." Whatever the connection between the unknown parent and Bernhard's play *Der Zimmerer* (*The Carpenter*), in which experiments with the psyche (i.e., psychoanalysis) of the mentally unstable title character are shown destroying his identity, perhaps the real carpenter, like the fictional one, was a sociopath and victim of lack of education.

After a year, no longer able to provide support, Thomas's mother admitted his existence to her parents and moved with the child to the family home in Vienna. Her father, Johannes Freumbichler,[3] an eccentric writer of independent,

---

[3] Caroline Markolin's biography of Freumbichler, *Die Grossväter sind lehrer: Johannes Freumbichler und sein enkel Thomas Bernhard* (Salzburg: Otto Müller, 1988), contends that the Bernhard protagonist of the fanatically dedicated intellectual pursuit is incipient in the grandfather's writings.

nihilist views, would become the central figure in Bernhard's life: "The only person I really loved.... Everything I know I owe to this man ... who himself was taught by Montaigne, just as I in turn was taught by him." Bernhard's first published piece, "Before the Grave of the Poet," written at age nineteen, commemorates the first anniversary of Freumbichler's death.

Freumbichler taught the boy to believe in his own superior intelligence. At an early age, "through being constantly close to my grandfather," Thomas also became aware of "the monstrous effort involved in literary endeavor," and at the same time paradoxically aware—to use the words of Reger, a composite of Bernhard and his grandfather in one of his last novels, *Old Masters*—that "ultimately everything one writes turns out to be nonsense."

The first part of *Gathering Evidence*, a record of mental and physical suffering, endurance, and will, begins with Bernhard's earliest recollections and ends in his thirteenth year as he is about to enter a Salzburg boarding school. The child yearned to be near his mother, especially while she was reading ("leaning on my mother's shoulder, happy just to hear her breathing"), to receive some sign of affection from her, instead of which she relentlessly punished him—and, as the intelligent and sensitive child understood, his father in him. Like many emotionally disturbed children, he was a chronic bed-wetter, which his mother cruelly and stupidly sought to cure by disgracing him, displaying his soiled sheets so that the neighbors could see them. Eventually he was sent to a home in Germany for, as he later learned, "maladjusted children."

Bernhard later took his revenge on motherhood in a portrait of the Mother in his last novel, *Extinction*, as well as in the "Wittgenstein novel," *Correction*, with its portrait of the "unbearable Eferding woman," a butcher's daughter with "the vulgarity of all her gender," who repeats to her son the curses that Bernhard's mother shouted at him: "You're all I needed!" Significantly, the woman from Eferding and the Mother in *Extinction* are Bernhard's only major female characters, and arguably the only major characters who are not in any particular a description of himself.

Without presuming to diagnose the misogyny that pervades his work,[4] we can safely say that the origins must lie partly in his mother's rejection, her open hatred, of him as a child. As Sven Birkerts notes, in Bernhard's world "compulsive males are pitted against small-minded, intractable women," and "everything

---

[4] See Chantal Thomas's *Thomas Bernhard* (Paris: Editions Seuil, 1990) for an analysis of this subject. She presents the case for the opposite in Bernhard the man, who is quoted as saying that he limits his *"fréquentations"* to women: "I can't stand men, I am allergic to their talk" (conversation with Asta Scheib, *Libération*, April 17, 1987).

in the female psyche exists for the sole purpose of affronting the man."[5] Bernhard rarely praises a woman and, when he does, as with Hoeller's wife in *Correction*, the sentiment is quaint: "Never a loud word, never the first to speak, everything in and about her was oriented toward taking care of things around her." But then, Bernhard praised Ingeborg Bachmann (like him, a fervent admirer of the life and work of Ludwig Wittgenstein), probably the only contemporary Austrian writer whose international stature is within measuring distance of his own, with the crude comment "an intelligent woman, a rare combination."[6]

No doubt grandfather Freumbichler's precept that women are Liliths who intrude into and bring about the decline of the patriarchal society also encouraged Bernhard's misogyny. Certainly the old man did not trouble to conceal his "asperity" toward his wife and daughter, Bernhard's mother. In Bernhard's world, virtually devoid of sexuality, a remark like the following from *The Loser*[7] is extremely rare: "The innkeeper wipes the dirt from the wardrobe door with her bare fingers [and] enjoyed the fact that I watched her do it.... Now I suddenly understood why Wertheimer had slept with her." The incestuous form of marriage, Isis and Osiris, or, in German mythology, Siegmund and Sieglinde ("the concept of genius applies more [to Wagner] than [to] anyone else"), is the only acceptable kind. Even so, in *Wittgenstein's Nephew* he attributes his own "survival" to an unnamed woman (actually Hedy Stawianiczek) who shared his life for more than thirty years, and who was thirty years his senior.

In the autumn of 1943 Thomas entered the Salzburg National Socialist Home For Boys where he remained for a year. (In *The Loser* Salzburg is "the sworn enemy of all art and culture.") Freumbichler had taught him that teachers are "idiots," and warned him that "the community always seeks out the weakest member and exposes him to its pitiless laughter," advice that undoubtedly helped Thomas to endure the brutality of the school, where he was taunted for not having respected parents and for living in a poor lodging. Freumbichler's reflection that "man's most precious possession [is] his freedom to take leave of the world by suicide" may have been helpful at the school. During Thomas's incarceration there, four fellow pupils committed suicide by jumping out of win-

---

[5] *New Republic*, 13 and 20 August 1984.

[6] *Aus Gesprächen mit Thomas Bernhard* (Vienna: Löcker Verlag, 1988). Bernhard, however, is outdone by Cyril Connolly on Mary McCarthy: "That rare thing, an intelligent woman writer who has not played down her masculine mind."

[7] Translated from the German by Jack Dawson. New York: Knopf, distributed by Random House, 1991.

dows or hanging themselves ("In the last six months in my dormitory alone three students have killed themselves," the schoolboy narrator says in *Gargoyles*), and still others, who lived at home in the city, threw themselves over a cliff, Suicide Mountain, as it is called in *The Loser*: "Every week at least three or four people throw themselves off it into the void." Thomas, too, tried to hang himself in the closet to which he was confined for violin practice—his violin lessons were, he says, his only refuge—but he concluded that he did not wish to die because he was "too full of curiosity." When later in life an interviewer asked Bernhard whether he wrote about suicide to keep from hanging himself, he replied, "Could be, yes, sure."

Many of Bernhard's sympathetic characters resort to taking their own lives, among them the "Persian woman" in *Yes* ("with no other person had I ever been able to talk about absolutely anything with a greater intensity," the narrator says); Joana in *Woodcutters*, who has already hanged herself before the novel begins, and from whose death the story takes off; the brother / sister lovers in *On the Timber Line*; the general in *The Hunting Party* (1974); Roithamer in *Correction*, the writer-architect protagonist, based on Ludwig Wittgenstein; and, in *The Loser*, both Wertheimer (the "loser," Glenn Gould's nickname for him) and Gould, whose death is explained as a result of pushing himself to the limit in the pursuit of artistic perfection. Indeed, Gould, with his eccentricities and his reclusiveness ("He had barricaded himself in his house. For life"), and his musical perfectionism, is the natural, prototypical Bernhardian hero.

The account in *Gathering Evidence* of Salzburg during the last months of the war should be read in conjunction with the writings of Primo Levi about still more horrifying experiences in an even more infamous part of Nazi Europe. As an adolescent Bernhard witnessed air raids in which cellars were turned into graves reeking of burnt flesh; he was threatened with asphyxiation in mountain cave bomb shelters; and he saw scattered bodies and parts of bodies, as well as rows of corpses covered with sheets and stripped of shoes. People lived "simply for the next distribution of rations, intent only upon surviving and not caring how."

Freumbichler had instilled his grandson with the resolve not to let himself "be impressed by either variety of idiocy, the Catholic or the Nazi," both of them "infectious diseases of the mind"; in *The Loser*, Catholicism and the Socialist Party, "are the two most disgusting institutions of our time." Bernhard describes how, with the American occupation, the National Socialist Home became the Catholic Johanneum, with the difference that Hitler's portrait was replaced by "a large cross"—convincing the boy "that our relations with Jesus Christ were in reality no different from those we had had with Adolf Hitler six months or a year earlier"—the Nazi salute at breakfast by saying grace, the Nazi director by a no less sinister priest, Uncle Franz (actually Franz Wesenauer, whose thinly-disguised portrait in *Evidence* led to a libel suit in 1976).

In the next stage of his autobiography, Bernhard, now a school dropout, finds a job as a grocer's apprentice in the basement of a "low-cost, soul-destroying housing project," where he nevertheless finds being "usefully employed, working for human beings among human beings," preferable to school. He even allows that his "boyish charm ... friendly manner and quick wit"—possibly the most upbeat remark ever to escape him—may have been responsible for his success in his new life. But in fairness, this consummate misanthrope's chronicle of work in the cellar is uncomplaining, and his gruelingly vivid depictions of the destitute customers, "half-witted and drunk," are almost compassionate. This must be said because Bernhard is no egalitarian, and his fiction is as contemptuous of "the people" as it is of the middle classes and the nouveaux riches.

In the cellar he soon begins to develop a philosophy. "In the end all that matters is the truth-content of the lie," he announces, having seen in his own experience how truth degenerates into half-truth and truism. Thinking of music as a possible career, he takes lessons in music theory and singing. "I was ... crazy about [music] and intent upon making it the supreme justification for my existence, my only true passion, the essence of my life." When in *Old Masters*, Reger, the elderly music critic for the London *Times*, avows that "music is still alive within me and it is as alive in me as on the day I was born.... [I am] saved anew by music every morning, from all the atrocities and hideousnesses ... to be made once more into a thinking and feeling individual by music,..." the voice is Bernhard's own.

One is struck throughout Bernhard's work by the veneration for Schopenhauer. "I had inherited *The World as Will and Idea* from the library of my maternal grandfather," he writes in *Yes* (1978), "from earliest youth to me the most important of all philosophical books.... [N]o work of literature had ever made a deeper impression on me." What Bernhard admired most in Schopenhauer is his anti-Christian skepticism and his clarity of intellect and language, formed, in part, during his term at Wimbledon School,[8] which must have reminded Bernhard of his own boarding school. The veneration was reinforced by Schopenhauer's preoccupation with music, his separation of music from the phenomenal world, his perception that music represented "the inner essence of

---

[8] See *Arthur Schopenhauer's English Schooling*, by Patrick Bridgewater. New York: Routledge, 1988.

the heart."[9] For the solipsist Bernhard—"there is nothing outside of heads"— words can only emphasize the isolation of the individual, the barrier between verbal language and the world. Music alone communicates.

In his novels and plays, Bernhard attempts to make writing come as close to music as is possible with words, by means of such formal techniques as variation, both of phrases and in the imitation of theme-and-variations structures in narrative. (His plays *Der Weltverbesserer* and *Der Schein Traugt* are said to incorporate principles of sonata form, but this would be true of any literature employing exposition, development, recapitulation.) The repetition of words and phrases in beguiling rhythms is characteristic of Bernhard's style. The anaphora: "We need someone for our work, we also need no one. Sometimes we need someone, sometimes no one, and sometimes we need someone and no one"; this might have come from Gertrude Stein, with whose work he was familiar. In any case, music, and talk about music and musicians, figures importantly in his novels and plays. A recording of Beethoven's Fifth Symphony in the play *Eve of Retirement* (1979), however, animadverts on the composer in the sense that the Nazi characters see themselves as ennobled and uplifted by the genius of their fellow German. Composers and even a few performing musicians—Klemperer, Glenn Gould—are seen as heroic figures.

In the final chapters of *Evidence*, Bernhard tells how he contracted severe pleurisy, a result of ignoring a chill while unloading potatoes in the cellar, and how, after undergoing a thoracic puncture, he was sent to a hospital "death ward." Here the doctors knew "practically nothing" and could "achieve practically nothing." The patients gave the doctors the slip by dying ahead of schedule, and the often unpunctual chaplain administered extreme unction to the already dead. Here, too, some wet washing fell only an inch or two from Bernhard's face where it would have smothered him. He attributes his own recovery to his ability to imagine "whole movements [of] Mozart and Schubert":

> This imagined music which I listened to in my corner bed became one of the most important elements, if not *the* most important, in my progress towards recovery. Everything within me had been almost deadened, but now I had the joy of discovering that it was not completely dead, that it could be brought back to life and developed.

From the death ward Bernhard was transferred by ambulance to a tubercu-

---

[9] See Carl Dahlhaus's *The Idea of Absolute Music*, translated by Roger Lustig. Chicago: University of Chicago Press, 1990.

losis sanitarium—"one realm of despair to another"—to cure a disease he did not have but was infected with there. His repulsive picture of the consumptives toting their mucus bottles and fever charts about with them is relieved by mordant moments, such as the disappointment of the doctors when at first he fails to test positive for TB.

It was then that he realized the importance of literature in his life. Dostoevsky's *The Demons* "told me that I was on the right [path], *the one that led out.* I had felt the impact of a work that was both wild and great." The incipient writer begins to see that his genius lies in his "capacity for intense observation": and he has learned that *"Durch den Tod wird das Leben verstärkt"* ("Life is intensified by means of death").

Since the revelations of Karl Hennetmair,[10] Bernhard's Ohlsdorf friend, companion, and protector of privacy, who had kept a diary of his ten-year association, the novel *Yes* can only be read as straightforward autobiography of the period 1965–1975. Bernhard purchased the farm house, his last home, from Hennetmair, called "Moritz" in the book, the only character with a name, and the description of him, of walks with him, and of evenings and dinners in his home, tally exactly with what has been made known of the contents of Hennetmair's manuscript. The narrator is gentle, even affectionate toward Moritz, and critical of his own prickly behavior, his long spells of isolation and his eccentricities as Moritz must perceive them. No doubt the "Persian woman" in *Yes* has some of the qualities of Hedy Stawianiczek.

But *Yes* is important above all for the self-portrait and for the account of how Bernhard listened to music—by reading scores silently and in a virtually soundless room—in this case scores by Schumann, of whom he shows a profound appreciation. "All my life I had been concerned with Schumann as with no other composer.... Schumann's music had always been my salvation.... I had the ability ... to withdraw with a full score and to hear the music noted down in the score, I did not need any instruments...."

Wittgenstein's Nephew, written in the same year (1982) as the first, but last composed, chapter of *Evidence*, is also an installment of autobiography, but this time directly, and the period recalled is later.[11] In 1967 Bernhard and his friend

---

[10] *Die Zeit*, August 4, 1989.

[11] Bernhard's later "Conversations" (1988; see note 6) are a memoir covering the period immediately beyond the formal autobiography, when he was a court reporter, but the book should be read for its comments on "the literary life," including the complaint that invitations to P.E.N. Congresses "usually say that 'Umberto Eco has already accepted.'"

Paul Wittgenstein were confined to adjoining wings in a Vienna hospital. Bernhard was thirty-six and recovering from surgery for pulmonary sarcoidosis. Paul Wittgenstein, aged sixty, was a mental patient who had undergone electroconvulsive therapy. "Paul the madman was just as philosophical as his uncle Ludwig, while Ludwig the philosopher was just as mad as his nephew Paul," Bernhard predicates, completing the equation with the remark that, unlike Ludwig, Paul did not "publish his brain" but *"put his brain into practice."* Besides illness, the bonds in this spiritual friendship were a shared love of music (Paul would "lecture on Stravinsky or *Die Frau ohne Schatten* in the middle of the street"), shared neuroses, including compulsive counting (Roithamer, Ludwig Wittgenstein's model in *Correction*, counts his steps as he paces up and down), the need to travel "simply in order to get away from one place and go to another," and mutual rage against Austria. This last is expressed with more vehement vituperation in *Correction* as "a permanent condition of perversity and prostitution in the form of a state ... a rummage sale of intellectual and cultural history ... with nothing left, apart from its congenital imbecility, but its hypocrisy."

The bonds were reinforced when Paul Wittgenstein accompanied Bernhard to the ceremony at which he received the Grillparzer Prize for Literature, an occasion which Bernhard presents only as an indignity to himself, though he describes it as high comedy:

> Just before the ceremony, in great haste and with the greatest reluctance, I had jotted down a few sentences, amounting to a small philosophical digression, the upshot of which was that man was a wretched creature and death a certainty. After I had delivered my speech, which lasted altogether no more than three minutes, the minister, who had understood nothing of what I had said, indignantly jumped up from his seat and shook his fist in my face.... For a moment complete silence reigned, as they say. And then the strangest thing happened: the whole assembly, whom I can describe only as an opportunistic rabble, rushed after the minister.... They were the best known, most celebrated, and most respected names in Austrian letters. They all raced out of the audience chamber and down the stairs after the minister, leaving me standing there with my companion. Like a leper. None of them stayed behind with us; they all rushed out, past the buffet which had been prepared for them, and followed the minister down the stairs—all except Paul. He was the only one who stayed with me and my companion, horrified, yet at the same time amused, by the incident.

The title *Wittgenstein's Nephew* is an obvious allusion to Diderot's *Neveu de*

Rameau, Paul Wittgenstein having been Ludwig's second cousin, not his nephew, though Paul, like the composer's nephew, was mad. Like Diderot, Bernhard plays with the thin line between madness and reason, and both writers "send up" the notion of the *philosophes* that, as Goya famously illustrated, *"The Sleep of Reason Produces Monsters."*[12]

* * *

Bernhard has been promoted as another Kafka (in their shared sense of entrapment), a new Musil (the narrator in *The Loser* tries to reread *Törless* after twenty years but manages only one page because "I no longer tolerate descriptions"), a recorder *à la* Robbe-Grillet, a Beckettian. Yet some of Bernhard's catalogs of lesser calamities are closer to Woody Allen farce than to any of these. Martin Esslin has drawn the similarities and parallels between Bernhard and Beckett[13] in, for instance, the frequent use of long monologues, and of pairs of interdependent characters (the "deadly togetherness" of Konrad and his half-sister / wife in Bernhard's *The Lime Works*), and concluded that they are the result of "affinities" rather than a direct Beckett influence.[14]

In most ways, it seems to me, Bernhard and Beckett are opposite sides of the same coin. Bernhard's work, unlike Beckett's, is transparently autobiographical, and his narrators and characters are very evident extensions of himself. In contrast to Beckett's settings in limbo, Bernhard's place-names are real and on the (Austrian) map, though also, of course, imagined and unreal. Moreover, Bernhard levels the borders between art and life, mixing historical people—Glenn Gould, Paul Wittgenstein—with fictional ones. Whereas Beckett remained personally detached from the world, Bernhard became a public figure, appearing on television, noisily resigning from the West German Society of Poets when the

---

[12] At this point we might remind ourselves that incest, insanity, suicide, and illegitimacy mark the reign of the last Austrian monarchy. The emperor and empress, first cousins, were also so closely related otherwise that the Archduke Rudolph had only half the usual number of grandparents. The empress's second cousins, Wagner's Ludwig II and his brother, were incurably insane before the age of forty, and Rudolph a victim of venereal disease and a morphine addict, was probably insane. The empress's niece, Countess Marie Larisch (the same who told Eliot the sledding story in *The Waste Land*), arranged the liaisons of Rudolph and Maria Vetsera that ended in their suicide at Mayerling, and provoked the suicide of her own son when he learned of his mother's role in the affair.

[13] *Modern Austrian Literature* 18, no. 2 (1985).

[14] *The Lime Works*, translated by Sophie Wilkins. Chicago: University of Chicago Press, 1986.

ex-Nazi ex-President of West Germany was made an honorary member, libeling prominent political figures, attacking the Austrian "blend of National Socialism and Catholicism" as well as each separately. Reger (in *Old Masters*) invites the reader to "step into Saint Peter's and free yourself completely of those hundreds, thousands and millions of Catholic lies about history," while Bernhard, both in his fictions and in his own name, continually execrates his native country (occasionally neglecting to hide the love-hate aspect of the relationship[15]). "I love this people, but I won't have anything to do with this state," the narrator says in *The Loser*, and Bernhard told a BBC interviewer that in Austria

> everyone behaves as though they were sick or mad.... I too am sick and mad. The Germans have too little sense of humor to be really mad.... [T]hey are too pessimistic.... The Austrians are not too pessimistic so that they can be sick and mad. For that there has to be a certain greatness.

Nevertheless, Bernhard's will states:

> I explicitly stress that I want nothing to do with the Austrian state and I reject not only every intervention, but also every attempt by this Austrian state to associate itself with my person and my work for all time.

The will also forbids the performance of any of his plays in Austria for their full copyright term of seventy years. By a contract signed before Bernhard's death, the Burgtheater has continued to stage the five plays already in its repertory, among them *Heldenplatz* (the name of the square where Hitler was welcomed by hundreds of thousands in 1938), one of the theater's greatest successes, seen by more than 85,000 people, despite, or because of, the efforts of the Waldheim government to ban it, and of skinheads to blockade the theater by dumping a heap of manure in front of the Ringstrasse entrance. But Bernhard's own posthumous ban is otherwise in force, according to Dr. Peter Fabjan, his sole executor, who has testified that the writer repeatedly made his intentions clear to him and to friends.[16]

The theater pieces, at least those at present available in English versions, are much less substantial than the prose fictions. Simply to follow, let alone evaluate, Bernhard's stagecraft from the scanty directions in the texts (*cf.* Beck-

---

[15] Gitta Honegger (*Performing Arts Journal 13*, vol. 6, no. 6 [1983]: 6), remarks that Bernhard "includes himself in the culture he attacks." Helmut Schödel, in *Die Zeit* (August 4, 1989), compares Bernhard's maledictions against Austria to those of "a rejected lover."

[16] Fabjan, Bernhard's physician, was with the writer on the night of his death.

ett), to say nothing of the verbal art of the plays—the disjunctions, the free-verse stress, the use of enjambment (in the absence of punctuation)—is next to impossible. The earlier ones are absurdist, in the tradition of *Ubu Roi*, *The Bald Soprano* and other classics of the genre. "Absurdity [*lächerlich*] is the only way forward," Bernhard asserted, though to judge by the critical reviews he published in Salzburg newspapers during the 1950s, the contemporary theater that he first admired was the naturalistic (*Death of a Salesman*).

In his first widely performed play, *A Party For Boris* (1968), a rich lady who has lost her legs (and her husband) in an accident and does not wish to be surrounded by ambulating people, has established a home for legless cripples, thereby becoming "the good woman," though her philanthropy is exposed as ultimately selfish and cruel. She gives a party for Boris, her new (legless) husband, during which fifteen wheelchairs career about the stage—or sixteen, since the lady has had her female companion strapped into one as well. The jokes are that the legless people complain about the beds being too short, and that the woman's presents for Boris are long underwear and a pair of boots. Since most of the better lines are spoken by the woman ("people have no ideas / because they have no time for ideas and they have no time / because they have no ideas"), and since Boris, the other star-actor part, utters only twenty-six words—otherwise merely nodding, laughing, beating a drum, and, unnoticed, dying—the reader can only surmise that the success of the play depends on stage business, sight-gags, and other means not evident in the text.

Four of the other so-far translated plays, *The President*, *The Hunting Party*, *Force of Habit* and *Histrionics*,[17] also belong to the absurdist or *cruauté* category. An attempt to assassinate the president of an unnamed country during his visit to the Unknown Soldier's Memorial misfires when he raises his cane to point to a blue-jay, and the casualties, instead, are a colonel and the president's wife's beloved dog, who dies of a heart attack. Thereafter when "the death" is referred to, she thinks of the dog instead of the colonel. In *The Hunting Party*, a parody of *The Cherry Orchard*, the dialogue is largely confined to a writer—Bernhard himself ("Each of us carries a terminal disease / Daily we awake to our terminal disease")—and the wife of a general crippled at Stalingrad who shoots himself as his beloved forest is cut down. The general is aware that his life is being turned

---

[17] *The President; and Eve of Retirement*, translated by Gitta Honegger (New York: Performing Arts Journal Publishers, 1982); *The Hunting Party*, translated by Gitta Honegger in *Performing Arts Journal* 13, vol. 5 (1980): 101–31; *The Force of Habit, a Comedy*, translated by Neville and Stephen Plaice (London: Heinemann), 1976; *Histrionics*, translated by Peter Jansen and Kenneth Northcott (Chicago: University of Chicago Press, 1990).

into a play by the writer, and the audience recognizes this play as the one it is seeing.

The dramatis personae of *Force of Habit* and *Histrionics* are the members of, respectively, a family circus and a family theater. In the former, a musical ring-master, a clown, a bareback rider, a lion tamer and a juggler have been rehearsing Schubert's *Trout* Quintet for twenty-two years in the unrealizable hope of achieving a perfect performance. "We do not want life / but it must be lived / We hate *The Trout* / but it must be played," the juggler says, without elaborating. In *Histrionics*, the action consists of a rehearsal of a play, *Wheel of History*, an insane historical diatribe ("Nero Metternich Hitler / historic constellation / Churchill the link"), written by Bruscon, a bullying megalomaniac and misogynist ("Women have no concept of art"; "the female sex / ... they always prevent us / from blossoming"). Suffice it to say that here the familiar Bernhard attitudes—"If we think clearly / we're bound to do away with ourselves"—sound jejune.

Eve of Retirement[18] reveals the continuing obsession with Nazism in the German psyche. The action takes place on Heinrich Himmler's birthday, annually observed by Rudolph, a former deputy commandant of a concentration camp and now a retiring West German chief justice (a "decent law-abiding citizen" who should be protected from "dredging up the past"), and by Vera, his like-minded sister and lover—the incestuous relationship began during his ten years in hiding in their cellar after the war. On this "most important day of the year" they have in the past forced Clara, their paraplegic sister, who opposes their unrepentant National Socialist mentality, to wear the striped jacket of a camp inmate and have her head shaved. Rudolph enters, saying that some Jewish boys have attacked him, and not coincidentally ("There is a connection / between today's date / and the way those youngsters came at me"). He and Vera exchange clichés: "Poverty is caused / by the poor themselves"; "the Germans hate the Jews ... / that's the German nature"; Americanization and democratization have "destroyed German culture."

Rudolph dresses up in his SS uniform and he and Vera turn the pages of a family album in which photos of themselves as children have been placed side by side with pictures of piled up corpses and other Nazi atrocities. At the end of the play, Rudolph threatens to shoot Clara but collapses from a heart attack. Vera, trying to remove his uniform, telephones their (Jewish) doctor.

Vera is something slightly more than a two-dimensional cutout, a woman who seems to have doubts about her past life and the moral rectitude of her

[18] See note 17.

Germany. If Bernhard only hints at this, the probable reason is that to have explored her inner life any further would have been to exceed the boundaries of black melodrama. She has the play's only telling line: "None of us can get away," and Rudolph its only comic one: In the war "the Poles were ruthless / always in ambush."

If *Ritter, Dene, Voss* (1984)[19] is the most substantial of the dramas so far translated, one reason is the skill with which Bernhard exploits his fascination with Ludwig Wittgenstein. The dominant personality traits of many of Bernhard's central characters might have been modeled on Wittgenstein's, including the love of music (Wittgenstein to Bertrand Russell, 1912: "Mozart and Beethoven ... are the actual sons of God"); the reclusiveness; the constant revising, or inability to complete, writings; the inclination to suicide (three of Wittgenstein's four brothers were suicides); and the misanthropy, with special odium for Austrians, although to take as a typical remark, that to Russell, 1921: "While human beings are not worth much anywhere, the people at Trattenbach are much less good for anything than [people] anywhere else"—Russell challenged this as illogical—seems mild compared to Bernhard at his most venomous.

As the play opens, two sisters of Voss (Wittgenstein, referred to by them as "Ludwig") are preparing to transfer him from a mental institution ("the whole time he said / *Well-Tempered Clavier* / while I was signing the release") to the Vienna home of their childhood. The sisters are jealous of each other, and, in imagination at least, incestuously involved with their "anti-Kant," as they refer to their brother (misleadingly, since Wittgenstein seems to have known Kant's philosophy only as filtered through Schopenhauer, whose notion of the transcendental ego comes from Kant).

"It's always the same with him / difficulties of interpretation," Dene, the more solicitous sibling says of her brother. (She may have been suggested by Margarethe Stonborough-Wittgenstein, famous for the portrait of her by Klimt.) Voss is vulnerable, subject to phobias and unorthodox behavior, including long periods of isolation and silence. He fears, and has a borderline struggle with, insanity, and his relations with his sisters are sexually infantile: "He insisted that I stay in the bathroom / until he was completely naked." Voss believes that he can "overcome everything / just by thinking / not by being thoughtful / by thinking." ("To think," the Wittgenstein alter ego says in *Correction*, "is to regain and recover everything previously thought.") Voss's thoughts—"what is philosophy if not mathematics / mathematics on the brink";

---

[19] Frankfurt am Main: Surhkamp, 1984.

"self-realization / what a disgusting word … / you are after all realized, and you are yourself"—would be readily accepted as genuine Wittgenstein obiter dicta if attributed to him by one of his students. But the resemblances between Bernhard's style and that of the man who diverted Western philosophy away from epistemology toward the study of meaning are even more striking the other way around, Wittgenstein sounding like Bernhard. The statement that philosophy should "set limits to what cannot be thought by working outwards through what can be thought" might have come from *Correction*, as well as from the *Tractatus*.

* * *

Bernhard's novels consist for the most part of monologues, some of them first-person narratives, some transmitted by a narrator directly from a speaker (or from his writings), and some from third parties. The main characters are all solitary, paranoid (according to the writer Roithamer, "Experience teaches you to keep your distance … because people only come close and close in on you to disturb and destroy you"), mentally unbalanced scientists and obsessive / compulsive artists engaged in hopeless pursuits, caught in their own lucubrations and unable to finish or even to start their books, or endlessly revising them. (Bernhard's grandfather himself failed to complete the book that had "occupied him for the last fifteen years of his life.") This condition is more than symbolic; it is the main subject matter on which the plots turn. In a 1971 interview, Bernhard, referring to E. M. Forster and Virginia Woolf, remarked that "something finished, something beautiful is becoming more and more suspect."

For years, Rudolph in *Concrete*[20]—like Diderot's Jacques and Musil's Ulrich, most of Bernhard's characters have only one name—has gathered material for a study of Mendelssohn but has not been able to formulate the first sentence (though *he* at least promises himself to begin "if not today, then tomorrow, if not tomorrow then the day after, and so on"). After two decades of preparation, Konrad, in *The Lime Works*, cannot bring himself to write even a single line of his book. The speaker in *Yes* is unable to engage in his scientific studies on the antibodies in nature. The industrialist in *Gargoyles* revises his philosophical treatise every day. In *The Loser*, the narrator has been working on his manuscript, "About Glenn Gould," for nine years but is constantly destroying and re-writing it until "nothing remained except the title *The Loser*." In *Correction*, Roithamer has "totally corrected [his manuscript] into the exact opposite of what he had started out to

---

[20] *Concrete*, translated from the German by David McLintock. New York: Knopf, 1984.

say," but he vows to "correct the corrections and correct again the resulting corrections" with the eventual intention of correcting it "out of existence"; the narrator cites numerous passages in Roithamer's manuscript, that were "first underlined, then crossed out, then stetted." Death, of course, is the ultimate, existential correction.

Correspondingly, the monologues in all the novels are largely made up of pretexts for not writing. The most likely model for the procrastinations is Oblomov, with the difference that Bernhard's characters are fanatically industrious. Bernhard has an unerring sense of timing as the movement of consciousness in his protagonists changes focus, and he is dazzlingly inventive in the way in which he says the same things differently, the explicitation and exaggerated precision with which he conveys the workings of the obsessive-compulsive minds of his autistic authors.

The central characters resemble each other, and the novels sometimes appear to belong to a series, or to make up one long unified work. For example, Paul Wittgenstein, and Joana, in the *Woodcutters*, are referred to in the later book *Concrete*, and an article by Adelbert Stifter about "the local limestone" is mentioned in the book which followed *The Lime Works*. Situations and relationships are also held over from book to book. In *Lime Works*, Konrad, watching from a window, is mysteriously struck by the sight of Hoeller chopping wood, and in the next novel, *Correction*, the narrator, also watching from a window, is similarly fixated by the sight of a taxidermist, coincidentally named Hoeller, stuffing a bird. Both watchers are disturbed by an awareness that the men they are watching are reciprocally watching them, a similitude suggesting the recall of scenes from opera to opera in *The Ring*.

Like his later novels, Bernhard's earliest, *Frost* (1963)—his *Magic Mountain*, despite his declared abomination of Thomas Mann ("truly stupid ... a petty bourgeois writing strictly for the petty bourgeoisie")—portrays post-1945 Austria as physically, spiritually, and mentally ill. A young medical student reminiscent of Hans Castorp is sent from Vienna to examine Strauch, an ailing painter (product of a loveless childhood, it goes almost without saying) self-exiled in a remote mountain village. The one-sided discussions between them—the isolated and paranoid Strauch is the first of Bernhard's monologists—range from the medical to the philosophical, the sociological, and the political. Strauch vents his considerable spleen on the responsibility of women in the decay of culture, on the useless and parasitic role of the Church, and on the wretchedness of the human condition. In the end, Strauch disappears in a snowstorm. Eventually, a great frost will destroy the world, Strauch has maintained, at which time "the stars will shine like nails with which the heavens have been shut close," an image worthy of *Wozzeck*. The relentless negativism of the novel, and the gore, which in later books Bernhard turned into comic romps, can seem gratuitous, but the book establishes the author's thematic obsessions, typical characters, and technique.

Gargoyles, four years later, is also set in a landscape that is malignant both naturally and humanly: homicidal, mentally unbalanced, incestuous, sick, cruel, avaricious, and stupid. In this nightmarish Bildungsroman, a doctor invites his teenage son, the book's narrator, to accompany him on his rounds through a remote mountain gorge. The first of his deranged patients is so hermetic that he has had all of the birds and animals in the surrounding forest shot to protect his, and his half-sister/lover's, privacy. The last patient, Prince Saurau, the doomster resident-owner of a mountaintop castle, gives an account of his insane father's suicide. Saurau senior, shortly before shooting himself, ate some pages from *The World as Will and Idea* (shades of the Aristotelian repast of Eco's Jorge of Burgos), explaining in a suicide note that "Schopenhauer has always been the best nourishment for me." Afterward the prince describes how

> the women … carried the body into the bathroom to wash it. Under the direction of the district doctor they tried to hold the shattered skull together with clothespins. They stuffed the bullet hole with cotton dipped in wax. Meanwhile a few women were clearing out the pavilion, so that we could lay Father out in there. Because of the play that had been given there a few weeks before … the pavilion was still full of dozens of sets, props, costumes, and chairs. He had been surprised at the speed with which the workmen transformed the pavilion into a mortuary hall, the prince commented. As the women carried the body across the yard to the pavilion, they let it drop, so the son had carried his dead father into the pavilion all alone. They merely wrapped him in sheets and covered him with sheets. For several hours blood continued to flow from his head, and from his mouth and ears, which necessitated frequent changing of the sheets.

In context, the description is so extreme and the delivery so flat as to become richly comic.

The Lime Works (1970) is a superior book, unified in structure—the episodic scheme of *Gargoyles* is replaced by a single, closely focused story—more deeply thought and felt, and with far greater penetration into the mind of its main character. It is narrated by an unnamed life-insurance salesman, one of many ironies. Konrad and his half-sister/wife, who has been "crippled by decades of taking the wrong medications," live next to an abandoned lime works. The story opens on Christmas eve, but the action is over before the curtain rises. He has just blown her head off with the carbine with which he had taught her to shoot at intruders: "Konrad felt that his decision and his ruthless determination had been the correct decision and the correct ruthlessness." Konrad, with a history of shooting at passersby, has been imprisoned some fifteen times for aggravated assault. The uxoricide and its aftermath, more titillating than horripilating, are variously described in differently informed rumors: "Konrad is supposed to have said"; "Konrad thought, says Wieser." But since the outcome is known at the beginning, the discrepancies have little significance in the *Roshomon* sense, showing instead that nobody gets anything right. It is the closest the novel comes to a "message."

Lime Works is Bernhard's most relentlessly lugubrious creation. Konrad, who, according to the magistrate, "had Schridde's hair syndrome, a symptom of stomach cancer," dragged the corpse back to the room, "blood pouring from it harder all the time"; it took him "over an hour to get the heavy, lifeless woman's body that kept slipping down on him back into that [wheel]chair." The several bottles of schnapps that Konrad gives to the police who come to arrest him are consumed "in the patrol wagon, though to gain the necessary time they chose a detour of about sixty or seventy miles."

Konrad had been conducting Urbantschitsch Method experiments on his wife for his projected book, *The Sense of Hearing*, a work not yet begun because of the threat of interruptions. These daily sessions, which lasted "only a brief three or four hours, or a longer six or seven hours," began "in the early twilight before dawn" with, in one instance, Konrad reciting

> a series of sentences with the short *i* sound, such as 'In the Inn district it is still dim,' a hundred times slowly, then a hundred times rapidly and finally about two hundred times as fast as possible.... When he was done he demanded an immediate description of the effect his sentences had on her ear and her brain.

Afterwards, he would play Mozart's *Haffner* Symphony for her, "always the same record year after year," and forcefeed books to her, reciting incomprehensible passages from Wittgenstein's *Tractatus*, or reading aloud Kropotkin's autobiography, which she deeply hated.

In the latter part of the book we get a glimpse of the other side of this "marital hell." Konrad's wife sends him to the cellar every five minutes for a glass of cider, instead of allowing him to bring a large jug of it. But her sadism is no match for his, nor, it must be said, since she is this mad intellectual jailbird's prisoner, is it quite believable. Yet the novel has a sustained intensity of tone and suspense—we are continually led to expect some imminent but never forthcoming revelation about the origins of the couple's symbiosis of hate—and the sheer awfulness of both scene and story provide some wild comedy. Best of all are Konrad's observations about writing:

> The intervals in which he thought it would be possible for him to write the book were growing shorter, while the intervals in which the book seemed to be a lost cause were growing longer.

The writings of Roithamer (Wittgenstein) in *Correction* (1975) are different in that they contain prescriptions for positive resolves:

> We enter a world which precedes us but is not prepared for us.... [I]f we survive ... we must take care to turn this world ... a given world but not made for us or ready for us ... we must turn it into a world to suit our own ideas ... so that we can say *we were living in our own world, not in some previous world.*

Roithamer has actually achieved his goal of building a conic[21] house for his beloved sister ("the highest expression of this love he had envisioned and undertaken and accomplished and completed the building of the Cone"):

> By studying ... my sister and trying to think ... my sister through ... in accordance with [her] character ... everything about her, corresponding to her eyes and ears, her hearing, feeling, intelligence, alertness, attention I enabled myself to build the Cone ... as if I had lived, existed, all along, all those years of development, which were nothing else than my development in the direction of the Cone ... the giving embodiment to an idea.

"This idea," Roithamer writes in another of his meditations, "was to make my sister perfectly happy by means of a construction perfectly adapted to her person...." This three-level construction, "an edifice of stone and brick, glass and iron," is partitioned into seventeen rooms, nine of them, including the meditation chamber, "the true center of the Cone," without windows.[22]

---

[21] Translators disagree as to whether the word *"Kegel"* should be rendered by "cone" or "skittle." The book refers to the top of the structure as its "tip," which would indicate a conical rather than a ninepin shape, but the latent incest motive cannot be understood without the sexual symbolism of the "female," Matriushka-doll, skittle.

[22] See Bernhard Leitner's *The Architecture of Ludwig Wittgenstein*, Press of the Nova Scotia College of Art and Design, 1973. Bernhard must have seen the manuscript of Hermine Wittgenstein's "My Brother, Ludwig Wittgenstein" (first published in Leitner's book) through the intermediary of Paul Wittgenstein.

At the novel's opening, Roithamer, distraught over his sister's death, has hanged himself. The narrator,[23] a friend since early schooldays, has gone to the house of Hoeller, another mutual boyhood friend, to sort out Roithamer's legacy there in the garret in which Roithamer had written those "thousands of slips and a bulky manuscript, 'About Altersam'" (Ancient Seed), a chronicle about the family estate, bequeathed to Roithamer by his father in order to destroy him ("parents seen as the first *destroyers* of their children ... leaving it [Altersam] to the son who hated it").

The literary-executor narrator's admiration for Roithamer's intellect and integrity is mixed with feelings of envy ("I had never been a match for Roithamer's ideas") and fear ("I fully expected to be annihilated or at least destroyed by his writings"). Gradually, imperceptibly, the narrator, seen from the first as Roithamer's double, merges with him into a single voice. The narrator is quick to see that "perfecting and presenting the Cone to [Roithamer's] sister must result in her death"—"A person like Roithamer's sister cannot endure so climactic a condition," the narrator says, whereupon she duly succumbs to a mortal disease—and, in consequence, Roithamer's. The structure is completed; thus the Cone has eventually destroyed them both, partly for the reason that "young men ... tend to push an idea ... until they have made it a reality.... [E]veryone has an idea that kills him in the end"—and partly because the sister understands that the Cone is an expression of incestuous desire.

Roithamer, like Ludwig Wittgenstein, has taught at Cambridge, followed austere personal habits, experienced an unhappy and rebellious childhood, and spent years as an architect. (Wittgenstein actually built a house in Vienna, now the Bulgarian Embassy, for his sister.) The book is not a *roman à clef*, however, but an attempt to enter a powerful mind at its highest pitch of concentration. Bernhard once explained to a critic,

> The question is not "How do I write about Wittgenstein?" but rather: "Is it possible for me to be Wittgenstein for just *one* moment without destroying either him (W) or myself (B)?"[24]

---

[23] The narrator shares several points of intersection with Bernhard, such as the recollection of winter walks with Roithamer and Hoeller through the woods to school together ("While we were always suitably dressed for our way to school, we weren't always suitably dressed for our way through life"), the three of them bringing logs for the classroom stove, the wealthy Roithamer carrying a larger one than the poor Hoeller and the narrator; the identical story appears in *Gathering Evidence*. Roithamer hangs himself in a forest clearing that he frequented as a boy, thus finding his end in his beginning. See Richard Gilman, *Nation*, July 19, 1980.

[24] Quoted in Mark Anderson's "Notes on Thomas Bernhard," Raritan, Summer 1987.

The impossibility of crossing the barrier between self and other is one of Bernhard's obsessions. The narrator who resuscitates the dead Roithamer through the study of his writings does so at the cost of his own subjectivity: he becomes Roithamer's double.

Correction may be Bernhard's most profound book, but its repetitive misogyny seriously undermines its power: "The female sex is incapable of going beyond the first impulse in the direction of the life of the mind," is a characteristic Roithamer remark, and it is said of Roithamer's nephew's suicide that "six months after they noticed he was gone, his young wife hadn't missed him until then."

The Cheap-Eaters (1980) marks a major shift toward simplification, both in style and meaning. Short, immediately comprehensible on every level, traditionally punctuated with clauses set off by commas, and not inordinately long sentences by periods, it is the Bernhard novel to read first. The main theme, the unrealized scientific pursuit, is familiar, as are the ironies and paradoxes ("he needed people around him in order to be alone"), but the mood, in spite of the "sad" outcome of the story, is comic, an effect achieved in large part by the repetitive rhythms of the characteristic Bernhardian "redundancy": his subject "meant everything to him while everything else meant nothing"; "his mutilation and disfigurement, and his repellent aspect eventually quite naturally stemming from that mutilation and disfigurement"; "He might have gone to the Old Ash and not to the Old Oak, but suddenly he had gone not to the Old Ash but to the Old Oak."

As in *Correction*, the "tragic" history of Koller, the already dead protagonist, is narrated by a childhood school-friend who envyingly admires his superior intellect. Like Roithamer's, Koller's life work, the *Theory of Physiognomy*, survives only in notes in the possession of the narrator:

> [The theory] had for a long time been put aside ... an essay on the successful completion of which eventually depended a further essay, and on the successful completion of that actually yet another essay [on which] depended a fourth essay.

But no matter, since the narrator realizes that Koller "truly was his own work," the result "of his physiognomical thinking."

On a certain October 31, sixteen years before the narration begins, Koller happened to go to Vienna's Türkenschanz Park rather than to the Wertheimstein Park, and in consequence was bitten in the left leg by Weller's dog, tearing free from his leash; Weller, a wealthy glass manufacturer who also frequented both parks, might also have been in the other one, as the narrator observes more than once. Due to medical incompetence, Koller's leg had to be amputated. On the first day of his discharge from the hospital, he breaks a long habit and goes "not to the Old Ash but to the Old Oak" to eat in the Vienna Public Kitchen with the "cheap-eaters," one of whom is the narrator. This fortuitous disruption changes the direction of Koller's work, when he eventually becomes aware, though "not until this past week," that the four cheap-eaters, whose table he shares, are the real material, "the central chapter" of his physiognomical study. Whereas the narrator regards the dog bite as the misfortune of Koller's life, Koller regards it as his "life's good fortune," to which he owes his theory of physiognomy: "The dog bite had opened up to him his way of thinking, which until then had been shut to him." At mid-point in the novel, the narrator is seized by the idea that Koller, by the force of his willpower, had attracted the Weller dog, whose "bite must have had its place in the Koller concept even before it was in fact executed."

The last part of the book consists of the biographies of the four cheap-eaters, whose physiognomical readings Koller is on the eve of expounding to the narrator when, because of his artificial leg, he falls on his stairway and dies from the resulting head injury. Thus the misfortune which Koller had understood as good fortune turned again into misfortune, except that the narrator's book preserves Koller's story as an embodiment of his theory. The reader is left thinking about questions of chance in his own life, the time he turned left instead of right.

It may be that two of Koller's aspects were suggested to Bernhard by the example of the Austrian philosopher Rudolph Kassner, best known in the English-speaking world through his correspondence with Rilke; Kassner lost a leg in World War One, and his greatest book is the *Physiognomik*.

In *Concrete* (1982), Rudolph, like his author, is constantly anticipating death and forever fulminating against such unchallengeable enemies as "human imbecility." Rudolph suffers from alternating nothing-and-everything patterns of thinking, and a large part of the novel simply traces his vacillations concerning a possible trip to Majorca, where he has spent winters in the past. The unfavorable consequences in both eventualities, to go or not to go, are weighed back and forth and over and over, until at last he packs his bags, then decides not to go, then changes his mind when he imagines his housekeeper returning and finding him "unpacking my bags two days after I've gone away for three or four months."

Finally in Majorca ("[I have] the knack of taking myself by surprise") he remembers that during his last visit a young woman told him that her husband had just died in a fall, probably a suicide, from the balcony of their hotel room, and that she intended to return to Munich to settle his estate. Now, going to the cemetery on impulse to look for the husband's grave, Rudolph learns that she committed suicide instead and is buried with him. Whether the title refers to their tomb or to the actuality of the tragedy—as opposed to Rudolph's many abstract imagined ones—the discovery is not an edifying one for him. It does not become a real event but merely another of his paranoid nightmares. Partly for that reason the Majorcan episode seems tacked-on, and the book lacks the tension of *The Lime Works* and the sense of passionate argument of *Correction*.

The narrator of *The Loser* (1983), an accomplished pianist, and his pianist friend Wertheimer, had known their coeval Glenn Gould in Salzburg twenty years earlier. The entire novel consists of the narrator's interior monologue, the subject of which is the destructive, paralyzing effect on Wertheimer, who, after twelve years of preparing for the career of a piano virtuoso, hears Gould play the first bars of the *Goldberg Variations*: "Wertheimer had recognized the genius Glenn Gould and was mortally wounded."

The narrator lives in Madrid but was in his Vienna apartment when a telegram from Wertheimer's sister in Chur, Switzerland, whom Wertheimer had virtually incarcerated until at age forty-six she escaped and married a Swiss businessman (Wertheimer had loved her, "by the way, although he hated her like no one else in the world"). In response, Wertheimer goes to Chur and hangs himself from a tree one hundred feet from her home.

At the beginning of the novel, the narrator, returning from Wertheimer's funeral, is entering the Dichtel Mill Inn in Wankham, a village near the Wertheimer estate at Traich, which he wishes to visit. The substance of the book is composed of the narrator's thoughts about "Glenn, Wertheimer and I" and their differences of character and personality. These unparagraphed thoughts are punctuated by the phrase, "I thought to myself as I entered the inn," repeated with, eventually, variants progressing to "I thought in the inn," and "I thought standing in the inn waiting for the innkeeper." When the innkeeper, who was Wertheimer's mistress, finally appears, two-thirds of the way through, she questions the narrator about the funeral. But here the novel veers off course in a digression on her uncle, a convicted murderer, that provides Bernhard with an opportunity to vent his familiar misanthropies and oppugn the Austrian jury system.

Gould was "killed by the impasse he had *played* himself into for almost forty years," the narrator says, "whereas Wertheimer and I gave up the piano because we never attained the inhuman state that Glenn attained." Discrepancies emerge between Bernhard's brilliantly imagined Gould and the real-life subject of the biographies, as in the narrator's anecdote of an ash tree outside Gould's window, the sight of which inhibits his playing to the extent that he cuts it down with an axe and a saw. No sooner was it lying on the ground than "he realized that he had only needed to draw the curtains and close the shutters." The story shows an understanding of the real Gould's character, but it overlooks the protective manias of the man who wore fingerless gloves when practicing, never shook hands but bathed his in warm milk, and would never have risked a callus or a sprain. Slips of this kind suggest that the novel was written at high speed, as do such other contradictions as the narrator's avowal, halfway through, that he did not anticipate Wertheimer's suicide, following an earlier remark that "Wertheimer had to commit suicide.... He'd used himself up, had run out of existence coupons."

The ending is neatly symmetrical. The narrator goes to Wertheimer's room in Traich where Franz, the keeper, describes how his master burned all of his writings, then had the piano sent in, which he played incessantly for weeks. The narrator notices the Glenn Gould recording of the *Goldberg Variations* lying on Wertheimer's still open record player.

Woodcutters[25] (1984) is Bernhard's most nearly traditional novel, the only one populated by ordinary nasty people, instead of fanatics and cranks, and in an urban social milieu, instead of an isolated mountain landscape. Much of it is a comedy of manners that Bernhard might have turned into a play. The text is the interior monologue of its grouchy narrator—who, again like Bernhard, has lung trouble, has attended the Mozarteum, and is devoted to Wittgenstein. On the same day that a girlfriend, Joana, hangs herself, the narrator encounters his and her former friends, the Auersbergers, a failed composer ("Webern's successor," whom "I am bound to describe as the almost noteless composer"[26]) and his rich, socially ambitious wife. "Not having the presence of mind to refuse," he accepts the Auersbergers' invitation to a late dinner party after the premiere of a new production at the Burgtheater ("the world's first theatrical whorehouse") of *The Wild Duck*, in which a young girl commits suicide for similar reasons": Ibsen's neurotic women—Hedda, Nora, Mrs. Solness—are ancestors of Bernhard's.

Waiting in a wing chair in the Auersberger home for the guest of honor, the actor playing Ekdal, the narrator soliloquizes about Joana and Jeannie, another guest, a would-be writer whom he detests (a "derivative literary virgin" who has "progressed [from] her Virginia Woolf fixation to her Virginia Woolf

[25] More correctly Woodcutting (*Holzfällen*).

[26] In 1984, the composer Gerhard Lampersberg, seeing himself ridiculed as Auersberger, filed a libel suit. The Austrian police promptly banned the book, thereby making it a mail-order bestseller from West Germany. In February 1985, the suit was dropped, but the paperback edition suffers some deletions. Lampersberg had been a close friend of Bernhard in the late 1950s and had set his *Five Movements for Ballet, Voice and Orchestra* to music.

posture"). The locution, "I thought, sitting in the wing chair," reiterated some two hundred times, both hypnotizes and brings the reader back to the immediate scene while reminding him or her that nothing is actually being said aloud.

With the arrival of the actor ("the archetypal mindless ham") the scene shifts to the dining room table and his vain talk. When Jeannie begins to needle him (her "malice had been laying in wait all evening"), the narrator begins to find him sympathetic. In the end, Herr Auersberger—who thinks that "the human race should be abolished," and that "we should all kill one another"—has drunk himself into a "thoroughly infantile condition." The narrator then makes up with Frau Auersberger, then despises himself for this "base and contemptible mendacity." As Bernhard intends, the repetition, the hyperbole, the irascible wit, get "on our nerves," to borrow his phrase describing the effect of the real-life actor he most admired, but also achieves a penetrating portrait of Vienna bourgeois society: philistine, social-climbing, and pretentious.

In *Old Masters* (1985), Bernhard's most enjoyable novel, subtitled, "a comedy," Reger, an eighty-two-year-old musicologist, has been visiting Vienna's Kunsthistorisches Museum for thirty-six years, three times weekly on alternate days, to contemplate Tintoretto's *White Bearded Man*. When the story begins, Reger has invited Atzbacher, his young friend, and the book's narrator, to meet him there on a successive day, an interruption of the routine that constitutes the suspenseless and inconsequential "plot." Irrsigler, a museum guard, parrots Reger's observations ("ninety-nine percent of humanity has no interest whatever in art, as Irrsigler says, quoting Reger word for word"), and provides Bernhard with the means for three-way word-games: as Atzbacher says, "I reflected, while regarding Reger, who was in turn regarding Tintoretto's *White Bearded Man* and who, for his part, was being regarded by Irrsigler."

Irrsigler is a purely comic figure: he had wanted to be a policeman "in order to solve his clothing problem," but the museum attendant's uniform serves the same purpose and bespeaks a more exalted cultural level. His uncle's family used to come to the Museum "once in every few years, on free-admission Saturdays or Sundays." Reger also has his comic side. He hates his parents, who "never forgave me for having made me," and his wife for having died "with all that enormous knowledge which I conveyed to her, that she should have taken that enormous knowledge into death with her [is] an enormity far worse than the fact that she is dead." But most of the book is filled with Reger's revilings of such Austrian institutions as Adelbert Stifter's prose "packed with distorted metaphors,"[27] Vienna's lavatories, and the contents of the museum: the Hapsburgs "had an ear

---

[27] Bernhard's attack on Stifter is generally thought to have been aimed at Peter Handke as well.

for music, certainly, but no understanding of art." Even Beethoven is not im-mune: The Tempest Sonata is "ridiculously serious," so "doom-laden" as to qual-ify as "kitsch"; in Beethoven "everything is *really marching* ... and the marching-tune dullwittedness [is manifest] even in his chamber music."

The best of the book's several set pieces is aimed at Martin Heidegger,[28]

that ridiculous Nazi philistine in plus-fours ... sitting on his wooden bench outside his Black Forest house, alongside his wife who ... ceaselessly knits winter socks for him from the wool she has herself shorn from their own Heidegger sheep.... [H]e was a genuine German philosophical ruminant, a ceaselessly gravid German philosophical cow ... which grazed upon Ger-man philosophy and thereupon for decades lets its smart little cow-pats drop on it.... True, the Heidegger cow has become thinner but the Hei-degger cow is still being milked. Heidegger ... in front of that lie of a log cabin ... the philosophical philistine with his crocheted black Black Forest cap on his head, under which, when all is said and done, nothing but Ger-man feeble-mindedness is warmed up over and over again.... His *nothing is without reason* is the most ludicrous thing ever. [In] a series of photographs Heidegger is just climbing out of bed, or Heidegger is climbing into bed, or Heidegger is sleeping, or waking up, putting on his underpants, pulling on his socks ... [s]tepping out of his log cabin and looking toward the hori-zon, whittling away at his stick, putting on his cap, taking off his cap, hold-ing his cap in his hands ... cutting a slice of bread (baked by himself), opening a book (written by himself), closing a book (written by him-self)....

* * *

Extinction,[29] Bernhard's final novel (1986), is a seamlessly written mono-logue in two well-structured and balanced parts. The narrator, Franz-Josef Murau, a wealthy middle-aged Austrian intellectual living in Rome, has given books by Jean Paul, Kafka, Musil, Thomas Bernhard (*Amras*), and Broch to Gam-betti, his close friend, pupil, and alter-ego ("he outdoes me in doubting"). The last line of the text identifies Murau as the recently deceased author of a novel called *Extinction*.

The first half consists of Murau's account, during a walk in the Pincio with Gambetti, of Wolfsegg, his Upper Austrian ancestral home ("a citadel of brain-

---

[28] In *Aus Gesprächen mit Thomas Bernhard*, the author attributes some of the success of his early years as a journalist to his insertion of meaningless phrases that he pretended were quotes from Heidegger ("as Heidegger said").

[29] *Extinction*, translated from the German by David McLintock, New York: Knopf, 1995.

lessness"),[30] and a description of his family. Earlier in the afternoon Murau has received a telegram from his sisters in Wolfsegg announcing the death of their parents and older brother in an accident. The news does not shock or even greatly move Murau, whose immediate concern is that having left Wolfsegg only three days ago, after the wedding of one of his sisters, he must already return. He thinks of inviting Gambetti to accompany him in order to see "the hand I was dealt at birth," but instead expatiates on the subject in a lengthy diatribe in which "We both laughed more than ever before."

Murau's father was a "lusterless farmer" with "an atrophied brain"; his mother, who married him only "to get her hands on his fortune," was "the most avaricious person I've ever known"; and his brother was "irremediably stupid." "Our parents naturally love us," Murau tells Gambetti, "but suddenly we realize that equally naturally they hate us.... They had not reckoned with my eyes which probably saw everything I was not meant to see when I first opened them.... One day, I *saw through them* and they never forgave me.... I was implacably opposed to them from the first moment."

The shortcomings of Murau's sisters are too extensive to be inventoried here, but can be sampled in a passage near the beginning of the book:

> [They spend] their winters knitting sweaters that fit no one.... Either the sleeves were unequal in length, the back was too wide, or the waist and the neck too narrow.... [M]y sisters would force us into them pulling and stretching in all directions. At Christmas their hideous knitwear was placed under the tree and we had to perform the most incredible contortions to get into it.... [O]n Christmas Eve the whole family sat around in my sisters knitwear like a bunch of cripples.

Murau regards his mother, "the bane of Wolfsegg," as "the epitome of evil." She always "ran up the Nazi flag on Hitler's birthday," and is "a Nazi to this day, notwithstanding her Catholic hypocrisy." Further, she is the mistress of Archbishop Spadolini, a high-up Vatican official "kept" by her for his hotel and travel expenses. Her brief visits to her son in Rome are pretexts to spend longer ones before and after with Spadolini. This "born falsifier ... born opportunist, born prince of the Church" alternately repels Murau and, because he possesses "verbal artistry" and is "well-schooled intellectually," fascinates him, but Murau

---

[30] The place-name is ironic in that Count Walsegg commissioned Mozart's Requiem anonymously, intending to pass it off as his own work. The reader with any knowledge of Mozart will associate the word with fraudulence.

does not object to the secretiveness of the affair "between a lying mother and a hypocritical ecclesiastic."

Meeting Spadolini at Wolfsegg the night before the funeral, Murau is appalled by the fulsomeness and mendacity with which the Archbishop speaks of his deceased mistress and her husband, but at the funeral itself, cannot help admiring the way Spadolini's "Catholic histrionics" steal the show, even though he is not officiating: "The priests' seminary is actually the ecclesiastical equivalent of a drama school." Since Bernhard does not describe any of the physical attributes of the deceased mother, and since she has never read a book, knows nothing about the arts, and lacks all social graces, her relationship with the polished and highly educated ecclesiastic is not quite believable.

The second part of the novel is titled "The Will," though little is said about it until the denouement when Murau decides to "pay his sisters off" and give the estate to the Jewish community of Vienna. Shortly after arriving at Wolfsegg, Murau happens to hear the local wind band practicing a piece by Haydn for the burial service. He rates the villagers' music-making no less highly than "so-called serious music" because the latter would be "inconceivable without popular music," and the players "have the advantage of being amateurs, of playing for love, but not professional ambition."

He then learns that the accident was a consequence of a musical evening. The family had driven to Linz to attend a Bruckner concert (a deadly Bernhardian touch) "in the Brucknerhaus by the Danube, one of the ghastliest cultural centers of the world...." Leaving the concert, "with my father at the wheel ... they had collided with a truck, and an iron bar from it had almost decapitated my mother." Murau has already read a newspaper description of her body as "beyond recognition," and seen a newspaper photo of the headless cadaver. Viewing the sealed coffin of his mother, and the corpses of his father and brother, Murau does not dwell on "the three bodies which no longer have anything to do with the human beings they once were." But he avoids meeting the eighty or so funeral guests, shakes no hands, and, during the liturgy, does not kneel.

Some of Bernhard's targets are new: "Worldwide stultification was set in motion by photographic images and attained its present deadly momentum when the images began to move." Goethe is "the gravedigger of the German mind, the megalomaniac patrician in the world of women ... an alarmingly small figure. The prince of poets—what a ridiculous notion! ... Hölderlin is the great lyricist, Musil the great prose writer, and Kleist the great dramatist. Goethe fails on all three counts."

But most are familiar, the degeneracy of the Austrian people, the blight of the Austrian Government, "literary brokers" (as distinguished from writers), Catholicism: "To say that we had a Catholic upbringing amounts to saying that we were utterly destroyed ... the Catholic Church won't tolerate any human being other than the Catholic human being." Even the Austrian "efflorescence of music" is attributed to

> the Catholic extirpion of thought.... The mind having been suppressed for centuries, Austria became the land of music ... having been driven out of our mind by Catholicism we have allowed music to flourish. True, this has given us Mozart, Haydn, and Schubert.... [Y]et I can't applaud the fact that we have Mozart but lost our mind, that we have Haydn but have forgotten how to think and given up trying, that we have Schubert but have become more or less brainless.

This owes something to Hugo von Hofmannsthal, who wrote in 1906 that "Austria found its spirit in music and its music has conquered the world."

Murau's Wolfsegg estate has five libraries, but he is the only family member who has ever used them, or, for that matter, ever read a book. "While my brother spent his time waiting in the cowshed for a cow to calve, I was busy in the library decoding a sentence by Novalis ... waiting for Novalis's idea to be born in my head." Murau advises Gambetti not to visit places associated with writers, poets, philosophers, saying that he had gone to Sils Maria thinking he might "understand Nietzsche better," only to discover afterward that "I no longer understand him at all.... My visit to Sils Maria finished off Nietzsche." Murau's highest encomia are reserved for Kafka: "the only one who produced not bureaucratic literature but great literature.... I remember Kafka as a great writer ... but when I reread him I am absolutely convinced that I've read an even greater writer." (One of Murau's friends in Rome, Maria, a poet and "the most intelligent woman I ever met," is to some extent a portrait of Ingeborg Bachmann, who lived there and was the one female writer Bernhard greatly admired.)[31]

As expected, Bernhard digresses on the procrastinations of writers, a strange obsession in the case of a writer so prolific himself. New, and surprising, is his, or rather Murau's, confession:

> I seize on all available persons, one after another, and tear them apart, denigrate them, demolish everything about them and denude them of more or

---

[31] For Bachmann's high opinion of Bernhard, see her *Werke* (Munich: Piper, 1978), 4: 362.

less all their virtues, so that I can rescue myself and breathe freely again.

* * *

The new Europe, which has already rendered obsolete our literature of current history and politics, "secret" intelligence and the romance of espionage, will have little effect on Bernhard's work, both because he writes only about unchanged Austria and because events are unlikely to disprove his main theme, that injustice prevails everywhere. Bernhard, the essentially comic writer for whom Death is always just offstage, is already defined by, protected by, his period.

More than a year after Bernhard's death, his hold on Viennese theatergoers was so great that in May 1990 numerous busloads of them rode eighty miles, *hin und zurück*, to Bratislava, Czechoslovakia, to see his 1987 play, *Elizabeth II*, in a production by the Schiller Theater of West Berlin. Bernhard's wishes had been carried out, his will upheld. One imagines the pleasure he would have had in the spectacle of Burgtheater patrons being bussed beyond the border to see his play, which depicts a luncheon for the British Queen on her official visit to Vienna, and which features the contumacious comments of one Herr Herrenstein, crippled and confined to a wheelchair, on the Burgtheater, the Vienna State Opera, the polluted air of the country as well as the city, and the ex- and not-so-ex-Nazis surrounding him.

By way of an envoi, we predict of Thomas Bernhard, as in his play one of Wittgenstein's sisters does of *him*, that "one day they'll be working on him at all the universities in America."

Bali B'hai

Carol J. Oja's biography of Colin McPhee,[1] the Canadian-born (1900) writer, composer, pianist and ethnomusicologist, provides a survey of his compositions, or at least the fewer than half of them not lost, with a generous selection of examples in music type. As one in a series on American composers, the book naturally gives more space to McPhee's music than to his far more prized writings (if apples may be preferred to oranges), particularly his memoir, A House in Bali,[2] but also his technical study Music in Bali.[3] But the facts of his life are of interest in themselves.

A House in Bali is a minor literary masterpiece. No critic seems to have recognized or acknowledged this when it appeared, in 1946, and the few musicians who read it did so largely out of curiosity about a colleague. Today the musician is largely forgotten, his book widely admired, both for its observations of cultures in conflict and its sophisticated but unaffected narrative style.

A first-person-singular account of life on the island in the 1930s, A House in Bali, does not hint at the existence, much less the close proximity, of McPhee's wife, Jane Belo, the anthropologist whom he married in 1930 and who, as Oja reveals, shared with him both the house and enthusiasm for Balinese culture. Though this does not cast doubt on the veracity of the story as a whole, it raises questions. Since both McPhees wrote about some of the same ceremonies, it is unclear which of the events he describes she also witnessed, and when and how their experiences intersected. In the case of the Balinese women's court dance-drama, Legong, for instance, Jane Belo and Margaret Mead, a Bali neighbor, provide detailed, minute-by-minute, notes. McPhee's account, not necessarily of the same occasion, is casual and impressionistic. In the acknowledgments to her scholarly book, Trance in Bali (1960), Belo generously refers to her husband's

---

[1] Colin McPhee: A Composer in Two Worlds. By Carol J. Oja. Washington: Smithsonian, 1991.

[2] A House in Bali. New York: Oxford University Press, 1989.

[3] Music in Bali: A Study of Form and Instrumental Organization in Balinese Orchestral Music. New Haven: Yale University Press, 1966.

work in Balinese music as "a stimulating parallel," and expresses gratitude for his help; but her and Mead's account of the Legong, unlike his, says nothing about the gamelan[4] music that is one of its major elements.

The McPhees arrived in Bali together, according to Belo's *Traditional Balinese Culture*. But Colin's account in *A House in Bali* describes his immediate traversal of the island alone except for a driver. Six months later, when the pair returned to Paris to renew their visas, three Balinese friends, hers as well as his, accompanied them to the steamship, whose electrical and plumbing facilities left them awestruck. Colin excized his wife from this scene as well, though she paid for the trip and indeed supported him in toto during their seven years together. True, he also concealed the real nature of his relationships with the young male dancers, musicians and houseboys who are the principals in his cast of characters, but this becomes obvious in the book, and, given the publishing restrictions of the time, could not have been made more explicit.

Oja attributes the breakup of the McPhees' marriage in 1938, while they were still in Bali, to Jane's increasing humiliation from Colin's ever more openly flaunted homosexuality—pederasty, rather, since the reference is probably to Sampih, his adopted pre-teenage boy. McPhee himself cites the same cause in a letter to his Woodstock (New York) friend Sidney Cowell, wife of the composer Henry Cowell (who had spent four years in San Quentin for the same "crime" before being proved innocent), but blames Jane's "vanity." Walter Spies, the German painter and musician and McPhee's closest European friend on the island, mentions what must have been a contributing factor, that McPhee "drank heavily and had an ugly temper when drunk" (he died of cirrhosis of the liver), but curmudgeonly conduct does not in itself explain why, as McPhee told Carlos Chávez, in the otherwise direct and candid *A House in Bali*, "I give no indication of having been married," and why, as he wrote to Sidney Cowell, he had been harsher to Jane than to anyone else.

Jane was fully aware of her husband's sexual proclivities from the beginning, as well as of her own inclinations toward women. (In the late 1930s the Dutch Police, on a witch hunt, interrogated thirty-four young female dancers in Jane's village concerning her sexual behavior.[5]) The marriage had been an

---

[4] In *Traditions of Gamelan Music in Java: Musical Pluralism and Regional Identity*. New York: Cambridge University Press, 1991, R. Anderson Sutton says that the ensemble consists predominantly of metal instruments, ideophones (bronze or iron gongs, gong chimes, and metallophones), and one or more double-headed drums.

[5] An account of this stage of the island's history is found in Steven Runciman's *A Traveller's Alphabet* (London: Thames & Hudson, 1991). "Almost all" European and American men and women

arrangement between people with similar temperaments, even to the extent that both of them in later years were patients in psychiatric hospitals, in her case for "repeated stays" between 1944 and 1955. Both were attracted by the exotic, both wrote poetry, both were interested in drawing, and both were fascinated by African-American culture ("the moment I am among Negroes," McPhee wrote, "I feel strangely at peace and happy, and always wish I lived in Harlem"). One of Jane's college classmates and closest friends was Zora Neale Hurston.

As a student of Franz Boas and Ruth Benedict at Barnard, Jane became absorbed in anthropology, and when she and Colin first sailed to Bali in 1931, she seems to have been as attracted to the island as an opportunity for fieldwork as he was to its music. Margaret Mead's Preface to Belo's *Trance in Bali*[6] describes her as "one of the most gifted observers and interviewers [in ethnological fieldwork] whom it has been my good fortune to know," and credits her earlier writings on Balinese art and ritual, published in periodicals during the 1930s, for her own decision to go there in 1936. In later years Mead and Benedict became the trusted confidantes of both McPhees separately, and Benedict vetted Jane's book. Belo's personal papers and medical records are part of the Library of Congress's Margaret Mead collection, but they contain little biographical information about her, no more, Oja says, than a one-page undated resumé, an apparent job application, and a New York driver's license.

Early in her relationship with McPhee, Belo wrote to her ex-husband, the painter George Biddle:

> My present state of being in love with a feminine man has aspects of masculine protest.... Heaven knows what stages of change I still have to go through, and how long it will take before I can be the mature female.

But however bitter she may have felt at the time of divorcing McPhee, back in New York she continued to send him her writings about Bali, to which he responded kindly. Though he told Chávez that she had been infuriated by being censored out of *A House in Bali*, when the divorcees met by accident in New

---

had "become rather too intimate with the natives," Sir Steven writes, and "when the government in Java had at last become aware of these shocking activities, the male settlers had been taken off to be tried and gaoled in Java, while the women settlers were ordered to leave the country." This may have been the case with Belo and Mead. Sir Steven goes on to say that when "a tourist ship was arriving, the maidens all hastened to bare their bosoms, knowing that that was what the visitors liked, dressing respectably again as soon as the tourists departed."

[6] *Trance in Bali*, by Jane Belo. New York: Columbia University Press, 1960.

York's Museum of Natural History in 1952, McPhee described the occasion to Chávez as a "reconciliation," and even mentioned the possibility that it might endure. Her "sad, aged" appearance, he said, "would break your heart."

Born in Toronto of Scottish forebears, Colin McPhee displayed remarkable musical gifts at an early age, giving promise of a piano virtuoso's career while "still in knickerbockers." At fifteen he presented a recital program of his own compositions. Oja reproduces a chorus written three years later that indicates a feeling for harmony. In the same year, 1918, he entered the Peabody Conservatory in Baltimore, where he eventually performed a piano concerto of his own on a program with Beethoven's G Major Concerto.

Returning to Toronto after graduation, he contributed incidental music to a play, identified by Oja in a distracted moment as "Hippolytus's *Euripides.*" A spell in Paris followed, with piano lessons from Isidor Philipp, Stravinsky's teacher at the same time (preparing to play his piano concerto), and further efforts at composition. An excerpt printed from a 1926 opus looks like a near copy of the octave and two-part-counterpoint style of Stravinsky's 1924 Sonata. In Paris, McPhee met Jane Belo, a wealthy Texan, then the wife of Biddle, scion of the socially prominent Philadelphia family.

Back in New York, McPhee lived for more than a year in a room rented from Edgard Varèse at 188 Sullivan Street. In 1927 he played one of the four piano parts (and Aaron Copland another) in the Carnegie Hall performance of George Antheil's *Ballet mécanique.* McPhee's own music of the period, in the samples Oja prints, derives from neoclassic models of the day and shows little individuality. Near the end of the decade, hearing a Balinese gamelan orchestra in the German-made Odeon and Beka recordings (five of its ninety-eight sides were released commercially in the U.S. in 1931), and captivated by the rhythms and sonorities of the music, he resolved to learn it at first hand. He was also encouraged in this by many of the people he and Jane Belo met at parties in Carl Van Vechten's West Fifty-fifth Street apartment, one of whom, the Mexican painter Miguel Covarrubias, traveled to Bali six months before Colin and Jane.

The culture of the island's million or so inhabitants was in turmoil when the McPhees arrived there. In 1906, when the Dutch "deposed" the Balinese royalty, the entire royal retinue committed mass suicide by walking into the guns of their colonial masters. The Dutch educators were determined to stamp out every trace of the native culture, even forbidding children in art classes to represent trees, flowers, and birds in the traditional decorative style, teaching them instead to draw realistically and in accordance with the laws of perspective. Missionaries brought pictures of the Virgin that the natives mistook for the

Queen of Holland, but they became Christians only briefly—Bali is apparently immune to Islamic and Christian conversion—and then mainly to avoid costly cremations.

The destruction of the culture came with the growth of the tourist industry. McPhee remarks on the difference between 1932, when a man seeing an automobile could still ask, "How can it be? A chariot going like that without horse or cow?" and 1935, when the motor traffic was well on the way to the present-day gridlock of tour buses.

The house in Bali was constructed in 1932, after McPhee, during an interlude in Paris, had found that symphony orchestras seemed "torpid and mechanized," and that "the endless *legato* of the violins" contrasted dully with the metallic spangles of sound produced by the Balinese *gangsas*. Their new home, in the comparatively cool and salubrious hill climate near the village of Sayan, consisted of a house in the style of a theater pavilion, a sleeping house (separate quarters as far apart as possible for husband and wife), a bath house, a music studio, a kitchen, garage, temple, and shrines. The furnishings included a Steinway grand purchased in Java, peacock chairs, doors carved in Chinese style, and a menagerie of monkeys, an iguana, a small python, a flying fox, red and green parrots that slept hanging upside down from their perches.

The compound had been built next to a cemetery, and McPhee tells us that the superstitious villagers soon began to complain of demonic deeds. The first portent was an earthquake in the wrong month; the right ones, in Bali, are assigned by deities. Others began to occur in the McPhee household when, for no apparent reason, the cat fell off the roof and was killed, bicycle bells were heard ringing in the empty garage, and drops of blood were found on the floor, washed away, but found again in the same places the next day.

Balinese demons can be exorcized only by *Leyaks*, invisible supernatural sorcerers, who in turn can be summoned only by top holy men. The price in sacrificial animals and birds levied by the guru whom McPhee solicited was both onerous and impractical—a chicken with feathers growing the wrong way ("frizzled," in Flannery O'Connor's word)—but the old man was open to compromise, especially when primed with glasses of arac which he "tossed down with the sudden quickness of a lizard that has seen a fly." To McPhee's remark, "I thought priests might not drink strong drinks," a houseboy responds with "He is very holy and may do as he pleases." On another occasion, the village imposed a 24-hour curfew in the hope that, with everyone indoors and all lights out, "the demons would think the village deserted and pass it by."

McPhee's thumbnail portraits are wonderfully vivid. An ancient holy man, "white hair tied up in a knot on the crown of his head ... piled on top of a slow-moving pony [and] holding a paper umbrella over his head" reminds him of "a Chinese painting of a Taoist monk." A prince with whom McPhee eats fruit, spits the mangosteen, litchi, and pomelo pips on the floor where they are "immediately gathered by an attendant," a human spitoon who "carried the royal discard in his hands." The face of the visiting Regent of the district is "a masterpiece of sensuality, cruelty and cunning. His sarong and headcloth were arranged in extravagant folds. Enormous moonstones buttoned his white official jacket, and his fingers were heavy with rings." When one of McPhee's handsome young retainers brings tea, the regent's gaze settles on the boy, after which "his eyes met mine in a glance of insolent penetration."

Bali, when the McPhees landed there, was the most musical land on the planet:

> The air was constantly stirred by musical sounds. At night hills and valleys faintly echoed with the vibrant tones of great bronze gongs. By day drums thundered along the roads to the clash of cymbals as chanting processions of men and women carried offerings to the far-off sea.... Bells were fixed to oxen yokes, weavers' shuttles, pony carts ... and tiny ones were hung to the feet of domestic pigeons, whose tail feathers were attached with bamboo whistles.

The Balinese gamelan is a mallet instrument resembling a marimba. A gamelan orchestra is an ensemble of them joined by gongs, drums, and cymbals. Its music is based on five tones, cosmologically signifying the gods linked to the five directions, north, east, south, west, and the center, the omphalos of the world where Siva, the Creator-Destroyer, sits in the middle of a lotus. The sole purpose of music is to please the gods; the pleasure of humans is coincidental. Like some Indian ragas and the canonic hours of the West, it has a "scale of midnight" and "a mode of dawn." It is also anonymous and, apart from the barest outlines encoded in a few virtually uninterpretable scratches on dried palm leaves, unwritten—a fugitive art, therefore, with no theory, no notation, no indication of rhythm, melody, and the interweaving of sonorities; every phrase, note, detail of the accompaniment is learned by ear and by "careful and infinitely patient listening to a teacher."

During what seems to be McPhee's first experience of a live gamelan orchestra, he felt

> a sensation of indescribable freshness. There was none of the perfume and sultriness of so much music in the East, for there is nothing purer than the bright, clean sound of metal, cool and ringing and dissolving in the air. Nor

was it personal and romantic in the manner of our own effusive music, but rather sound broken up into beautiful patterns. Gongs of different sizes punctuated this stream of sound, divided and subdivided it into sections and inner sections, giving it meter and meaning.

Nyoman, a Balinese musician for whom McPhee played specimens of Western music on an upright piano, complained that it sounds "like someone crying.... Up and down, up and down, for no reason at all." McPhee tells us that since the piano has twelve pitches and Nyoman's instrument only five, irregularly tuned, Western music can have no meaning for the native ear: "The Balinese taste for Bach, in tourists' tales," is an impossibility. For Nyoman and his people, Western European art music is "a complicated noise, without order, tempestuous and baffling in its emotional climaxes, dragging on and on and leading nowhere." Music, for these people, is remote from emotional self-revelation:

> Without effort, with eyes closed, or staring out into the night as though each player were in an isolated world of his own, the men performed their isolated parts with mysterious unity.... I wondered at their natural ease, the almost casual way in which they played.... As I listened to the musicians, watched them, I could think only of a flock of birds wheeling in the sky, turning with one accord, now this way, now that.

McPhee is a keen observer of many aspects of Balinese culture. Where do the gods stay when here on earth? he wonders, and eventually deduces that they hide in the tiniest objects, in stones and bits of wood, and in little golden figurines fashioned for them and kept locked up in temples. He is fascinated by foods and their preparation, whether dragon-fly larvae on shredded and toasted coconut or curried anteater. "A whole etiquette revealed itself in the way people sit," he writes, introducing a discussion of the hierarchical relationships between man and man in the island's caste system, though this complex subject, with its distinctions of language, manners, and dress, different in every district and village, and of the effects of Dutch authority instated over the four existing Hindu castes, is more comprehensively examined in the methodical writings of Jane Belo and Margaret Mead.

In a chapter on the puppet shadow-plays and traditional dramas based on the ancient legends, McPhee refers to the dance as "music made visible," Balanchine's artistic credo, except that Balanchine would have objected to the Balinese theater's obscuring of the borders where dancing ends and acting begins. When McPhee finally decides to undertake a serious study of the island's music, which later became *Music in Bali*, he pitches a tent in distant places in search of ancient primitive instruments, such as are seen in relief sculptures on Javanese temples. He is shown several unfamiliar kinds of drums and gongs and a kind of rattle, a harp-shaped frame hung with different sizes of bamboo tubes. McPhee's inquiries are not confined to technicalities. "How does a musician earn a living?" he asks, and the answer is: "Oh, his wives weave mats."

A House in Bali was written in the early 1940s at Yaddo, in the house of Henry Cowell at Shady (Woodstock), New York, and in the top-floor apartment of the Brooklyn Heights brownstone whose other tenants included W. H. Auden, Carson McCullers, Gypsy Rose Lee, Oliver Smith, Benjamin Britten, and Peter Pears. (McPhee's Balinese transcriptions undeniably influenced Britten's *The Prince of the Pagodas*.) Paul and Jane Bowles were also residents in the Brooklyn house while McPhee lived there, and the reader inevitably remarks on the resemblances between the two couples, and on the two men themselves, both of them having wedded unusual "Janes," lived as expatriates and preservers of indigenous cultures, worked as music critics, and been more successful as writers than as composers.

While at work on *A House in Bali*, McPhee recognized that "I write so much better than I compose." (Virgil Thomson might have made the same observation concerning his own gifts, though he would hardly have said so, and also Harry Partch, author of the lucidly argued *Genesis of a Music* and composer of sounds remote from Western musical traditions.) McPhee elaborates in a letter:

> I've been trained as a musician, and feel words the way I feel tones. The sentences must float ... [j]ust as the music of Mozart floats, while Beethoven ... and Bach too at times, sinks to the bottom of the glass.

He told Margaret Mead, a close friend despite her tiresome "YMCA energy," "I was a fool to be so fussy about what I thought was style, but ... at last when I had a subject, I could not resist playing with it self-indulgently. At the same time I was trying to make a complex experience crystal-clear."

Fussed over or not—three versions of *A House in Bali* are mentioned and McPhee admitted that "little, trivial things seem able to disturb me for hours. You'd think I was James or Flaubert"—McPhee's book displays remarkable descriptive dexterity. In the tiny town of Buleleng

> the dentists were Japanese, and their offices held no secrets from the passer-by. In the center of each a plush chair balanced on uncertain machinery; the walls were covered with terrifying charts, while glass cases exhibited pearly molars and sets of golden teeth.

A House in Bali, *Music in Bali*, the children's story *A Club of Small Men*, the music criticism, and the letters attest to a a "natural" literary gift. So do McPhee's unpublished Balinese field notes:

> Spent the day sailing in praus across the straits of Java ... walking over the coral reefs.... Small fish of indescribable brilliance, gold, scarlet, crimson, ultramarine and silver; enormous starfish ... giant clams—the same whose shells are used in Cathedrals of France for *l'eau bénit*.

McPhee's music criticism, the 140 or so pages of it published in Mina Lederman's *Modern Music* between 1939 and 1946, as well as his record reviews in *Mademoiselle* and the more substantial essays on Balinese music in *Dance Index* and *The Musical Quarterly*, expose a more audacious side of his personality, and an honesty that such friends as Virgil Thomson and Aaron Copland must have respected, even as it may have irritated them (Benjamin Britten was "grieved" by McPhee's dismissal of *Sonnets of Michelangelo* as "baroque and pompous show pieces"). Thomson's "chaste and Lilliputian" Third Piano Sonata, McPhee writes, might better be described as *"Adventure in C* ... a sharp would be as disturbing as a coarse word at a church social"; the "eloquent simplicity of [Copland's *Lincoln Portrait*] somehow does not ring quite true to my ears"; and "the sexy and goonlike voices of the Andrews Sisters, those Rhine maidens of the jukebox," provide an object-lesson "in the degradation of a Negro tune." He might have been thinking of Stokowski, with whom he had had some experience, in noting that the gamelan orchestra has "no conductor's stick to beat time, no over-eloquent hands to urge or subdue."

McPhee had a "natural" musical gift as well, if not a creative one of any size. He was a time-to-time composer whose best efforts depend on formal, rhythmic, melodic, and instrumental Balinese examples. Oja is not deaf to the weaknesses of the music, its minimalist repetition and its monotonous syncopation. She extravagantly praises two of the late pieces, the *Nocturne* for chamber orchestra and the Second Symphony ("sublimely beautiful"), but is well aware that McPhee's importance is less in his own music than in his explication of the music of an Oriental culture, in helping the twain to meet. If, as Steve Reich claims, non-Western music has become "an increasingly important source for Western composers," McPhee provided one of the first bridges.

In New York in the 1940s and 1950s, McPhee was obliged to scrounge for a living. He thumbed along the familiar route of the Guggenheim grant, the Bollingen fellowship, the Fulbright. He had no success on the lecture circuit, succeeded as a reviewer but made no money, scripted radio programs on the history of jazz for the OWI, worked as an arranger, and tried to wangle commissions—Lincoln Kirstein sponsored one for chamber ensemble arrangements of McPhee's transcriptions of Javanese court dances, which were performed in two Ballet Society concerts in 1947.

At one point McPhee lamented to a friend, "The only things in life I want are the things money can buy," and though he recognized that the separation from Jane marked the beginning of his decline, he blamed the divorce on "bad luck." Though remarried, she silently continued to give him money, indicating at least a residue of affection for him. After a six-year hiatus from composing, he took a teaching position in Los Angeles, where he died in 1964.

McPhee's life after Bali contains many lows and only a few highs—a recording of his music for two pianos that he made with Benjamin Britten, and the performance by Béla Bartók and his wife at Amherst College in 1942 of some of the Balinese 2-piano transcriptions. In 1943, in a depressive psychosis, and in sad contrast to the sustained euphoria of A House in Bali, he confessed to Dr. William Mayer (husband of Elizabeth Mayer, Auden's friend and his co-translator of Goethe's Italian Journey), director of the psychiatric hospital in Amityville, Long Island:

> Many times there was a decision to make between some important opportunity and a sexual (homosexual) relationship which was purely sensual. I never hesitated to choose the latter. The Balinese period was simply a long extension of this.

Yet his best years were those on the sexually ambidextrous island which inspired his two books, his lasting achievement.

The cover of Music in Bali, whose principal dedicatee is Margaret Mead, reproduces one of the stone reliefs depicting musicians at Borobudur, the colossal ninth-century Mahayana Buddhist shrine in central Java. The photograph is not credited, but may have been taken by Walter Spies, who had been commissioned by the Dutch Government to paint a diorama of village life at the foot of Borobudur as he might imagine it to have been when the building was completed (tenth century). Borobudur had been documented by camera from as early as 1845, and Gauguin had studied photos of its relief sculptures. Since the 1980s, the monument, visited by one to two million tourists a year, has been filmed (Brian Brake's Borobudur: The Cosmic Mountain, the mountain that connects heaven and earth).

McPhee would have known about Borobudur from his reading of Sir Thomas Raffles's History of Java (1818). In any case, Music in Bali includes a survey of the musical instruments depicted in the Borobudur sculptures, the flutes, shell horns, cymbals, gongs, paired drums, bow harps, lutes, reed mouth-organs, archaic xylophones and metallophones, elephant bells—strung to the animal's sides like jingle bells, to illustrate an episode in the *Gandavyuha*, the Mahayana sutra, which is the subject matter of the highest level of the reliefs.

Paul Bowles's Pipe Dreams

"For the American Academic, Paul Bowles is still odd man out; he writes as if *Moby Dick* had never been written." Melville apart, Gore Vidal's remark remains true today. The laureate of loneliness and dislocation, of damaged psyches, of lives out of control or slipping through the net, is very different from the present-day practitioners of the literature of delinquency to which Bowles opened the floodgates forty years ago. At the same time, an "American academic" biography has appeared,[1] nearly all of the books have been reprinted, and a film of the best-selling novel *The Sheltering Sky* has come (and quickly gone). Despite the kicking and screaming author, the mantle, or djellaba, of canonization as a comfy classic of American literature is in the making.

Sawyer-Lauçanno's life of the uncategorizable artist and social outsider appears less than a year after Bowles published sections of his diary disavowing it. ("Twice or three times a year L. arrives from Boston, where he's busy writing that biography which I rejected before he started").[2] The book provides more facts than Bowles's autobiography, *Without Stopping* (1972), but the same incidents are more skillfully told in the latter. To these two versions must be added the newly published "autobiography" of Mohammed Mrabet,[3] the central figure in Bowles's life for the last quarter of a century, whose tales in Moghrebi Arabic[4] Bowles has been translating since the late sixties. Here Mrabet reveals above all a propensity to personal violence and a taste for exhibitions of homosexual sadism; Bowles and his wife appear in the latter part of the book.

The descendant of old New England families, Paul Bowles was born in

---

[1] *An Invisible Spectator: A Biography of Paul Bowles*, by Christopher Sawyer-Lauçanno. New York: Weidenfeld & Nicolson, 1989.

[2] *Antaeus*, Autumn 1988.

[3] *Look and Move On by Mohammed Mrabet. An Autobiography as Told to Paul Bowles*. London: Peter Owen, 1989.

[4] The dialect language of more than twenty books, most of them credited to Mohammed Mrabet, that Bowles later tape-recorded and transcribed into English.

Queens in 1910. A precocious, exceptionally intelligent only child, he was writing poems and stories by the age of nine, and at the same time receiving lessons in piano and music theory. Bullied by his dentist father, the boy retreated into himself. Indeed, his whole life can be explained as an *épater-le-bourgeoisie* rebellion against the values and mores of his parent, and the fatherland he represented. Paul's abandonment of college and escape to Paris at age seventeen fit this description, as do other gestures of revolt such as his marriage to the flamboyantly lesbian writer, Jane Auer, his decision to live in Tangier, his strong opposition to Christianity, and his use and advocacy of drugs: he was ether-sniffing already in his first semester at the University of Virginia in Charlottesville. Bowles is the last of the "Lost" Generation and the first of the "Beats," the peer of many of the former, a better artist than any of the latter.

Sawyer-Lauçanno helps to relate the life to the work and events in the fiction to their real-life sources, and he provides useful summaries and critical cribs of Bowles's four novels. The reader's obstacles are not here but in the more than half of the book devoted to Bowles's career as a musician. His music is virtually unknown, and, except for a few recorded piano pieces and a recent release of eleven songs,[5] unavailable. Since most of it consists of incidental scores for some twenty-two plays, an appreciation of it is likely to remain next to impossible. If concert suites could be stitched together from his theater-music fragments—185 of them in separate cues for the 1942 Theater Guild production of *Twelfth Night*—Bowles would doubtless have done so himself.

Sawyer-Lauçanno does not venture to compare Bowles's strikingly different musical and literary personalities; and since the wry, light-hearted side of his music corresponds to nothing in the morbid world of his fiction, we are left with two apparently unrelated faces rather than a composite visage. Nor does the biographer examine the music close up, telling us instead, unhelpfully, that one of Bowles's film scores came through "in a finely tuned manner," and quoting the verbiage of daily and hebomedal reviewers. A *New York Times* drama critic wrote that Bowles had contributed "spidery and tinkling music of exquisite texture" to *Sweet Bird of Youth*, and another New York newspaper reported that the score of Bowles's opera based on Lorca's *Yerma* sounded "haunting … mystical [and] modern." Whether or not traditional operatic forms were employed is not vouchsafed, nor is there any discussion of the melodic, harmonic, rhythmic, vocal, and instrumental language.

---

[5] *American Songs: Works by Paul Bowles, Lee Holby, Richard Hudley, Eric Klein, John Misto and Virgil Thomson*. William Sharp, baritone; Stephen Blier, piano. New World NW369. CD and LP.

Bowles's growth as a musician is fully, orally and archivally, chronicled. The teenage composer showed his music to Henry Cowell, who passed him on to Aaron Copland for lessons in composition. At nineteen, Bowles accompanied Copland to Berlin, Paris, and Morocco. The last was love at first sight for Bowles (not for Copland), a love that was consummated in 1947, when he settled there for good, becoming more writer than composer.

Sawyer-Lauçanno's picture of New York musical life between the late 1930s and the early 1950s tells us more about promotional finagling than about prevailing currents in musical philosophy. Bowles's progress is charted from opus to opus until, in the mid-1930s, he was launched as a film, ballet and theater composer. In a review of his incidental music for the 1937 Orson Welles Mercury Theater production of Marlowe's *Dr. Faustus*, Virgil Thomson welcomed the young composer's entry into "musical big-time." Three years later Thomson devoted a column in the *Herald Tribune* to the *Twelfth Night* score, an unprecedented step for a music critic, given the lowly status of the genre. But when in the late Forties Bowles switched from music to writing, Thomson's comment, according to Sawyer-Lauçanno, was that "Bowles's lack of formal musical education began to hinder his ability to create the more serious classical compositions expected of a composer in middle age":

> Anybody without a musical education copies what's around, and Paul's music was always sweet and charming but the most advanced thing he knew or could handle was Ravel.

Yet with the possible exception of the two female voices at the beginning of *A Picnic Cantata* (1953, set to a poem by James Schuyler) superficially suggesting *L'Enfant et les sortilèges*, Bowles's music is remote from Ravel's, while, in the treatment of the voice and the word-setting in cadences of quotidian speech, close to Thomson's own. The most conspicuous influence in Bowles's earliest music is Satie, and, after him, neither Thomson nor Copland, but George Antheil, the composer of *Ballet mécanique*. What can safely be asserted about Bowles as a composer is that the songs and other music with words are more successful than such "abstract"—his word—instrumental pieces as the Concerto and the Sonata for Two-Pianos, commissioned and first performed by Robert Fizdale and Arthur Gold.

Bowles, the born exile ("I'm always happy leaving the United States"), attributes his change of professions to an aversion to New York. "I couldn't make a living as a composer without remaining all the time in New York. I was very much fed up with being in New York." But if his musical drive had been stronger, surely even "the city" would have been bearable. His friend Ned

Rorem points out that the "writing brought him far more accolades" than the music, and Thomson, not seeing that the composer of promise might also be a writer of high accomplishment, said that money was the deciding factor. Yet while the biography shows the young Bowles to be an opportunist in various minor ways, he could not have been one in having seriously committed his talent once he realized that his natural gifts and temperament were more effective in literature than in music. In a 1952 interview in the *New York Times*, Bowles explained that "there were a great many things I wanted to say that were too precise to express in musical terms." This is revealing, for the hundred-percent composer would start at the opposite end, with Mendelssohn's "What music says cannot be expressed in words because *music* is too precise."

The essays, "The Rif, To Music" and "The Route to Tassemsit," in the collection of travel essays *Their Heads Are Green And Their Hands Are Blue,*[6] describe portions of Bowles's 25,000 miles of Moroccan travel in 1959 on a Rockefeller Foundation grant to record indigenous music for the Library of Congress. He had begun to collect recordings of Moroccan music in 1934, and, in 1956, with modern equipment, portable Ampex, earphones and microphones, to tape it. The 1959 project, a major ethnomusicological undertaking, was abetted by U.S. Embassy support but nearly blocked by the Moroccans. "I detest all folk music and particularly ours here in Morocco," an official in the Moroccan government told him. "It sounds like the noises made by savages. Why should I help you to export a thing which we are trying to destroy?" Bowles nevertheless succeeded in gathering a precious legacy, and in 1972 the Library of Congress finally issued recordings of a small part of it.

Music is "the most important single element in Moroccan folk culture," Bowles declares at the outset of "The Rif, to Music," and he observes that Moroccans have a "magnificent and highly evolved sense of rhythm." But he does not acknowledge that, while the counter-rhythms and syncopations of South Moroccan drum music are fascinating for a time, the music as a whole lacks structure in comparison to that of the highly developed musical cultures of, for example, Bali and India. Bowles is especially struck by the Moroccan manner of vocalizing, by the restriction in range to three adjacent pitches, and by the use of such Berber instruments as the double-reed zamar and the low-register reed-flute qsbah. When he invited a qsbah player to record a solo, the response was a corollary to Mendelssohn: "How is anybody going to know what the qsbah is

---

[6] *Their Heads Are Green And Their Hands Are Blue, Scenes From The Non-Christian World,* by Paul Bowles, with photographs by the author. New York: Ecco, 1987.

saying all by itself unless there is somebody to sing the words?" But Bowles's remark that the music of qsbah, "more than any other I know, most completely expresses the essence of solitude," perhaps best explains its appeal to him.

In this charming book, so "normal," sane and sensible, the along-the-road anecdotes ("The flies crawl on our faces trying to drink from our eyes") are as interesting as those in Bowles's fiction. Here, as in the fiction, this subtle intelligence ("it takes an exceedingly insensitive person today to continue being an artist") is a no less acute recorder of sensual experience. His description of scenery, sonorities (a tape of "an old-fashioned rubber-bulbed Parisian taxi horn run off at double speed"), palpations, flavor (revolting foods), and nauseating, especially excremental, odors are particularly keen—and frequently off-putting.

Bowles's description of a civilization that is dying is central to understanding his work. He sees a world where the basic wisdom of the people has been destroyed and cannot be replaced; religion may be superstition, but the sense of the helplessness of life based on beliefs that "'it is written' has given way to an even more unfortunate belief that man can alter his destiny." For

> the partially educated young Moroccan material progress has become such an important symbol that he would be willing to sacrifice the religion, culture, happiness, and even the lives of his compatriots in order to achieve even a modicum of it.

* * *

"Creativity is an eruption of the unconscious," Bowles wrote in 1985. In "the light of reason, this subterranean material generally discovers the uses to which it will be put." As first set forth in the short stories collected in *The Delicate Prey*[7] (1950), the principal props in his imagined world are landscapes, especially god-forsaken ones. "It seems a practical procedure to let the place determine the characters who will inhabit it," he wrote in January 1989. The landscapes are more important than the inhabitants, whose interior lives are left unexplained, and who undergo practically no development. Sometimes Bowles's characters emerge only through brief dialogue. In "The Echo," for instance, the tomboy temperament of Prue, Aileen's mother's "peculiar" friend, is established mainly through bits of pugnacious talk: "What the hell d'you think life is, one long coming-out party?"

These early stories are distinguished, too, by their simplicity of plot, their detachment, and a lucid and laconic style free of cumbersome clauses. Occa-

---

[7] *The Delicate Prey and Other Stories* by Paul Bowles. New York: Ecco, 1950.

sionally an aphorism slips through: "It is only when one is not fully happy that one is meticulous about time," aptly in this case ("Pages from Cold Point"), less so, given the inebriation at the origin, in the later story "Tapiama": "What is freedom ... other than the state of being totally, instead of only partially, subject to the tyranny of chance?"

The perspective in these stories is usually that of the primitive mind observing people from alien cultures and fellow members of its own. Bowles's most common subject is the tale of the uncomprehending American or European encountering local life in Latin America, Northwest Africa and, exceptionally, Southeast Asia. He also describes both the allure of the Muslim and the difficulties faced by even the most devoted and intelligent Europeans in trying to understand it, as in the late story "The Time of Friendship," an account of the bond between a spinster Swiss schoolteacher and a young Algerian boy:

> Across the seasons of their friendship she had come to think of him as being very nearly like herself.... Now she saw the dangerous vanity at the core of that fantasy: she had assumed that somehow his association with her had automatically been for his ultimate good, that inevitably he had been undergoing a process of improvement as a result of knowing her. In her desire to see him change, she had begun to forget what [he] was really like.

The stories in *The Delicate Prey* were written during a period of four years in which Bowles also composed an impressive body of music and translated Sartre's *No Exit* (Bowles's title, suggested by a sign in the subway) for its first New York production, as well as completed *The Sheltering Sky*. As Bowles described the novel to Ned Rorem:

> Really it is an adventure story in which the adventure takes place on two planes simultaneously: in the actual desert, and in the inner desert of the spirit.... The occasional oasis provides relief from the natural desert, but the ... sexual adventures fail to provide relief. The shade is insufficient, the glare is always brighter as the journey continues. And the journey must continue—there is no oasis in which one can remain.

Tennessee Williams, setting some kind of record for vagueness, describes *The Sheltering Sky* as an "allegory of the spiritual adventure of the fully conscious person into modern experience," and he compares the author to Camus, probably because of the North African locale, although the adventures of Bowles's naive Americans in the Sahara have little in common with *L'Etranger*. The success of the novel must be attributed to its sustained suspense and scandalous, for

1949, subject matter, the repeated rape of an American woman, her abduction to a seraglio, and her mental breakdown. But by the measure of its single plot and three-character cast it is more an extended short story than a novel.

The most disturbing pieces in *The Delicate Prey* are concerned with cultural collision and the world of drug fantasies. The United States is the setting of only one, "You Are Not I," in which the author enters the locked-in mind of a psychopath to decipher its suspicions of other people's motives. All seventeen stories are remarkable, but now, at a forty-year distance, the most memorable are still the two most shocking, the title pieces of this and the later volume, *A Distant Episode*, both of them considered unpublishable in Britain until 1968 and still not advisable for the squeamish.

Sexual stimulation from hashish triggers the atrocities in "The Delicate Prey," a grisly tale of an encounter in the Sahara between members of enemy tribes:

> The [Mongari] moved and surveyed the young body lying on the stones. He ran his finger along the razor's blade; a pleasant excitement took possession of him. He stepped over, looked down, and saw the sex that sprouted from the base of the belly. Not entirely conscious of what he was doing, he took it in one hand and brought his arm down with the motion of a reaper wielding a sickle. It was swiftly severed.... [After cutting a pouch in the boy's entrails and stuffing the organ there, a] new idea came to him. It would be pleasant to inflict an ultimate indignity upon the young Filali. He threw himself down; this time he was vociferous and leisurely in his enjoyment.... [Later] the Mongari turned him over and pushed the blade back and forth with a sawing motion into his neck until he was certain he had severed the windpipe.

The sexual mutilation and humiliation, the pathology of seduction and cruelty, the linking of sex and death remind us of Robert Mapplethorpe's "X Portfolio," except that in Bowles's art, unlike the photographer's, sexual fantasies are rare.

In the less lethal and marginally less horrifying "A Distant Episode" (1945), a French professor comes to North Africa to study Moghrebi Arabic and is captured by nomads, who cut out his tongue (linguistics is his subject), tie tin cans to the rags they have exchanged for his clothes, and force him to dance clownishly for their amusement. He finally escapes but by that time, crazed, he has assumed the identity the nomads have given him, and instead of going to the police returns to the desert. Sawyer-Lauçanno does not mention the story's striking resemblance to the professor in *The Blue Angel* who becomes a geek.

Spirits and ghosts appear frequently, as in "The Circular Valley." In this tale of Poe-like weirdness and intensity, a derelict monastery in Mexico is haunted by an invisible djinn, who "possesses" some gringo visitors there, directing their actions in mysterious ways. But Bowles's most original stories are about drug-induced transferences, as in "Allal," in which a Moroccan boy who becomes infatuated with a poisonous snake and, after a whiff of kif too many (kif is a mixture of cannibis and tobacco that exalts and sexually excites), boundaries blurred and traversed, he exchanges personalities and corporealities with it. The ending is ferally frightening:

> It was beautiful to caress the earth with the length of his belly.... On catching sight of a man ahead, he left the road and hid behind a rock.... [A boy] was so close that Allal went straight up to him and bit him in the leg.... Swiftly [Allal] glided through into the alcove. The brown body [Allal in his human incarnation] still lay near the door.... Allal needed time to get back to it, to lie close to its head and say: "Come here." As he stared ... at the body, there was a great pounding at the door. The boy was on his feet at the first blow, as if a spring had been released, and Allal saw with despair the expression of total terror in his face, and the eyes with no mind behind them.... [He would] be sent one day soon to the hospital at Berrechid.... Allal lay in the alcove dozing.... The men nearest him were on their hands and knees, and Allal had the joy of pushing his fangs into two of them before a third severed his head with an axe.

The mordant exchanges in "Call at Corazon" (1946) bare the raw hatred between a newlywed couple on a tramp-steamer calling along the Central American coast. When the husband remarks that one doesn't "take a honeymoon alone," his sexually unsatisfied, solitary-drinking bride replies: "*You* might." Though appalled by his wish to purchase a monkey, when he agrees not to she promptly about-faces: "I'll be more miserable if you don't, so please go and buy it.... I'd love to have it.... I think it's sweet." After the animal has made a shambles of their cabin, she pretends not to mind it. "What I mind is you. *He* can't help being a little horror, but he keeps reminding me that you could if you wanted." When the husband offers to get rid of it, she suggests that "you drop him overboard." The unspoken thoughts are no less bitchy: "She knew he would wait to be angry until she was unprepared for his attack." At night, discovering that she and the whiskey bottles she keeps in the cabin are missing, he goes in search, finds her and a member of the crew half-dressed and sprawled on the floor in an alcoholic stupor, and packs his bags. In the morning, he debarks and boards a train alone.

Sawyer-Lauçanno contends that the account of "marital tension" is "not pure invention" and that "the fictional renderings by both Bowles and his wife, the talented but deeply neurotic and incorrigible Jane Auer, confirm Virgil Thomson's testimony that the version of the marriage in Jane Bowles's own novel *Two Serious Ladies*[8] is, like "Call at Corazon," a "a thinly disguised story of their honeymoon." Both the similarities (the alcoholism) and the disguises (she is depicted as a heterosexual) are apparent in Bowles's story; moreover, he told Gertrude Stein that Jane hated monkeys. Yet the acerbic wife does not sound like the Jane Bowles in her published letters to her husband,[9] some of them running on to thousands of words, many of which, in the tradition of drinker's ink, are repetitious. But, then, Bowles's own terse style could not accommodate garrulity.

While acknowledging Bowles's homosexual temperament—he is "quite drawn toward homosexuals and homosexuality"—and allowing Thomson and Tennessee Williams to name male lovers, Sawyer-Lauçanno professes to believe that, apart from an early seduction in Paris by an older man, Bowles "stopped short of physical involvement." Granted that Bowles can put himself into other people's shoes, that he and his characters are sometimes perfectly fungible, and that he is much given to fantasizing, one doubts that the nuances of feeling in "Pages from Cold Point" could have been so convincingly conveyed by a writer who had not directly experienced them himself. The boy lay "asleep on his side, and naked," his homoerotic father writes in a memoir:

> I stood looking at him for a long time ... my eyes followed the curve of his arm, shoulder, back, thigh, leg.... I shall never know whether or not he was asleep all that time. Of course he couldn't have been, and yet he lay so still ... warm and firm, but still as death."

In this story, Vidal says, incidentally reminding us that in the pre-permissive society we had to read such things more closely, "nothing and everything happens." Sawyer-Lauçanno states the case for Ned Rorem as the model for the sixteen-year-old and Bowles himself for the parent, although Bowles has denied this:

---

[8] *Two Serious Ladies.* Jane Bowles. New York: Knopf, 1943.

[9] *Out In The World: Selected Letters of Jane Bowles 1935–1970*, edited by Millicent Dillon. Santa Barbara: Black Sparrow.

There is more than a bit of Bowles [in the father]. His response, for instance, to [his son's] homosexual promiscuity—feigning ignorance or indifference—is very much the response that Bowles was making to [his wife's lesbian] liaisons.

But the story as a whole is less than entirely successful; the pretense of gradually revealing the true nature of the son's adventures and of the father's incestuous desires is belied from the beginning, where both are obvious to the reader.

Some of the autobiographical correspondences in the stories are wholly transparent. The first-person voice of the writer wrestling with himself in "If I Should Open My Mouth" (1952) is identical to that of the author of *Without Stopping*:

> [When] sound asleep ... often the best things come to light and are recognized as such by a critical part of my mind which is there watching, quite capable of judging but utterly unable to command an awakening and a recording.

So, too, the six-year-old Donald (read Paul) and his tyrannical father at a family Christmas in Vermont in *"The Frozen Fields"* (1957), though the story is more engaging than either Bowles's own non-fictional account of the relationship in *Without Stopping* or the one by Sawyer-Lauçanno, with his theory that all of Bowles's anti-middle-class acts and attitudes are part of the pattern of rebellion against his father.

A precocious listener, Donald is aware that the grown-ups, in their conversation, "were being mysterious because of him," and an abrupt silence convinces him that "if he had not been there ... they would all have begun to talk at that point." Bowles exploits the potent clichés of memory inspired by the opening of Christmas presents: "How lovely! But it's too much!," and, to Donald, both before—"You just hold your horses"—and after he unwraps the inevitable sweater: "I got it big purposely so you could grow into it." One scene between Donald and his mother is an American period piece in itself:

> "Why does Mr. Gordon live at Uncle Ivor's?" "What was that?" she demanded sharply.... "Dear, don't you know that Uncle Ivor's what they call a male nurse?" ... "Is Mr. Gordon sick?" "Yes he is but we don't talk about it." "What's he got?" "I don't know dear."

Recent Bowles stories depict an America of violence, cupidity, and shallowness: "Unwelcome Words" and "In Absentia," both of them in the form of letters ("Every work suggests its own method"), "Massachusetts, 1932" (about shotgun uxoricides), and "Julian Vredon" (a parricide).

In the longest of these fabulations, "Here to Learn," Malika, a fetching fifteen-year-old from the Rif, owes her worldly ascent/descent to her elementary level education at a Spanish-speaking nunnery in Morocco. One day while she is sitting with a group of women in a roadside market, a "Nazarene" in a yellow convertible stops to photograph them. They ask Malika to make use of her Spanish and tell him to leave. Meanwhile, a swarm of baksheesh-demanding urchins has besieged him; he asks Malika to get into the car, then drives off with her. Having been alone with him, however briefly, she cannot rejoin the women. He takes her to his house in Tangier, where she is astonished by its modern equipment and turns the hot and cold taps on and off during the first night in her new home, "to see if sooner or later one of them would make a mistake." She becomes his mistress, but like most of Bowles's stories this one is devoid of erotic content.

On the eve of a quick trip to London, the Nazarene invites his friends Bobby and Peter to stay with her in his absence, assuring her that "they don't make love with girls." She concludes that they must be eunuchs and, when their friends visit, realized that "there were a good many more eunuchs in Tangier than she had suspected." Soon Tony, not a eunuch, brings her to Paris, depositing her there with his sister, who, in turn, passes her along to an Italian girlfriend with whom she goes to Cortina d'Ampezzo. There she meets a rich Texan, who marries her and carries her off to Los Angeles. After "Tex" is killed in an automobile accident, Malika, now a wealthy widow, returns to Tangier, where, on a visit to her native Riffian village, she learns that her mother is dead and that her former home and neighborhood have been bulldozed to make way for a new city. Like Malika, the reader is left to ponder the effects of her cultural disruption on her future. Sawyer-Lauçanno finds the story "wonderfully ironic" in its reversal of the situation of the Westerner in North Africa. But the ironies are freighted with moral lessons avoided in Bowles's best work.

In Sawyer-Lauçanno's judgment, Bowles's "greatest achievement" is the short "novel" *Points In Time* (1981), which the author describes as "lyrical history." Based on historical events in Morocco from the Roman period to 1980, expanded and presented in story and dialogue form, the eleven self-contained episodes are recounted with an economy quite literally cut-to-the-bone: "The Spaniard in the garrison starts from sleep to find his throat already slashed." Barbarous as much Moroccan history has been—and still is (Bowles's journal of May 3, 1988 describes an incident of Ramadan violence: "[A seller in the market] whipped out a long knife and slashed the other with a downward motion, severing his jugular")—the bloodthirstiness in this book provokes more flinching and wincing than in any other. The brief sections end with, respectively, decapitation, impaling on a spear (twice), evisceration by a stag's antlers ("his intestines coiling out of him into the dirt"), the slow amputation by dagger of a man's ten toes, which are flung one by one into his face. In one scene, pieces of a leper's flesh are caught on "thorns and remained hanging there." In another, one of the tortures rejected as "insufficiently drastic" is a proposal to flay the victim, then cut the skin at his waist and pull it upward over his head to twist it around his neck and strangle him.

Responding to a question about the choice of such material, Bowles said that

> the awakening of the sensation of horror through reading can result in a temporary smearing of the lens of consciousness. All perception is distorted by it. It's a dislocation. A good jolt of vicarious horror can cause a certain amount of questioning of values.

A large amount, one hopes, but the explanation seems incomplete without raising the question of sadism and Bowles's apparent imperviousness to the macabre.

The sensations and experiences of drug-users on their journeys out of the phenomenological world and into *les paradis artificiels* are a preoccupation. The consumer's reports found throughout Bowles's work tell us that majoun, derived from cannabis (which the pederastic Haddawa Sufis of Egypt smoked), induces a sense of physical and mental upward propulsion, enhances pleasant and italicizes unpleasant experience, and synergizes the artistic imagination: "The *majoun* provided a solution [for *The Sheltering Sky*] totally unlike whatever I should have found without it." In "Under The Sky," an early story set in Mexico, he describes the effects of marijuana, the staple of his own drug diet in Thailand in 1966:

> [He held] the smoke in his lungs until he felt it burning the edges of his soul. From the back of his head it moved down to his shoulders. It was as if he were wearing a tight metal garment.... He continued to smoke, going deeper and deeper into delight.

Sawyer-Lauçanno publishes a brilliant letter to Ned Rorem written under the influence of mescaline, which helps to explain, or at least reveal, Bowles's fascination with horror and suggests the degree to which drugs are the catalyst for his imaginative ideas:

Whatever mescaline does, it doesn't seem to make one coherent. But neither does it supply any feeling of there being an interior, unreachable cosmos. It says: See where you are? Look around. This is what it's like. Can you stand seeing it? Touching it, smelling it? Fortunately one draws no conclusions, since everything is far too real to be able to mean anything. As I say, you examine horror very closely, without even any interest. Disgust is what one would feel if one were alive. Instead of that, one knows that it's all artificial, the structure of reality itself. Disgust is something that ought to be felt *for* one by someone. But of course there is not even anyone to experience the disgust, so it remains there, unfelt, but all around one, unregistered loathing, unattainable nausea, as wide as the smile of the sea while it belches up corruption.

Bowles writes in the preface to the four stories in *A Hundred Camels in the Courtyard*, his "Kif Quartet":

> Moroccan kif-smokers like to speak of "two worlds," the one ruled by inexorable natural laws, and the other, the kif world, in which each person perceives "reality" according to the projections of his own essence, the state of consciousness in which the elements of the physical universe are automatically rearranged by cannabis to suit the requirements of the individuals.
>
> I believed that through the intermediary of kif the barriers separating the unrelated elements might be destroyed, and the disconnected episodes forced into a symbiotic relationship.

Kif has benign effects on the body politic. "A population of satisfied smokers ... offers no foothold to an ambitious demagogue.... You can't even get together a crowd of smokers: each man is alone and happy to stay that way." Not much support here for the U.S.'s drug war! Bowles, the *preux chevalier* preserver of the arts and traditions of the Third World, including, besides narcotics, the superstitions of animists and medicine men, is at least consistent. Reading about an outbreak of bubonic plague in India, he wonders whether

> the almost certain eventual victory over such diseases will prove to have been worth its price: the extinction of the beliefs and rituals which gave a satisfactory meaning to the period of consciousness that goes between birth and death.

Indeed, these attitudes are also in line with the only comments that Sawyer-Lauçanno manages to make about the Bowleses during a certain 1940s war: "[It] seemed to touch them little. Bowles felt no guilt, only relief at being 4F; and Jane, although Jewish, did not ... express strong sentiments about the annihilation of European Jews."

Bowles's condemnation of the modernizing and politicizing West has willy-nilly made him an opponent of "progress," as well as a renegade *non grata* in the eyes of the Moroccan government, which harasses him to the extent of censoring his mail, confiscating not only a copy of *Satanic Verses* from abroad but even the galleys of his own book. Interpreting his Aesopian parable about a hyena luring a stork into a cave with promises of friendship, then killing it, Bowles openly identifies the beast with "progress," the bird with tradition. Yet his eloquent address to the question of the relation of Africa to the West helps, in its depth of feeling, to adjust the received view of him as entirely narcissistic and indifferent:

> How greatly the West needs to study the religions, the music, and the dances of the doomed African cultures. How much we could learn from them about man's relationship to the cosmos, about his conscious connection with his own soul. Instead of which we talk about raising their standard of living! Where we could learn *why*, we try to teach them our all-important *how*, so that they may become as rootless and futile and materialistic as we are.

Against Interpretation

Milan Kundera begins his impeachment[1] of the betrayal of the writer by the well-meaning but misguided disciple or custodian, and of the composer by the performer, with an examination of the relations between Kafka and Max Brod. Since it is no longer news that, *pace* Brod, Kafka did not ask him to destroy all of his work after his death—Kafka on his deathbed was correcting the galley proofs of "A Hunger Artist" for publication—an account of their friendship, fanatic veneration on Brod's side, need not be retold in a brief review. But Kundera goes on to reveal some of the damage that Brod wrought on Kafka's work, including deletions and impeding re-articulations by re-paragraphing and added punctuation. Kundera also dissects three French translations of an excerpt from *The Trial* as an example of the distortions of and losses to Kafka's art in its rendering in another language.

Kundera's analysis of *The Trial* is categorical. K. is guilty "not because he's committed a crime but because he's been accused." K.'s guilt is not doubted because "Society has adopted the accusation." K. is to be interrogated at a house in the suburbs, but not knowing at what time, and feeling pressed for time, he runs across the entire city; "*i.e.*, he does not take the streetcar, which follows the same route, for the reason that he had no desire to humble himself by too scrupulous punctuality." Since the tribunal refuses to declare the charge against him, K. "ends up looking for the crime himself."

Comparing *The Trial* to Orwell's *1984*, Kundera remarks that whereas Kafka's power is in reshaping the world by an immense poetic imagination, "the Englishman's novel is firmly closed to poetry." Moreover, it is merely "political thought disguised as a novel." Its pernicious influence resides in its "implacable reduction of a reality to its political dimension alone....I refuse to forgive this reduction on the grounds that it is useful as propaganda in the struggle against totalitarian evil. For that evil is precisely the reduction of life to politics, and of politics to propaganda."

---

[1] *Testaments Betrayed. An Essay in Nine Parts*, by Milan Kundera. Translated from the French by Linda Asher. New York: HarperCollins. New York. 1995.

Kundera's preoccupations with the novel as art form emerge in his comparison of Thomas Mann's *The Magic Mountain* and Robert Musil's *The Man Without Qualities*. Whereas Mann fills long passages "with data on the characters, on their pasts, their way of dressing, their way of speaking, the social customs of the time," and whereas his "intellectuality shows mainly in the dialogues about ideas carried on before the backdrop of a descriptive novel," in Musil, "the intellectuality is manifest at every instant." Against Mann's descriptive novel, Musil's is a "thinking" one. The events are set in a concrete milieu and in a concrete moment, the same as in *The Magic Mountain*, just before the 1914 War. But while Mann's Davos is described in detail, Musil's Vienna is barely identified. Mann makes use of every means offered by the various branches of knowledge—sociology, political science, medicine, history, physics, chemistry—to illuminate this or that theme, but in Musil,

> The novelist doesn't set up as a scholar, a doctor, a sociologist, a historian, he analyses human situations that are not part of some scientific field but are simply part of life. This is how Broch and Musil saw the historical task for the novel after the era of psychological realism.... [I]n Musil everything becomes theme (existential questioning). If everything becomes theme, the background disappears and ... there is nothing but foreground. It is this abolition of the background that I consider to be the structural revolution Musil brought about.

Kundera's humanism speaks out on every page of the book. In an illuminating discussion of Nietzsche, for example, he remarks that the philosopher's "refusal of systematic thought has another consequence: an immense broadening of theme; barriers between the various philosophical disciplines, which have kept the real world from being seen in its full range, are fallen, and from then on everything human can become the object of a philosopher's thought. That too brings philosophy nearer the novel: for the first time philosophy is pondering not epistemology, not aesthetics or ethics, the phenomenology of mind or the critique of reason, etc., but everything human."

The greatest surprise for most readers of *Testaments Betrayed* will be the discovery of Kundera's deep musicality and musical knowledge. His father was a musician who encouraged his son's talents with piano lessons and instruction in harmony, counterpoint, and composition. The son's musical perceptions are acute, highly original, and on a more sophisticated level than those of all but a few musicologists. A third or more of the book is devoted to Janáček and Stravinsky. If some of Kundera's descriptions of Beethoven's and Chopin's "strategies," as he calls them, irritate academics, they can only agree with his comments on the modern composers, which are both remarkably apt and remote from the going views. In a discussion of Beethoven's piano sonatas, he dares to laugh a little at the behemoth:

> The most important, most dramatic, longest movement is the first: the sequence of movements is thus a devolution: from the gravest to the lightest…. Imagine all the great symphonists, including Haydn and Mozart, Schumann and Brahms, weeping in their adagios and then turning into little children when the last movement starts, darting into the schoolyard to dance, hop, and holler that all's well that ends well.

The chapter on Janáček, with Kafka the other "great Czech artist of the century," is the best introduction to the composer that I have read, immeasurably superior to the one by Max Brod, who, in thrall to the composer to almost the same extent as he was to Kafka, published the first monograph on him. Like his biography of Kafka, it confines the composer to a provincial role, keeping him in the company of other Czech musicians only; Berg is mentioned in passing, but Bartók not at all. Failing to grasp Janáček's true stature and place in the international scene, Brod classifies him in relation to Smetana, that mediocrity who was and still is the national idol.

Janáček must be distinguished from the other great modernists, Kundera writes, in that his style is without influence from any of them, and his roots and genesis are radically different. Kundera begins in a Paris record shop, where he fails to find even adequate performances of Janáček's concert music. Nearly all renditions of the piano pieces are "wrong in both spirit and structure," Kundera asserts, and he sensibly attaches part of the blame for this on the solo medium itself, "undefended against *rubato*," as it is. Examples in music type are provided to show how the available recordings neglect the dynamic markings and do not produce the necessary tension. No less importantly, Kundera calls attention to the characteristic absence in Janáček of "transitions, developments, the mechanics of contrapuntal filler, routine orchestration." And he contrasts Janáček's expressionism, "an enormously rich emotional range, a dizzyingly tight transitionless juxtaposition of tenderness and brutality, fury and peace," with German Expressionism, which is characterized by "a predilection for excessive states—delirium, madness."

Turning to Janáček's operas, Kundera understandably ranks *From The House of the Dead* with *Wozzeck* as one of the two greatest operas "of our dark century," and rightly rejects *The Excursions of Mr. Brouček* as a failure. The most absorbing part of the essay deals with Janáček's "self-imposed accumulation of obstacles," foremost among them the centrality of the Czech language in his work, but also the "psychological meaning of the [verbal] melodic phrase," which is more important than the melody itself. Kundera acknowledges the impossibility of translation, while conceding that the operas could be known internationally at first only in their German versions. Brod, who did not understand Janáček's true value, was nevertheless his most effective advocate, translating all of the operas into German and thereby launching them into the international sphere. French, Kundera notes, cannot accommodate the first-syllable stress of Czech words, and the French language is hopelessly unable to convey any of the psychological nuances of the original.

Among the other obstructions in Janáček's decision to concentrate his "inner power" on opera is that the medium exposes him to "the mercy of the most conservative bourgeois audience imaginable." Added to this is the fierce hostility that the composer faced as the citizen of a small nation. He never left home, the province of Brno, and, unlike Schoenberg in Vienna, was not supported there by disciples or truly dedicated performers. For fourteen years, the conductor of the National Theater of Prague blocked the presentation of *Jenůfa*, Janáček's first great opera—Mahler wanted it for Vienna in 1904, but no German version was available—finally presenting it in 1916, in a version of his own, mutilated by cuts and countless changes, but a triumph nevertheless, for which Janáček was expected to show gratitude.

Kundera's insights into Stravinsky are worth more than most book-length studies of the composer. Partly from his experiences as a refugee himself, Kundera could see that "Without a doubt Stravinsky ... bore within him the wound of his immigration.... The start of his journey through the history of music coincides roughly with the moment when his native country ceases to exist for him.... He finds his only homeland in music ... his only compatriots ... from Pérotin to Webern.... [H]e did all he could to feel at home there: he lingered in each room of that mansion, touched every corner, stroked every piece of the furniture [from] Monteverdi to Hugo Wolf ... to the twelve-tone system ... in which, eventually, after Schoenberg's death (1951), he recognized yet another room in his home." Kundera remarks elsewhere that "the term 'neo-classicism,' commonly pinned on Stravinsky, is misleading, for his most decisive excursions into the past reach into eras earlier than the Classic."

Kundera goes on to say that the inclination to re-evaluate the entire history of music is common to all the great modernists, "the mark that distinguishes great modern art from modernist trumpery." Still, it is Stravinsky "who expresses it more clearly than anyone else." Kundera then proceeds to demolish the composer's chief detractors, first, Ansermet, who argued that Stravinsky's "diversity of style amounts to the absence of style." Discussing the notorious quarrel between the conductor and the composer, Kundera perceives, as no one else did, that Ansermet's anger can only be seen as that of "the performer who cannot tolerate the author's proud behavior and tries to limit his power."

Adorno, the other major detractor, with his "fearsome facility" in linking "works of art to political (sociological) causes," contended that Stravinsky's music is "music about music." Kundera refutes this by pointing out that "like no other composer before or after him, Stravinsky turned for inspiration to the whole span of music, which in no way lessens the originality of his art.... It is precisely his vagabondage through musical history—his conscious, purposeful 'eclecticism,' gigantic and unmatched—that is his total and incomparable originality." Expanding on the delight in Stravinsky's music, Kundera notes that it "bears the mark of humor," and wonders if "a fatal lack of humor makes Adorno so unreceptive to Stravinsky's music?"

Kundera tells us that when he was younger, "Stravinsky was one of those figures who would open doors onto distances I saw as boundless." At the time, Kundera thought of modern art as an "infinite journey." He now thinks that it was a short one, which implies that the great musical explosion in the early part of the century has fizzled out in the latter part. He presents his opinion of rock music piquantly: "Now anyone can suck his thumb as he likes."

II
∾ The Arts

Painting as a
Metaphor for Literature

*It is the business of a painter not to contend with nature ...
but to make something out of nothing.*

—John Constable, 1824

Dust-jacket pin-ups, whether intended to reveal, conceal, or merely appeal, are inevitably read as indices of the author's self-image. Here is John Updike,[1] grinning broadly and walking tall, in the dark suit of a business executive. And John Ashbery,[2] coatless, cravatless, half invisible through a half-open door, eyes wide open but blocking any attempt "to find the mind's construction in the face." And Robert Hughes,[3] a swivel away from his computer, ready for work, suspenders and rolled-up sleeves like a sheriff without the badge, dead seriousness not belied by the curl in the middle of the forehead. All three, in their different configurations, write about some of the same art, and, of course, write extremely well.

The shortest, best illustrated and most polished product is *Just Looking*, John Updike's soft-spoken literary readings of a variety of art works presented with his customary concinnity. In his description of Antonella Da Messina's *St Jerome in His Study*, writer identifies with writer, noting the quality of the light, the probable room temperature, the clutter of half-open and place-marked books, the no-doubt-noisy avians, and the lurking threat of interruption by the lion with the thorn in its paw. The furnishings of the study and its domestic birds and animals set the scene of a story, albeit not told. Updike's iconographic inventory of the picture duly notes the white of Jerome's sleeves and the open page of his Book, his strong features and unbent back, and the thought that his

---

[1] *Just Looking: Essays on Art*, by John Updike. New York: Knopf, 1989.

[2] Cover of *Self-Portrait in a Convex Mirror: Poems*, by John Ashbery. New York: Viking, 1975.

[3] *Nothing If Not Critical. Selected Essays on Art and Artists*, by Robert Hughes. New York: Knopf, 1990.

over-ample cassock would require a train-bearer. As for plot and mood, the novelist suggests that Jerome may be cogitating a point of theology. But about the painting as painting—the different background perspectives on either side, the absolute centering of the middle windows, the shadows, the dominance of reddish brown—nothing is said.

Roughly a third of the book is devoted to American art from Erastus Field to Wyeth; avoiding the argy-bargy over the "Helga" pictures, Updike suggests that "we resent broody poses in Wyeth and accept them from Hopper" because of the "glamorizing touch" in the former, and because "broodiness feels more excusable in Hopper's urban than in Wyeth's rural settings." All but one picture in Updike's gallery is of the representational kind. The exception, Richard Diebenkorn's *Ocean Park No. 79*, provokes an astute remark, "Abstraction removes painting from the secondary realm of imitation and enrolls it in the primary order of mute objects," as well as other comments that expose a difficulty with the genre: "The written word, and the mode of thinking that words shape, still stand embarrassed before abstract art. What is it *about*? What is *happening*?" Abstract Expressionism's shift of focus from product to process glamorizes the painter, "making him, rather than the sitter or the landscape or the Virgin, the star." In Robert Hughes's words, photos of Pollock "seemed to depict not his art but his mythic power of creating it"; in Updike's formulation, "Pollock painting is the subject of Pollock's paintings."

In the Diebenkorn, Updike asks us to try to see the sea in a large blue square, as well as, possibly, a beach in a sand-colored strip on the upper border of the blue. When we fail, he concludes for us, nothing can be ventured about the picture except that it conveys a "sensation of ocean." With this, and an acknowledgment of its "balanced tones," he dismisses the painting as "an expensive variety of wallpaper. Inarticulate ... we pass on, as if the canvas has said to us, 'Have a nice day.'"

In his commentary on a dozen or so John Singer Sargent "paughtraits," Updike draws attention to the "unreal" elongated figure and arms and the exaggerated decolletage of the Duchess of Sutherland; to the edge-of-chair "tension" of Mrs. Charles Thursby, "as if she is about to leap up past the painter and mount a horse sidesaddle"; and to Catherine Vlasto's hand "oddly flattening several keys of the piano she leans against," though odder still is why in the first place a woman of such conspicuous wealth would have an upright. But, then, the clothes, millinery, furniture, and unnatural poses of most of Sargent's sitters are more interesting than what he reveals of their characters. Comparing Sargent's painting of the black-stockinged *Daughters of Edward De Boit* to Winslow Homer's *Boys in a Pasture*, Updike reflects that "childhood and youth are seen in our democracy as classes that cut across class distinctions." All the same, children adopt the class-consciousness of their parents, and in the presence of those patrician Bostonian girls the two barefoot farm boys would probably be made aware of social barriers.

Most of the essays deal with twentieth- and late nineteenth-century art, while those on Old Masters are ingeniously contemporized. Cranach's *Eve* raises the thought that her "luminous skin" has never been striped by a "bathing suit tan." The Rouen reliquary sculpture of the Irish-French Saint Saens's hand raised in benediction provides an opportunity to digress on the evolutionary trend in non-primate mammals *away* from elongated fingers toward paws and hooves. The amphibian who crawled up on land hundreds of millions of years ago had "five digits fore and aft," and some two-legged dinosaurs had "hands not so different from ours," Updike informs us, before going on to the hand in art, a subject too large even to touch on in the present brief note. One wishes he had mentioned, and won new readers for, Henri Focillon's "In Praise of Hands," but the comment that Durer's praying hands have been "turned into a pious cliché" will help to deter buyers of Christmas cards.

Some of the biographical information in the essay on Vermeer is out of date. The painter did not marry "a local girl," from Delft, but one from Gouda, whose mother obliged him to become a Catholic, and he married at a slightly older age than the one Updike gives. In the case of this most enigmatic of painters, even the smallest new fact is important, as in John Michael Montias's recent discoveries that the artist had definitely known Gerard Ter Borch in Delft, which helps to sustain assumptions of artistic parallels between them; and that Leonhaert Bramer was a witness at Vermeer's wedding, which establishes a connection between the musical instruments in Bramer's *Vanity*, now in Vienna, and the foreground viol in Vermeer's *Music Lesson*.

Turning to the *Dixneuvième*, so far from just looking, Updike sees. After shuffling for an hour in a queue at a Renoir retrospective—why would he do that?—he perceives that in the case of this artist "Background is mostly backdrop," that the voluptuous nude *Bathers* of 1882 and 1895 have little girls' heads, and that the paintings are "dutifully consumed by the eyeball" until they "deposit on the retina an accumulated taste of artificial sweetener." .

But when Updike says that Cézanne might have chosen the landscape in *Pines and Rocks* "by setting his easel down almost anywhere," we doubt the choice was quite that haphazard. The same topographical features are repeated numerous times in the "Bibemus Quarry" and "Forest Near Chateau Noir" series, though the taupe-gray and purplish rocks in *Pines and Rocks*—Updike does not include purple in his account of the picture's pigments—have persuaded some scholars that the scene is near Fontainebleau.

The report on the 1988 Dégas exhibition at the Metropolitan, the ideally unsuitable place for this reticent, intensely private artist, contains a trivial error—the musician in the painter's ballet orchestra is blowing the stem of his bassoon, not of his oboe—and an important one, the description of *The Little Fourteen-Year Old Dancer* as "the most winsome of unforgettable statues." Unforgettable, certainly, but hardly "winsome." The tired, prematurely-lined and somewhat simian face of this *petit ballet rat* makes us feel uneasy, as Huysmans wrote when it was first exhibited, and the contrapposto—the uptilted chin and bow-like arch of the torso, the forward and out-turned, fourth-position right foot, the long thin arms stretched behind the back and the laced fingers—is painful. Moreover, the effigy is disturbingly lifelike, or for those of us who find Mme Tussaud's people morbid, deathlike. The mixture of reality and art, what with its real silk hair-ribbon, actual horse's hair, braids obtained from a supplier for dolls, linen bodice, tulle tutu, stockings, ballet slippers is mummifying, a collage.

To judge by the large number of drawings Dégas made for the wax statuette, as well as by the concluding line of his poem "The Fleeting Girl Dancer" ("And you come, you come tormenting an old faun"), not to mention his admission to the dealer, Vollard, after destroying a failed attempt to complete it, "You are thinking what it was worth, but a hatful of diamonds could not have matched my pleasure in destroying the thing for the joy of starting all over again"—which sounds like Pygmalion and Galatea—*The Little Dancer* obsessed him. Dégas did not allow any of his sculpture, his semi-secret art—some 150 wax models with his finger marks were found in his studio after his death—to be cast in bronze in his lifetime, bronze being "a substance for eternity," which "places too much responsibility on the artist," but for this image he constructed a glass display case of a kind used for scientific exhibits, and exhibited the empty box first.

Updike remarks that in Renaissance pictures nudity was virtually restricted to goddesses—he is forgetting Susannah—and that the perfect "modern excuse for the female nude," as Dégas discovered, was the bath. As the women emerged toweling from the tub, the body was displayed in the contorted poses that he wished to paint and sculpt, and had earlier introduced in the strangely erotic *Scene of War in the Middle Ages*. The posterior amplitudes, the foci of these stooping, squatting, crouching, shrugging figures—"like cats licking themselves," Dégas said—are thrust outward, which, as Updike sees, "excited" Dégas. (And not only Dégas; the most desirable females in certain primitive societies, Darwin wrote, were those "who project furthest *a tergo*.") Here Updike is responding to Manet's malicious remark that Dégas was impotent because he did not seem to have a mistress. But only on Seurat's death did his closest friends learn that he had one and a child by her.

The essay on the little-known 1920s *New Yorker* cartoonist Ralph Waldo Emerson Barton is the longest and most engrossing in the book, partly because Barton's life is such a good story; his explosively claustrophobic art is interesting largely for the clues it contains to his violently manic depressive personality. The intelligent and gifted Missouri-born caricaturist[4] was also a philanderer whose second and third wives moved on to, respectively, e. e. cummings and Eugene O'Neill. Wife number four, the composer Germaine Tailleferre, was already estranged when, at age thirty-nine, no longer able to manage his up and down swings, he committed suicide. Updike quotes most of the self-diagnosing letter that Barton left behind, for the good reason that "a man within minutes of ending his life must be listened to." It spares none of his women and was published in its entirety on the front page of the *New York Times*.

* * *

Somewhere in the 30-year harvest of his art chronicles,[5] John Ashbery remarks that art is a "critic-heavy industry," so heavy that "to create a work of art that the critic cannot even begin to talk about ought to be the artist's chief concern." Though hardly a "concern" of Rembrandt's, his self portraits, as Ashbery says, "leave one speechless by saying everything there is to say." Ashbery himself has many illuminating things to say, and he does so in the most graceful way. Admirers of his poetry who nevertheless complain of difficulties in "getting inside of it" should read his always lucid and easy-going prose ("nature doesn't kid around"). The same man wrote both.

Like Updike, Ashbery reads pictures for their stories, even describing the "scenario" in the case of Kitaj's *Study for the World Body*:

> What we see is a couple embracing in what is apparently an empty house; a light socket with no bulb hangs from the ceiling, a coathanger hangs from a nail in a bare wall. The uncurtained window admits light but frames no view: it is partially blocked by an ominous black rectangular shape whose position in space is ambiguous—is it standing next to the couple or

[4] See *The Last Dandy, Ralph Barton: American Artist, 1891–1931*, by Bruce Kellner. Columbia: University of Missouri Press, 1991.

[5] *Reported Sightings: Art Chronicles 1957–1987*, by John Ashbery, edited by David Bergman. New York: Knopf, 1989.

behind them, against the window? They have just been disturbed apparently; the man who has his back to the viewer is turning around to look at something that the woman retaining him with a white hand on his shoulder gazes at, too. Perhaps there is danger.

Ashbery devotes another hundred words or so, and some lines by Auden, to the couple, but says nothing about the picture as painting, the composition based on a dead-center pillar, the ghostly bluish white of the girl's complexion, the pinkish tan of the man's, and the garish rutilence of the ceiling and wall, which contributes more to the effect of ominousness than the black rectangle.

Ashbery copes with a wide assortment of American artists, among them Grandma Moses ("Her landscapes have depth.... [T]he landscape is composed of varied tones"), Edwin Dickinson ("a greater and more elevated painter" than Hopper, "in his seeming indifference to specific moods, in his search for the kind of universal specificness"), and Fairfield Porter, "perhaps the major American artist of the century," a claim that matches Updike's description of Porter's work as "a miracle, an Intimism with American spaciousness, a color-drunk hymn to ... things as they are." (Ashbery characterizes Vuillard, the major influence on Porter, as an "intimist," and Robert Hughes devotes most of his essay on the English painter Howard Hodgkin to the French tradition of Intimism.) But both estimates seem somewhat high. Porter could not paint faces, or even the backs of heads: those of the two children in the otherwise masterly landscape, *The Cliff of Isle au Haut*, turn the picture into a magazine illustration.

The claim for Porter, exposing the chronicler's preponderantly representationalist perspectives, should be placed in the context of Ashbery's conviction that Balthus and Giacometti are "the two major artists of postwar France." This widely-shared judgment emerges in discussions of their relationship to André Derain, the *Fauve* who "may yet prove to have had the greatest influence of any painter of his generation, Picasso included." The rehabilitation is finally underway, with the 1991 exhibitions at Oxford (*The Late Derain*), the Metropolitan Museum (the *Fauves*), and the new monograph by Jane Lee.

As an apprentice-reviewer for the Paris *Herald Tribune* in the 1960s, Ashbery kept tabs on Franco-American friction ("the reluctance of the Paris public to contemplate anything new, especially of American origin"), and, in addition, wrote an amount of reportage (the artist Jennifer Bartlett is "expecting her first child in August") and *vernissage* publicity—on, for example, Niki de Saint-Phalle, who elicits a polysyllabic growl from Robert Hughes ("steatopygous baubles").

Ashbery also conducted interviews, including a devastating one with Warhol: "'Maybe I won't give up painting.... Why should I give up something that is so easy? ... I thought the French would probably like flowers because of Renoir and so on. Anyway my last show in New York was flowers and it didn't seem worthwhile trying to think up something new.'" A dozen years later Warhol is on Ashbery's list of "today's acknowledged masters" (Gulp!). But, then, he is a generous, encouraging, if diffident critic, who almost on principle instills a desire in us to see more of the artist's work.

One blank spot in the book, not necessarily indicating a taste, is the absence of German art, with the curious exception of Max Klinger; Klee is mentioned (but just), Klimt, Schiele, Kokoschka not at all, and only in passing Anselm Kiefer, in Hughes's view "the best painter of his generation."

Otherwise Ashbery covers the contemporary scene in all its heterodoxy, from the latest and most marginal—the flavor-of-the month, trendier-than-thou exhibitions ("the zeitgeist as of last week")—to the mammoth monochrome oblongs and quadrilaterals of the School of New York. The Abstract Expressionists were "overexposed," he says. "Their heads were turned. They pontificated. One had to ignore their statements about their art if one wanted to go on loving it." He includes pieces on environmental art, the art of the insane, textiles, ceramics, origami, wallpaper, and Frank Lloyd Wright ("one of our greatest creators in any branch of the arts"). But the only Old Masters discussed, and these briefly, are Chardin, Fuseli, Piranesi and Parmigianino, whose *Self Portrait in a Convex Mirror* provided the title, and more, for Ashbery's best-known longer poem before *Flow Chart*.

De Chirico, Ashbery believes, is "one of the greatest painters of this century," and when William Rubin ranked him "just under Picasso and Matisse, Kandinsky and Miró " (*Miró ?*), Ashbery argued for a higher place, nothing less than "a special Elysium of his own." Like Eliot on James, the Italian master "exists in a sphere beyond the reach of interesting ideas." More questionable is the assessment of Dufy, "the full range" of whose genius is described as "almost Mozartian." One doubts, too, "unfairly underrated" though he may be and as Robert Hughes asserts, that Dufy might eventually be "classed with Picasso, Matisse and Bonnard as one of the great innovators of our century."

Surrealism and its world of dreamlike and romantic things is near the center of Ashbery's taste, and the essay on Tanguy is one of his most thoughtful. Tanguy's works are "Self-created, totally autonomous, they exist in a world where time, space and light are functions of other natural laws than ours." The death of the surrealist movement is attributed partly to natural, historical causes, partly to the many excommunications under Breton's dictatorship: "It is difficult to impose limitations on the unconscious," Ashbery remarks. But surrealism lives on, "absorbed into our daily lives, in movies, in interior decoration, in verbal imagery."

In Ashbery's view, Realism is a state of mind, and an Impressionist scene can be as Realist as one by a genre painter. Redon's realistic paintings are "more fantastic than the imaginary [imagined?] ones," he writes, and "because of its total commitment to realism," Neil Welliver's "great picture" *Shadow* "is more haunting than anything Magritte ever did." Ashbery tells us that the still-lives and shrubs and flowers of the pre-Impressionist French Realist Léon Bonvin, "seen through the mist of early morning or twilight have a finesse that few artists have ever achieved in watercolor," whereas his biography reads like a plot that "Zola or the Goncourt brothers would have rejected as too grim to be plausible."

Not surprisingly, Ashbery's criticism teems with literary allusions, Baudelaire to De Chirico's *Hebdomeros*, "that masterpiece of surrealist literature," and on to, of all people, John Dewey, who acquits himself brilliantly: "As long as art is the beauty parlor of civilization, neither art nor civilization is secure." An epigraph borrowed from "The Song for Simeon" at the head of one review reminds us of Ashbery's deep involvement with Eliot, occasionally overpronounced:

> But this was the way we had chosen,
> The way that leads to understanding.

The critic's most arresting remarks often appear as simple asides: "Art isn't about ideas but *is* ideas"; "To restrict something proclaimed as 'total' is to turn it into its limited opposite"; "We would all believe in God if we knew He existed, but would this be much fun?" The original use of a word, as when Saul Steinberg, in conversation, is described as having allowed a pause to "accumulate," recalls the same power in Ashbery's poetry:

> leaves still blowing around
> self-importantly after winter was well underway
>
> . . . .
>
> The almost-full moon
> Yawned, we could see it had other places
> To be, yet was loath to depart.

Indeed, the most memorable line in *Reported Sightings* stands comparison with the most memorable lines in Ashbery's poetry: "No sooner has the artist dealt with his reactions to the art of the past than he finds himself being wound on the spool of art history and is done unto as he would do unto others."

* * *

Unlike Updike and Ashbery, belletrists both, Robert Hughes is a full-time critic of art in its moral, social, political, and commercial contexts. His comparatively rare purely aesthetic judgments often disagree with those of the other two critics, tacitly in the case of Fairfield Porter, whom he does not mention, aggressively in that of Toulouse-Lautrec, who, for Ashbery, is on the wrong side of "the borderline between talent and genius," and whose paintings depend "too much on their subject matter for their effect," but for Hughes "one of the creators of modernism itself."

Earthier than either Updike or Ashbery, Hughes refers to a "pair of pert jugs" in *Playboy*, to journalism as practiced by "moist Radcliffe girls," and to the "pubes" in Courbet's *La Source*, which is to overlook the clearing for the forest. In repudiating "the cultural gorge and puke of the early eighties," he does not shy away from such pretty epithets as sleezeballs, glop, gunk. But he also describes the materials and techniques of contemporary artists in greater detail than either of the other two critics.

Attacking "cultural Reaganism" for its "private opulence and public squalor," Hughes contrasts the "weeks of private viewings" that preceded the opening at the Met of "Van Gogh in Arles," with the viewing offered to the general public of "about 30 seconds per picture," albeit soothed by the voice "on their Acoustiguides [of] the Met's director, Philippe de Montebello, on the merits of the deceased." The masterpiece "laden with fetishistic value," is wryly remarked upon in another context as having "lost today a certain freedom of access."

Hughes does not play the social game ("Many stones lie unturned but no breech is left unkissed") and is not afraid to name names. Henry Geldzahler is a "popinjay." The Washington show "Treasure Houses of Britain" is described as a "marriage of the fantasies of Reaganism with the opportunism of the English toff—a marriage made in heaven, to be consummated on Chippendale sofas with Carter Brown fluttering like an eager putto with many a coy glance between the withered participants." Elsewhere Brown is identified as the "rich kid being groomed for a future in the art world holding the lap robe" of Berenson as aged sage. To the revelation by Julian Schnabel (whose "cackhandedness is not feigned") that "there are so few people who know how to make art," Hughes administers the coup-de-grace: "Indeed; and one less than he thinks."

Hughes takes on the whole of the American art scene, from the dominance of received ideas in American taste to the cluttering of big cities with "abstract ironmongery: sculpture that means nothing but is part of the perfunctory etiquette of urban development." Lambasting the role of art teaching—"drawing from life … has practically been wiped out of art training in the last twenty years"—he remarks that Cal Arts, in "El Lay," epitomizes the present state of the schools: "no drawing, just do your own thing." The "cult of creativity as therapy," he observes in another book,[6] helped "wreck the standard of late modernist art education in America."

The essays on the corrupting influence of connoisseurs and dealers, from Berenson (who practiced both but called the former "conosching") to the greed and knavery of the Marlborough Gallery-Rothko-estate scandal, are the best of their kind. The sale prices discussed in the 1984 essay "Art and Money" already seem diminutive compared to today's auctions, and the statement that the most preposterously inflated ones are "what happens when Americans get into the act" is in need of updating. But Hughes's main thesis, that "in the past, art was not used as a form of investment," has never been more pertinent; one did not buy paintings "in the expectation that they would make one richer," or with an eye to future tax write-offs. The same can be said of his definitions: "The word *masterpiece*, which used to mean a work that proved an artist's graduation into full professional skill, now means an object whose aura and accumulated myth strike people blind temporarily"; and, "a fair price" in the art world is "the highest one a collector can be induced to pay. Once it is established it shows its fairness by reforming the level of the market."

Hughes is occasionally careless with language. One wonders how anything can be "almost inchoate" (p. 284) and "almost conundrumlike" (p. 289), and how the "ineffable" can be "quoted" (p. 199). Then, too, "proleptic hints of art to come" is tautological. He is also careless with matters of fact. Luigi Russolo was a Futurist musician, not a painter. Borobudur is in Java, not India. Klimt did not belong to Kokoschka's "circle," as Kokoschka's autobiography makes clear. "Far beyond Munch, Klimt and Schiele," Hughes says, Hans Makart, the Austrian history painter, was "the most famous Northern artist in the 1890s"; but Schiele was an infant during that decade. (The latitude of Vienna is south of the Paris latitude, but Hughes means Northern in spirit.) "The work" of six artists Hughes names "would not exist unless someone paid for them [sic] and paid well." But no one knows how well Piero della Francesca, one of the six, was paid.

Hughes's best *bon mots* are those on Francesco Clemente ("its decadence never fails to make collectors want to cuddle it"); on Sandro Chia ("if this show turns out not to be a passing phase, a minor artist will be in major difficulty");

---

[6] *Frank Auerbach*, by Robert Hughes. New York: Thames & Hudson, 1990.

on De Chirico ("if modernist critics ... were going to make capital from his youth while insulting his maturity, then let them eat fake"). He writes wisely of Giorgio Morandi as a "seraphic misfit," and "not a *petit maitre* but a major," and of Joseph Cornell: "chaos, accident and libido" outside the boxes; "sublimation, memory and peace" inside.

The Piero Quincentennial

The late John Pope-Hennessy's *The Piero Della Francesca Trail*[1] repeats his contention, put forth in a 1986 essay, "Whose Flagellation?"[2] that the tortured man in the background of the Urbino painting is not Christ but St. Jerome. Sir John argues that the aureole surrounding the Christ's head, the gilded classical figure on top of the column, and the "neon" lighting are found in no other picture of the flagellation. Since these three conditions, "inexplicable" in the Piero, are "integral" to Jerome's dream as described in his letter to Eustochium, Sir John asserts that Matteo di Giovanni's *Dream of St. Jerome* in the Chicago Art Institute, though it lacks a gilded classical statue, confirms his interpretation.

In Piero's foreground trio, the two richly dressed and fully hosed figures are "discussing the *locus classicus* for humanists," Sir John continues, on grounds that Jerome's reading of pagan literature (Cicero and Plautus) provoked the punishment in his dream. The barefoot youth between them, he goes on, is an angel attesting that "*Convenerunt in unum*," "Agreement was reached," the caption known to have been on the picture's poplar frame in 1839. Further, "There is not a shred of evidence that the intention behind the foreground figures is historical." (Case dismissed.)

The most immediately obvious fallacies here are that Jerome's captors would have been Christians, whereas one of Christ's wears a "Turkish" turban; that Piero's foreground figures are not looking at each other, which suggests that a discussion, humanist or otherwise, is not likely; and that the left arm akimbo with turned-in back of hand and weight on one leg of an "angel" with no wings is an uncharacteristic posture for this endangered species: the hand on hip is a well-known gesture in Renaissance painting signifying social and political power and authority.[3] Leonardo wrote that "the intention of the mind" can

---

[1] New York: Thames & Hudson, 1991.

[2] *Apollo* 124, no. 295 (September 1986).

[3] See "The Renaissance Elbow" by Joaneath Spicer in *A Cultural History of Gesture*, edited by Jan Bremmer and Herman Roodenburg. Ithaca, N.Y.: Cornell University Press, 1992. Spicer does not cite pictorial examples before the 1490s, but she cites a manual of etiquette from the 1500s to

be represented through body language, which is to say "gestures and movements of the limbs."

Despite Sir John's papal put-down, some of the "shreds" in support of a historical interpretation of Piero's picture will not go away. Consider the enthroned figure. *"Convenerunt in unum,"* the second verse of Psalm 2 in "The Acts of the Apostles" unmistakably refers to Pontius Pilate. Moreover, Piero's Pilate has been identified by his clothing. In 1883, a German scholar remarked that the Emperor Constantine in Piero's "True Cross" frescoes is a portrait of John Paleologus VIII of Byzantium: both Emperors wear the same distinctive headgear, described by a chronicler when Paleologus entered Florence, February 15, 1439, for an Ecumenical Council on the unification of the Eastern and Western churches: "a hat coming to a point in front on which he had a ruby bigger than a pigeon's egg...."[4] In that same year, or in Ferrara in 1438, Pisanello made a medallion profile of Paleologus sporting this millinery, a portrait that Piero must have seen: the correspondence between the details in the Pisanello and Piero's Constantine cannot be coincidental, though Piero, who was in Florence in 1439, could have witnessed Paleologus's procession himself and made his own drawing.

Recently, the miniature portrait of Paleologus as Theseus[5]—identical to the Pisanello except that it is in color (red hair and beard, blue tunic and hat superstructure, purple baldachin[6])—has been dated to the mid-1450s; the *Flagellation* was painted about the same time, which is to say before 1458, when Piero was in Rome, and after 1450–52, when Piero became familiar with Leon Battista Alberti's architecture in the Tempio Malatestiana in Rimini and incorporated it in the *Flagellation*. The "third master" of the Plutarch manuscript has been iden-

---

the effect that a protruding elbow was considered an effrontery; nor does she mention Piero's hand-on-hip portraits of Hercules (in Boston), a prophet (in Arezzo), the *Madonna del Parto* (Monterchi), typical of a pregnant women balancing her new weight, and the tallest female attendant of the Queen of Sheba (Arezzo). The repertory of hand and arm gesticulation in Piero's "True Cross" frescoes (Arezzo)—outflung arms, hands folded in prayer or extended in supplication, the handshake of Solomon and Sheba, spread fingers and pointing index fingers—is an uninvestigated subject.

[4] See Creighton Gilbert's *Change in Piero della Francesca*, Locust Valley, N.Y.: J. J. Augustin, 1968, and *Piero della Francesca's Flagellation: the Figures in the Foreground. Art Bulletin* 53 (1971).

[5] This is in the illuminated manuscript of Plutarch's *Lives*. in the Malatestiana Library in Cesena. See *Le Muse E Il Principe*. Vol 1, *Saggi;* Vol. 2, *Catalogo,* by.Alessandra Mottola Molfino and Mauro Natale. Milan: Franco Cosimo Panini, 1991.

[6] See the *Oxford Dictionary of Byzantium*, vol. 1, "Insignia," for a discussion of the significance of color in Imperial Byzantine raiment.

tified as Piero's collaborator Giuliano Amadei.

The 1883 discovery went unnoticed, but in 1911 A. Venturi, and in 1912 Aby Warburg, reached the same conclusion independently. Then in 1930, J. Babelon noted that the Pilate in *The Flagellation* is still another portrait of Paleologus wearing his long-peaked hat.[7] Pilate is the archetype of the accomplice, of course, and Paleologus, on returning to Constantinople, had bowed to opposition and nullified the Florentine decree ending the schism. In 1976 T. Gouma Peterson remarked that Pilate's crimson stockings were part of Paleologus's regalia.[8]

In 1953, Rudolph Wittkower and B. A. R. Carter's landmark analysis of the picture-space in *The Flagellation* revealed that the architecture in the painting follows the measurements of real architecture. It is constructed on a geometric framework. The unit of measure, one-tenth the width of the canvas, is the horizontal black bar above the head of the bearded foreground figure. Mathematical ratios relate this measurement to the square ceiling panels and the squares of the pavement, as well as to columns, figures, and the radius of the circle in which Christ is bound.[9] Further, the height of the Christ corresponds to the *"mensura Christi,"* which is one and a half *braccia* (just under five feet tall), a popular *quattrocento* belief. Thus it can be claimed that Piero achieved a symbiosis between the human figure and architecture.

More mysterious than the mathematical inspiration of the picture, however, are the identities of the three foreground figures. (As Carlo Bertelli points out,[10] seven of the eight Flagellations by Jacopo Bellini also included bystanders, "to give credibility to the story.") Kenneth Clark[11] was apparently the first to suggest that the background scene embodies the thoughts of the foreground threesome, and that the picture is an allegory of the sufferings of Christianity under Muslim rule. The background represents the past, the foreground the present (i.e., the 1450s after the fall of Constantinople in 1453), a temporal partitioning emphasized both spatially and by the turned backs of the foreground figures.

[7] *Jean Paléologue et Ponce Pilate. Gazette des Beaux Arts* ser. 6, vol. 4 (1930).

[8] "Piero della Francesca's Flagellation; On Historical Interpretation," by T. Gouma Peterson, *Storia dell'arte* 28 (1976).

[9] See "The Perspective of Piero della Francesca's 'Flagellation,'" *Journal of the Warburg and Courtauld Institutes* 16 (1953).

[10] Carlo Bertelli, *Piero della Francesca*, translated by Edward Farrelly. New Haven: Yale University Press, 1992.

[11] Kenneth Clark, *Piero della Francesca*, 2d edition, revised. New York: Phaidon, 1969.

Clark construes the three men as (l. to r.): "a type of learned Greek with a certain resemblance to the Emperor John Paleologus"; a "bucolic figure similar in appearance to the angels in [Piero's] *Baptism*"; and "a person of rank." For Marilyn Aronberg Lavin[12] they are Ottaviano Ubaldini (from a profile of him by Joos van Ghent that to some eyes bears little resemblance); Ottaviano's son Bernardino, deceased; and Ludovico Gonzaga (whose features, made unforgettable by Mantegna, are to other viewers in no way similar to those of the Piero figure). Lavin's case for Ubaldini, nephew of Federigo da Montefeltre, the notched-nosed, one-eyed Duke of Urbino, had already been undermined by Creighton Gilbert's discovery that beards were not worn by Italian men in *quattrocento* paintings until about 1485, appearing only in depictions of foreigners and figures from the past.[13] But Lavin's Bernardino candidacy clearly provided Carlo Ginzburg with the clue to his identification of the central figure.

Pope-Hennessy denounces Ginzburg's book[14] as a "mythomaniacal study, filled with imaginary history." But its history, whatever may be said about the chain of hypotheses connecting it to Piero's picture, is solidly founded.[15] The book endeavors to establish the principal personages in Piero's life and the political events that must have had an effect on him. It proposes that the figure on the left is Cardinal John Bessarion, the Protector of the Franciscan Order and Paleologus's mediator. Previous scholars have ruled out Bessarion because his pictured age is younger than his actual one, assuming that the time of the foreground is the "present," and because he is not in religious habit: he was a convert to the Roman Catholic Church and before that had been Metropolitan of Nicea. The figure on the right, Ginzburg believes, is Giovanni Bacci, a minor Aretine humanist whose family commissioned Piero's "True Cross" frescoes. Ginzburg connects him to Bessarion in that he is holding the scarlet ribbon which he presented in Constantinople as the Pope's emissary there in 1440, when Bessarion was made a Cardinal of the Church of Rome.

In Ginzburg's reconstruction, the subject of both the Constantine fresco and the Flagellation is the Crusade preached both by Piero's patron, Pius II, and Bessarion, but opposed by the Bacci family, except Giovanni, whose drug and

---

[12] Bertelli.

[13] "Piero della Francesca's Flagellation: The Figures in the Foreground," *Art Bulletin* 53 (1971). Donatello is bearded in the portraits of him attributed to Masaccio and Uccello, and beards are found in some group scenes, but these are exceptions that prove the rule.

[14] *The Enigma of Piero.* London: Verso, 1985.

[15] See Trevor-Roper's review of the book, printed as an introduction to the paperback edition.

spice business depended on trade with the Infidel. Ginzburg's thesis that Bessarion and Giovanni Bacci were the most important people in Piero's life has not been, perhaps cannot be, documented, apart from Vasari's testimony that "a portrait of Bessarion" was included in Piero's destroyed Vatican frescoes. Nor does any written reference associate Piero and Bacci, though they *had* to have known each other during the painting of the Arezzo frescoes and the *Misericordia*.

In Ginzburg's projection, the "angel" figure in the center is the seventeen-year-old Buonconte da Montefeltro, the intellectually distinguished pupil of Bessarion and the illegitimate son of Federigo. In the summer of 1458, Buonconte and his friend Bernardino Ubaldini journeyed from Urbino to Naples not knowing that it was in the throes of a plague. Retreating too late, both young men died. Lavin refers to Bernardino's companion as simply "another local prince." But as a Montefeltro (he had been legitimized), and as a youth of recognized gifts and promise, Buonconte seems a more logical choice than Bernardino. Ginzburg's hypothesis requires a slightly later dating of the Plutarch manuscript at Cesena.

Both Clark and Lavin fail to recognize, or to concede, that Ginzburg's Giovanni Bacci is also the kneeling person, front left, under the Madonna's cloak in Piero's *Misericordia*. This is puzzling, the more so in Clark's case since, following Vasari, he acknowledges that the kneeler is the same man in profile to the left of Khosru, the about-to-be-decapitated Sassanid monarch in the Arezzo fresco. Clark's reason for rejecting the triple identification and dismissing the Bacci in the *Flagellation* as a "physiognomic type" is a flimsy one: the figure is dressed in a richly brocaded robe, whereas "the citizens of Borgo and Arezzo who appear in Piero's other works are always dressed in the plain tunics of the bourgeoisie." Similarly, Clark rejected the claim that the St. Peter Martyr figure in Piero's Brera alterpiece is a portrait of the mathematician Luca Pacioli, on grounds that a Franciscan friar cannot be shown, as the Saint is in the picture, in the habit of a Dominican. Whether or not clothes make the man, Pope-Hennessy is unquestionably correct in identifying the Peter Martyr with the authenticated portrait of Pacioli by Jacopo de Barbari at Naples.

Clark is also mistaken about larger questions, including what might have been thought the central and least problematic scene in the frescoes, *"The Annunciation,"* which occupies the center wall between the larger lateral walls, meaning that the Incarnation is seen as the nexus between the Old and the New Testaments, *The True Cross* as a concordance between them. Clark's counterproposal goes overboard: the fresco does not depict the Annunciation at all but the inspiring of Constantine's mother, Helena, with the mission to discover the

Cross. His argument is based on the absence of the Annunciation symbols, the dove of the Holy Spirit and the lily of purity, here replaced by a palm frond, the emblem of martyrdom and of victory over death. But surely the martyrdom is Christ's, as the Annunciate's aggrieved expression tells us, and so is the victory. Inconsistently, Clark fails to mention the absence of Helena's symbols, the crown (she has a nimbus instead), the cross, the hammer and nails, as well as the presence of the redoubtable Mary symbol, the book in the left hand. The position of her index finger halfway through the text may suggest that she is dividing the two Testaments, or perhaps pointing to the allusion in Psalm 139, "in thy book all my members were written." In most Annunciations the book is closed, but she reads in the one by Lippo Lippi in the National Gallery, London, while the one in Fra Angelico's fresco shows blank pages on which, we assume, the cosmic secret will be recorded.

Clark's conclusion is in error in more elementary ways. First, God the Father, commonly represented by a hand extending from a cloud, is here fully embodied, thereby obviating the dove, as the dove in Piero's *Baptism* obviates God. And second, the positioning of the genuflecting Gabriel, traditionally the only *female* among the either male or androgynous heavenly host—for a male to have announced the impending pregnancy would have been an impropriety—could have signified nothing else for Piero's contemporaries. Neither Clark nor any other Pierologist remarks that the Gabriel does not have a halo and is a human being in every respect except the wings.

The deeper unplumbed mystery of the Annunciation is the upper right quarter of the picture, an area as large as God's and perspectively closer. Here, outside an open upstairs window, an iron loop dangles on a short cord from a wooden transom sustained by iron brackets that extend a foot or so from the wall. The apparatus reminds Clark of a windlass in a picture by Seurat, Maurice Guillaud[16] of "a receptacle for harvest"—apparently meaning that the room inside the window is a granary—and Lavin of a simple roof support. (Neither Clark, nor Lavin, remarks that the shape of the window and the horizontal strips of black marble in the background building are the same as in the Arezzo *Annunciation*.)

The same fixture in Fra Angelico's St. Nicolas predella in Rome establishes that, whatever else, the transom was used to suspend drying laundry, as it is today in Spoleto and other Umbrian towns. The loop, which is very like those

---

[16] *Piero della Francesca: Poet of Form*, by Jacqueline and Maurice Guillaud. New York: Crown, 1988.

in Christ's binding in several pictures of the flagellation, seems to have further significance, however, and, displayed on a linen cloth in the center foreground of an anonymous *Entombment* in the Kress Collection, it upstages the dead Christ. Two octagonal columns "with some rings of iron," supposedly from Pontius Pilate's house in Jerusalem, were among the Lateran relics that Piero could have seen in Rome in 1458–59. Whether or not the dark upper-storey room symbolizes the cave of the entombment and the transom the cross, this segment of the picture is clearly part of the web of relationships underlying the whole.

The continuing credulity and obsession with the efficacy of relics in the humanist *quattrocento*, in view of the utter preposterousness of their actually being what they were alleged to be, are beside the point, which is that, like the architecture, certain objects in the Lateran collection may be literally as well as symbolically represented in *The Flagellation*. Ginzburg suggests that the Piero of the True Cross murals must have known about the fragment of the Cross owned by the Paleolugi and brought to Italy by the Patriarch of Constantinople in August 1451. Bessarion inherited it during the Vatican Council at Mantua in May 1459 and in 1472 bequeathed it to the Scuola Grande della Carità (now the Accademia) in Venice, where it resides today.

The Lateran collection reputedly included not only the stone on which the thirty pieces of silver were counted out and on which soldiers diced for Christ's clothes, but also a staircase, the "Scala Santa," twenty-eight steps carved from one block of marble, said to come from Pontius Pilate's praetorium, supposedly climbed by Christ for His interview with him, and now at San Giovanni Laterano. An account of a voyage to Jerusalem between September 1457 and April 1458 in the Vatican Library[17] contains a description of the stairway and a throne. Both appear in *The Flagellation*, although the throne is a curule in the style contemporary to Piero.

* * *

To return to Pope-Hennessy's objection that no other flagellation has a gilt

---

[17] Another Vatican manuscript, an illuminated Latin version of Ptolemy's *Cosmographia*, contains an illustrated view of Jerusalem showing Pilate's house, a two-storey, flat-roofed building with a sequence of arched windows in the upper floor, exactly as in Piero's picture; since the translation was commissioned by Piero's patron, Federigo da Montefeltro, the painter could have seen the illustration. While in Rome, too, he might have known the fragment of a pillar, the "Santa Colonna," to which Christ was traditionally believed to have been bound for the flagellation, brought from Jerusalem in 1223 and now in Santa Prassede.

statue of a nude man from classical antiquity at the top of the column to which Piero's Christ is bound—must all objects in Renaissance pictures have precedents?—one wonders why it cannot simply represent the Roman world of Pilate's time. Ginzburg follows earlier suppositions that Piero's source is a giant statue from the Roman Temple of the Sun, fragments of which, the head and the hand holding the ball (the *"palla Sansonis"*), were part of the papal collection when Piero was in Rome in 1458–1459. Lavin has learned that a statue of the sun god "Sol" was still standing in the *quattrocento* on a column near the Colisseum. But the statue most resembling Piero's is the one in Masolino's fresco in Rome showing St. Catherine appealing to the Emperor to destroy it as a pagan idol.

Describing himself as "no friend of iconologists," Pope-Hennessy says that Piero's paintings "mean no more than what they appear to mean," as if that were self-evident. Sir John himself knew, of course, that unicorns indicate chastity, fig trees concupiscence, and that in Piero's *Senigallia Madonna* the box on the upper shelf represents the Host of the Eucharist, the wicker basket on the shelf below the cradle in which the infant Moses was found in the Nile bulrushes. But who else, without being told, knew that the ostrich egg in Piero's Brera altarpiece, suspended over the Madonna from the ceiling scallop, "appears to" represent parthenogenesis (the Immaculate Conception), that the ostrich egg is an emblem of the Montefeltro family for whom the picture was painted, and that traditionally the *ovum strathionus* was suspended from the apses of Abyssinian and Near Eastern churches.

In his final years, Sir John had been making a case for the inferiority in some respects of Piero to Giovanni Bellini, whose "power of description far exceeded Piero's and the geometry of [whose] paintings is correspondingly less evident." Sir John quotes Berenson: "[Piero] seems to have been opposed to manifestations of feeling. One is almost compelled to conclude that [he] was not interested in human beings as living animals.... [P]erchance he would have exchanged [them] for pillars and arches...." True, most of Piero's faces do not advertise emotions. But Berenson also wrote that "impersonality" is Piero's "most distinguished virtue—one which he shares with ... Velasquez, who painted without ever betraying an emotion." Still, the exceptions cannot be ignored. The eyes of the young warrior with bow-shaped lips and a headband in the Khosru fresco are eloquent with awe, dread, pain, weariness, grief.

The more than one hundred color photographs in the Guillauds' *Piero della Francesca* include close-ups of scenes from the *True Cross* cycle that can be made out in the originals only from ladders or scaffolds, and then less distinctly. Transferred to onion-skin paper, the reproductions set new standards in translucence and, except for scale, greatly surpass the badly damaged reality. In the Church of St. Francis, moreover, the many empty, faded, and color-neutral patches interrupt the narrative. But to compare the Guillaud reproductions with any others is to be dismayed by the poor quality of the competition. For only one instance, the light and colors in *The Dream of Constantine* in the monograph by Antonio Paolucci[18] are bright and the sky is near daybreak, in contrast to the deep-night subfusc and the pale yellow in the Guillaud.

But the photographs deserve better texts; indeed, worse ones would be difficult to imagine. Piero's lateral, sharply-pointed clouds are likened to "candyfloss," and Maurice Guillaud accompanies Piero's "poems of form" with some puerile "poetry" of his own, this following a scarcely believable introduction in which he articulates the painter's thoughts while contemplating the chapel's empty walls! "I shall strew the surface with visual scents," Guillaud's Piero warbles, if "I can manage to convey instances of the absolute." Guillaud's no less floridly fatuous captions ("Radiant fulsomeness [*sic*] in dialogue with shadowy void") are made even less palatable by arty distributions of the words on the page, framing a picture, canting toward it from the corners, curving in correspondence to a "poem" of his about "well rounded forms." Green letters are placed in a strip of white paper on an otherwise blank sheet, and the type-size is toyed with in the neoteric "cAlifOrnia STYLe," to no evident purpose: "iN thE wEAry eYEs of the vanquished King."

To Margherita Lenzini, Coordinator of the Arezzo Restoration Project, falls the impossible task of providing the "art-historical background." Her version of it is deficient in every aspect of the subject: long-discredited conjectures masquerade as attested facts, whereas nothing is said about the techniques and the labile chemistry of fresco painting, of the transferring ("pouncing") of full-sized cartoons to fresh plaster, and the soaking of pigments in tempera (casein, oil, egg-white), which are then applied to comparatively dry plaster. She is more interesting and reliable on the history of the depredations down to the present stage of apparently unstoppable deterioration from pollution, seismic shocks, seepage (which crystallizes the calcium nitrates, thereby breaking up the paint layers), destruction by Napoleon's soldiers billeted in the church—bullet holes, graffiti—as well as by more recent ones, in the reverberations of World War II bombing in the area. But restoration has been more ruinous than any of these, especially that of Gaetano Bianchi in the late 1850s, as we see from ultraviolet-ray photos showing the very different pictures beneath those

[18] *Piero della Francesca*. Florence: Cantini, 1989.

that he repainted. But then, as long ago as 1842 Lord Lindsay had described the frescoes as being "absolutely in the last agonies of dissolution, hanging in flakes from the walls."

Pope-Hennessy and Bruce Cole[19] are in disagreement on several issues. Cole narrows Sir John's "Piero was born about 1420" to not later than 1418, since "a recent archival discovery proves that Piero was at least eighteen in 1436"; in that year, in his native San Sepolcro, he worked with Antonio d'Anghiari painting papal insignia to go over the four gates of the town. Cole tells us that Sir John's *terminus a quo* dating of Piero's *Misericordia*, "after 1450," on grounds that San Bernardino was not canonized until 1450, is not watertight, since halos were sometimes painted before canonization. Subsequent documentary evidence has been uncovered revealing that Piero was recalled to San Sepolcro in 1454 to complete the painting. As for differences in evaluation, Cole considers the Khosru fresco, in the "sheer scope and scale of surging, close-knit combat ... one of the most remarkable scenes of action from the middle of the fifteenth century." Pope-Hennessy thinks the Khosru soldiers are "static and motionless," not "lifelike" and not "clearly differentiated."

One of Cole's other discussions is major. He contends that the *Battle Between Constantine and Maxentius*, the title that Pope-Hennessy retains, should be called the *Battle Between Constantine and the Barbarians at the Danube*. The subject of the scene is incontestably that of the first version of Jacopo da Voragine's *Legenda Aurea (The Golden Legend)*. The Maxentius of the second version died crossing a bridge that snapped under him, and Piero's picture does not show a bridge. In the first version, too, and not in the second, an angel appears to Constantine in the night, as in Piero, with a cross lettered in gold: "With this sign shalt thou conquer." Furthermore, the flags of the fleeing army display the barbarian emblems of a dragon and a Moor's head, but no Imperial Roman standard, which would have been a *sine qua non* for the army of the Emperor Maxentius.

Paolucci's monograph is the most comprehensive to date. It provides many more established dates than any book in English, and while some of them are concerned with such ancillary matters as the acquisition of real estate by the painter's brothers, the details help to form a family portrait; all except five dates—in Florence, Rimini, Rome, Arezzo, Urbino (the second, year-long stay, in 1482)—are from San Sepolcro. Paolucci also identifies people not mentioned in the other books, such as Giovanni Santi and Giovanni Testa Cilenio, and he supplies the results of stratigraphic studies, chemical analyses of pigments, sum-

---

[19] *Piero della Francesca: Tradition and Innovation in Renaissance Art.* New York: Icon, 1991.

maries of the principal iconological and stylistic critical writings about the pictures. Finally, he gives the provenances of the paintings, telling us, for instance, that the *Flagellation* was not transferred from the sacristy of the Urbino Cathedral to the museum there until 1916, and that the "Hercules," purchased by Isabella Gardner from a Paris dealer in 1908, was discovered in the 1860s in the Palazzo Graziani in San Sepolcro. He does not comment on the contents of the small but richly bound library of the penitent Jerome on a rock in the desert. Cicero? Plautus?

According to Vasari's 1558 life of the artist, Piero della Francesca was blinded by cataracts at age sixty. In the 1550s, one Marco di Longaro, a lantern maker, told a friend that as a child in San Sepolcro he had led the elderly Piero by the hand; whether or not influenced by these sources, art historians have propounded a failure-of-eyesight theory in connection with the late paintings (1470s). Piero died in his mid-seventies, and was interred on the same day, October 12, 1492, as the portentous event thousands of miles to the west recorded by his more famous countryman from Genoa.

Who Savoureth Musicke

Most of the illustrations in *Five Centuries of Music in Venice*[1] evoke sonorities, as does the cover showing two of Carpaccio's clamant trumpeters sounding their tantaras while miraculously walking on water. Many of the pictures, some 175 in black and white, forty pages of them in color, portray musicians playing instruments. What the book lacks is an insert of a tape or compact disc containing an Andrea Gabrieli canzona, a Monteverdi madrigal, one of Diomedes Cato's lute pieces, Barbara Strozzi's *Astratto* aria, a Vivaldi concerto.

And an intelligent text. True, its quoted passages, beginning with Torkington in 1517, would form an attractive pocket anthology: Wotton, Nashe, Coryate, John Evelyn; during the Carnival of 1640 Evelyn heard "three noble Operas ... with incomparable Voices and Music," but he also attributed the corruption of English to the "affectation of travellers." Addison, Mary Wortley Montague, Beckford, Howells and James are here, but not the music chronicler Dr. Burney, which would have salvaged the chapter on the eighteenth century, also the *Childe Harold* canto, Wordsworth's "gorgeous east in fee," and Browning's *Galuppi*, but of these heart throbs only the Browning relates to music. Best of all is Cassiodorus, writing from Ravenna: the Venetians live "like sea birds, with their homes dispersed ... across the surface of the water, secured only by osier and wattle against the wildness of the sea."

John Julius Norwich's introduction is peculiar. He poaches a patch of Ruskin's deepest purple to describe St. Mark's (the "vaulted porches" are "ceiled with fair mosaic"), but turns to the Doge's Palace on his own. Its color, he says, varies from "the palest apricot in the morning sun to the colour—and apparent texture—of smoked salmon after a rainstorm." But smoked salmon comes in many shades, rainstorms notwithstanding, and can be grainy as well as smooth. More peculiar still are Lord Norwich's composer-painter analogies, in which

---

[1] *Five Centuries of Music In Venice*, by H. C. Robbins Landon and John Julius Norwich. New York: Schirmer, 1991.

Titian is the Mozart of Venetian painting, Veronese its Liszt, and Tintoretto, "there can be no doubt," its Beethoven, this in a book that does not include the one picture that might have been expressly painted for it, Veronese's *Marriage at Cana,* in the Louvre, with its portraits of Titian playing the double-bass, Tintoretto the viol, and Veronese himself the viola da braccio.

Remarking on how little Venice has changed in the last two centuries, Norwich tells us that the acoustic properties of St. Mark's "swamped complex counterpoint," and that "this is as true today as it was in the time of the Gabrielis" (hardly a surprise, the building being the same). But in comparing Bellotto's eighteenth-century view of the Scuola di San Marco with a recent photograph from the same perspective, Norwich's occluded eye fails to notice the subsidence of Venice itself, the thirteen steps from canal to terra firma in the Bellotto vs. the three steps today.

Norwich's text is swamped, too, but with redundancies ("pointing forward to the future"), adverbs that negate the statements they are intended to modify (Titian's "almost uncanny sureness of touch" confirms that his touch remains merely canny), and adjectives that favor subjective-emotive expletives over specificity. A Giovanni Bellini altarpiece is "sublime," Venetian architecture is "exquisite," and nearly everything about the city is "superb," from Sansovino's "superb Marciano Library," some unidentified but "superb statuary" (Antonio Rizzo? the Bregno brothers?), the "superb flowering" of Venetian painting, and Vivaldi fiddling "superbly."

H. C. Robbins Landon is an equally slapdash writer ("the use of two choirs, placed in different parts of the church, began"), and his presentation is sometimes confusing: Heinrich Schütz's nineteen Italian madrigals were published in Venice in 1611, he tells us, then in the next sentence but one refers to "the twelfth and last of these extremely sophisticated madrigals...." Gabrieli, he writes, "sought to be a bright optimistic composer," though what Gabrieli "sought" to be is unknown, and "optimism" is an anachronistic concept. We read that his music "lacks sentimentality"—generally, as well as in this case, a commendable "lack." But unlike his co-author, Robbins Landon appears to have only the slightest acquaintance with the city. He refers to the *Sestiere* of Canareggio, one of the city's seven main districts, as an "unfashionable Venetian suburb." But could Venice *have* a suburb, as distinguished from an archipelago?

The chapter "Monteverdi and the Seventeenth Century" repeats the same potted information found in Lord Norwich's introduction to it, but deviates into great writing—Thomas Nashe's—to describe the Venetian bordello, "Tabitha the Temptresses." The pander, "a notable practitioner in the pollicie of baudrie," who conducted Nashe to this establishment "spoke several languages" and "en-

tertained us in our owne tongue very paraphrastically and eloquently, and mau-
gre all other pretended acquaintance...." Tabitha, the Turkish wench who received the English client and his knavish companion, "could set as civill a face
on it as chastities first martyr Lucrecia.... On her beds there was not a wrinkle
of any wallowing to be found...." Ben Jonson's epitaph for Nashe, his *"amici delec-
tissimi,"* has recently been found. It begins:

> Here lies
> Conquered by destiny and turn'd to earthe
> The man whose want hath caused a generall dearth
> Of wit; throughout this land: none left behind
> to equal him in his ingenious kind....

More than half of the Monteverdi essay is devoted to the composer's pre-
Venice years in the service of the Duke of Mantua, where, ill-paid when at all,
he was "on the edge of a nervous breakdown." The well-known letter from
Monteverdi's father pleading his son's cause to the Duchess is quoted at length
and said to be "a shame to the Gonzaga name," which, being synonymous with
murder these four hundred years, might be difficult to tarnish any further. But
whereas generous extracts are given from Monteverdi's letters petitioning the
Duke for promotion and back pay, nothing is said of the two crucial manifestos
of his Venetian period, the letter of 1616 to a patron and the preface to the
Madrigali Guerrieri, et Amorosi (1638).

The first of these, defining the goal of opera as "touching the emotions,"
protests against a "dialogue of the winds," the Zephyrs and the Boreals, in an allegorical libretto: "Ariadne moved us because she was a woman, and similarly
Orpheus because he was a man and not a wind." The second identifies wrath
(Ira), moderation *(Temperanza),* and entreaty *(Humilità o Supplicatione)* as the three
predominant emotions that animate musical drama. The wrath that Monteverdi
means is of the Achilles kind, lost since the Greeks. He believed he had found
and could express it musically through contrasts: "It is only opposites *(gli con-
trari)* which powerfully move *(movono)* our souls." In musical terms *"Ira"* is rendered by *"concitato"* and entreaty by *"molle,"* while the resolution of dramatic
conflict is achieved with the middle emotion, *temperato,* moderation.

All of which is the substance of Monteverdi's Second Practice, not named
in the book and hence not distinguished from the First, whose masterpiece, the
Vespers of 1610, receives less than its due in Robbins Landon's language: "one of"
Monteverdi's "loveliest works; in its Magnificat, the searingly beautiful old
plainchant floats through and over the rich tapestry of orchestral sound," which
suggests Mahler rather than the six instruments of Monteverdi's score.

A dozen or so lines are allotted to Barbara Strozzi, a bravura performer on the viola da gamba and one of history's few renowned female composers—whose presumed father had written the librettos for two lost Monteverdi operas. Nothing is said of her music—she published eight songbooks that display distinctive melodic and rhythmic gifts—but this oversight may be blamed on the portrait of her with charms distractingly undraped. Feminists outraged by the foregoing phallogocentric remark should in fairness consider the sexist aspect of the female orchestras of the *ospedali* in eighteenth-century Venice. These foundling hospitals "were established to receive orphaned (and largely illegitimate) girls," Robbins Landon writes, though in fact boys were sheltered as well, but trained only in trades. The musically gifted of the gender were taught to sing and play instruments, and since the art of music cannot be learned by the tone-deaf and the untalented, this is proof positive that music is at least as much an aptitude of the female half of the human race as of the male.

Lord Norwich remarks that the printer Aldus Manutius came to Venice in 1490, and that when he died there twenty-five years later the city had sixty-five presses, three times as many as Rome. Nothing is said of music printing until the Monteverdi period, yet by the first decade of the sixteenth-century, the Venetian Ottaviano Petrucci was printing polyphonic music from movable type. In 1502 Petrucci published partbooks of several masses by Josquin Desprez, and two years later a volume of the same composer's motets, as well as works by Isaac, Agricola, Compère, and others.

Important omissions must be mentioned. Robbins Landon's roster of the great composers who resided in Venice includes Orlando di Lasso, Handel, the younger Scarlatti, Rossini, Verdi, Wagner, and Stravinsky, whose *Canticum Sacrum* reflects the architecture of St. Mark's in some of the same ways as Guillaume Dufay's motet *Nuper rosarum flores* mirrors the structure of Brunelleschi's dome in Florence. But not the fifteen-year-old Mozart, who gave a public "academy" during which, and in front of an audience, he composed a fugue on a subject by a local composer. Mozart and his father lodged with the Ceseletti family, February 11-March 12, 1771, opposite San Fantin, on the transpontine side of the canal, a residence commemorated two centuries later by a plaque. The elder Mozart described the city as "the most dangerous place in all Italy," in its licentiousness, which apparently extended to the Ceseletti home, where seven daughters attempted to spank the younger Mozart in what they pretended was a Venetian initiation rite.

A still more astonishing absence is that of a discussion of bell music, the only kind that has perdured in Venice throughout the five centuries of the book's title. Unlike the stationary Buddhist bell, struck from the outside with a mallet or ramrod, the oscillating, corybantic clapper bells of Venice ring at different speeds according to size, the smaller, higher-pitched, overtaking and surpassing the larger ones. When three or four bells of different sizes tintinnabulate from a single campanile, the fluxing rhythmic relationships among them can mesmerize the mathematical as well as the musical mind. In Venice, bells still announce epithalamiums and deaths—the transitory sound of a bell is a *momento mori* in itself—and Venetians still live by bells, called to work by the *marangona*, to prayer by the tolling of the canonic hours (nones, complines), to bed by the midnight bells, five of them, uniquely, of St. Mark's.

The illustrations include color reproductions of musicians' portraits—Lasso giving the beat to his Munich orchestra, Domenico Fetti's Monteverdi as an old man, and Rembrandt's Heinrich Schütz, the greatest of the composers schooled in the early seventeenth-century Venetian style. The paintings, drawings, woodcuts of opera-house interiors and *ridotti* long since disappeared, of organ and orchestra lofts—Canaletto's picture of a choir in a balcony in St Mark's reading from a single large score—of musical instruments, of concerts and musical balls, make this a book to treasure. Buy it for the pictures, or for the *pittoresco*-period pin-up of *maestra* Strozzi. But read it only for the borrowed texts: "Musicke," Castiglione wrote, makes "sweete the mindes of men ... and who so savoureth it not, a man may assuredly thinke him to be not well in his wits."

Women Musicians of Venice
and the Red Priest

"Not a single evening goes by without a concert somewhere. The people run along the canal to hear it.... [Y]ou cannot imagine how crazy the city is about this art.... The transcendent music is that of the *ospedali*. There are four of them, made up of illegitimate and orphaned girls and those whose parents are not in a position to raise them. They are brought up at the expense of the state and trained solely to excel in music. They sing like angels and play the violin, the flute, the organ, the oboe, the cello, and the bassoon.... They are cloistered like nuns ... about forty girls take part in each concert." (Charles de Brosses, from *Le Président de Brosses en Italie: Lettres familières écrites d'Italie en 1739 et 1740. 1858, 1969.*)

During the century and a half before the center of musical activities relocated in Vienna, the orchestras and choruses of the *ospedali grandi*, Venice's female charitable institutions-cum-conservatories of music, were the most highly esteemed in all Europe. A Russian visitor, Count P. A. Tolstoy, noted in 1698 that "in Venice there are convents where the women play the organ and other instruments, and sing so wonderfully that ... people come from all parts of the world to refresh themselves with these *angelic* songs...." Henry III of France, Gustavus III of Sweden, Frederick IV of Norway and Denmark, the future Tsar Nicholas heard and admired them, as did Rousseau and Goethe, who described an oratorio in one of them as "infinitely beautiful," the "voices, behind a grille"—"a delicate cage," he called it—"were magnificent." In the summer of 1771, Charles Burney, the music historian and father of Fanny, wrote that a *Salve Regina* performed in an *ospedale* was

> new, spirited, and full of ingenious contrivances for the instruments.... [T]here seemed to be as much genius in this composition as in any that I had heard since my arrival in Italy.... [T]he Venetian is a good school for counterpoint.

Dr. Baldauf-Berdes disarmingly describes her account[1] of Baroque music's

[1] *Women Musicians of Venice: Musical Foundations, 1525–1855*, by Jane Baldauf-Berdes. Oxford. Clarendon, 1993.

162

most curious phenomenon as a barely adequate introduction to the subject. But whatever the size of the dent, her book is a major contribution to our knowledge of Venetian culture. John Hale's recent *The Civilization of Europe in the Renaissance*[2] mentions only one of the *ospedali*, which he calls a "reformatory," while Brian Pullan's *Rich and Poor in Renaissance Venice*[3] discusses them as social but not musical institutions. Dr. Baldauf-Berdes's extra-musical, religious, social, political, civic, economic scope—Venice, she writes, was a "salvation-based social welfare economy" with "an ellipsoidal church and state form of government"—far exceeds the promise of its name. It must also be admitted, however, that the title, *Women Musicians of Venice: Musical Foundations, 1525–1855* is misleading, since Baldauf-Berdes touches only in passing on secular female musicians, the female madrigal singers and the prima donnas of the opera houses that flourished contemporaneously with the *ospedali*.

The four musical "convents" were located on the city's three principal waterfronts, most centrally the *Pio Ospedale della Pietà* (House of Mercy) on the Riva degli Schiavoni, founded in 1346, whose composer, *maestro dei concerti*, and violin teacher for thirty years was Antonio Vivaldi. Illegitimacy was a prerequisite for wards of the Pietà, which gave names to the infants it rescued, baptized them, and, before farming them out to wet-nurses, branded them with a "P." By 1677 the Pietà, part of which is now part of the Hotel Metropole, had become a foster home for some six thousand *esposti* (foundlings), an unprecedented acceptance of responsibility on such a scale by a state.

Like the Pietà, two of the other *ospedali*, the Derelitti (orphanage and boarding school) and the S. Lazzaro dei Mendicanti (originally a home for beggars, and before that the world's first lazaret), are near each other on the *de citra* side of the Grand Canal; the Mendicanti, much the largest of the four, with two cloisters, abuts on the northern lagoon in a monastery built by Longhena; Scamozzo is the architect of the church itself. The fourth, the *Ospedale degl'Incurabili* (hospice for the chronically ill, as well as, later, a school and conservatory of music), on the *de ultra* side (the Fondamenta De Ca' Bragadin at the Zattere intersection of the Rio S. Vio), was demolished in 1821, though its high brick and stone walls, topped by *putti*, still survive. It was founded as a hospital in the modern sense—Venice had the world's first public health department (1485)—dispensing medicines and medical care and providing food and lodging. Later, as a college of music, superior to the others, Burney thought, at least when under the direction of Baldassare Galuppi, who

[2] New York: Simon & Schuster, 1994.
[3] Cambridge: Harvard University Press, 1971.

was at the same time *maestro di cappella* at the Basilica of St. Mark's. The Incurabili, divided into male and female halves (a *monasterium duplex*), provided a model for the others in both architecture and management, and its members enjoyed an elevated social standing.

Dr. Baldauf-Berdes devotes ample space to the structure of Venetian society in the Renaissance and Baroque periods, and to the growth of the Serenissima from corporate communities to state, nation, and empire. While this political history is familiar, and available in countless other books, her account of class calibration beneath the Doges, who were elected by the nobles, is worth some attention. The aristocrats, immediately below, formed the powerful Council of Ten and served as senators and procurators (administrators); some of the latter were women, most famously the eighteenth-century *procuratessa* Mocenigo, from the family that produced seven doges and patronized Palladio.

Five percent of the population of 88,000, according to a mid-seventeenth-century census, were members of the aristocracy. They were subject to a strict code that allowed males to marry beneath their class only on condition that their children did not inherit their father's patrician status, and that, in order to keep substantial dowries within the city, forbade wealthy females to marry non-Venetians. Patricians were also barred from acquiring skills: the nobleman composer Benedetto Marcello was not permitted to conduct or play an instrument in his own works, for that would have been thought shameful. Baldauf-Berdes writes that musicians outside the *ospedali* were comparatively prosperous.

Religiosi comprised 4.7 percent of the population, which rose to 6 percent in the seventeenth century, the *popolani*, or commoners, 75 percent. Otherwise a strict caste system obtained among workers, skilled (gondoliers, artisans, fishermen, lace-makers, merchants), and unskilled (vendors, manservants, ladies' maids). Even the very poor were divided into three social classes. Strict social barriers notwithstanding, it seems that by 1700 wealth and power in Venice were concentrated in about ten families.

Life in the *ospedali*, too, Baldauf-Berdes tells us, was highly regulated. The sequestered women rose with the sun, recited prayers aloud while dressing, dined in silence in refectories while spiritually edifying texts were read to them. They were required to attend Mass daily, the services of the canonical hours at least three time a week, and to confess frequently. Between times, and betwixt other duties, they sewed sails, worked in the kitchens and laundries, and the musical among them copied music, for which extra lamp oil was provided. Older musical sisters, the elite *privilegiate del coro*, taught the younger ones to play instruments, as well as performance practice, solmization, ear-training, theory and harmony. The teachers took the names of the instruments they played: "*Maestra* Lucretia della Viola, *Maestra* Catterina dal Cornetto, *Maestra* Silvia dal Violina, *Maestra* Luciana Organista."[4] Singers repeated vocal exercises and instrumentalists rehearsed by themselves and in ensembles.

Close relatives, for those who had them—the *ospedali* served as boarding schools for upper class non-musical girls, *figlie del commune*, who were seeking a general education in Latin, arithmetic, religion—could visit only once a month and only in the presence of an official. Correspondence was censored or not delivered at all. Only one day of vacation a year was granted to each member, but as groups they were taken "on holiday excursions." The tendency of the *ospedali*, Dr. Baldauf-Berdes writes, was to make "Aspasias out of the girls rather than nuns" (perhaps forgetting that the name is synonymous with "mistress" as well as with "woman of intellectual distinction").

Discipline was strict. The penalties for "casual talk," "frivolity," and "obstreperousness," let alone serious infractions such as tardiness and leaving Mass or other Office (to relieve nature, one supposes), included haircutting (heads were shaved), fines, the withholding of income (Baldauf-Berdes tells us that performers were paid, but not how much or in what proportion), a bread and water diet, solitary confinement, and deprivation of the privilege of wear-ing the *ospedale* uniform, blue (faith) at the Incurabili, red (charity) at the Pietà, white (virginity) at the Derelitti, and purple (mourning) at the Mendicanti. Harsh as the *ospedale* regime sounds, it was regarded as enviable in a society that permitted parents to sell their children into slavery and their sons as gal-ley oarsmen.

Marriage was the only generally accepted reason for withdrawal from the "asylums," and upwardly mobile matches, like that of Elizabetta Torogood, an English-born violinist at the Derelitti who married a nobleman and received a handsome legacy, where promoted. But permission had to be obtained from *governatori* known for refusing it to musicians of outstanding ability (the *privile-giate*) and hence of value to the *ospedali*. These governors, one of whom was the painter Lorenzo Lotto, also served as talent scouts, combing the city for chil-dren to enclose. It was said that the primary reason for seeking the young *ospedali* women in marriage was their innocence of worldly experience. One wonders how the bachelor and widower suitors of the vestals became acquainted with them in their cloistered environments, but Dr. Baldauf-Berdes

[4] The quotation is from H. C. Robbins Landon's *Vivaldi: Voice of the Baroque* (London: Thames & Hudson, 1993), p.28.

reveals that the performing musicians were allowed to mingle with their audiences after outside concerts such as those portrayed by Guardi at the Sala dei Filarmonici and the Ca'Rezzonico; in the latter picture one notes that the hundred or so performers are being led by a *maestra*, possibly one of those mentioned by Charles de Brosses:

> There is nothing so diverting as the sight of a young and pretty nun in a white habit, with a bunch of pomegranate blossoms over her ear, conducting the orchestra and beating time with all the grace and precision imaginable.

Those who did not find husbands, among them the indigent offspring of impoverished nobles, not dowried and therefore not marriageable, were taught to think of themselves as being married to music, and thus metaphorically to Christ, music being the *ancilla religionis*, the art that mirrored the Divine Order and was practiced in Heaven, where angels sang and played instruments. If the older unmarried women of the choirs lost their voices, they were transferred to the *ripieni*, the back-stand string sections of the orchestras, which testifies to the broadness of the *ospedali* musical training: everyone was taught to play every instrument.

Some of the *ospedali* musicians aspired to careers beyond the grille, and some, such as the violinist Regina Strinasacchi, from the Pietà, did achieve eminence as itinerant virtuosi; Mozart composed his Sonata K. 451 for her, and performed it with her in Vienna in 1784, writing to his father afterward that she is "a very good violinist who has a great deal of taste and feeling in her playing." A number of *ospedali* singers became prima donnas in opera houses throughout Europe, among them Nancy Storace, for whom Mozart wrote the soprano *scena* "Chi'io mi scordi di te," K. 505, and who created the role of Susanna in *Le Nozze di Figaro*. In the revival of the opera, the Mendicanti-trained Adriana Ferraresi sang the same role, with two new arias composed for her by Mozart, and went on to create the part of Fiordiligi in *Così fan tutte*. Biancha Sacchetti, for whom Haydn composed a cantata, was a former prioress and organist at the Mendicanti, and Caterina Giusti, another alumna, held the position of chief organist at the Basilica of San Marco for more than a dozen years against all male competition.

The *ospedali* welcomed reformed prostitutes. In 1608, Thomas Coryate (1577–1617), author of *Crudities* (1611), estimated the population of the *unre*formed to be about 20,000, which helps to explain the large number of foundlings, as well as the spread of venereal disease. Dr. Baldauf-Berdes 's sources show that members who had been granted "sick-leave" had been known to spend it in the palaces and country villas of noblemen, but she does not stoop to rebut charges of promiscuous involvement in such cases. Or, indeed, in larger ones. The report of a Vatican secret agent taken from the archives of the Holy Inquisition at Venice in 1720—a few years earlier the chief censor of Venetian opera libretti[5] was the Grand Inquisitor himself— states that one Anzola Trevisana, known as *La Galinera*, practiced the oldest profession at an address near the Madonnetta, and that her procuresses were "the mistresses of the Pietà," from whence, moreover, girls were "frequently brought in." Hester Thrale, Dr. Johnson's sometime friend, repeated similar tales about *ospedali* girls, and a letter by de Brosses mentions "a furious dispute among three convents in the city to decide which will have the advantage of giving a mistress to the new nuncio."

Dr. Baldauf-Berdes does not provide answers, even hypothetical ones, for questions that will occur to many readers. "Musical activity began in the *ospedali* in 1525," she writes, which would be during Andrea Gritti's term as doge, but how this came about, whether through connections with older institutions of a similar sort in Constantinople and Rome (the Schola Cantorum) is not explained. And what *kind* of "activity" is meant? The date precedes the era of the Gabrielis and the *cori spezzati*, the music bandied from balcony to balcony in St. Mark's. By 1565, however, the year of the earliest music known to have been composed specifically for an *ospedale*, this style was flourishing, and the facing balconies of the Mendicanti confirm that it had been introduced there. (Architectural historians now believe that the curved walls of Palladio's San Giorgio in Venice were conceived as sounding boards for the *cori spezzati* of St. Mark's, who accompanied the doge to the church on St. Stephen's Day and, divided in half, sang motets back and forth between the choir and the apsidal transepts.) The organ would have been the principal instrument at first, along with, as can be seen in paintings of processions in the Piazza, the *tromba da caccia* and the trombone; Galuppi himself sponsored the *ospedale* candidacy of two sisters who played the former.

Four thousand musical manuscripts survive, dating from 1565 to the end of the eighteenth century, some by members of the *ospedali*, some by composers, including Vivaldi and Galuppi, living outside the schools. This trove, Dr. Baldauf-Berdes tells us, has yet to be catalogued and studied, so we can only suppose that the instrumental music would feature organ *sonate da chiesa*, and, later, with the development of the string orchestra by Torelli, Albinoni,

[5] For an account of the background of ecclesiastical censorship see Paul Grendler's *The Roman Inquisition and the Venetian Press, 1540–1605*. Princeton, N.J.: Princeton University Press, 1977.

Corelli, and Vivaldi, sinfonias and concertos. Burney heard fugues in the Mendicanti, though he found the subjects "trite" and the choruses only "slightly put together." Masses and motets, Magnificats and Misereres were sung, as well as arias and antiphons, cantatas and complines, Te Deums, Passions, responsories. On festive occasions, oratorios and religious music dramas were performed, some of them lasting as long as two hours, which implies a degree of structural complexity heretofore unknown for the early seventeeth century, and raises a thought about possible cross-fertilization from secular music. In 1709 a French visitor, C. Freschot, wrote that in the churches and *ospedali* one heard "the same arias that one has heard at the opera," with different words, so that "instead of expressing, for example, the loves of Pyramus and Thisbe, [they] say something of the life of the saint whose feast day it is." Dr. Baldauf-Berdes does not tell us this, or that orphanage girls must have been allowed to sing in opera. In 1715 "Marietta from the Pietà" appeared at the Teatro San Angelo in Handel's *Agrippina*.

Nor does Dr. Baldauf-Berdes speculate on musical aptitudes in females as compared to those in males, or on the question of whether aristocratic Venetian society considered musical training more suitable for girls than for boys, as was the case in bourgeois America sixty years ago, when piano lessons were held to be more appropriate to the education of girls than of boys, for whom they bore a taint of effeminacy. (When Byron remarked that an interest in music was an indication of this, Leigh Hunt controverted him with the argument, "It would be difficult to persuade the world that Alfred and Epaminondas, Martin Luther and Frederick the Second, all lovers of music, were effeminate men.")

Male foundlings did not receive the same musical training as females, though until age ten, boys, who functioned mainly as acolytes, attended classes and religious services together with girls and apparently received the same musical instruction. In the sixteenth century, groups of eight boys from the *ospedale*, playing wind instruments and led by a fugleman or priest, took "alms walks" to the *campi* seeking donations for their "begging baskets." In 1628 the Mendicanti extended the musical education of its young males, but stopped doing so abruptly for reasons Dr. Baldauf-Berdes does not vouchsafe. The *ospedali* accommodated far fewer boys than girls—one census at the Derelitti lists forty for the one sex against 125 for the other—but of course boys were employable in the outside world.

Dr. Baldauf-Berdes has little to say about whether or not music composed by women is, or should be, different from music composed by men, a contested issue frustrated by the circumstance that the art's images of femaleness were created by men. Still, as the editor of violin concertos by the *ospedale* violinist and composer Maddalena Lombardini, she might have confided either a discovery of, or a failure to discover, some quality of emotion, or grace, not expressed in quite the same way in music composed by a female. Perhaps the uniformity of styles during this period, the second half of the eighteenth century, would tend to obscure sexual differentiation, but this could also be the case in the opposite situation of today's smorgasbord of them.

The author remarks, justly, that the musical attainments of the *ospedali* are "all the more praiseworthy" in that "they took place in oligarchic and, therefore, overwhelmingly patriarchal Venice," but adds unjustly that "the women musicians of Venice might still [in the 1990s?] be conducting new experiments … if it were not for … the actions of some who felt threatened with the loss of status as the result of women's achievements." No. The decline of the *ospedali* was a result of the destruction of Venetian social structure and economy which began with the arrival of Napoleon in 1797, not of a conspiracy by threatened males. She is unfair, as well, to some female musicians in asserting that Alfred Einstein's discussion of women musicians in Venice is limited to "courtesans"— i.e., "kept women," or "prostitutes"—since the word can hardly apply to *all* female singers in the madrigals that are Einstein's subject.

* * *

Dr. Baldauf-Berdes tells us, disapprovingly, that "as regards Venetian music history, investigative energies have been directed over the past half-century toward collections of works by Antonio Vivaldi…." And when, in the prologue to his book, *Vivaldi. Voice of the Baroque*, H. C. Robbins Landon informs us that the Reverend Don Antonio Vivaldi's inescapable *Four Seasons* (pub. 1725) has become the most popular piece of classical music in the 1990s, with more than 150 recordings on the market, we are hardly surprised. Of Vivaldi's nearly five hundred concertos, these four were always the most widely known and admired; even Joseph Haydn, in far away Hungary, had a copy of them. Twenty years after Vivaldi's death in Vienna, 1741, aged 63, Carlo Goldoni referred to him as "the famous composer of the *Quattro Stagioni*." In Paris, the *Primavera* Concerto, "*applaudissait toujours avec transport*," had been repeated by demand in 1729, and in the following year Louis Quinze expressly asked for it. Yet no performance seems to have taken place between 1803 and its revival after World War II, during which century and a half Vivaldi sunk into oblivion.

Ezra Pound's contribution to the rediscovery of the composer is well known. In the mid-1930s the poet persuaded the American violinist Olga

Rudge to catalog the more than three hundred manuscript pieces of instrumental music by Vivaldi in the National Library in Turin. Following this work, she and an Italian musicologist founded the Centro di Studiani Vivaldiani in Siena, where a Vivaldi festival was held in September 1939. In 1947 publication of the music began, and, in 1950, Gian Francesco Malipiero's edition of *Le Stagioni* appeared. Since then, the opus has been climbing to the top of the charts, overtaking Tchaikovsky and Mahler on the way, a mood swing, parallel to the fall of serialism and rise of minimalism, from the Romantic Agonies to the simple emotions and constructions of a comparatively remote period.

The Vivaldi boom has increased to the extent that in 1991 a single autograph letter from him to the Marchese Guido Bentivoglio, his patron in Ferrara, fetched over $100,000 at a New York auction. Robbins Landon confesses that he was inspired to write this book by the "extraordinary phenomenon" of Vivaldi's renown, going on to say, and compounding redundancy with fatuity, "Pieces of music do not arrive at such an august position—one of solitary splendor which not even Mozart has managed to approach—without some reason."

The facts of Vivaldi's life remain scant, but have increased apace, and Robbins Landon's new book provides a useful updating. Even the exact date of the composer's birth (March 4, 1678) was unknown before the 1960s, but now facsimiles of the entry of this event in the register of San Giovanni in Bràgora (May 6, 1678) are sold as tourist tchotchkes to be treasured alongside the glass grotesques of Murano. Manuscripts of works known and unknown have been recovered, and letters, though many fewer from the composer than to and about him.

Vivaldi's grandfather was a musician, his father a barber and a violinist in the orchestra of St. Mark's. The bambino Antonio seems to have been born prematurely, and in any case was baptized at birth by the midwife, who thought him near death. As the oldest of six children in a poor family he was destined for the priesthood, but was found to be musically precocious, and at age eleven was able to deputize for his father during an absence from Venice. In 1703 he became a violin teacher at the Pietà.

Vivaldi himself is the only source, in a letter to Marchese Bentivoglio, for the facts concerning his ecclesiastical career. He took first holy orders at age fifteen-and-a-half, but did not become an ordained priest until ten years later. Piety was undoubtedly a lesser motive in this decision than the guarantee of security. (Other composers of secular music had also been priests, among them the madrigalist Orazio Vecchi and the Escorial's Padre Antonio Soler who, in reference to the radical modulations in his keyboard sonatas acknowledged a debt to Gesualdo.)

In his letter Vivaldi tells Bentivoglio that he had said Mass in the Pietà for a year, but on one occasion had to leave the altar three times without being able to finish. He no longer says Mass, the letter goes on, nor did he do so while in Mantua, where he spent three years (1718–1720) as *maestro di cappella da camera* to the Habsburg governor. The reason is that he has suffered since birth from a constriction in the chest combined with asthma. Because of this disability he leaves home only in the afternoon, and only in a gondola or sedan chair, and on his journeys outside Venice requires the assistance of four or five people, which is very costly. Here it must be said that this tale seems somewhat incongruous, for the most immediately apparent quality of Vivaldi's music is its robustness and high-speed movement. If he were unable to stand for long at the altar, he nevertheless presumably remained upright and did not have to depart while conducting the orchestra at the Pietà and playing the violin in concerts.

At the beginning of his career at the Pietà, Vivaldi published a set of trio sonatas that show the influence of Corelli but have also the characteristically Vivaldian rhythmic propulsion and grasp of form. Henceforth the few known facts of Vivaldi's life concern his travels as a performer and producer of his work, his involvement in litigations, and his scandalous connection, as a priest, with Anna Giraud, "La Girò," his favorite singer in the Pietà and later his stellar opera performer, presumed to be his mistress.

Only recently, with the discovery of a letter from him to the Principessa Borghese, has anything been known about his stay in Rome in 1723 to produce one of his operas, *Ercole sul Termodonte*. Another of them, *Giustino*, staged there the following year, introduced the Lombardian rhythm, or Scottish snap, that became the rage of Rome and apparently brought him greater success than he had ever experienced in a Venetian theater. The Pope invited him to play the violin in the Vatican, and he was well received by Prince Colonna and Cardinal Ottoboni, Corelli's patron. (After Ottoboni's death, a part of his music library, including a batch of twelve Vivaldi violin sonatas and a version of the sempiternal *Stagioni*, found its way to Manchester, England.)

Forty-odd Vivaldi operas have been preserved, not all of them complete. Only two of the three acts of both *Armida* and *Catone*, for example, are extant. Some of the operas, moreover, are only partly by him, and some of the later ones, including *Bajazet* and *Rosmira*, are largely compilations from the works of other composers, such as Pergolesi, Leo, Galuppi, Hasse, and even Handel. Vivaldi's first opera dates from 1713, and there is no evidence of his interest in the theater before Handel's arrival in Venice in 1709. No doubt Vivaldi realized that composing operas could be more lucrative than teaching at the Pietà, and that producing them and assuming the role of impresario could be financially profitable, if sometimes risky. Later, when his own operas had fallen from fashion, he readily mounted those of other composers. In Venice, where "all is fashion," De Brosses observed in 1739 or 1740, "Vivaldi is an old man, who has a fury of prodigious composition ... [but] his music has been about for a long time and the music of last year no longer earns money."

Robbins Landon has little to say about Vivaldi's operas, summarily dismissing them as "static," "undramatic," and unpalatable for today's audience. Other Vivaldi scholars, including Michael Talbot, author of the entry on him in *Grove* and one of the few familiar with many of the operas—musicians in general know only one, *Orlando*—have remarked on their admirable "control of pace," their "secure sense of form," "gift of succinct characterization," and the use of stock characters, which enabled the composer to fit arias with new words and insert them into other operas. Vivaldi seems to have reserved arias for scene endings, after which the singer would acknowledge applause and exit. One also would like to know more about the "lavish sets" and the stage pictures of Vivaldi's Mexico (*Montezuma*), China (*Il Teuzzone*), and his operatic Egypt (*Armida*), Persia (*Bajazet*), Macedonia (*Filippo*), Scotland (*Ginevra, Principessa di Scozia*).

In November 1737, two days before Vivaldi was due to leave Venice for Ferrara to produce an opera there, Tomaso Ruffo, Cardinal of the Este city, ordered him not to come, partly on grounds of his relationship with "La Girò," who by this time was popularly known as "Annina of the red priest." Vivaldi, who had large sums at stake in contractual obligations to singers, dancers, and other participants, wrote to Bentivoglio denying the allegation of impropriety with Giraud and asking him to intercede and protect his interests. The composer protests that Anna resides at a great distance from him. But in connection with a writ against him, one Antonio Mauro, a scene painter Vivaldi had asked to precede him to Ferrara, states that it was delivered to the Reverend Don Antonio's house and "was given to a woman." Carlo Goldoni's memoirs further establish that Annina and her sister Paulina shared the composer's house, and that Annina had "a good figure, beautiful eyes and hair, and a shining warmth."

Vivaldi's living arrangements are attested to by other sources. Robbins Landon quotes a description of a party given by the Spanish ambassador in Venice: "The music was by the singer La Girò, who lives at the house of the *abate* Vivaldi; the composer himself sat at the harpsichord and indicated the tempo to the instruments.... The music went on until three o'clock in the morning." Taking La Girò's defense in a lawsuit, Vivaldi stated that she lives near Santa Maria in Formosa, which is not far from S. Giovanni in Bràgora and may have been his residence as well. The claimant in the suit was an instrument maker from whom she purchased a harpsichord with "money from an admirer," the Duke of Massa Carrara. (The builder contended that she had not handed over all of the money, but his case was dismissed as without merit.) A letter of 1726 from the Neapolitan ambassador to his government on the subject of Venetian licentiousness also refers to her:

> It's just as with us, one makes love all day long.... [E]veryone sings and there are fine voices ... [such as] that of Annina from the Pietà who is now creating a furore at all the best theaters.... Here they sing and play in boats....

Mauro's writ also accuses Vivaldi of cheating, dishonesty, untruthfulness, and sharp business practices: "Neither God nor the world can applaud [your] trickery and dealings." Vivaldi responded by charging Mauro with theft and ingratitude, but the composer is less straightforward and less convincing. From this and other evidence, it was clear that Vivaldi was a contentious arm-twister, always seeking advantage. He drove hard bargains, charging a guinea for each of his concertos, which was considered exorbitant. "Vivaldi has become my intimate friend for the purpose of selling me some very expensive concertos," de Brosses wrote. Another feature of the composer's character was a servility and groveling before superiors in dedications and letters excessive even for the age: "I beg to lie at the feet of all the illustrious members of your house." But the other side of the ledger, and of the personality, is inferable from the vivaciousness and the gentle sentiments of his music.

Vivaldi's claim that he never ventured outside on foot is contradicted by the visiting German violin virtuoso Pisendel, who recalled "walking with Herr Vivaldi in St. Mark's Square" and from there to his house. And, expensive or not, the composer is known to have traveled a great deal, slipping off to Amsterdam in 1739 to produce a theatrical spectacle, conduct, and play one or two of his violin concertos, and to Bohemia in 1729 or 1730, as well as, probably, Moravia (autograph parts of three Marian antiphons survive in Brno); two of his operas were staged in Prague in the latter year. In Trieste, the Habsburg Emperor Charles VI, an accomplished musician, ennobled Vivaldi, gave him money as well as a gold chain and medal, and was presented in turn with a clutch of concertos.

* * *

Robbins Landon's chapter on the *Stagioni* serves notice that "it is not the purpose of this book to enter into complicated musical analyses." Since the clockwork *ritornelli* and alternating *tutti/soli* of these simple pieces could hardly warrant or sustain anything of the sort, what the book does enter into, none too successfully, are the music's uncomplicated, not to say banal, "programmatic" aspects. According to Robbins Landon, the slow movement of the *Inverno* (Winter) Concerto depicts the retreat indoors from a "driving" rain to a "roaring open fire," when to at least one listener, this lovely, tranquil piece neither "drives" nor "roars." In warmer weather, the violin trills believably imitate bird calls, and loud repeated notes and upward-flashing scales can suggest thunder and lightning. But what is one to make of the claim that with an "incredible stroke of genius" Vivaldi evokes a growling dog? This miracle is achieved by assigning the lowest line to violas (instead of to *basso continuo*), who play two notes in slow tempo and in the same rhythm in every measure, the second note twice as long as the first and at the same pitch. This sounds like "woof-*woof*," "woof-*woof*" to the eminent scholar, though even the best-trained performing pooches neither growl nor bark in rhythmically steady, evenly-held tones. The music further reminds him of a canine, "howling or barking at the moon on a still moonlit night in a solitary northern Italian landscape."

Robbins Landon believes that the core of Vivaldi's artistic thought is sacred music, which he had been composing from at least the age of thirteen, according to the date on his manuscript of a *Laetatus* now in Turin. He cites a movement of another religious piece as "a trance of beauty," and mentions fugal and polyphonic passages in various Credos, Kyries, and Glorias, but instead of examples in music type offers only adjectival descriptions, forgetting that an "incredible pedal point on the dominant" (where else?) and "cascades of choral sound," mean nothing to readers without scores.

In Graz, in October 1740, La Girò sang in Vivaldi's opera *Catone in Utica*, and it seems likely that the *"prete rosso,"* though doubtless the *"prete bianco"* by then, accompanied her there, since he is next located in Vienna, February 7, 1741, as a guest of the Duke of Sachsen-Meiningen. (Vivaldi's imperial patron, Charles VI, had died a few months earlier from eating poisonous mushrooms.) The composer is heard from only once more, on June 28, when he signed a receipt, now in the Moravian Library in Brno, for a sale of his music to the Count of Collalto, a name that occurs in the history of the child Mozart. A month later, on July 28, Vivaldi was dead from "internal inflammation," which, whatever that means, was also given as a cause of Mozart's death.

The facts of Vivaldi's funeral in Vienna read like a rehearsal for Mozart's fifty years later. Both composers had known periods of comparatively good earnings, yet both died poor, a result of "disorderly prodigality" in Vivaldi's case, according to a Venetian obituary, and something similar was intimated of Mozart. Vivaldi's service, with the nine-year-old Joseph Haydn as one of six choirboys, took place in the Stephanskirche, as Mozart's did. And, like Mozart, Vivaldi was buried in an unmarked pauper's grave.

"A Certain Sigr. Mozzart"[1]

H. C. Robbins Landon's Mozart biography begins at the end, in *1791 Mozart's Last Year*, and progresses by stages backwards. This generates suspense: the subsequent installment, *Mozart: The Golden Years 1781–1791*,[2] leaves the reader wondering whether its successor will be called *The Silver Years*, and the one after that *The Enamel Age* (the teething prodigy). But the retrograde approach requires recapitulations of the future, and, more important, it lacks the coherence that can be achieved only by tracing the composer's development from the beginning.

Since the bicentenary (1956), and the elevation of Mozart above all other composers, the literature has increased exponentially, and with it the specialization. Entire tomes are now devoted to single subjects ranging from Masonic symbolism in *The Magic Flute* to questions of tempo, ornamentation, and the dating of the manuscripts by ink and watermarks, the latter showing, for example, that supposedly early church music was actually composed in Vienna in the late years. New sources have been uncovered and old ones reopened to further research, with the result that among other drastic revisions in our knowledge of the composer, we now know that he did far more sketching than had hitherto been assumed, thus making him seem at the same time more human and still not less god-like.

Robbins Landon himself, starting with his early 1950s edition of the Mass in C minor, has contributed substantially to the new scholarship. His most recent biographical discovery constitutes a fascinating chapter of *The Golden Years*. In 1791 the Austrian government began to suspect a conspiracy against the Emperor by the Illuminati, an anti-Jesuit, pro-French-Revolutionary branch of Freemasonry. Mozart's name does not appear in the documents, but a suspicion animadverted upon him through his association with Baron Van Swieten, the Royal Librarian who was Mozart's patron and Masonic brother. On October 14, 1791, the tutor of the Crown Prince, appointed by Van Swieten, was se-

---

[1] The Royal Court Councillor von Gebler in a letter dated Vienna, December 13, 1773.
[2] *Mozart, the Golden Years 1781–1791*, by H. C. Robbins Landon. New York: Schirmer, 1989.

cretly denounced to the Emperor as the head of the Illuminati, and a few weeks later, on the same day as Mozart's death, December 5, 1791, Van Swieten was accused of disloyalty to the Crown and stripped of his government offices. Yet he was given responsibility for arranging Mozart's hasty funeral at St. Stephen's and interment (first stage) at St. Marx's. The reader thirsts for more.

Robbins Landon's discussion of the relationship between Haydn and Mozart in musical interchanges and in comparisons between their very different musical personalities is another feature of the book, not surprisingly from our foremost Haydn authority. Of particular interest is an analysis of similar schemes of tonal organization in Haydn's opera *La fedeltà premiata* and, vastly more developed—"a musical edifice of formidable intellectual power and effectiveness"—in Mozart's (later) opera *Così fan tutte*. Also on the subject of Haydn and his Esterhazy employers, *The Golden Years* identifies Mozart's Esterhazy patron as Count Johann (instead of, as previously thought, his brother Count Franz), and sorts out an old confusion of authorship in a work by Michael Haydn, Joseph's brother and one of Mozart's closest friends. On an occasion when illness had prevented Michael from completing a requirement to compose a set of six duets for violin and viola, Mozart wrote the missing two pieces for him (in G and B flat, K 423 and K 429), ingeniously disguising his own style while imitating his friend's (and to some extent Joseph Haydn's), another instance—the composer of *Figaro* contributed many insert numbers to Italian operas—of Mozart writing not only his own music but also the best of other composers' (and even non-composers: he wrote music for his friend, the botanist Nikolaus von Jacquin, and consented to its publication under Jacquin's name).

Robbins Landon recognizes the need for books "that try to explain ... complex music to the general reader in terms he or she can understand," and claims a measure of success in his "middle course between a scholarly treatment and a more journalistic" one.[3] But his catalogs of keys and harmonic progressions help neither the non-musician, for whom the information is meaningless, nor the musically literate, who do not have to be told. "The slow Kyrie then modulates to the relative major," he says, though what this conveys to anyone uninstructed in major-minor relations is hard to imagine. So, too, the statement that a certain rhythm is introduced "in bar 3" and repeated "in bars 7, 11, 13, and so forth," is useless for the reader without score, and too obvious to mention for

---

[3] In a later book, *The Mozart Essays*, New York: Thames & Hudson, 1995, Robbins Landon compliments himself on having "tried to apply the Berensonian principle of using a clear stylistic 'fingerprint' to support the other evidence in a quite revealing fashion."

the reader with one.

The inconsistencies in *The Golden Years* may have been designed to keep the reader alert: beginning an account of the "Gran Partita" for winds, the longest of Mozart's instrumental works, the biographer notes that "brevity is a prerequisite for wind-band writing." Irrelevancies are also effectively employed to the same purpose, as in an example in music-type of how Mozart did *not* write the beginning of the *Figaro* Overture, and in an inventory, with no conceivable bearing on Mozart, of the possessions of Prince Galitzin—"fourteen carriages, eleven horses and 552 bottles of rare wines," etc. False trails are started, too, as in a reference to the Piano Concerto K 271 as "forward looking," though Mozart neither developed nor returned to the direction of this marvel-unto-itself.

More seriously in error is the classification of the composer's last symphonies in terms of "cyclothymic" disorders. Can the G minor, with its ineffable tenderness and countless perfections, really betoken a "frantic and anguished neuroticism," a "near-hysteria"? And if the *Jupiter* Symphony, "produced during a manic mood swing," has "the same kind of depth as those mysterious landscapes in the background of many a *quattrocento* Italian painting," what kind of depth is that, and which landscapes are the mysterious ones? Elsewhere we cringe, reading that the second movement of the E-flat Symphony is "as inscrutably beautiful as the smile in Leonardo's *Mona Lisa.*"

Inevitably, the best parts of any Mozart biography are the excerpts from the composer's correspondence. *The Golden Years* offers two 24-carat samples, both from letters to his father. The first explains the conception of Osmin's music in *The Abduction from the Seraglio:*

> a man who is in such a rage completely loses control and breaks all the rules, not being himself—and thus the music mustn't know what it is doing either. But since the passions, violent or not, must never be expressed in an offensive manner; music, even in the most appalling situations, must never offend the ear, must always remain music.

The second defines the transcendent artistic philosophy embodied in three just-completed, immortal, piano concertos:

> Here and there only connoisseurs can derive satisfaction, but in such a way that the non-connoisseur will be pleased without knowing why.

Which reminds us of Leon Battista Alberti's "[Painting should be] pleasant both to the educated and to those who are not."

* * *

The first 150 years of Mozart biography are characterized by romantic myth-making, the last fifty by greater knowledge and understanding, but also by distorting interpretation. William Stafford convinces us of this in a book[4] intended to supercede those of the most eminent Mozartians of even a few years ago. But Stafford is mistaken in thinking that Wolfgang Hildesheimer's suspicion that Mozart's letters are dissembling (they are) "rests on an implausible account of his personality," and that Volkmar Braunbehrens's portrait of Mozart-as-social-rebel dissolves with a shake of the kaleidoscope (it doesn't). On the other hand, he correctly argues that Braunbehrens's and H. C. Robbins Landon's replacement of the neglected and improvident composer of popular tradition with a lionized and affluent one is a gross overcorrection. Stafford is well aware, of course, that Mozart studies will not be put on hold and that his own reinvestigation will be overtaken as well. Too many questions can never be answered, too many arguments are *ex silentio*.

The death is both starting point and focus of *The Mozart Myths*, which attempts to explain the myth-making process that began immediately after it, in terms of the life as a whole. Stafford's review of the medical history, or symptomatology, concludes with the "almost certainty" that the last illness was rheumatic fever, which had afflicted Mozart as a child, and/or infective endocarditis—the difference was not known in 1791—and that "he probably died of heart failure resulting from those illnesses and the [iatrogenic] treatment." The latter probably consisted of bloodletting, emetics, and poisoning by antimony, which is also an emetic. The doctors who attended him "did not think he had been poisoned," Stafford writes, not telling us how he knows what they might have thought; nor is anything known of the origins of the poisoning rumor published in a Berlin newspaper three weeks after the death. Mozart's widow described trajectory vomiting: "He began to vomit—it spat out of him in an arch—it was brown, and he was dead." One wonders to what the doctors attributed the presence of brown (old) blood in the stomach, and why vomiting was induced, if it was induced, in a patient thought to be suffering from a rheumatoid disease and unable to move without agonizing pain.

Two of Stafford's "absolute certainties" are that Mozart in 1791 was "not having thoughts of death," and was "not burnt out and ready to die," as the inferiority of the Clarinet Concerto of October 1791 to the earlier Clarinet Quintet suggests. The grounds for the former are the high spirits in the composer's

---

[4] *The Mozart Myths: A Critical Reassessment*, by William Stafford. Stanford, Calif.: Stanford University Press, 1991.

last letters and, for the latter, Alan Tyson's study of datable manuscript fragments indicating that at the time of death Mozart had been working on a horn concerto, a violin sonata, a string quintet, and a new mass. But the strongest evidence for both is Mozart's own catalog of his works, in the many pages of ruled staves at the end intended for the incipits of future creations.

Stafford's presentation of the "burnt-out" view notes that Mozart was apparently unable to finish the six string quartets supposedly commissioned by the King of Prussia, and that his last works are those of a "fulfilled" composer, written in a "late style" corresponding to Beethoven's "third period ... spare, simple, pure" (hardly the qualities that come to mind in connection with the *Hammerklavier* and the *Grosse Fuge*). But these arguments are offset by those for the continuing growth of Mozart's powers as manifest in the greater succinctness of the introductions and codas in *The Magic Flute*, the exploitation of wider spacing, as in the octave and a sixth between the melodic lines of the strings in the first movement of the *"Jupiter"* Symphony, and the new role of trombones and bassoons in the dramatic music.

Mozart died on December 5, 1791, at fifty-five minutes past midnight, and was buried on December 6. Contending that interment on that day would have been in violation of a law requiring an elapse of forty-eight hours between death and burial, Stafford suggests that the register entry is a mistake. But since winter burials in Vienna did not take place before 6 p.m., Mozart would have been dead more than forty-one hours by that time, which might have been thought long enough, particularly if, as his sister-in-law and young son testified, the body had a putrid odor. In any case, a recent discovery confirms that the funeral procession, from the Mozart apartment to St. Stephen's Cathedral, took place on the sixth, and, since the cross-bearer and four pallbearers were followed by four choirboys carrying candle lamps, after sundown. The widow followed them, and Baron van Swieten (who paid for the funeral), then three of Mozart's pupils and three musician friends, one of whom was Antonio Salieri.

The enigma of the obsequies is less of an issue than that of the botched burial in an unknown grave. Stafford tells us that "individual graves could be obtained by special dispensation," and that "quite ordinary people" had them, along with headstones, and that "Mozart's unceremonious burial was normal for that rationalist time." But surely Baron van Swieten realized that Mozart's fame throughout Europe demanded that an exception be made, a "special dispensation" at the very least. Three London newspapers announced Mozart's death within two weeks of the event.

Inexplicably, Stafford devotes only a few lines to "the Hofdemel affair," while at the same time admitting that it is "the most damaging scandal associated with Mozart's name." Franz Hofdemel, a government official and Mozart's lodge-brother, had on occasion loaned money to the composer. Magdalena Hofdemel, his wife, may or may not have been Mozart's pupil, but he knew her as a neighbor living a five-minute walk away, and as the daughter of a man from whom he had borrowed money in 1790 in Brno; Mozart gave him a watch as collateral; it surfaced in 1956.

According to gossip that reached Beethoven's deaf ears, Magdalena was Mozart's mistress. (Hearing her name from Karl Czerny, Beethoven's pupil, the composer asked whether she was "the woman who had the affair with Mozart?" a remark that Czerny repeated to Otto Jahn, Mozart's first comprehensive biographer who, like many others, believed it.) On the day of Mozart's funeral, Hofdemel tried to kill his five-months-pregnant wife with a razor, then successfully killed himself with it. A workman, overhearing her screams, went to fetch a locksmith, two witnesses, and a doctor, who found the widow in a faint but managed to save her life. Stafford does not mention these events and evidently does not suspect that coincidences might have roots, in this case that Magdalena, in a high emotional state, confessed feelings about Mozart to her husband who, perhaps having doubts about the paternity of her unborn child, flew into a jealous rage. That the government made an effort to hide the connection between the Hofdemels and Mozart is not a matter of conjecture, however: the name of the suicide was witheld until a week after his death, at which time it was published in Graz but not in Vienna.

Some of Stafford's pronouncements are puzzling. He tells us that "many will find the view of [Mozart] as transcendent genius more convincing than that of him as outstanding musical craftsman." But surely craftsmanship, which goes nowhere by itself, is not an alternative to "transcendent genius," and, as surely, Mozart was both. The "centrality" of the piano concerto "is significant," Stafford observes, "for the debate between soloist and orchestra symbolizes the growing alienation of the non-aristocratic individual from the society of the *ancien régime.*" But "debate" is not the right word, the kinds of relationship between piano and orchestra being far more complex that that of mere opposition.

* * *

Ivan Nagel's *Autonomy & Mercy,* [5] the standout book in English translation of the Mozart year, is for readers already steeped in the operas. Some of Nagel's

[5] *Autonomy and Mercy: Reflections on Mozart's Operas,* by Ivan Nagel, translated from the German by the author and Marian Faber. Cambridge: Harvard University Press, 1991.

references—Alfieri, Beccaria, Brentano, Kleist, and Corneille, whose *Cinna* is crucial to the discussion of *opera seria*—are not part of most American cultural backgrounds. Indeed, the American musical public might object that Nagel has made Mozart into a conceptual thinker. But a few quotations will give an idea of the quality of Nagel's intellectually stimulating discourse: "Not a single note in [Don Giovanni's] marriage vow to Zerlina ... or in his declaration of love to Elvira ... suggests that he does not believe what he is singing, and the fact that Mozart would not, could not, show what it means to live a lie ... is what creates the abyss in *Così fan tutte*"; in *Don Giovanni*, alone of all the operas, "there is neither forgiveness nor mercy.... How could *Don Giovanni* end with mercy? Giovanni does not entreat"; in Mozart's four greatest operas "there is not a single figure who is not animated by a human soul, thanks to Mozart's love for his or her unique being. One exception proves the rule ... the Stone Guest: *a statue.*"

***

Haplessly, Cliff Eisen's updating of the Mozart documentation[6] seems to have gone to press just before the publication of the two major finds of the last forty years, though the first of these, the discovery in the Vienna Hofkammerarchiv of a lawsuit against Mozart by Prince Carl von Lichnowsky for the repayment of a debt of 1,435 florins, was in print by November 1990. On November 12, 1791, three weeks and two days before Mozart's death, a court ruled that half of his salary as Imperial Royal Chamber Composer be garnisheed and the remainder of the money raised by impounding and selling his goods and chattels. Since the Prince had been Mozart's lodge brother and two years earlier had taken the composer with him part of the way to Berlin, this bombshell raises many questions and revives the large one concerning the mystery of Mozart's ever-deepening indebtedness.

The second discovery, published in Salzburg in the summer of 1991, came about in the course of an examination of the archives of St. Michael's, the Vienna court chapel: a Requiem Mass for Mozart was held there on December 10, 1791. The program of the memorial, organized by Emanuel Schikaneder, librettist of *The Magic Flute*, and his colleague Joseph von Bauernfeld, on behalf of Vienna's opera and court musicians, apparently included the first and second movements, the latter with simple fill-in orchestration by Mozart's pupil, Franz Jacob Freystadtler, of Mozart's *Requiem.*

---

6 *New Mozart Documents: A Supplement to O. E. Deutsch's Documentary Biography*, by Cliff Eisen. Stanford, Calif.: Stanford University Press, 1991.

The 120 or so new hard facts that Eisen presents bring the realities of the period closer. One item is the comment by the Russian Ambassador to Dresden in 1789 that in Mozart's music, "not a single melody emanates from the heart." Another, by the representative of a London music publisher calling on Mozart in 1785, remarks that the composer had been hard at work until the interruption and that he "continued to put down occasional notes during our conversation." He was small, "of very slight build," and "His face was not particularly striking," the English visitor goes on, unwittingly describing the colossus of the species homo sapiens.

A Little Mozart Tour

June 8, 1991. New York. To see the exhibition, "Mozart: Prodigy of Nature," at the Morgan Library, is a humbling experience.[7] Some fifty Mozart manuscripts are displayed, ranging from four pieces composed at age five to a draft page of the Requiem, together with the copy in Beethoven's hand of Mozart's Quartet K 387. Fourteen autograph letters, early and late, are here, too, and among other invaluable documents, Mozart's marriage contract. John Russell's report in the *New York Times* begins by remarking that "great music falls from the air" and "in almost every case the autograph manuscript of that music is right there beneath our noses.... The thing heard and the thing seen are one."

Yes, and except that we cannot turn the pages, the union would be synergistic; speaking for myself, I could only stop, *not* look, and listen when one of the Queen of Night's arias began to fall from the air while I was studying a sketch for the Priests' March in the *Magic Flute*, being unable to read one score while my ear is monopolized by another. But the recorded concert does feature performances of the manuscript music on display, and after two or three visits, and on an uncrowded morning, the visitor would probably be able to chase from one showcase to another in time to glimpse the first few measures of whichever concerto, sonata, aria, quartet, symphony has come up on the tape.

Mozart's manuscripts are neat. Johann Anton Andre, who purchased the bulk of them from Mozart's widow in 1799, remarked that the notes are "small, fully-shaped and show no signs of hesitation." But to follow them during performances, which is now possible in facsimile publications of several works, is an acquired skill. The lack of vertical alignment, the long note or long rest

---

[7] *Mozart: Prodigy of Nature*, an exhibition at the the Pierpont Morgan Library, 1991; an incomplete catalog of the exhibition was published by the library in association with the British Library, 1991.

placed in the middle, instead of at the beginning, of the bar, is an impediment. Another is that musicians have become accustomed to reading Mozart's appoggiaturas in written-out form.

The Morgan exhibition is for the musically literate. And for those who read German: only a few passages from the letters on display have been translated, and none of the marginalia. One of Mozart's scatological letters to his cousin Maria Anna Thekla Mozart is left entirely in the original language over a caption describing the contents as "vulgar to the point of being unprintable." Dear me! Do musicologists not read contemporary fiction and not go to the movies? Nor is the catalog's sniffy dismissal of the "Basle" letters (Maria Anna's nickname) as "notorious" any help. What might have been explained is that Mozart's unprintable humor is strictly gastro-intestinal, never genito-urinary.

Twelve of the autograph scores are of symphonies—the *Haffner* reveals interesting crossings-out and corrections of octave placement—twenty-one of chamber-music (quintets, quartets, trios, duos), and twelve of keyboard works, including the *Preambulae* and the great A-minor Sonata. Only four operas are represented, the *Magic Flute*, as aforesaid; *Tito* by the Act I duettino; *Figaro* by the draft of an aria, and an arrangement for violin and piano of another, "*Non so più cosa son*"; the *Impresario* by the complete full score, from which differences in ink-quality and color in the Overture (black and white only in the catalog), reveal that the top line and bass were notated first.

Otherwise the two most important treasures in the display cases are the thematic catalog, the "*Verzeichnuss aller meine Werke,*" that Mozart kept from 1784 to 1791, and the 280-page Thomas Attwood exercise book, the record of this English pupil's lessons with the composer, twelve pages of it entirely in Mozart's hand, 115 in his (the annotations in red) and Attwood's. One of the disappointments of the bicentenary of the composer's death is that the exercise book for the niece of Stadler, Mozart's clarinetist friend, has not appeared in facsimile, along with a book on what is known about Mozart's other pupils, the physician Joseph Frank, who remarked that the composer had "fleshy hands," and the many females: the gifted Barbara (Babette) Ployer (whose exercise book, containing the only source for the theme in the Benediction in Mozart's *Requiem*, has been published both in facsimile and in type); the blind pianist Marie-Thérèse von Paradies (for whom Mozart wrote a concerto); Josepha Auernhammer (who fell in love with him); the pianist and composer Frau Schulz (who concertized in Russia); the fifteen-year-old Thérèse Pierron Serrarius (harpist and daughter of the flutist Comte de Guines, wrongly "Duke" in the Morgan catalog); the eighteen-year-old Thérèse von Trattner (for whom Mozart wrote the Sonata K 457); the thirteen-year-old Rosa Cannabich (for

whom he wrote the Sonata K 309); Maximiliana Valentina and her sister Wal-
burga Willmann; Countess Thérèse Cobenzl (the dedicatee of three piano
sonatas); Countess Thiennes de Rumbeke; and Countess Khevenhüller-Metsch.

The exhibition catalog invites some quibbles. The *Prague* Symphony is not
in the key of "E flat." A map of "Europe in Mozart's time," without Scandinavia
and the Iberian and Greek peninsulas, traces the extent of his travels but oddly
omits many of the cities in which he performed, including such important ones
as Dresden and Leipzig, while locating some in which he did not. Odder still is
a reference to *Don Giovanni* and the "polymetric preparation for the ball. (The
great Sextet in Act III also bears memorable witness to Mozart's musico-dramatic genius.)" But the *music* is polymetric, not the preparation for the ball, and
the parenthetical non sequitur prompts one to wonder which pieces in *Don Giovanni* do *not* bear witness to the same.

More serious is the catalog's assurance that "Mozart's legacy, unlike Bach's,
would be little diminished had he never composed a note for the Church." This
must be protested: the legacy would be cruelly diminished by the loss, among
late works, of the *Ave verum corpus*, the D-minor Kyrie, and the Requiem's Introitus and Fugue; sadly reduced by the subtraction of the *Vesperae solennes* from
the last Salzburg years, and by the disappearance of the most popular of all the
early vocal pieces, the castrato cantata, *Exultate Jubilate*. It would be profoundly,
inestimably poorer by the deletion of the the the C-minor Mass, in which the stupendous *"Qui tollis peccata mundi,"* dismissed by Robbins Landon as an "old-fashioned" chorus,[8] is an isolated peak different in kind from any of the composer's
other creations, a work without successor, like the K 271 Piano Concerto and
the Sinfonia concertante and, like them, a glimpse into undeveloped dimensions of Mozart's creative universe. But neither can the Offertory and Litany
composed in Munich in 1775–1776, and the five complete Masses from the
same period, be disregarded.

The thematic catalog is of course open to only one page, but the beautiful
new facsimile edition of it, introduced and transcribed by Albi Rosenthal and
Alan Tyson,[9] is on sale. Rosenthal's history of the volume brings Mozart to life
in two glimpses of him taken from A. H. Andre's not-yet-translated, *Zür
Geschichte der Familie Andre* (Offenbach am Main).[10] The author's ancestor, Jo-

---

[8] Landon, *Mozart Essays*, p. 188.

[9] *Mozart's Thematic Catalogue: A Facsimile*, Introduction and Commentary by Albi Rosenthal and
Alan Tyson. Ithaca, New York: Cornell University Press, 1991.

[10] Offenbach. 1962. The book is not listed in Eisen's *New Mozart Documents*, nor in the bibli-
ographies of H. C. Robbins Landon's *Mozart Compendium*.

hann Andre, head of a publishing firm in Offenbach and father of the Johann Anton Andre mentioned above, received a visit from Mozart during the composer's 1790 stay (September 28–October 15) in nearby Frankfurt:

> Clad in a grey travel coat with short collar, Mozart stopped in front of the Andre house. No sooner had he alighted from the coach than he was attracted by the dance music: the male and female workers of the firm had been given permission to hold a dance. Mozart mixed with them quickly, chose the prettiest girl and danced with her for a long time to his heart's content.

(The Offenbach excursion is not recorded in any biography of Mozart; perhaps the "lost" October 17 letter ostensibly sent to his wife from Mainz mentions it, though scholars now doubt that he in fact wrote it, despite his reference to the date.) In Mannheim, on October 23, Johann Anton Andre, aged fifteen, attended a rehearsal for *Figaro* (wrongly *Don Giovanni* in Rosenthal) during which "Mozart complained about Kapellmeister Franzl's slow tempi and asked for livelier ones." (This can only have been Ignaz Franzl, whose brother Friedrich married Johann Anton's sister.) On this occasion Johann Anton described Mozart as "a small, nervous man of rather pallid complexion, but with reddish cheeks and a large prominent nose."

In 1805, Johann Anton Andre published the *Verzeichnuss*, said to be the first book produced by the lithographic process. A facsimile, appearing in Vienna in 1938 in an edition of only two hundred, was reissued in New York in 1956. But Rosenthal-Tyson are the first to reproduce the final fourteen pages, ruled with five pairs of staves like the preceding twenty-nine, indicating that he expected to continue to compose. (Did Mozart ever suffer from tendinitis and carpal tunnel syndrome, writers' cramp?) The empty staves are painfully poignant.

Allan Tyson's meticulous description of the book discusses, *inter alia*, discrepancies in tempo indications with the autograph scores, the peculiarities of Mozart's spelling, his abbreviations, the care he took to include the instrumentation and the names of the performers. In a few cases the transcription of Mozart's text leaves the reader thirsting for more information, e.g., the note on the orchestral song *"Ein teutsches Kriegslied für den Jungern Baumann"* says nothing about the connection between the composer and the young Friedrich Baumann, a popular comedian at the theater in the Vienna suburb of Leopoldstadt.

Again and again the reader marvels at the dates of the entries, above all of the E-flat Symphony on June 26, 1788, of the G-minor Symphony on July 25, and of the *Jupiter* Symphony on August 10, with six smaller works appearing between the first two. How can even the greatest thinking-feeling intelligence produce three utterly different masterpieces at such speed and without the slightest slip? Not believing in thaumaturgy, we turn to Wordsworth about the human mind being "of substance and of fabric more divine" than the world of nature. Six scores fully described by the composer in the *Verzeichnuss* have been lost, though in two cases not their Masonic texts. From oversight or other reasons, twenty that are not included survive.

June 11. Vienna. The whole city is selling, living on, excusing itself through, Mozart. What passes for his likeness is everywhere, most often in the Barbara Krafft portrait (painted twenty-seven years after his death): on walls and kiosks, streetcars and buses, T-shirts, handkerchiefs, embroideries, posters and postcards, plates and placemats, calendars and gold-edged playing cards, candy boxes, tote bags, baubles and souvenirs of every kind—dolls of Mozart as child prodigy—and subliminally in television commercials. The music stores advertise the complete works in forty-five volumes of compact discs with a running time of 184 hours, the book stores display dozens of new titles (including important ones on Mozart's widow and sister and the heretofore insufficiently explored contents of their correspondence after his death). A 5,000 Schilling note ($500) bearing Mozart's image has been issued. Austrian Airlines passengers receive free Mozart CDs, and at bedtime Vienna hotel guests find a chocolate mint in a Mozart wrapper on their turned-down duvets.

Tourists are herded to the sites of Mozart's residences, and from church to church (the St. Stephen's Cathedral of his marriage and funeral and the St. Marx of his first Mass, conducted, aged 12, in the presence of Empress Maria Theresa), from cemetery to cemetery (the one, with his statue next to Beethoven's, where he is not buried, to the one in which he is but nobody knows where). They go afterward to the Café Mozart and the Mozart Bar, then to the Mozart Sängerknaben, the "Wiener Mozart Konzert"—whose orchestra and other performers are dressed in eighteenth-century costumes—or to Mozart operas in several theaters.

All-Mozart programs are pandemic, too, and pernicious, thanks to too many major keys, too many minuets, perfect cadences, protracted, out-of-style, and stupid cadenzas, obligatory repeats (the pedantry in this regard of that excellent Mozart conductor John Eliot Gardiner is regrettable), and too much merely well-made music (like the *Haffner* Serenade and that very long opera *La Finta Giardiniera*, which keeps promising to take off but does not). None of the programs offers even a touch of experiment, such as performing the A Major Violin Concerto with the less good second version of the slow movement alongside the first one that Brunetti, the Salzburg violinist, rejected as "artificial," meaning that it was over his head and he could not play it.

In the park across from the Karlsdom, an ambulant theater performs its version of the *Impresario*, with incorporations from *Figaro* and *Don Giovanni*. The singers try to synchronize with, or overdub, the tape of an orchestral soundtrack, with varying degrees of success. Rustic, amateurish, and farcical though it is, I watch for almost an hour. The audience knows every phrase of the music.

The Mozart *Ausstellung* in the Kunstlerhaus, presented by the Historisches Museums der Stadt Wien, is a huge, labyrinthine affair for only the most enterprising Mozartians, and the catalog, *Zaubertöne, Mozart in Wien 1781–1791*, is too heavy to schlep even for them. Even so, as many of the 614 pages as I have worked through so far contain information encountered nowhere else, such as that the onetime owner of the score of the Six German Dances K 571 was the ill-fated Emperor Maximilian of Mexico, and that after his death and until October 1927 it was kept in Schloss Miramar near Trieste.

The walls just inside the entrance display maps that chart all eighteen of Mozart's journeys, distinguishing them by colored lines. As in New York, a perpetual Mozart concert is piped in, but the volume is lower and in the furthermost rooms mercifully faint. Fewer autographed scores are shown than in New York (about thirty, but including the G minor Symphony, the D minor Concerto, and part of the second act of *Così*), but a great many more autograph letters. Dioramas reproduce vignettes of Viennese life in the 1780s with which Mozart would have been familiar. At any rate, he must have known the same kinds of beds, chamberpots, furniture, kitchen utensils, and tableware, and *did* know similar billiard tables. Mannequins dressed in the costumes of the period confirm that his Viennese contemporaries were a smaller race than ours (and he himself, as noted in every description, was unusually small among them).

Portraits of the people in Mozart's life, friends and family (Joseph Lange's *Constanze*), royal and titled patrons, librettists, singers, entrepreneurs, other composers (George Dance's drawing of Haydn), and those, like Beaumarchais, who influenced him so deeply from far away, are on the walls. The pictorial side of the exhibition is too extensive to describe—the Vienna cityscapes include oils by Belotto and Longhi—but the largest part of it is devoted to the theater, maquettes and costume designs together with scaled reconstructions of scenes from Mozart's operas as staged at the time.

The sciences are represented by pictures and reproductions of some of the actual machinery of Volta's and Galvani's experiments in electricity; by drawings of Linnaeus's botanical and histological work; by displays indicating the state of contemporary knowledge in anatomy, optics, chemistry, and medicine, this last terrifying in the case of clysters that injected tobacco-smoke, and surgical instruments—for phlebotomy, scarifying, and obstetrics (*Geburtshilfe*)—less so in the pills, powders, and sticking plasters of the typical traveler's pharmacy. Considerable space is devoted to Mozart's friend Mesmer, but no parallel is drawn between his and Freud's studies in hysteria and their respective uses of magnetism and hypnosis.

The catalog essay on Mozart's literary world, illustrated by books, a hand press, and writing materials, emphasizes the *Aufklärung* philosophy of the time and supports the view that Mozart's April 4, 1787 letter to his father on death derives in part from Moses Mendelssohn's *Phädon: The Immortality of the Soul.* Mozart's library, which included this volume and the works of six other Enlightenment authors, as well as the works of Ovid, Wieland, Molière, and Metastasio, is exhibited here in the editions that he owned, and in at least one case by his own copy.

* * *

During the overture to *Così* at the Volksoper, the "philosopher" Don Alfonso emerges from the orchestra pit, crosses to a puppet theater at the side of the stage, manipulates the figures inside to positions opposite those in which he had found them, takes pen and paper and makes notes, all much to his amusement. But not to mine, in this or any of the other distracting and tiresome stage business. I would prefer a tacky backdrop of Naples and Vesuvius to the nondescript panels on the revolving, merry-go-round set, which creates the wrong kind of tension: will the actors get on or off the treadmill in time? The chorus, ghostly in white clothes and white masks, is, as should be, not involved in the action. The principals "wife"-swap on stage-front beds (up to a blackout point), but this overemphasizes the unresolvable point of the plot: clearly the new partners are better matched than the old, hence to return to the past would be impossible. The music tells us that Mozart's sympathies are with the women (the sisters).

I am undergoing one of my seasonal changes about *Così*. Though Mozart quickly distinguishes the personalities in his symmetrical pairs, the equations are too pat, Despina's insolence too far below the level of Figaro's, the Don too sardonic by half, and the long-foreseen conclusion too slow in coming. But except for the marches, the music, all two-and-a-half hours of it, is incomparable joy. Since the performance is in German, which turns the fast pieces into tongue-twisters, I focus on the orchestra, and from my seat over it, am able to follow the rotation of instrumental timbres at the employment level, clocking the horns and the trumpets as the players leave the pit in turn for two and even three successive numbers. The orchestra is superb; its *piano-pianissimo,* articulation, phrasing, and intonation are far superior to those of any ensemble of the size that I have heard in London or New York.

In contrast, *The Magic Flute*, by the Hamburg Opera at the Theater an der Wien, is a torture. The prompter, wearing a stuffed parrot hat, stands in full view throughout, the serpent exposes a bare, human, but larger-than-life, bottom, the Sarastro is feeble when he should be stentorian, and the Queen of Night is a screech owl.

* * *

The Kunsthistorisches Museum's auditory exhibition, *Die Klangwelt Mozarts*, is a revelation. Earphones transmit tapes of the old instruments on display, each played alone, first in demonstration, then in ensembles, and, for comparison, in juxtaposition to tapes of the modern versions of the same instruments. The result is a triumph for the "period instrument" lobby, if not for period-instrument performance; the latter, reacting to a romanticizing style, makes the music sound artificially archaic, which is not the way it sounded in its own time.

The largest collections are of the string family—an Amati violin with white frets traditionally thought to have belonged to Mozart's father—and the keyboard instruments, organs, clavichords (first mentioned in Austria in 1407, according to the only-slightly-less-voluminous catalog), pianos (including a replica of the small one that accompanied Mozart on his travels), glockenspiels. The winds include eight sizes of block flute, curved oboes, English horns bent like bows, bassoons, serpents, basset horns (Rube Goldberg contraptions with prosthetic metal braces), small-bell trombones, and several sizes of trumpets together with their wooden mutes. The percussion section includes cymbals, triangles, tambourines, cupboard-like sets of musical glasses, side and bass drums, and timpani, both large (bombinating) and small (hum-drum?). The lutes and mandolins, zithers and pedal harps are the most beautiful instruments, but the curiosity of the exhibition is the glass harmonica, invented by Benjamin Franklin: Mozart (*MOZART!*) had a musical debt to America.

The *"Mozart Requiem"* exhibition in the Austrian National Library—still another large catalog—is padded with Requiems of no value by precursors and successors. The score-book of Mozart's is opened, movingly, to the *"Lacrimosa,"* the last page in his hand.

In the street outside the entrance, a flute-playing panhandler is blowing the accursed *Nachtmusik*, but I refrain from stopping my ears and instead give him Schillings. Mozart worship is not the worst religion the world has had to endure.

* * *

Two recent, vastly superior studies of Mozart greatly expand our knowledge of him and are at the same time so dissimilar in subject emphases that overlapping rarely occurs. Georg Knepler's *Wolfgang Amadé Mozart*[11] explores biographical, psychological, historical, and musical-analytical aspects of the subject without following chronology or attempting a full survey. Knepler's Mozart is a disciple of Diderot and the Enlightenment, through Mme d'Épinay and Baron Melchior Grimm, whose Paris household the composer shared for several months in 1778. Maynard Solomon's Mozart[12] is in some ways a normal as well as a phenomenal person, a son, brother, husband, father, and Freemason. He is also a socio-political being and profound humanist, but at some remove from Knepler's incipient Jacobin.

Mozart: A Life is a comprehensive biography for general readers, psychoanalytical to a degree but illuminatingly, especially concerning the growth of the *wunderkind* in relation to his family and the ongoing oedipal contest between Wolfgang and his suffocatingly possessive father. Leopold Mozart, as source of the son's genetic inheritance, as well as his teacher, caretaker and exploiter of his talents, is the book's second subject. Mr. Solomon persuasively contends that father and son led parallel lives, that Leopold subconsciously reenacted situations of his own unhappy youth. By proposing to elope to Italy with his future wife's older sister, with whom he was infatuated, Wolfgang enraged his father, and when his mother attempted to mediate, Leopold revealed a paranoid streak by accusing her of collusion with their son. A few years later, when Mozart moved to Vienna to lead an independent life and pursue a freelance musician's career, thereby liberating himself from both his father and his detested employer, the Archbishop of Salzburg, Leopold, losing his equanimity, attempted to fill the void by taking an eleven-year-old pupil, Heinrich Marchand, his daughter's son, with the incredible intention of making him into another Wolfgang. Further, Leopold vindictively bequeathed his estate not to his son, who had married against his wishes, but to his far-from-needy daughter, the same reason his own mother had cut him off. But Leopold was flagrantly dishonest in this, since his substantial legacy could only have been earned by Wolfgang's early concert tours and was therefore rightfully his.

After the rupture between them, Leopold refused to receive Wolfgang's wife and wrote recriminating letters nagging him to return to Salzburg, re-establish their partnership there (pooling their salaries), and accept a humiliating sinecure in the provincial city. This can be deduced from Leopold's letters to third parties, among them the Baroness Waldstätten, to whom he complained

[11] Cambridge: Cambridge University Press, 1994.
[12] *Mozart: A Life*. New York: HarperCollins, 1995.

of the moral and material "degradations" that his son had inflicted on him, and from Wolfgang's letters to his father, of which the other side of the correspondence was destroyed, probably by Mozart himself.

Leopold, a composer and virtuoso violinist, gave his son a thorough musical education, while tutoring him in academic subjects and instructing him in proper social behavior and court etiquette. He advised the young man to "train" his "reason by reading good books in several languages," though at a still younger age Mozart had already read *The Arabian Nights* in Italian and Fenélon's *Les Aventures de Télémaque* in French. Mozart's letters, verbally inventive, witty, marvelously thoughtful, suggest that no form of mentation was beyond his powers. His library at the time of his death contained three treatises on the natural sciences, in addition to works of philosophy and history, poetry, and plays.

Leopold, the tyrannical husband and parent was also an able entrepreneur. Purse-proud at first with the profits pocketed from his performing-animal exhibitions of his son, he learned, after Mozart outgrew his marketability as a prodigy, that poor-mouthing was wiser. But Leopold's mendacity is apparent from early on, as when he tells Wolfgang that "what I wrote about my health is all quite untrue ... you must, however, spread the news everywhere that I was ill." What had come most deeply between them by the time of Wolfgang's resettlement in Vienna was that his new compositions had far surpassed Leopold's expectations and comprehension of him: he simply did not understand the unfathomable depth and scope of his son's genius. Mr. Solomon percipiently remarks that Mozart's "creativity became a hallmark of their estrangement, and of [Leopold's] own impotence, even as it thrilled him to consider that he had fathered, shaped, and nurtured so miraculous a being."

Mozart: A Life reveals as much as may ever be known about the composer's mother, whose letters to her son do not survive. She was excluded from the long Italian journeys, unlike the earlier family ones, ostensibly because of the expense, much exaggerated by Leopold, who would have preferred to live in Italy if Wolfgang had been able to secure a good post there. (A vacant one in Hapsburg Mantua was withheld from him by the Empress because she considered Leopold's money-making activities and crass promotional tactics in bad taste.) In 1777, Frau Mozart, without Leopold but at his insistence, accompanied the twenty-one-year-old Wolfgang to Augsburg, where for a fortnight he frolicked amorously with his cousin Thekla, afterward writing her letters unrivaled in coprophilic literature until those of Joyce to Nora from Dublin in 1909.

Mother and son continued to Mannheim and from there to Paris, first (March 23, 1778) on the Rue Bourg l'Abbé, later (in April) *chez* the Marquise d'Épinay on the Rue du Sentier. In the latter, on July 3, after four lonely months—Mozart worked at another address—his mother died. We can scarcely imagine Mozart's feelings and plight following this first death that he had experienced. Evidently he had not understood the seriousness of her illness and, respecting her wishes to see only a German doctor, found one who thought that "rhubarb powder, in wine" would cure her. When Mozart finally appealed to Grimm and d'Épinay for help it was too late. Leopold cruelly accused his son of negligence, even though he had not wanted his mother to undertake the journey in the first place and had begged his father to allow her to return to Salzburg. Although Mozart composed music in Paris that raised his art to a new firmament, in other respects his six-month sojourn there was disappointing.

Mr. Solomon is not entirely successful in his attempts to relate the traumas of the Paris period to some of the slow movements that Mozart composed there. That these connections exist is not in doubt, but only that words can describe them. Mr. Solomon knows that "there is an imagery in music that is beyond literal referentiality and extra-musical indications," but he cannot resist adding that our "intuitive responses and imaginative capacities ... are capable of symbolizing vast realms of experience and feeling." The difficulty here is that great music can mean different things to different imaginations. Mozart's greatest music gives meaning to human existence itself, but as music, not as symbol, or substitute religion, or philosophical analogy—which is not to deny that it may be a drug or a therapy. Mr. Solomon tells us that while listening to the Andante of the A-minor Sonata he has experienced "sensations of surpassing intensity—oceanic, comforting, and rapturous," and at different moments has perceived a "strange mixture of beatitude and terror," "inexpressible ecstasy," and "unthinkable anxiety." But whatever this conveys about the musicologist, it says nothing about the music. The crucial event in the Andante of the Sonata is Mozart's discovery of the power in the melodic interval of the upward major-sixth.

Mr. Solomon's analyses of the fusion of operatic (vocal) and sonata (instrumental, symphonic) forms and procedures in *Figaro* and *Don Giovanni* are more fruitful. But he does not mention the opposite, the transference of operatic melody into instrumental music, as in the oboe and clarinet arias in the slow movements of the "Gran Partita," K 361, which Mozart may have composed during the four-year period when he examined and rejected more that one hundred libretti before choosing *Figaro*.

In the first half of his last decade in Vienna (1781–1791), Mozart was unceasingly productive, prosperous, and a popular performer favored by the Emperor, who called out "Bravo Mozart" after hearing him play one of his piano concertos. He enjoyed the company of the city's intellectual, social, and artistic elite. Then, in the latter half of the period, all of this was reversed. His concerts were fewer in number, ill-attended and under-subscribed. His productivity was attenuated for a time and he fell deeply into debt. The accepted explanation for this change in fortune is that he had been overexposed as both performer and composer, which would account for the decline in the quantity of piano concertos and the return, in 1788, to the symphony.

Speculation about the financial side of the volte-face has centered on Mozart's spendthrift habits, possible gambling debts, and blackmail. Mr. Solomon's ledger of the known and the probable income during the Viennese decade shows that although Mozart was not exactly destitute in 1789–1790, and his earnings had dwindled, he was living above his means. Yet this does not explain the enigma of the large debts and the desperate tone of his letters to creditors. He literally begs for the smallest amount, if a larger one cannot be forthcoming, and pledges repayment in a pitifully wheedling manner. Why, one wonders, did his friend, fellow Mason, and pupil Prince Lichnowsky, who had invited the composer to accompany him to Berlin in 1789, bring a lawsuit against him in 1791, only three and a half weeks before his death, as it happened, for the recovery of a large loan? (The question might possibly be answered if the Lichnowsky archives, now in South America, are opened to scholars, but the only mention of the affair is in the Vienna court register; Mozart's widow and the Lichnowskys never referred to it.) Nor has any evidence of blackmail or gambling debts been found, but Lichnowsky's suit for the substantial sum of 1435 gulden, more than ten times Joseph Haydn's *per annum* salary as Esterhazy composer, suggests something of the sort.

Mr. Solomon's most explosive chapter, devoted to the two-month Berlin journey, exposes Mozart's lies in his letters to his wife, some of them in the enumeration of letters that he did not send or even write. The author justifiably doubts the composer's claim that the Prussian King had invited him to Potsdam, citing documentation that proves he was definitely not expected. Clearly Mozart was not commissioned to write "six quartets" for the King or "six easy sonatas" for Princess Frederike; he did not even begin the sonatas and published the three quartets that he did finish without the Royal dedication. He went directly from Vienna to Prague (not Potsdam), where he called on the Duscheks, whose house guest he had been at the time of *Don Giovanni*. He was informed that Frau Duschek, his former pupil (who was twenty-three years younger than her spouse), was in Dresden where, coincidentally, Mozart had a concert. Staying three days after it with her, he then made a wide detour to Leipzig, rather than going directly to Berlin and Potsdam, to arrange for a concert with her there as his vocal soloist, on his return from Berlin three weeks later.

Mr. Solomon refers to Mozart's "driving sexuality" and his "apparent inability to remain faithful to his wife." The composer's late letters to his extremely jealous wife show him to have been an accomplished dissimulator, as he had doubtless learned to be during life with father. They are cover-ups, Mr. Solomon contends, and Constanze had reason to be suspicious. Did Mozart have affairs with his female pupils and with his operatic leading ladies, among them the Papagena and the Pamina in the first *Magic Flute?* Did he live alone in the cottage provided for him by the opera's librettist, the notoriously promiscuous Schikaneder? Sex, after all, is the subject of Mozart's greatest operas. His Vienna obituary refers to his "overwhelming sensuality," which seems an odd time and place to publish such an observation.

During the 1786 carnival of Vienna, a masquerader in the Hofburg, actually Mozart costumed as an Oriental philosopher, distributed copies of a broadside sheet containing eight riddles and fourteen proverbs that he had written under the title *Fragments of Zoroaster.* He sent one to his father, who showed it to the editor of a Salzburg paper which then published seven of the proverbs and one of the riddles. Predictably, Leopold thought the proverbs edifying—they seem apodictic and unremarkable to us—but objected to the "oracular" style of the riddles and asked for plainer explanations. (The printed one is transparently erotic.) Though no copy of the broadside is extant, a draft in Mozart's hand of the other seven riddles was recently placed on deposit in the Berlin State Library. They show Mozart as something of a psycho-physiologist, as in the remark, which sounds like a precognition of DNA, that "whatever passions a man finds himself in at the time when he grants me life I will surely bring those along into the world." However that may be, the riddles are grist for Mr. Solomon's psychoanalytic mode, which he supports with quotations from Bakhtin, Ricoeur, and the like. The author's assertion that "materials such as these are better suited for psychological analysis than are structural works of art," is indisputable.

Oddly, Mr. Solomon does not mention the recently discovered two-page account in Mozart's hand of his expenses and income ("My cash") for 1786, first published in the *Prince Lichnowsky Newsletter* for November 1993,[13] but the sequence of numbers "99, 55, 33, 66, 88" under the expenditures surely indicates a secret cipher.

In all but a few instances Mozart signed himself "Wolfgang Amadé," and his marriage contract reads Wolfgang Amadé Mozart." In his preliminary marriage documents, however, and in his own hand in the petition to the Police for permission to marry, as well as in the marriage register at St. Stephen's Cathedral, Vienna, 4 August 1784, the name is Wolfgang Adam Mozart." What could he have meant by this reference to the progenitor of mankind?

---

[13] The motto of this curious publication, launched in Austria in 1991, is "All the News that fits the Prince."

Love in a Cold Climate

hen the correspondence[1] between Pyotr Ilich Tchaikovsky and Nadezhda Filaretovna von Meck began, in December 1876, the bachelor of thirty-six was the most promising of Russian composers and the most highly regarded abroad; four months earlier, at Bayreuth for the first *Ring of the Nibelung*, he had been warmly—he thought obsequiously—received by Liszt. Shortly after returning from Germany, morbidly fearful of public exposure of his homosexuality, he wrote to his homosexual brother Modest: "I should like to marry or enter into an open liaison with some woman so as to shut the mouths of assorted contemptible gossipers." The woman of his dreams, or nightmares, should not expect any consummation of conjugal rights.

Nadezhda Filaretovna was forty-five, recently widowed, prodigally wealthy—her husband's rise from engineer to railroad tycoon is generally attributed to her business acumen—and passionately musical. Her household staff included a violinist ("I have a good Stradivarius") and a cellist, and in the summer months it would soon include the teenage Claude Debussy, who could read orchestral scores at the piano and play piano duets with her. She had been a polyphiloprogenitive, if not a strictly faithful, wife: her husband's discovery that the youngest and favorite of her eighteen children was illegitimate had brought on his fatal heart attack; years later, when one of her daughters revealed the secret of the illegitimacy to one of her sons-in-law—as well as, probably, the secret that the child's father was also the husband of her eldest daughter—he would use it to blackmail her.

Two brief exchanges are followed by Mme von Meck's third letter, which runs to nearly 1,500 words and includes three musical quotations from Tchaikovsky's early opera *Oprichnik*, which now embarrassed him ("poor stuff, written hastily and in places without inspiration"), but which she would "like to die hearing." Before dying, however, she wants him to contrive a four-hand fu-

---

[1] *"To my best friend": Correspondence between Tchaikovsky and Nadezhda von Meck (1876–1878)*, translated by Galina von Meck, edited by Edward Garden and Nigel Gotteri, with an introduction by Edward Garden. New York: Oxford University Press, 1993.

neral march from it. At the instigation of their mutual friend, Nikolai Rubinstein, virtuoso pianist and Tchaikovsky's superior at the Moscow Conservatory, the financially straitened composer had written her asking for a loan. Rubinstein suggested that she commission pieces from him, thus initiating her role as Tchaikovsky's benefactress.

Tchaikovsky's commensurately expanded third letter remarks on her apparent lack of interest in meeting him. She replies that the reasons he supposes for this are mistaken, but whatever the right ones—"the more fascinated I am by you, the more I fear acquaintance"—the condition that they never meet seems to have been understood. They lived near each other at times, saw each other at a distance in the theater—she had first glimpsed him bowing, "hurriedly and reluctantly," after a performance of one of his works—and twice by accident close up, Tchaikovsky raising his hat as they silently passed by. The *Oprichnik* march makes her "nerves tingle [and] want to cry, want to die, want another life."

The principal event in their personal lives during the two-years covered by the correspondence in the present selection is Tchaikovsky's marriage. He did not know Antonina Ivanovna Miliukova when in May 1877 he received her declaration of love. Ignoring the aberrancy of her behavior, he replied and was soon agreeing to see her, partly because she had threatened suicide if he did not. He took the precaution of interviewing her former piano teacher at the Conservatory, but went to the meeting undeterred by this colleague's uncomplimentary description of her.

Tchaikovsky immediately recognized that he and Antonina Ivanovna had nothing in common ("she's a very limited person," he confided to his brother Anatoly), were in fact extreme opposites in every way, and he felt "total repugnance" for her physical presence. That he nevertheless proposed to her on his second and last visit before their nuptials confirms that his rational faculties had suffered a breakdown. Later, to Mme von Meck, he would blame his self-destructive act on "fate," on family and social pressures—above all his eighty-two-year-old father's long-standing wish to see him married—and on his unbalanced mental state at the time. She urged him to seek a divorce, promising a huge settlement on his wife, but this did not take place, and the marriage would harrow him until 1881, when his publisher learned that Antonina Tchaikovskaya had abandoned an illegitimate child—she had several of them in all—in a foundling home. Four years after Tchaikovsky's death, she was committed to an insane asylum near St. Petersburg, where she died in 1917.

The wedding, July 18, 1877, was semi-secret and somber, devoid of all epithalamia. The unimaginably awful honeymoon began with a visit to his family in St. Petersburg. During the train journey he was rescued from the obligation to converse with his bride by a chance fellow passenger, Prince Meshchersky, an intimate friend from his years at the St. Petersburg School of Jurisprudence. He was rescued again in a Petersburg hotel by doses of valerian. After returning to Moscow for a similar visit to her "weird family," as Tchaikovsky described it, she remained in the city to prepare their future residence, while he left for Kiev and Kamenka. Back in Moscow at the end of September, he attempted to commit suicide by exposure, wading into the icy Moscow River. On October 6 he fled to St. Petersburg, where a doctor told him he could recover his equilibrium only by a permanent separation from his wife. Later, from Switzerland, he portrayed her to Mme von Meck in a letter that displays the mordant side of his personality. She is twenty-eight, he says, which was old by the current parameters of nubility, as well as

> fairly unhandsome in appearance.... Her eyes are ... expressionless; her lips are too thin.... She is very affected and there is not a single movement or gesture which is straightforward.... That was the easy part of the description. But, now that I come to describe her character and intellect, I meet an unsurmountable difficulty. Her head and heart are both completely empty.... She has never once expressed a single idea.... Never once did she display the least desire to find out what I was doing.... She had told me that she had been in love with me for four years; and also that she was quite a reasonable musician ... [yet] she didn't know a *single note of my compositions* and ... had never been to concerts ... of the Musical Society, while knowing that she could see the object of her four-year love there at any time. She is very garrulous.... Hour by hour she would tell me endless stories about the countless men who had nursed tender feelings for her. Most frequently they were generals, nephews of famous bankers, and even members of the imperial family....

The compensating, retributive event of Tchaikovsky's life occurred soon after, when Mme von Meck responded to his appeal for money with a generous sum and a pledge that henceforth he would receive a monthly allowance of 1500 francs. The "well-known-unknown" ideal friend, who posed no threat of personal contact, now became his provider as well. For a time, Tchaikovsky's sister sheltered and coped with his wife, but he continued to support her from his new stipend. Before long, however, he was lamenting to Mme von Meck that the "unbearable shackle" has "brazenly taken off her mask" and is sending him letters that show her to be "untruthful and vicious." He can no longer bear the sound of her name or anything that reminds him of her, he says, and from then on both correspondents refer to her as "a certain personage," or "a certain matter."

If Mme von Meck's distancing congratulatory letter on receiving Tchaikovsky's news of his engagement betrays a twinge of disappointment, her elation on hearing of the fiasco of the marriage is undisguised. "Pyotr Ilich," she asks, "have you ever loved? I think not. You love music too much to be able to fall in love with a woman," which is to forget such lovers of music *and* women as Liszt and Wagner. She persists: "Have you ever known non-Platonic love?" And he equivocates, "Yes and no," then formulates her question in a different way: has he ever experienced "full happiness in love." The answer to this is a vehement "no, no, and again no," but he tells her to look for the answer to the question in his music. (Chopin was "an awful character," she wrote later, "one can hear it in his music.") In dismissing platonic love as semi-love, "not the feeling that goes deep into a person's flesh and blood," she remarks parenthetically that this was "not at all the way Plato loved," unwittingly brushing against the truth. But the last part of this cryptic, venturesome letter is missing, as are all passages in the correspondence that would seem to contain references to his sexual inclinations. Modest was an efficient censor, both for his brother and himself, going so far in his own case as to become the tutor of a nine-year-old deaf-mute who also became his charge and, to judge from an allusion to the relationship by Tchaikovsky, his catamite.

In fact Mme von Meck seems to have had no inkling of Tchaikovsky's sexual inclinations, not only failing to recognize his account of the marriage as a description of sexual panic, but actually concluding that Antonina Ivanovna did not want to have his child. She would soon revise this assumption, telling him that his wife must be made to realize that "one person seeks only *certain* marital relations and another will not be satisfied *with only that one thing*" (her emphasis), which seems to mean that she thought sexual intercourse was the only marital relationship that Antonina Ivanovna was capable of sharing with him—as may have been the case with von Meck's husband in her own marriage. Yet one wonders how this worldly, experienced woman could fail to recognize the sexual temperament behind Tchaikovsky's avowed wish for her to comfort him "like a child in its mother's arms," and his wish to be for his younger brothers "what a mother is for her children," knowing "the indelible mark that maternal caresses leave on a child's heart." Leo Tolstoy was more percipient. After spending two evenings in Moscow with the composer, and weeping during a performance of his first string quartet, the author of the "excruciatingly brilliant" *The Death of Ivan Ilich*, as Tchaikovsky called it, would remember him after his death as "a man about whom there was something not altogether clear."

By the end of the first year, both correspondents are emotionally dependent on their "chats" with each other. "I can't sleep and I am sitting down for another chat with you," Tchaikovsky begins a letter to his mother-confessor. "I am now used to telling you everything," he says, while assiduously avoiding any reference to the real reason for his marriage and its dissolution. Mme von Meck decides that this is the propitious moment to adopt the intimate form of address, but she has not yet taken the full measure of his intensely private, hypersensitive nature. He declines her proposal, protesting that the "thou" form would be awkward for him, the breaking of a convention on which he depends. In an ambivalent afterthought, prompted, perhaps, by a reminder that she is his patroness, he concedes that he might be able to adjust to the change, although the form of address will not affect the feeling.

"Our sufferings are identical," Tchaikovsky avers at one point, and Mme von Meck is constantly noting the similarities between them, one of which is "our need for profound emotions," as distinguished from "accepted" ones. A "supernatural affinity of ideas and feelings [is] apparent in almost every one of our letters," she grandly claims. Yet the more open they are with each other, the more they expose the antagonisms in their tastes and temperaments, leading the reader to suspect that Tchaikovsky would have been even more miserable, however differently, if he had married her instead of Antonina Ivanovna. Her favorite pastimes at Brailov, her vast Ukrainian estate, are billiards, boating ("I always take the helm"), driving a trap, and target practice with a revolver, none of which can have greatly appealed to him. Their "philosophies" are in contradiction. He abhors the "realism," or "ideal materialism," that she professes, and takes "the liberty of disputing your description of yourself." A true realist, he corrects her, would "never seek consolation and reconciliation in music, ... the most utterly ideal of all the arts.... The realist cares nothing for art, especially music, for music responds to an inquiry which forms no part of his limited nature." The quality of character common to both of their personalities, he insists, is "misanthropy."

Nor do they agree about religion: "People like Spinoza, Goethe, and Kant have managed without [it]," he observes, and "intelligent people must be skeptics"; like you, "I've lost all faith in doctrine long ago." But he warns that "those who break with traditional beliefs rush vainly from one philosophical theory to another without finding the strength with which believers are armed." He cannot accept the notion of immortality—"and, anyway, would it be eternal happiness?"—yet is unable to reconcile himself to the thought that his mother, who died from cholera when he was fourteen, the revenant he cannot exorcise, has disappeared forever. For him, if not for Mme von Meck, the rituals of the Orthodox Church have "retained much poetic charm," and the Liturgy of St. John Chrysostom is "one of the greatest of all artistic creations," as indeed Tchaikovsky's setting of it is one of his.

Worse still, the "beloved friends" are far apart on important musical judgments, and Mozart's music uncovers the unabridgeable gulf between them. She reviles it as "vacuous," "a pleasing tickling of the ears" that cannot "move a single fiber of the human soul." Her tone is ranting:

> I love depth, power, grandeur.... I can't have anything superficial, objective.... He is so ... imperturbably jolly that it arouses my indignation.... I wonder how someone who had written such a gripping and shattering thing as the first movement of the Fourth Symphony in F minor can be enthusiastic about Mozart.

"Of the old classics in music," she tells him, "I like Bach, Beethoven, and Hummel [!!] in his two concertos." Tchaikovsky, who "bows" before Beethoven but does not "love" him, only partly conceals the extent to which his patience must have been tried: "Nobody has ever expressed so beautifully in music the feeling of resigned and hopeless grief" as Mozart in the Adagio of the G minor Quintet. Further, "I love the music of *Don Giovanni* so much ... that I can't speak calmly about it.... It is thanks to Mozart that I dedicated my life to music."

Of the great composers only Schumann, whom she compares unfavorably in some respects to Tchaikovsky, is mutually admired in something of the same way. True, both correspondents abominate Brahms, whose first symphony Tchaikovsky condemns as "dark, cold, and full of pretensions to profundity," but they do not know much of his music. Mme von Meck scorns Wagner as "a profaner of art," but Tchaikovsky recognizes the "genius" in this "symphonist by nature," paralyzed "by the theory he has invented." *Die Walküre* does not have a "single broad, complete melody which allows the singer room to blossom," he continues, and though the *Ring* includes "plenty of passages of surprising, but purely symphonic, power," some of them, including the "Ride of the Valkyries," make a "huge impression" in the concert hall but "lose all pictorial effect in the theatre." Tchaikovsky confided his deeper appreciation of Wagner to Modest— "something has been achieved at Bayreuth which our children and great-grandchildren will not forget"—no doubt foreseeing that Mme von Meck would dispute the appraisal, but in a letter to her beyond the short period of the present book, he describes Wagner's musical talent as "colossal."

The first movement of Tchaikovsky's Violin Concerto does not affect her as much as "those works of his in which one hears despondency or turbulent passion," she tells him, spelling out the cathexis in his music that had infatuated her in the first place. *Francesca da Rimini* excites these emotions in her, while *Marche Slav*, of all pieces, brings "such bliss that the tears come to my eyes." Tears well up frequently and readily in both of them, along with, in her case, instant prostration. In his, a "flood" of them can induce sound sleep.

Their literary perspectives rarely align. When Tchaikovsky discloses his intention to compose an opera on *Eugene Onegin*, a poem that has enthralled him since childhood, she flaunts her preference for Pisarev and Chernyshevsky, which "will tell you my attitude to Pushkin." He challenges this:

> Forgive my defending Pushkin and attacking Pisarev ... but I respect the former as much as I detest the latter.... [In Pushkin] there is something in the very verse, in the succession of sounds, which penetrates to the very depth of the soul. That *something is music.*

When she enthuses over Nekrasov, he puts her down with: "Talent ... doesn't make an artist.... [H]is last works are unbearably boring, and the aim of his satire is shallow, vulgar, trivial ... humor of the lowest kind." In one of his many letters to the Grand Duke and poetaster Konstantin Romanov, Nekrasov's muse is described as "crawling along the ground."

The composer's letters to his brother Anatoly indicate that the obligation to write to his "best friend" could become onerous, as it frequently was in the 1880s. "It is hard forever to be thanking and thanking," he complains, and "one cannot keep on inventing new phrases to express gratitude." On receiving an eight-page letter from her, he explains that "of course I had to reply with a long letter, too." Twice in the autumn of 1878 he turns down proposals to reside for a spell on the opposite side of Lake Como from her, but when she moves to her Villa Oppenheim on the outskirts of Florence, he accepts her invitation to live in an apartment on the same Viale and only three hundred yards away: "The knowledge that I'll be close to you will make me feel warm and comfortable." To avoid encounters, she gives him advance notice of the hours of her outings, but he is soon tattling to Anatoly: "I feel embarrassed in general at her being so near.... When she passes my house, she stops [her carriage] and tries to get a glimpse of me"—as, it follows, he did of her—whereupon he closed the shutters after dark. To Modest he wrote that he found her physical proximity "oppressive," and, after she had left Florence, told him of his "astonishment" at missing her, which casts his hundred-percent sincerity at other times into doubt but helps to prepare readers of his biography for his vindictive outbursts against her a dozen years later when she canceled his allowance: "My confidence in her unbounded readiness to support me ... has been deceived.... I know perfectly well that she's still terribly rich."

Mme von Meck's inquiries about his creative processes are almost always rewarded. He composes some pieces in response to an "irresistible inner need," others on "request" or "to order," but the quality is independent of the circumstance. The "moment of emotional intensity" is not the determinant because feelings are "always expressed retrospectively.... What was written in the heat of the moment has to be corrected, filled out." She wishes to know whether in the Scherzo of the Fourth Symphony the melody or the pizzicato instrumentation came to him first. He tells her, in a letter written in exalté mood—"everything I have written today will have the power to enter the heart and make a lasting impression on it"—that his musical ideas and their orchestration are conceived simultaneously. So, too, a melody can never appear in his head apart from its harmony and rhythm. When she presses him to reveal the "program" of the Fourth, which is dedicated to her and has made her immortal, he asks, reasonably, "How can one recount the undefined feelings one goes through when an instrumental composition without a definite subject is being written?" but then provides a jejune commentary, illustrating it with the four principal themes of the first movement, tagging them "Fate" motive (of the introduction and recurrently), the "fruitless languishing" motive, the "daydreams," and the "happiness" motive. The author of so many melodies now abused by "tenors" and "baritones" in their showers does not reveal to her that he sings loudly while composing.

The editing of *To My Best Friend* is unsatisfactory on several counts. Only the first thirty-eight letters are given in their entirety, and many of the subsequent 238 (of a total of 1200 for the thirteen-year period) are merely summarized (wholly, as well as in part), which may be justified in the case of the discursive Mme von Meck, but not in that of Tchaikovsky, an elegant and resourceful writer whose lucid expositions and arguments must to some extent reflect his seven years as a student in the St. Petersburg School of Jurisprudence. One of the editors tells us that the translations are "substantially" those of Galina von Meck (d. 1985), Nadezhda's granddaughter and Tchaikovsky's great-niece—Nadezhda's second son had married the composer's niece—but that her renderings of certain unspecified musical particulars had to be revised. Other improvements are said to include the matching of colloquialisms and archaisms with "their counterparts in English," but the result is a considerable number of jarring solecisms; *viz*, Tchaikovsky enjoys "tickling the ivories."

Equivalencies for rubles and francs in 1990s yen are not provided, leaving the reader with no idea of the size of Mme von Meck's allowance, and when the correspondents do not include New Style, as well as Old Style, dates, neither do the editors. Most frustrating of all, however, is the indexing of the wife of

Alexander Volshin as "E. K." (Elizaveta Karlovna in other books) "*née* von Meck," without identifying her as Nadezhda Filaretovna's oldest daughter, born 1848. John Warrack's *Tchaikovsky* (London, 1973) gives the full genealogical tree.

* * *

In the fourth and final volume of his comprehensive biography, David Brown's evaluations of the music composed during Tchaikovsky's last years have not changed since his 1981 essay in *Grove's Dictionary of Music and Musicians*. He objected there that the scenario of *Shchelkunchik* (the onomatopoeic original of the *Nutcracker*)

> provided no opportunity for the expression of human feelings beyond the most trivial, confining Tchaikovsky mostly to the world of tinsel, sweets and fantasy. [The music] is essentially simple, even trite.... There is no really strong tune anywhere in the work.

The new book downgrades the masterpiece still further, excluding it and its "appalling limitations" of subject not only from the company of Tchaikovsky's "greatest compositions," *The Sleeping Beauty*, the Sixth Symphony, "perhaps" *Eugene Onegin*, but also from that of the slightly lower category of his "finest works," the Fifth Symphony and *Pikovaya Dama*. "Both *Swan Lake* and *The Sleeping Beauty* had been dramatically meaty and deeply serious," Brown polemicizes, whereas *Shchelkunchik* is "meaningless in the profoundest sense." Precisely. And for these reasons—its vegetarian avoidance of meaty drama, and the absence of deep seriousness, with the despair, yearning, and pleas for sympathy that this entails—many will continue to prefer the ballet to the other two, as well as protest that the tune at the beginning of Act II, repeated in the Apotheosis, is one of the most affecting Tchaikovsky ever wrote.

Some listeners will also demur from Brown's classification of the Sixth Symphony as "stupendous"; by their lights, the maudlin song in the first movement and the swirling scales in the march come dangerously close to high camp. Neither here nor in his second volume, *The Crisis Years*, 1874–1878, does Brown attempt to refute Vladimir Nabokov's crucial reservation about Tchaikovsky's *Eugene Onegin*, namely that Pushkin's people are beyond operatic characterization.

Tchaikovsky recognized that *Onegin* "does not give scope to full operatic treatment," yet believed that "the richness of the poetry, the simple, human subject ... will compensate for whatever it lacks in other ways." Rich poetry is not a necessary ingredient for opera, however, and to cast a narrative poem in an operatic mold seems possible only by resorting, as Wagner did, to declamation. *Onegin* is additionally handicapped by its own institutional status as the best-known poem in the language. The fault of the libretto is not in its language, which incorporates a high proportion of Pushkin's lines, but in the nature of the operatic medium, which cannot project the psychology and the sophistication of the poem.

Tchaikovsky was deeply mistaken in his belief that Pushkin's "simple, human subject" would compensate for what the poem "lacks in other ways," though in truth the opera's insufficiencies lie in the limitations of the music, not in those of the poem—an unusual case in that the music in other operas (Mozart's) says so much more than the words, and mistaken in his belief that he could identify with people and situations in the story and compose music that would portray Tatyana's feelings.

Vladimir Nabokov's criticisms are justified: "The long-drawn and dejected tone of the musical phrase '*Nachryom pozhaluy*' ('Yes, if you like, let's start'), given to the tenor ... makes a whining weakling of Pushkin's virile Lenski...." Before the duel, as well, Lenski is in a trance-like, absent, psychologically complex state, but from his aria, the high point of the opera, the audience is aware of no more than the two-way emotional pull.

Nabokov also argues convincingly that Pushkin does not show Tatyana's decision to remain with her husband to be irrevocable: "Her answer to Onegin does not at all ring with sure dignified finality, as commentators have supposed it to do. Mark the intonations in XLVII, the speech, the anguished, poignant, palpitating, almost voluptuous, almost alluring enjambments (1-2, 2-3, 3-4, 5-6, 6-7, 8-9, 10-11), a veritable orgy of run-ons, culminating in a love that must have made Eugene's experienced heart leap with joy."

Further, the opera's final scene is superfluous, having been obviated in the previous one by the aria of Tatyana's husband, for which Pushkin does not have any parallel. Tchaikovsky's reason for interpolating the piece, to give the husband reality, is obvious and valid, but the subsequent scene comes as an anti-climax. "In the opera ... everything ... insults Pushkin's masterpiece," Nabokov writes, with more than a little exaggeration, but he should have included Tchaikovsky's copy of the poem among the appendices to his edition of it. The composer's annotations, alterations, and adaptations, are a valuable monitory of the countless hazards in attempting to adapt a work of art from one medium to another.

Brown's long awaited account of Tchaikovsky's last years contains no surprises. On the subject of the von Meck correspondence, Brown defines the relationship for her, as for Tchaikovsky as, apparently,

Revulsion against physical relations with the opposite sex. The death of her husband in 1876 had released her from sexual demands, and, now, evidently frigid, she could idealize Tchaikovsky as revealed in his music.

To bear a love-child at age forty-one, however, and to conduct a love affair with its father, her husband's young secretary—*after* the birth, for all anyone knows, as well as before—is hardly a sign of frigidity. Her husband's belief that the child was his indicates that she had been cohabiting with the two men contemporaneously.

Brown's discussion of the composer's death merely endorses Alexandra Orlova's suicide-by-poison theory[2] as more plausible than Alexander Poznansky's more thoroughly elucidated and convincing version of the death by cholera and uremia in his *Tchaikovsky: The Quest for the Inner Man*.[3] The "inner man" is the bowdlerized one, of course, deleted first by his brother, then by Soviet moralists. Because of the lack of documents, itself an *argumentum ex absentia* indictment, the book has been attacked for turning suppositions into facts and filling lacunas by speculation and invention. Poznansky's Tchaikovsky is sexually involved with his valet and other male servants, with his brother and nephew (the dedicatee of the Sixth Symphony), with male prostitutes, with friends in his homosexual entourage—some of whom, Prince Vladimir Argutinsky-Dolgorukov for one, and Modest himself for a time, would later join the entourage of Serge Diaghilev. Poznansky's critics have pointed to the absence of proof for active relationships with any of these younger men.[4] But Tchaikovsky himself provided an answer in the one letter to Modest that escaped his "scissors." Printed in the USSR in 1940 in a book suppressed before publication, a non-book therefore, it may be taken as an example in kind of excised passages: "I am so confirmed in my habits and tastes," the composer wrote, "that it is impossible to cast them off like an old glove. Besides, I am far from possessing an iron will and since writing to you I have already given way three times to my natural inclinations."

The known facts about Tchaikovsky's death are as follows. In St. Petersburg, on October 28, 1893, the composer conducted the premiere of his "Sixth

---

[2] Alexandra Orlova, *Tchaikovsky: A Self-Portrait*, translated by R. M. Davidson, with a foreword by David Brown. Oxford: Oxford University Press, 1990.

[3] Alexander Poznansky, *Tchaikovsky: The Quest for the Inner Man*. New York: Schirmer, 1991.

[4] Tchaikovsky's inscription to one of them on a copy of the Bieber (Hamburg) photograph, in Stravinsky's possession, uses the feminine form of address.

Symphony in B minor," as the program listed it. The four rehearsals had been enervating; bewildered by the music, the orchestra could not play it with any confidence, and the work did not make much impression at the concert. But if Tchaikovsky were greatly upset, he did not show it. Three days later he attended a performance of Anton Rubinstein's opera *The Maccabees*, and the day after that a play by Ostrovsky, dining afterward at Leiner's restaurant with, among others, the young Alexander Glazunov. Shortly after 1 a.m. Tchaikovsky walked with Modest to his apartment. The next day, November 2, the composer complained of upset stomach during the night, but nevertheless went out in the late morning.

From here on the history is debatable. At lunch, Modest was to claim, Tchaikovsky drank a glass of unboiled water, then retired to his room and slept; but Modest was only sporadically present on November 2 (owing to rehearsals of a comedy of his that opened on the night of his brother's funeral and was described in the press as "the second burial of the day"). In the early evening Tchaikovsky's condition was radically worse, and a doctor, Vladimir Bertenson, was sent for; he arrived sometime after 8 p.m. Seeing that the illness was serious, suspecting cholera but never having treated the disease, he called for his brother, Lev Bertenson, a high-ranking imperial court physician, who arrived at ten and by midnight had diagnosed cholera in the collapse stage.

Brown rejects this account on grounds that the incubation period for cholera is at least twelve hours, that unboiled water would certainly not have been on Modest's table. Moreover, Brown contends that what happened on November 6, after the composer's death, is inconsistent with a government regulation that the corpses of cholera victims must be removed immediately and in closed coffins, whereas Tchaikovsky's body was openly displayed in Modest's apartment, where two requiem services were held on November 6, one of them with the male chorus of the Imperial Opera singing the liturgy in an adjoining room, and two more on November 7, also with choruses. Rimsky-Korsakov, paying his respects, was surprised to see a cellist of his acquaintance kissing the deceased composer's uncovered face and head.

Poznansky rebuts these objections with the arguments that the cholera bacillus could have been ingested in food—unboiled water was not the only carrier—and that the period of incubation might have been a day or longer. He also cites a resolution of the Control Medical Council in the spring of 1893 to the effect that by that date cholera was considered less contagious than had been supposed, and that quarantines in cholera deaths were no longer compulsory: funerals could be public and open caskets allowed. Tchaikovsky's was closed when it was taken to Kazan Cathedral from Modest's apartment, where, in the presence of a sanitary inspector and police, the body had been wrapped in a sheet soaked in mercuric chloride against the spread of the disease.

Poznansky's hour-to-hour medical history, derived from the accounts of doctors and other witnesses and recounted by newspapers, suggests that Tchaikovsky may have recovered from the cholera: after the crisis in the night of November 2–3 his condition improved, for which reason the doctors delayed the hot-bath treatment traditionally prescribed for cholera patients until November 5, and then only in the hope of galvanizing his totally inactive kidneys. The ultimate cause of death seems to have been uremia. A medical bulletin issued by Lev Bertenson after the bath had failed to restore the kidney function announced "complete retention of the urine," and a second bulletin, posted at half-past ten in the evening, states that a sanitation inspector and police official had been called. Tchaikovsky died at a few minutes after three in the morning.

Alexandra Orlova's very different version of the death was told to her in 1966 by an octogenarian alumnus of the School of Jurisprudence, who had heard it in 1913 from the widow of a certain N. B. Jacobi, an official in the Department of Criminal Appeal. Mme Jacobi reportedly said that because Tchaikovsky had been paying "improper attention" to the young nephew of a Count Stenbock-Fermor, the latter wrote a letter complaining to the Tsar and gave it to Jacobi for delivery. As the widow's narrative continues, Tchaikovsky was summoned to Jacobi's apartment and tried before a kangaroo court consisting of eight of his former fellow students at the School of Jurisprudence. The composer was told that the honor of the School must be protected from the public scandal that would result unless the letter was suppressed, which could be effected only by the event of his death. As Mme Jacobi recalled, twenty years later, the proceedings lasted five hours, after which Tchaikovsky staggered outside. A day or two hence he committed suicide by drinking unboiled water, or taking poison, or both.

Poznansky does not dignify this tale with a refutation, but if he had, his first item would surely be that the Tsar, who knew Tchaikovsky, attended performances and rehearsals of his theater works, had granted him a lifetime pension, and was aware of his friendship with the Grand Duke, could not conceivably compromise himself by making the letter public; Tchaikovsky, with Tolstoy, was unassailably Russia's most famous creative artist, and any damage to his name would be against the national interest. (Further, would Jacobi have dared to open a letter addressed to the tsar?) The second item would be that the eight prigs of the jury, Tchaikovsky's only surviving classmates in the St. Petersburg area, included at least three good friends, the homosexual Prince Meshchersky, the composer's music publisher Bessel, and Vladimir Gerard, who delivered the graveside oration and is therefore unlikely to have voted for a death sentence; a photograph of him with the composer is still exhibited in the Tchaikovsky Museum at Klin. Utterly preposterous, too, is the thought of Tchaikovsky enduring denunciations of himself for five hours. But the weakest part of the Orlova case is that her story asks the reader to believe that the published medical history is actually a charade, a well-organized cover-up operation carried out by four deliberately falsifying doctors, a sanitary inspector, and the police.

No music has been subjected to as much familiarity, that great destroyer of originality, as that of Pyotr Ilich Tchaikovsky, but now, on the first centenary of his death, he remains a great original.

Diaghilev

Serge Diaghilev has never loomed larger than at present, despite the intangibility of his legacy. In Lynn Garafola's artistic, social and economic history of the Ballets Russes (1909–1929),[1] a full-length intellectual portrait of the great impresario emerges for the first time. Her skillfully written, critically perceptive, and compendious book is indispensable to anyone interested in what from our distance is clearly seen as this century's most fascinating movement in the arts.

Garafola shifts more perspectives than can be mentioned in a short review. Sufficient to say that Isadora Duncan, Konstantin Stanislavsky and Vsevolod Meyerhold are given greater importance than heretofore, as is Bronislava Nijinska, whose most durable ballet, *Les Noces*, was influenced both by Meyerhold and by the Constructivist painters Malevich and Tatlin. The role of Jean Cocteau, "gadfly of modernism," is also reassessed upward: in the years 1923–1926, Diaghilev's troupe "appeared to be a family begotten by Cocteau," Garafola writes. But the most consequential part of the Cocteau realignment is in her argument that his ballet *Parade* (1917) owed a debt to Italian Futurism, which, as she convincingly shows, had a more profound and lasting effect on Diaghilev than has been generally recognized.

A new emphasis is also placed on the anti-academic and "liberating aesthetic of Michel Fokine," who replaced the *poupée* ballerina of the Petipa period, during which the corps de ballets was little more than a frame for the solo dancer, with "ballet democracy" as expressed in harmonious groupings and hand-holding circles. Garafola does not comment on these Fokine features in the choreography of *The Rite of Spring*, or note that the hand-to-cheek gesture, already introduced in *Firebird*, is not likely to have been coincidentally discovered by Nijinsky, who alone is credited with the dances. Yet Bronislava Nijinska's statement that the last dance was her brother's "own" can only mean that Fokine had to some extent blocked out the remainder of the ballet before Nijinsky superseded him in June 1912.

[1] *Diaghilev's Ballets Russes*, by Lynn Garafola. New York: Oxford University Press, 1989.

Garafola's psychosexual approach to the ambisexual Nijinsky—a dancer "Masculine in the power of his leaps, feminine in the curving delicacy of his arms ... a living incarnation of the third sex"—reminds us that the Ballets Russes helped to make Uranianism, Sapphism, and androgynism acceptable (Auden's "What mad Nijinsky wrote / About Diaghilev / Is true of the normal heart"), and without neglecting Léon Bakst's heterosexual imagination, as the see-through harem pants of his odalisques attest. Nijinsky's uncertainty of his sexual identity is reflected in his Debussy ballets. In *The Afternoon of a Faun*, "the overt homosexual" declares himself "a covert heterosexual" who ultimately opts for "the safe haven of self-gratification"; and in *Jeux*, the one male and two female dancers who "flirt, embrace, pair off, exchange partners" are, in the choreographer's words, "three young men making love to each other." Alert to the general in the particular, Garafola describes the "Chosen Virgin" in Nijinsky's *The Rite of Spring*, as "a creation of twentieth-century male anxiety." Since the sacrificial maiden was conceived not by Nijinsky, however, but by Stravinsky, one of the least sexually "anxious" male artists of the era, "symbol" would seem more apt than "creation."

Diaghilev's intuitive genius and genius in artistic matchmaking, his depth of culture and manifold musical and theatrical talents are in evidence throughout the book. On the other side, he had a "streak of cruelty," was subject to "fits of panic and hysteria," and vindictiveness was one of his most pronounced qualities. Autocratic in both private and professional life, he abused his power to hire and fire in the pre-union 1920s, and underpaid rank and file dancers while overpaying his "stars"—which can be accounted for, if not excused, by his perpetual need of quick transfusions of money and his background of immense wealth in a Russia that had only recently emancipated the serfs. His high-handedness extended to his collaborations. He suppressed Cocteau's spoken text in *Parade*, pruned "bars and passages" as well as changed "chords, keys and tempi" in Ottorino Respighi's arrangement of Rossini pieces for the ballet *La Boutique fantasque*, and instructed his stage designers as to how their sets should look, including the shades of colors to be used. But this uncompromising man who quite wrongly informed Ravel that *La Valse* was not a ballet, dropped whole numbers from *Apollo* when Stravinsky was absent, and dictated to Picasso, had a unifying vision of his ballets not always shared by the creators of their constituent parts.

Garafola's analyses of the structure of Ballets Russes audiences are almost as engaging as her discussions of artistic innovations. Apart from incidental dance scenes in opera, ballet did not have an audience in the West before Diaghilev. Having begun as a producer of opera, he apparently understood how to effect the transition of the musical audience to the choreographic. Subscribers' rosters for his early Paris seasons establish that his "public" was an "amalgam of financiers, bankers and diplomats, members of the city's foreign and Franco-Jewish communities," assorted "personalities" from the art world, and a leavening of *le gratin*, the upper crust, including such bluebloods as the Comtesse Greffühle, the model for Proust's Duchesse de Guermantes.

Some readers may object that the lists detailing sums in francs and pounds are meaningful only to cambists who can equate them to present-day currencies, but the eye jumps over the figures. More importantly, the heretofore unexplored commercial history of the company reveals the extent to which money influenced artistic considerations. Soon after Coco Chanel sponsored the 1920 revival of *The Rite of Spring*, the Ballets Russes became a Chanel show room—her costumes for *Le Train Bleu* "might have come from her customers' wardrobes," Garafola remarks—as well as a Lanvin, and a Hermès. In the 1920s, stripped of his Russian sources of wealth, Diaghilev was obliged to cater to Parisian fashion and consumer chic. But his achievement lies in his "sense of the marketplace," and the "teaming of art and enterprise to serve the traditional ends of high art."

Does Garafola go too far in asserting that "far more than Stravinsky, period modernism's intriguing blend of tradition and experiment was spearheaded by Diaghilev"? True, by choosing "raw" materials from the eighteenth-century Diaghilev determined the stylistic direction and some of the musical parameters of the work. But these have nothing to do with the *Pulcinella* brand of modernism—"period modernism" is the book's buzz word—nor was Diaghilev pleased with what he heard. By the same token, the modernist identity of the Ballets Russes might be attributed primarily to music. Manifestly, the label did not apply before *Firebird*, *Petrushka* and *The Rite of Spring*. In the *Rite*, Garafola says, Nijinsky "created a twentieth-century icon, a summation of modernism at its most subversive." But surely this is what the music did, the ballet and its choreography having disappeared after a few performances, and surely it was the music that, willy-nilly, made the Ballets Russes the proprietor of a modernist image beyond the reach of its painters and choreographers.

The division of the book into chapters by subject—art, enterprise, audience—rather than straight all-encompassing chronological history inevitably involves an amount of repetition. But this is a small price to pay for the most comprehensive book so far published about Diaghilev's Ballets Russes.

Massine Centenary

The late Señor García-Márquez asserts[1] that Léonide Massine, "titan of the dance" and "artistic giant," was "Diaghilev's greatest creation—a young man made of uncommonly rich clay which Diaghilev modeled for the realization of his own needs." Actually Diaghilev's greatest creation was the Ballets Russes, but the author's claim makes an important distinction. Whereas Diaghilev gave Stravinsky and Nijinsky the opportunity to become what they already were, Massine had to be created—nurtured, trained, artistically educated, socially refined, endowed with an identity, and even taught to dance: the eighteen-year-old was primarily an actor when Diaghilev met him. The molding process continued as long as they were together.

These seven years occupy some 140 pages, while only thirty suffice to chronicle the seven lean ones that follow. Whereas Diaghilev provides his protégé with the greatest dancing masters, when teaching him music, the great impresario himself goes to the piano and plays opera and other scores. He also shows him how to draw, selects a library for him, and becomes his *cicerone* in Italy, where, "among other painters," the young man "admires Donatello." While on an automobile excursion in Tuscany, Massine writes to a friend that the landscape is that "of all Renaissance artists who have glorified ... sunsets." (*Sunsets?*) Moving on to Ravenna, he amazes historically minded readers by finding "much to admire in the sixteenth-century Byzantine mosaics."

Nevertheless, the pupil was a quick learner with native, especially histrionic gifts. And he was young. It seems scarcely credible that after only five months with Diaghilev, and still only eighteen, Massine is playing the title role in the Strauss-Hofmannsthal *Josephslegende*, which is to say working with the greatest theatrical team of the age. Hofmannsthal wrote to Strauss: "Our Joseph has just the quality of purity which is the antithesis of the female character"— thereby earning the librettist as high a score for political incorrectness as the composer in his Nazi period.

---

[1] *Massine: A Biography*, by Vicente García-Márquez. New York: Knopf, 1995.

This gossipy book tells us that by early January 1914 "sexual dominance of the younger man completed Diaghilev's conquest." But little more is said on this crucial matter. A year later, when the Ballets Russes was installed in Switzerland, the sexual intimacy between Diaghilev and his catamite "was discretely acknowledged by everyone." García-Márquez faults Massine for implying that on occasion he traveled or lived independently, when in fact "Diaghilev always knew where he was." But Diaghilev must soon have realized that Massine's sexuality was more hetero- than homo-, if indeed the latter orientation was not assumed opportunistically in the first place . The author comments that "during his formative years Massine appropriated much of his identity from Diaghilev's, and, admiring Diaghilev, wanted to please him."

The 1916 American tour of the Ballets Russes is the subject of one of the book's best chapters. In New York Massine found both an onstage and an offstage personality. Even at that date the American theater was ruled by the star-system, and Diaghilev was soon forced to meet the demand of audiences clamoring for Nijinsky, whom Diaghilev had dismissed because he felt betrayed by his marriage. Until Nijinsky arrived in the United States, Massine performed the great dancer's most famous roles, Petrushka and the Faun. The ballet of the latter, together with *Schéhérazade*, shocked the still provincial New York public. A *New York Tribune* review of *Schéhérazade* noted that Adolph Bolm's "remarkable impersonation of the Negro favorite of Zobeïde, Princess of Samarkande, will render the ballet impossible for production south of Mason & Dixon's line. Even to northern winds, it was repulsive." The *Catholic Theater Movement* objected so vehemently to the latter part of *The Afternoon of A Faun*, with its simulated masturbation, that Diaghilev was obliged to attend a hearing before a certain Judge McAdoo. Of this encounter, January 23, 1916, the *New York Sun* reported that "M. Diaghilev, half amused, half perturbed," said he believed that his "mind and the minds of those who planned and executed the ballets was less vicious than the minds of those that made the protest." Diaghilev nevertheless agreed to sanitize *The Faun*, and at the next performance had the discarded item of female drapery placed on a rock, while Massine sat gazing at its silken folds." (Arms outward, no doubt.) After the performance Diaghilev turned to the Director, Gatti-Casazza, and other officials of the Metropolitan Opera, exclaiming, in French, "America is saved."

The book quotes interesting comparisons of Massine's and Nijinsky's interpretations of Petrushka. Lydia Lopokova (later Lady Keynes), who had danced the Ballerina opposite both, noted that "Massine mimed the part ... with his hands stiff and hanging.... Nijinsky moved more with his whole body. Massine's was an intellectual creation, Nijinsky's of inward bodily genius, only half conscious." A New York critic thought that "Nijinsky paid more attention to the puppet's soul and less to his mechanism than Massine." Massine himself understood that Petrushka was his "most rewarding" role because "my sense of identification with the half-human puppet helped me to project much of my own personality." One is amazed that Massine was being judged in the same breath as Nijinsky.

Personally, offstage, Massine found his more famous colleague "aloof and removed." García-Márquez postulates that Nijinsky "probably resented the attention being paid to Massine and must have suffered injured pride in realizing that Massine had completely replaced him in Diaghilev's life." Nijinsky's opinion of his rival is found in the newly *un*expurgated *Cahiers*: "Boring. The Massine question is very simple. He wishes to enrich himself by taking everything that Diaghilev knows. Massine doesn't know anything." On a later occasion, in Madrid, Nijinsky came to Massine's dressing room to compliment him on his choreography for the *Good Humored Ladies*.

The year 1920 marks the zenith of Massine's creative life. He choreographed Stravinsky's *Song of the Nightingale*, the revival of *The Rite of Spring*, and *Pulcinella*, this last, from all accounts of his genius as a mime, also providing him with one of his greatest dancing roles. But none of this work survives, and the next year saw the termination of his career with Diaghilev. When Diaghilev learned that Massine had become infatuated with a female member of the company, Vera Savina, he invited her to his hotel suite, forced her to drink champagne until she was inebriated, stripped her naked, deposited her in Massine's bed in the adjoining room, and fired both of them.

García-Márquez concludes from his own late-in-life interviews with Massine that he was "inaccessible." Apparently this was always true. When he first joined the Ballets Russes, the dancer Lydia Sokolova found him "Impenetrable ... When he looked at you, his enormous eyes remained completely blank ... [he] would stare straight at you, but his eyes never smiled.... He overworked his dancers, and made them feel that they were mere tools for *his* artistic achievements." He was also "notoriously tightfisted, not above petty squabbling over money," and vain to the extent of locking himself in his dressing room on discovering that Lopokova's name, a more famous one than his at the time, appeared in slightly larger letters in a London program.

The bisexual practices for which Diaghilev discharged him left a trail of maltreated women but not a parallel one of broken-hearted men. (One of the latter, however, could have been T. S. Eliot, who in 1923 confided to a female friend that he had found "the dancer more beautiful than ever.... I quite fell in love with him.... Do you think Massine likes me? And would he come to see me, do you think?") Female dancers flirted openly with the choreographer and were ruthlessly exploited for their attentions. When still married to the young Eugenia Delarova of the Folies-Bérgères, he began an affair with the even younger Vera Zorina, who became the third member of his *ménage à trois* until the frustrations of the arrangement drove her to attempt suicide. Eventually, after she left him, he divorced Delarova and married Tatania Orlova, yet another dancer.

* * *

Diaghilev, the author writes, was "brilliant, often magnanimous, capable of radical devotion and self-sacrifice in the pursuit of artistic ideals," but also "tyrannical, merciless, mistrustful, possessive, and subject to uncontrolled fits of temper." However these qualities may balance out, Diaghilev is by so much the book's most fascinating figure that the reader's interest declines abruptly after the 1921 separation. It all but disappears with the logbook-style narrative of the later, career-foundering years, when Massine attempts to form new dance companies, to choreograph variety-show and opera ballets, as well as act in films (*Red Shoes*). His one great success, just before WW II is *Gaïté parisienne*, to Offenbach's music as chosen by, of all people, Nadia Boulanger.

According to García-Márquez, Massine's now forgotten 1930s "symphonic ballets," meaning his choreography for Beethoven's "Seventh," Tchaikovsky's "Fifth," Brahms's "Fourth," and others, derived from "dissection of the score.... [M]usical themes found their complement in a solo dancer or groups of dancers.... Dancers would represent sections of the orchestra, such as woodwinds or strings.... He wanted a choreographic rendition of the music's structure." But does a great symphony require or benefit from duplication of this kind? When we are further told that these visual lessons in music appreciation were achieved partly through "the interplay between masculine and feminine movements," we wonder if this is not true of all ballets.

The scenes that show Diaghilev's artistic talents and psychological acumen in operation are the book's most memorable. When he criticizes a passage in *Josephslegende* as "too long, and unnecessary," the composer of *Salome*, *Elektra*, and *Der Rosenkavalier* "takes his pencil and deletes about ten pages from the orchestra score." Even Picasso bows to Diaghilev's judgment and will, trashing (under protest) two versions of the *Pulcinella* decors before undertaking the one in Commedia del'Arte style that Diaghilev had conceived.

Even more remarkable is Diaghilev's manipulation of Matisse in their collaboration on the *Song of the Nightingale*. After the painter had refused to work with him at all, Diaghilev persuaded him to spend two weeks in London designing the ballet. Matisse recalled that he was unable to complete the curtain, and said "I've had enough, I leave you all the work I have done and I return to Paris.... Diaghilev stood up, picked up some white sheets of paper from a folder and a pencil and said to me, 'The idea you have for the front curtain is the following, is it not?' and he began to design vaguely the ideas I had told him. I objected, and said, 'Oh no, may I have the pencil ... and I began to design ... big Chinese griffins, white with green.... He let me do it and when I had finished he said, 'Well, there it is. Your front curtain is done. What is all this complaining about? You have just done it.'"

Martha Graham and the
Poetry of Motion

ong before her death at age ninety-six, April 1, 1991, Martha Graham had
become a part of world dance history, as well as of American history in
the largest sense. The genre known as modern dance, a distinctly American art form, derives essentially from the kinetic vocabulary that Graham began
to develop in the late 1920s and that enabled her to articulate a new psychological energy in her dance dramas. A discerning few, including Agnes deMille,
her biographer, disciple, and the future choreographer of *Oklahoma*, perceived
that Graham was on the way to enlarging the language of movement and thus
to creating a new means of communication.

Graham's leap into "the big league," as deMille calls it, dates from her appearance as the Sacrificial Maiden in Leonid Massine's version of *The Rite of
Spring*. As the first staging in America—Philadelphia and New York, April
1930—the performance was widely publicized, and Graham, in the solo part,
became a name in the dance world. Both she and deMille[1] devote a chapter to
the event, but without surrendering a word as to what actually happened on
stage. Instead, deMille explains that Graham had been cast in the role on the
recommendation of the dance-student wife of Leopold Stokowski, who conducted, and Graham, for her part, tattles on Stokowski for attempting to seduce
her.

Graham's lover at this time, deMille tells us, was Louis Horst, her musical
director (composer, conductor, rehearsal pianist), dance coach, true friend, and
the only male in her harem, the Graham company having been exclusively a sisterhood until the end of the 1930s. Graham met Horst in Los Angeles in 1916,
when he performed the same artistic functions in the Ruth St. Denis School of
Dance and Related Arts, in which she had enrolled. Principled, resourceful, encouraging, Horst is the most appealing character in both books. When Graham
broke with St. Denis in 1924 and moved to New York, Horst came with her.

---

[1] *Blood Memory*, by Martha Graham, New York: Doubleday, 1991; *Martha: The Life and Work of
Martha Graham*, by Agnes deMille. New York: Random House, 1991.

But with the advent of Erick Hawkins, one of whose performances in Lincoln Kirstein's Ballet Caravan Graham had seen in Bennington, Vermont, in the summer of 1936, Horst's "Jovian voice" was heard only from the sidelines.

In 1939, apparently in love with Hawkins, Graham made him the first male dancer in her company, the "prince consort in this female brigade." He was soon seeking equal status with her, but, lacking her gifts, could not compete. Nor was the duel in their professional relationship resolved when at long last, aged fifty-six, Graham married him. Her account of this flibbertygibbety act, though disingenuous in the extreme, is partly redeemed by a touch of wit: As they signed the marriage register, in Santa Fe in 1948, Martha was aware of the much younger Hawkins looking over her shoulder "to see what age I would put down; I took off the same fifteen years that I always had."

Graham suggests that the consummation of the marriage was their first experience of the kind, remarking that, after it, "Erick turned to me and said 'at last I'm free of this terrible thing.'" Then, while pretending not to know what he means, she wickedly quotes Ruth St. Denis on "the divine androgyny" in the dance world. DeMille, who testifies early on that Graham had always "advocated and practiced free love," tells us that the "bride and bridegroom settled in near her studio, where they had in fact been living together for years."

While extolling Graham's talents, her matching gifts of ambition ("She is a celebrity," Henry James said of Sarah Bernhardt, because "she desires with an intensity that has rarely been equaled, to be one"), and her grit, self-confidence, and good sense—in, for example, opposing improvisation because "she didn't trust the Spirit to be on call"—deMille also mounts the evidence of her monstrous vanity, vindictiveness, and egoism ("If she couldn't herself dance, she did not want any of the work to survive"). Graham's paroxysms of temper, moreover, could lead to physical violence, as when she "raked the chest of her partner with her nails, drawing blood," and grabbed one of her leading male dancers by the hair, snapping his head back until he "thought his neck was broken." Graham's hatred of men, not traced to its roots in deMille's biography, is undisguised in her own book: "Every woman is a Medea. Every woman is a Jocasta.... Clytemnestra is every woman when she kills. In most of the ballets I have done, the woman has absolutely and completely triumphed.... Woman kills, intends to kill." Graham's *Clytemnestra*, many agree, may be her greatest work.

DeMille's generally persuasive analysis of the artistic persona contends that in Graham's case ends justify means. But the apologist's language is excessive, hagiographic: "There was no false modesty.... Saints do not doubt their own worth." Once when deMille publicly rated Graham's achievement as "equivalent to Picasso's," one of the faithful demurred: the painter was undeserving of her company and even Wagner could be admitted to it only with a qualifying "maybe." When deMille claims that Graham possessed "One of the most extraordinary minds of this century," the reader would like to remind her of the dancer's own insistence that her poetry begins in the body.

Writing in the first person, and much of the time as part of the scene, deMille's portrait has an immediacy and sense of presence not likely to be equaled by any future biographer. She is also wonderfully forthright. When Graham proposes to cast her in the role of a boy, she protests that "I was a big-breasted, well-hipped, hale and hearty woman of blatant sexual appetites." Yummy! That said, one does not like to, but must, contradict her verdict that Webern's "Six Pieces" for the ballet *Episodes*—in which Graham's part far outshone Balanchine's—are "undramatic"; the largest of them, the *marcia funebre*, quickly convinces us of the opposite.

Graham's classes were punishing, apparently on the model of her own self-lacerations. DeMille says that one of her postures, the "swastika position," necessarily resulted in a "sprung crotch." During the two- to four-hour sessions, "no one laughed, chatted, gossiped," nor were "gooddays" exchanged, Martha being "tuned to rehearsal pitch and already at work when [the girls] entered the room.... The only speaking was when Martha told them what she wanted." She "never asked how [they] were getting on. She asked nothing about them personally." DeMille's sticking point is that the floor exercises, stretching the back, the arms, and the torso were "possibly Graham's most beautiful contribution to dance vocabulary."

The two books, Graham's brief and bitty late memoir and deMille's copious and long-gestated one, should be read side by side. Overlapping is minimal, and, of course, non-existent concerning the middle-age crisis that began with Graham's arthritis and crippling knee injury. "Years before," deMille reveals, "Martha was reliant on her daily dosage of Irish whiskey," but now, from the mid-1960s, she became "a real alcoholic," remaining home "sodden with drink," or "drunk throughout the rehearsal period," and, indeed, "drunk on most occasions." She performed for the last time in 1968.

The recovery began in 1973, slowly, gradually, teetotally. DeMille's tone turns evangelical: "Martha rose from the dead, and verily she was changed." But the change was in the decision "to become a superstar," from which moment *Blood Memory* degenerates into an agenda of Martha's encounters with the rich and famous and her record of their flattery. Some of the ill-assortments are droll in themselves—John Paul II and Swifty Lazar on the same afternoon—and so are some of the anecdotes, as when Graham asks her benefactress Bethsabée de Rothschild to take her to the Rothschild bank in Paris, in which, to her aston-

ishment, tellers and depositors are nowhere to be seen: "We don't really en-
courage depositors," Graham's hostess explains, "but yes, we do have one now
... the Pope."

Having undergone several face lifts, "after which she looked like a waxen
deity," Martha now gets about in a plane owned by Halston, who had made
many gowns for her and underwritten some of her costliest productions. She is
accompanied by a make-up supervisor, hairdresser, equerry, and a maid, while
far below, mindful or not of the diva's artistic creed in the improvident past,
"never to become involved in any enterprise primarily for the sake of money,"
the unenfranchised little people in her company head for the next engagement
on a bus.

The anti-ballet stance is more of an issue for deMille than it seems to have
been for the elderly Graham, who on one occasion appalled her biographer by
having been seen kissing Nureyev's hands after he had performed a piece of that
"technical superficiality against which she had set her life." In 1984, when she
received a Chevalier of the Légion d'Honneur, a French critic wrote that "Miss
Graham fought ... against the colonization of America by European classic
dance." True. But the colonialist cultivation of the traditions of classical ballet
in America does not now, if it ever did, pose a threat to modern dance, and from
the perspectives of today, some of the ex-Graham dance-makers, Paul Taylor
for one, have gained an edge and more over their classical ballet counterparts.
May they co-exist and continue to choreograph.

Dictionary of Divas

S tanley Sadie's elegant preface to his monumental *New Grove Dictionary of Opera*[1] emphasizes its independence from *The New Grove Dictionary of Music and Musicians* (1980): "Like most offspring," the new opus "has taken on a life of its own in the course of its compilation"; "at least 80 per cent" is not reprinted from the parent volumes but "newly written." Gilt-topped and handsomely bound in red boards, the books lie open on the table and are not too heavy for lightly cushioned laps—laps of luxury, albeit, for apart from Covent Garden and Metropolitan Opera box-holders they are beyond most opera-lovers' means.

Composers and their operas, individually synopsized in plot and action and analysed as drama and music, are the principal subjects of *Grove Opera*; the careers of singers, conductors, costume and set designers, stage directors, librettists and impresarios are recounted more succinctly. The contents are exhaustive, ranging from histories of the cities in which opera has flourished to histories of every genre of musical theatre involving voices, late sixteenth-century Florentine Camerata to Rock Opera (the subtitle of Lloyd Webber's *Jesus Christ Superstar*), and from such concomitant matters as theatre architecture and seating, stage machinery and lighting, to the evolution of opera glasses and the opera ticket (metal, ivory, bone, paper). Musical terminology and the jargon of vocal technique are defined and in some cases—appoggiatura, cadenza, ornamentation, portamento—illustrated in music type. The appendices catalog incipits, words only, of solos and ensembles and identify some 4,500 role names with the 850 operas in which they appear. No aria has been left unturned.

Bernard Williams's prolegomenon on the nature of opera, together with the essays by other contributors on the greatest opera composers, Monteverdi, Rameau, Handel (the longest single entry), Gluck, Mozart, Verdi, Wagner and those of the twentieth century, provide some of the dictionary's highest level of sustained reading. Williams predicates that the most powerful resource of opera as drama is its "capacity, through music, to deepen the action while advancing

---

[1] *The New Grove Dictionary of Opera*, edited by Stanley Sadie. London: Grove's, 1992.

it in time, thereby implying a complex relation between real and dramatic time." The music unfolds a sequence, "not of events, but of some other dimension of the action, often a state of mind, a mood or a motivation." He does not discuss the no less powerful resource of music's capacity both to interweave and distinguish the different feelings of two and more people simultaneously.

Williams contends that Boito's "much praised" elimination of the first act of *Othello*, by foreshortening the foundations of "the relations between the main" roles, moving Othello's character "sharply toward the pathological," and increasing the difficulty of Iago's inadequate motivation, actually makes the situation "less humanly credible," and is responsible for downgrading tragedy to melodrama. Turning to *Pelléas*, he concedes that "the basic sense of the indeterminacy of human relations" is difficult to stage, but he perceives that the opera is one of the few "to have engaged with the typically twentieth-century idea that reality is not merely given but both demands interpretation and can defeat it." His remarks on Mozart's Da Ponte operas are no less trenchant. Whereas each principal in *Figaro* has at least one self-revelatory aria, Don Giovanni, whose *modus vivendi* is action, never sings about himself. *Così fan tutte* creates the impression that "the elaborate conventional arias in the first act are public performances, occurring in real time, while the expressions of feeling later in the work, particularly from Fiordiligi, come from an inner world." The tenor's interruption in "her most affecting piece, *Fra gli amplessi*," gives the sense that "he has broken not just into her song, but into her life."

Julian Rushton's essays on style in Mozart and on each of the operas constitute some of the dictionary's most penetrating criticism. Considering anew the question of Susanna's and Figaro's relative strengths of personality and intelligence, and the musical convention that associates the dominant of the key, Figaro's terrain in the opening duet, with the dominant personality, Rushton observes that although the remainder of the opera "tends to support Susanna's claim to superior wit," the beginning of it, in which she twice "relaxes" to the tonic, "may be read as striking a balance emblematic of the compromises which make a successful marriage." (She sustains the dominant of the key again in the Act III Sextet.) Rushton understands that Mozart's key-schemes "can never be completely systematized as signs of character, social class, affect or even musical form," and that dance, stately aristocratic minuet, rapid, rustic and plebeian 6/8, is a more reliable index to social hierarchy. Similarly, though "Mozart's transmutation of the Sonata into a vehicle for drama may appear his most radical achievement," the other musical elements, tempo, rhythm, melody, harmony, and instrumentation, contribute more to mood and characterization than tonality.

Rushton offers fresh perceptions, contrasting, for example, the accelerating shifts of tempo in *Come scoglio* to the reverse procedure, "from fast (numerically) to slow (taxonomic)," in Leporello's inventory aria. *Così fan tutte*, he writes, "may be Da Ponte's most original libretto," and indeed would be if only for the reason that it is the rare or unique opera in which the seducers do not want to succeed. Going beyond the libretto's "potential triviality," Mozart found "ways to seek out hitherto unplumbed depths in the human psyche ... for an increasing number of commentators it is the profoundest of his Italian comedies." It is also, in some ways, the most attractive of them musically—the delectable terzettos, the headlong pace, the trumpet-tinctured orchestration—but what kinds of weighing apparatus can hold, or comparators measure, such towering masterpieces? No one will disagree with Rushton's conclusions that Mozart's operas "affected the minds of poets and philosophers"—Goethe, Kierkegaard—as well as musicians, that "he is the first operatic composer whose work has never needed to be revived," and that "it is likely to remain the touchstone of operatic achievement."

Strauss and Puccini, the only prolific twentieth-century composers of operas that have held the stage from the first, are freshly and fairly appraised. David Murray alerts us that the "downward curve" view of Strauss "from the bold atonal experiments of *Elektra* through a bourgeois retrenchment in *Der Rosenkavalier* and *Ariadne* ... to the *Rosenkavalier*-with-water *Arabella*," is the "dated" one, according to which "atonality was destined rather to supplant tonal music than merely to extend its resources." Yet this perspective, regardless of atonal determinism, is still the most widespread. Murray notes that Schoenberg composed *Erwartung* four years after *Salome*, but stops short of crediting the earlier work with the establishment of the overwrought style. Tracing Strauss's developing use of leitmotifs from mere name tags to larger devices of recall, Murray acknowledges that, unlike Wagner's, they are "always internal to the music drama" and have no independent "fictional" existence beyond the stage action.

Julian Budden astutely observes that Puccini's style enabled him to absorb modern ingredients. He spells it out: "diatonic melodies without chromatic inflection that move mostly by step while incorporating many a falling fifth; sequences with a heavy sub-dominant bias; successions of parallel, often unrelated chords; frequent use of odd notes, and unresolved dissonances; climaxes built on alternating progressions; and a habit of doubling the outer parts." Budden mentions the macabre aspects of *Gianni Schicchi*—the presence of a corpse on or offstage throughout, Schicchi dressing up in the deceased's night-garments and taking his place in bed, and the warning of the mutilation penalty for forgery—but does not invest them with any significance vis-à-vis the composer's psychological make-up. Puccini's artistic limitations were "spiritual," Budden forthrightly concludes. His values were those of "the bourgeois, unadventurous Italy before World War I. 'Great sorrows in little souls,' was his watchword." Bernard Williams perorates:

> Puccini's critical reputation is not as unqualified as his success, and many find it hard to dismiss a distinct sense of the cynical and manipulative.... It is hard to think of a parallel in another art to enduring works that are at once as effective and dubious.... [But Puccini] was exploiting something that is inherent to some degree in the performance of any opera, and that is why his talent, suspect as it is, is true to the nature of the form.... If [Puccini's operas] are not unqualified masterpieces, they are masterpieces of opera.

In the opinion of many, Leoš Janáček's last four operas, which have taken their place beside the Strauss and Puccini mainstays, are masterpieces of the unqualified kind. Together with *Wozzeck*, they articulate the feelings of Central Europeans of a certain time and endow them with a universalizing originality, directness and power. No matter that the plots are unpromising and "unoperatic." *Kat'a Kabanova* follows Ostrovsky's conventional story; *From The House of the Dead* is faithful to the horrors of Dostoevsky's Siberian prison; the beautiful woman in *The Makropulos Affair* is actually 337 years old; *The Cunning Little Vixen* with its cast of animals, avians, batrachians, and insects, and its scene in a badger's sett, threatens large-scale whimsicality (the marriage of the female of the title to a male of the species performed by a woodpecker). Instead, these subjects are transformed into music dramas of great tenderness and emotional intensity.

Janáček's musical language is new in every element. "No characters and no tunes," was Auden's verdict, but the tunes of the Blue Dragonfly's dance and the "autumn afternoon" interlude in the *Vixen* are immediately memorable. The rhythmic dialect of all the operas features a short first and a long second note, and, more importantly, a 6/4 meter that accommodates 2, 3, and 4 notes to the beat, in accordance with the naturalistic approach of Janáček's free-sounding speech-melody. Apart from interpolated dance pieces, the feeling of meter tends to dissolve, as it does even at the very beginning of *Kat'a Kabanova*. The instrumentation is a subject for a new treatise, but Janáček's colors are gorgeous as well as harsh, and the orchestra is almost always paramount.

The orchestra is the protagonist of *From the House of the Dead*. Berg is often invoked in connection with this posthumous opera and its pre-echoes of Auschwitz and Treblinka, but the not-yet performed *Wozzeck* comes to mind throughout *The Makropulos Affair* as well: in the jagged leaps after the reference to "that harlot," and in the dissonance, rhythm, and brass instrumentation in response to the Makropulos woman's "Do you want to spit in my face?" though the line itself, and one at the end of the opera, "there's no joy in goodness, no joy in evil," are *Wozzeck*ian. John Tyrrell's commentaries on Janáček and his operas are among the dictionary's finest contributions, but he does not place the composer in the context of modernism, properly as part of its center.

Among the living, Philip Glass, as the most popular original theatrical composer now in orbit—Lloyd Webber's musical idiom is derivative—is accorded more space than anyone except Michael Tippett. Tim Page evenhandedly chronicles the career, plumber and taxi driver to galactic "name," and the development of the style from the rejection of serialism to the lessons with Boulanger and the influence of Ravi Shankar. He prepares us not to expect such "Western musical events" as sudden changes of volume, and on the crucial rhythmic-structural element lets Glass speak for himself: "In Western music we divide time—as if you were to take a length of time and slice it the way you slice a loaf of bread. In Indian music … you take small units, or 'beats,' and string them together to make up larger time values." But Glass's stature is less impressively attested by what *Grove Opera* says about him than by its inclusion of an entry on *The Voyage*, first performed in New York on October 12, 1992; which is called up-to-date-manship.

In the history of opera "an interest in singers is older than an interest in composers," Bernard Williams reminds us, but none of the 2,500 biographies of singers is extensive, to judge from those of the most celebrated divas and divos (neither word has an entry). Backgrounds and schooling are covered in two or three sentences, the principal roles and the vocal, musical, and, if any, histrionic talents in a few more. The brevity may be attributed in part to the dearth of adjectives conventionally thought to evoke vocal texture ("velvety," "silken"), tone quality ("bright" or "dark"), temperature ("warm"), shape ("round"), and volume ("full"). Fischer-Dieskau's voice is "full, warm and resonant," Elizabeth Schwarzkopf's "full-toned," Pavarotti's "full and vibrant through the range," matching his "genial, eupeptic looks and generous figure." Marilyn Horne's is "tangy," a term borrowed from wine-tasting, but a more comprehensive notion of her attributes is found in the unexpected context of John Rosselli's entry on castratos. Remarking that these "18th-century equivalents of pop-stars" had wider ranges and more power and breathing capacities than normal singers, and that they sounded more "natural" and "true" ("*sincere*") than falsettists, Rosselli believes that Horne's execution of *fioritura* in her recording of Vivaldi's *Orlando* might approximate the performance "of a great castrato artist." Some of the dictionary's photographs of prima donnas in their get-ups for "mad" or "possessed" roles, Tetrazzini as Lucia, Anna Bahr-Mildenburg as Kundry, Aïno Acte as Salome, are terrifying.

Of the comparatively cramped space allotted to conductors, Thomas Beecham's share is smaller than Karajan's but larger than Mahler's, Toscanini's, Furtwängler's, and Weingartner's (whose performances are oddly remembered for their "lack of exaggeration"). The claim that Karl Böhm, in a biography that ignores his political acquiescence in the Nazi period, is "one of the outstanding conductors of the century," will be doubted. Of incumbent maestros, Muti generates "high-voltage electricity," while Abbado, more space than Muti, is "generally electrifying." James Levine's forte is "sustained intensity," Haitink's "patient concentration." Maazel is "bold, vigorous but variable" as an opera conductor, and he sometimes indulges in "crude orchestral color," which sounds more like a press notice than a judgment for the ages.

The essays on the libretto and on opera in translation—original languages are preferred and "a single internationally accepted language for each opera"—together with the biographies of some 550 librettists and their sources (uncounted), could be republished in spin-off booklets. Some of the statistics are arresting: between 1730 and 1795 Metastasio's *Artaserse* was set by eighty-five composers, among them Gluck, Paisiello, Cimarosa, J. C. Bach, Jommelli, Galuppi; thirty-one Shakespeare plays have been adapted into operas, *The Tempest* forty-seven times; and five operas—six according to *The Oxford Dictionary of Opera*, by John Warrack and Ewan West—were based on Scott's *The Bride of Lammermoor* before Donizetti's. But august ur-authors, including Yeats (Harbison's *A Full Moon in March*) and Eliot (Pizzetti's *Assassinio nello cattedrale*), are missing, as are some of their opera-inspiring works; the Stendhal entry does not mention *La Chartreuse de Parme* (Sauguet), and Henry James's omits the *Aspern Papers*, despite an illustration of the Argento opera based on the story and reference to it in the composer's biography (again compare *Oxford*).

David Pountney excepted, *Grove Opera* gives mixed reviews to the most conspicuous directors currently active on the most prestigious stages. Peter Sellars, whose *Figaro* and *Don Giovanni* were recognizable only by the music, is said to have an "unusual sensitivity to the theatrical workings of music in opera," but is nevertheless responsible for productions "in which the overlay of symbols and performance styles has seemed diffuse and complicated." Jonathan Miller's "fertile intellectual ideas" sometimes "failed to enliven the actual stagings." Robert Wilson (no entry in *Oxford*) may be "one of the most daring and creative figures in contemporary theatre," but his conceptions, "in which design is the main element," are "marathons of endurance for the audience." In a recent *Ob-*

server interview, James Levine served notice that the Metropolitan Opera seeks directors who "can steer a course between presenting dead imaginings of how operas might originally have been staged, and reinventing them as analogies of some contemporary situation.... [T]he updating or deconstruction or conceptualizing approaches don't work...."

The initial entry under "Opera" narrowly defines it as "drama in which the actors and actresses sing throughout," but the next sentence allows that "operatic works of the West include many in which some parts are spoken or mimed" and only some are sung. All the same, *Grove Opera* comprehends theatre pieces without singing, such as the melodramas of Georg Benda, admired by Mozart. Further, the restriction to "the West" excludes Peking Opera, as Sir Stanley's Preface forewarns: "Non-Western musical drama is not related to opera," and "cursory treatment [of it] would be inappropriate"—as it would be of most things. The "China" entry does not mention the indigenous form and is confined to a listing of European imports and nascent native productions of them. The account of Peking Opera in *Oxford* is substantial by its standards, no doubt for the reason that the oriental parallel form is universally known as "opera," and an opera lexicon would appear to be the logical source of information about it.

Readers of *Grove Opera* should acquire the *Oxford*, which supplements rather than duplicates the larger lexicon, offering second opinions and filling in blanks. A book of facts, modest in scope and without illustrations and music examples, it defines such terms as *"stretta," "tenuto," "congiura,"* not found under those headings in *Grove*, and provides histories, perhaps unique in English, of the art as it flourished or faded in such places as Dagestan and Yakutsk.

A sampling of stumbled-on omissions, mistakes of fact, and peculiarities (e.g., the "Metropolitan Opera" entry is inexplicably confined to the company's tours, its history relegated to "New York") points to a weak link near the convergence of the assembly lines. Boito's translation of Wagner's *Wesendonk Lieder* is listed but not his translation of *Rienzi*. Maria Malibran is said to have married for the second time in 1936. The "first performance in France of *Wozzeck*" did not take place in 1963 (*per* Vols. One and Four), but as we learn from *The New Grove* and from *New Grove Dictionary of Opera* (per Vol. 2), in 1950 conducted by Jascha Horenstein, while the first American performance of the completed *Lulu* took place in Santa Fe in 1979 (correct in *Oxford*), not in Chicago in 1987. Hermann Scherchen did not work with Schoenberg in 1911 "preparing" the as-yet-unwritten *Pierrot Lunaire*. The important first London performance of *Moses und Aron* is not listed under the opera, but the biography of Peter Hall, who staged it, states that the cast included four virgins, without explaining how this fact was determined. The location of the first American performance of the same opera is found under "Boston" and "Caldwell, Sarah," where few are likely to look for it, but the correct date is disclosed in *Oxford*. Schubert's *Fierrabras* is misspelled (III, p. 326) and a glitch mars the title line of IV, 1267.

The mention of trivia of this sort can only be understood as the highest compliment to the brilliant achievement of Stanley Sadie and his associates. The musical and musical-theatrical worlds are deeply in his and their debt.

Tycoons at the
Musical Top

Norman Lebrecht's exposé[1] of the business aspects of orchestral conducting focuses on the personalities, ambitions, vanities, rivalries, and greed of the highest-profile maestros of the moment rather than on their music making. His readings of character are shrewd, his assessments of talents and skills are not far from the mark, and his presentation is lively, whether the subject is a maestro (Stokowski "put the con into conducting"), a concert agent (his power was "in growing the best grapevine"), or an orchestral musician ("'I don't know what he's conducting. *We're* playing the *Pastoral*'").

The professional conductor, or conductor only, is a creation of the late-Wagner period. His school was the Central European opera house, where, as a repetiteur and orchestral assistant, he learned the performance traditions and routines of seventy or so operas at an early age and at first hand. The decline of the art can be attributed to the neglect of this system, the perforced neglect in less musically developed lands, in favor of the more general but less practical education of college or conservatory. Lebrecht's account of this shift covers such concomitant factors as the vitiating effects on orchestras of guest conductors and absentee music directors, and the dangers to musical culture of monopolizing artist managements and their mass marketing, consumerist goals. But most readers will wish to proceed immediately to cases.

The career of the late Herbert von Karajan, "the music director of the world" and "the richest musician who ever lived"—his estate has been estimated at half a billion dollars—is the referential center of the book. Lebrecht regards him as a continuation of Hitler. "In his own mind he *was* Hitler," a recording industry chief asserts, and according to one of his record producers, "he filled that void left by the death of Hitler in that part of the German psyche which craves for a leader." What can be said for certain is that Karajan applied to join the Nazi Party in Austria on the first day that this became possible (April 8, 1933), joined again in Germany three weeks later, and was rapidly advanced in the

---

[1] *The Maestro Myth: Great Conductors and the Pursuit of Power*, by Norman Lebrecht. Secaucus, N.J.: 1992.

Third Reich, at one time with the help of Hermann Goering, as a new *"Wunder."* During the war he conducted in the occupied countries (a concert in Paris included the *Horst Wessel* song), and in Berlin until late February 1945. What puzzles is that Karajan's past as a fervent Nazi was never an obstacle to his forty-year post-war reign, including his 1955 American tour.

Karajan's vindictiveness is shown in his boast that the Berlin Senate "would never dare" to exercise its right to invite Leonard Bernstein to cross "Checkpoint Herbie," and in his having "blocked the path to Berlin" of the "Kosher Nostra"—Daniel Barenboim ("the brains of a brilliant group" that "came snapping at both of Karajan's Achilles heels"), Itzhak Perlman, Pinchas Zuckerman, and Zubin Mehta. During a 1980s rehearsal in which everything went wrong, Karajan told his Berlin orchestra: "Gentlemen, do you know what I'd like? To tie a rope around all of you, pour gasoline on you and set you on fire." He later repeated this horrifying "jest" in a documentary film, not, of course, as an example of his monstrous imagination and the orchestra's abject servility, but of his "intimate" relationship with the players.

Lebrecht quotes unidentified "collaborators" of the *Generalmusikdirektor* to the effect that "the homosexual part was very strong in Karajan, and almost certainly active," and he attributes "homoerotic inclinations," and more than inclinations, to other conductors. But while deploring "homophobia" in the music world of the past—Dmitri Mitropoulos "was crucified for his sexuality rather than his musicality"—he does not scruple to repeat Thomas Beecham's notorious quips about Benjamin Britten and post-war Covent Garden, "The Twilight of the Sods," in which "unnatural vice" was rampant and the conductor John Pritchard was "a gay favorite" of the managing director.

Lebrecht's version of the dismissal of Daniel Barenboim as artistic director-elect of that $600m white elephant, the Opéra Bastille, blames the scandal on the personal animus of Pierre Bergé, a "brilliant entrepreneur," friend of minister of culture Jack Lang, and the "lover of Yves Saint-Laurent.... He and Yves owned a house in the high-class homosexual resort of Marrakech." Bergé disliked Barenboim's "plans and personality," but sympathy was on the side of the conductor until the size of his salary was leaked to the press, and until he accepted the directorship of the Chicago Symphony, making clear that his ambition was "to hold two overpaid dictatorships at one and the same time." By "grabbing greenbacks" in Chicago, Barenboim "confirmed in French minds everything Bergé insinuated."

Not sex but money is music's "last taboo," Lebrecht goes on, reminding us that only recently Joan Peyser's "prurient biographies of Boulez and Bernstein" revealed "everything she could discover of their sexual proclivities" but "did not discuss what they earned and what they owned." *The Maestro Myth*, citing the U.S. Freedom of Information Act, discusses both, telling us that the salary of New York's Kurt Masur is "over $700,000," that Mstislav Rostropovich, who "flails about tubbily when working the Washington rostrum," earns $687,000, or did in 1986, when he paid no taxes and "ran the orchestra into a four million dollar deficit," that Lorin Maazel's $1,000,000 Pittsburgh salary is a mere perk compared to the $4,500,000 he reportedly receives from the Bavarian State Orchestra (the second of his three music directorships), and that even the "lackluster" and "early burnout" Andre Previn can "expect to make two million dollars in an average year." "The post-Karajan conductor," Lebrecht writes, "has three homes, drives a red Rolls-Royce or Lamborghini, collects Henry Moores ... is clued into every conceivable tax dodge" and "has common interests with oilmen, stockbrokers, and corporate lawyers."

Lebrecht's jolliest chapter is devoted to such "Semi-Conductors" as Christopher Hogwood, "bachelor" and "Cambridge antiquarian," Roger Norrington, an "unprepossessing provincialist," and other British exponents of the "fringe culture" of "authenticity." The early music bandwagon began to roll in "post-industrial societies that were discovering wholewheat bread ... and open-toed sandals. Bespectacled, pallid figures ... plucked from the college library or organ loft," set out "to perform exactly what the composer wrote ... on the instruments and in the style of his time." The results were "distinctly painful to sensitive ears," but the movement came to grief for the different reason that its missionaries began to encroach on "maestro territory" (mid-nineteenth-century repertory) without maestro qualifications.

Lebrecht admires the "mavericks" Carlos Kleiber ("the most explicit and visible beat of any living conductor") and Klaus Tennstedt ("neither you nor he knows for sure that he will reach the podium without tripping, or that he will manage to conduct a whole movement. Then he does it, brilliantly"), as well as three conductors born after 1950 who have already become music directors: Riccardo Chailly (Amsterdam), Esa-Pekka Salonen (Los Angeles), Simon Rattle (Birmingham).

The treatment of many others is hard-hitting. Colin Davis's term at Covent Garden was "the longest and least edifying in the house's history." (Davis's recordings of music as different as the *Messiah*, Mozart's C-minor Mass, and *Tosca* are far the best on the market.) Claudio Abbado, Karajan's successor in Berlin, is "a great musician, but a feeble human being"—or so Lebrecht allows an orchestra player to say, without qualifying the remark. Zubin Mehta is charged with presiding over "the decline of two great orchestras" (New York and Israel), and Seiji Ozawa with Boston's drop "out of the creative frontline; ...

Boston, in the 1990s, barely holds its place among the Big Five U.S. orchestras." Ozawa's huge salary is "paid into a company ... in a legal dodge aimed at paying less in taxes to Uncle Sam. After thirty years at the head of North American orchestras, his English is ... barely functional."

Lebrecht's non-existent and tongue-twisting forms of familiar words ("virtuosically," catalizator") are minor deterrants. His razzle-dazzle, relentlessly alliterative style, and over-the-top exaggerations are adjuncts to his message about corruption, which is that even in the pursuit of high art "principled men perished and the morally flexible waxed exceedingly rich."

Furtwängler's Compromise

To judge from the intemperate responses to two recent accounts of Wilhelm Furtwängler's life during the Third Reich, his decision to remain in Nazi Germany throughout its twelve-year existence, as well as the nature of his relation to the regime, is at least as controversial now as at any time since 1945. On March 15, 1993, the conductor's widow entered the dispute with a letter to the *Times* of London criticizing Bernard Levin, who had "attempted a quasi-defense"—great musician, weak man—and challenging him to substantiate his characterization of Furtwängler as "an exceptionally unpleasant anti-Semite," which, as clearly shown by the historical evidence, he was not, and a "lamentable" human being, which is not the right adjective (though an apt one for this complex man would require elucidation).

Elisabeth Furtwängler conjectures that "the question of Furtwängler remaining in Nazi Germany may never be settled to everyone's satisfaction." Furtwängler himself, looking back, believed he made the wrong choice. In 1947, during his denazification trial, he was heard to say, "I should have left Germany in 1934," and it seems likely that the statement was an expression of genuine and longstanding regret.

The filmmaker Sam H. Shirakawa has written a full biography[1] extending to the nine postwar years of the conductor's life, and including an appraisal of his discography. Fred K. Prieberg, a German musicologist and author of the as yet untranslated *Musik in NS-Staat* (Frankfurt, 1982), has confined his account to the reign of terror. But overlapping of the two books even for those years is minimal, partly because some of their principal sources differ, and partly because the points of view are often at variance. Neither of them, however, supports the too simple rationale Furtwängler himself frequently expressed for having remained in the Reich, namely that great music, as transmitted by him could preserve the highest values of German culture. As we have learned, Germans could exult in the heroic emotions of Beethoven's music *and* work as

---

[1] *The Devil's Music Master: The Controversial Life and Career of Wilhelm Furtwängler*, by Sam H. Shirakawa. Oxford: Oxford University Press, 1992.

234

death-camp guards.

Both writers agree as well that the conductor was never a Nazi sympathizer and never an anti-Semite. It is clear from both accounts that Furtwängler helped a number of Jewish musicians, keeping them in the Berlin Philharmonic Orchestra in defiance of the regime. Shirakawa maintains that he was risking his life in doing so, Prieberg more plausibly contends that the conductor was "always aware of the advantage offered him by the regime's inability to take the severest measures against him," presumably meaning that before the war he was protected by his international prominence and by the importance of his presence in Germany to National Socialist propaganda, and that during it he was indispensable to the country's continuing and even intensifying musical life.

In 1942, when Himmler had him watched, and warned him that anything he did to help a Jew would henceforth be considered subversive, Furtwängler, according to Prieberg, showed no sign of being worried about his security. He had patrons. Hitler had sided with him in his rivalry with Herbert von Karajan, after the younger conductor's sensational Berlin debut in 1938. And politically prickly as Furtwängler was, Joseph Goebbels had come to his defense against Karajan, who was Göring's protégé, arranging to have the *Berlin Illustrierte* publish a picture of Furtwängler that was twice the size of the one of Karajan on the same page, accompanied by the remark that the older conductor was the most "spiritual and introspective" of all interpreters of symphonic music. Goebbels also warned Berlin journalists not to play off Karajan against Furtwängler, Hitler's favorite conductor, chosen by him again and again to lead important concert and opera performances. Prieberg tells us that the Führer considered Karajan "an arrogant fop."

Furtwängler protected only eight Jewish musicians in the Berlin Philharmonic, but among them were its star players—and therefore targets of jealousy—the concertmaster Simon Goldberg and the cellists Joseph Schuster and Gregor Piatigorsky. Shirakawa rightly sees this protection as a strong mitigating factor in Furtwängler's accommodation to the regime. He also cites the conductor's intervention with the government, in 1938, to help bring about the release from Dachau of a nephew of Fritz Zweig, the conductor and pupil of Schoenberg. Other documentary evidence reveals that Furtwängler aided at least eighty other Jews who were at risk, and "many more by talking to them in person or on the telephone." Prieberg appends a list of 108 prominent composers, conductors, instrumentalist, and singers, of whom a few, though not Jewish, were in political difficulties, and whom the conductor helped.

Furtwängler defended Jewish scholars as well as musicians, as in the case of the young Raymond Klibansky, whose critical edition of Nikolaus von Cucs had been suspended because of the "Aryan clause"; the conductor re-wrote Klibansky's résumé for him, gave his work the more eye-catching title, "Nicolas of Cusa and Meister Eckhart," and contributed a note describing the importance of publishing the work.[2] Regrettably, after the war Furtwängler apparently gave the U.S. authorities the files containing all of his correspondence from 1933, which might have brought more of his good work to light. In December 1946, shortly before his denazification trial, these papers mysteriously disappeared.

The initial grounds of Furtwängler's opposition to Nazi anti-Semitism, as stated publicly, are simply that it was a great stupidity, not that it was a monstrous evil. But his private views on racism were broader than that, as an unsent memo to Hitler written by the conductor in midsummer 1933 reveals. In the "Open Letter to Dr. Joseph Goebbels," published four months earlier in the liberal *Vossische Zeitung*, April 11, 1933, Furtwängler protests against National Socialism's anti-Semitic campaign strictly in the name of German music, not because it was morally wrong. It is "against the interests of our cultural life," he argues, adding, disconcertingly, that a campaign of the sort directed against performers, Jews and non-Jews, "who are out to impress through kitsch, empty virtuosity and the like," would be justified. "One cannot be too vigorous in one's opposition to such people and the spirit they represent." Here Furtwängler fails to recognize that kitsch and virtuosity for its own sake are ingredients of cultural life with as much right to exist as high art.[3]

Some weeks later, probably in June 1933, Furtwängler addressed a memorandum to Goebbels, though whether or not it was sent or received is not known:

> The Jewish question in musical spheres: A race of brilliant people! As a percentage of the orchestra Jews are not over-represented. As soloists they should be defended. [They are also an] indispensable audience.

"The influence of the Jewish [musical] press should be broken," however, for the reason that it has a "harmful influence on musical activity, to the benefit of 'modernism.'" Prieberg glosses this by saying that Furtwängler's real motive was to silence the critic Alfred Kerr, who had frequently attacked him and also antagonized Thomas Mann.

---

[2] Klibansky learned this only after the war from U.S. Colonel Nicolas Nabokov.

[3] *Trial of Strength: Wilhelm Furtwängler and the Third Reich*, by Fred K. Prieberg, translated by Christopher Dolan. Boston: Northeastern University Press, 1994.

While the equation of the disliked modernism with Jews is unfortunate, at about the same time Furtwängler sent a recommendation to one of Hitler's ministers warning that "among the Jewish international community [Schoenberg] is considered clearly the most significant musician of our time," and advising that they should not "make a martyr of him...." Schoenberg, whose name and reputation were far more widely known than his music, would become the symbol of Nazi persecution in England, France, and the United States. Already dismissed from his teaching position in Berlin, he was living in Paris in impecunious circumstances, and the mixture of personal concern for the composer's well-being and respect for him as a creative musician, while harboring at the same time an aversion to his music, warrants a digression as an example of the conductor's complex, and sometimes noble, character.

During the Weimar period Furtwängler had conducted the premieres of Schoenberg's Variations for Orchestra and the revised Five Pieces for Orchestra. Even so, "atonality" was a pejorative term to him, and was to become his synonym for musical pandemonium. He describes the atonal experience in a striking metaphor:

> If we let ourselves be guided by the atonal musicians we walk as it were through a dense forest. The strangest flowers and plants attract our attention by the side of the path. But we do not know where we are going nor whence we have come. The listener is seized by a feeling of being lost, of being ... faced with an all-powerful world of chaos. But of course it must be admitted that this strikes a chord in the apprehension of modern man.

Despite his dislike of "conscious history-making—only a work of art written for its own sake has the prospect of any historical significance"—Furtwängler's notebooks contain perceptive comments on Schoenberg's music: "Nothing says more for the importance of Schönberg's mind than the fact that he found the connection from Wagner to Brahms"; and, "the twelve-tone system of Schönberg ... as an auditory experience conveys the spirit of chaos but as a method of composition is the epitome of the world of modern science, the most highly rationalized system imaginable." In 1946, Schoenberg himself testified that he did not believe Furtwängler had been a Nazi and blamed the American ban against him on "the intrigue of one man" (i.e., Toscanini, who is not named). Schoenberg's sources and informants should be traced, however, since his remark that Furtwängler "is many times [Toscanini's] superior" sounds prejudiced.

On November 15, 1933, Goebbels created a Reichsmusikkammer, the musical branch of his cultural policy organization, as a means of establishing greater government control over music and musicians. Furtwängler was appointed vice-president, Richard Strauss president, and Hindemith a member of the executive council. The Musikkammer published an edict on "The Ten Principles of German Music." One principle was that "Judaism and German Music are opposites." Others were that "music arises from the deep and secret forces which are rooted in the people of the nation," that "the essence of music is melody," and that music "addresses our hearts and our feelings more than our minds."

At first, Furtwängler, then the director of both the Berlin Staatsoper and the Berlin Philharmonic, seems to have thought that his new political office would relieve him of managerial chores in connection with his two great artistic responsibilities, but the "Hindemith affair" brought his credulity to an end with a shock. On March 12, 1934, he had conducted the premiere of three symphonic excerpts from Hindemith's opera *Mathis der Maler*, to general acclaim from the liberal press and condemnation from the right wing, the latter in part because Hitler was known to detest the composer's music. The Führer had heard the earlier opera *Neues vom Tage* in 1929 and called it "degenerate."

In the summer of 1934 an attack on Hindemith's music was launched in the press with the claim that the composer had great ability but was an imitator with no genuine originality, one to whom "divine inspiration will always be denied." The diatribes soon became personal. Hindemith was declared "politically intolerable" as well as "closely related to non-Aryans" (his wife and her brother-in-law). Further performances of *Mathis* in any form were banned. Furtwängler published a letter of protest ("The Hindemith Case," *Deutsche Allgemeine Zeitung*, November 25, 1934), ending: "It is certain that no one of the younger generation has done more for the international prestige of German music than Paul Hindemith." That same day the conductor received an ovation at a morning rehearsal and several minutes of applause when he entered the pit of the Staatsoper in the evening.

Göring, who was present at the latter event, telephoned Hitler that the authority of the government was being challenged. Hitler then ordered the press to attack Furtwängler and instructed Göring to inform the conductor that unless he resigned from the vice presidency of the Musikkammer immediately, he would be dismissed from his musical posts as well. Furtwängler resigned from all three, and learned that Hitler had muzzled the press against any comment on the action. The delighted Göring sent a galling note, "I hope [to see] you again, perhaps as guest conductor, at my opera."

Furtwängler understood that "it will shortly become clear whether or not I shall be able to stay in Germany, but at least I am aware of what I am doing and that there is the possibility of leaving Germany for good." Anticipating this eventuality, Hitler promptly withdrew the conductor's passport. Two months later Goebbels informed him that he was free to leave but would not be allowed to return.[4] In what he later believed was the tragic mistake of his life, Furtwängler said that he had made up his mind to remain.

Prieberg attributes this decision in part to Furtwängler's fear that "he would go into a decline if he were forced to stay away [from Germany] for an extended period." Shirakawa attributes it to his sense of loyalty to his country and to political naiveté. Both are convincing, although "loyalty" may not be quite the word for the fervent, breast-beating nationalism (an artist "should never lose his beloved mother earth from under his feet") that colors the musician's writings.[5] In 1933, inviting the Jewish violinist Bronislaw Huberman to perform in the Germany that had only recently exiled him, Furtwängler employed the inane and tactless argument that "the tree of art is rooted in the worthy and inexhaustible soil of that mightily inspired collective we call the nation." (Huberman declined.)

The British historian Richard Evans draws attention to Furtwängler's "deeply ambivalent but by no means wholly hostile feelings" toward the Nazi regime, feelings rooted in the same "political conservatism and German nationalism"[6] that characterized the political philosophy of the July 1944 conspirators against Hitler with whom Furtwängler was briefly, though mistakenly, suspected of complicity. As late as 1944, Furtwängler proudly refers to Germany as "a completely unbroken nation," asking himself in a note, "Why will Germany win in this war?" and "Why will the authoritarian system necessarily win through with time?" and answering: "Because it is a feature of human nature that individuals cannot cope with limitless freedom."

Furtwängler's strong nationalist sentiment can also distort his musical perspectives. Germany was "the true creator of pure instrumental music," he foolishly proclaimed, ignoring Lord Herbert of Cherbury's Lute Book, Frescobaldi's organ toccatas, the French keyboard composers, and the Italian concerto grosso. "All symphonic music is German," he writes. "Half-symphonists such as Berlioz, César Franck, Tchaikovsky"—later he added Sibelius—"are in all essentials completely under the influence of Germany." In their symphonies, cer-

---

[4] Furtwängler might not have been warmly received in postwar Germany, which often regarded non-Jewish Germans returning from voluntary exile as traitors. Friedelind Wagner, the composer's anti-Nazi granddaughter, testified that "many people went back after the war, but the only ones who were welcomed were the Jews; those like me, who left on principle, were shunned."

[5] See *Furtwängler on Music*. Brookfield, Vt.: Scolar, 1991.

[6] *Times Literary Supplement*, December 11, 1992.

tainly, although this is untrue of such symphonic music as *Le Sacre du printemps* and the same composer's Symphony in Three Movements, both of which Furtwängler was the first German to conduct (though how he could have adjusted his delayed and contoured beat to the irregular meters of these pieces is difficult to visualize). He designates the sonata, moreover, a "purely German development," the "Germans' real contribution to world music, indeed to world art, its true original contribution." Yes, at the height of its development, but it is not "purely" German: Couperin, and Italian composers from Pasquini to Scarlatti, had something to do with it. "There has never been music which did not have the nation as its source," he goes on, overlooking Josquin, Lasso, and the other great masters who created music for the glory of God and the delectation of patrons.

Prieberg counters the plea of Furtwängler's political naiveté with evidence that the conductor was a cunning political manipulator on many occasions, as he would have had to be in his endeavors vis-à-vis the Jews and, in order "to reach such an exposed artistic peak" in the world of musical-political infighting. After Furtwängler's resignations from the Berlin Philharmonic and Staatsoper in 1934, the conductor "slipped into the role of cultural politician" compared to whom, at times, "Goebbels seemed the political bungler"—or so Prieberg thinks, further speculating that Goebbels and Furtwängler could almost have been each other's "second self," and that Goebbels's diaries betray a fascination with Furtwängler, suggesting that a kind of Castor and Pollux "mystical relationship" existed between them. "An artist like Furtwängler compels my deepest admiration," the minister of propaganda wrote in 1944. "He has never been a National Socialist. Nor does he ever make any bones about it."

Yet the artist had his own political ambitions. One of his early memos (1933–1934) indicates that he wanted to "pre-determine" German cultural policy, and that this would require "automatic access to the Führer at all times." The dictatorial side of his personality was already evident in 1933 when, "like a true 'Führer' himself," in Prieberg's words, Furtwängler "annulled" an election by the Berlin Philharmonic Orchestra that had ousted its management (apparently over a financial disagreement), promptly reinstated it, and forbade "any further discussion" of the matter.

The opportunity to emigrate had been allowed to pass at the very last moment when Furtwängler could have salvaged his reputation abroad. When Hitler attended his concert of May 3, 1935, and, at its conclusion, had the conductor photographed receiving roses and a handshake from him, the picture appeared throughout the world and the conductor's credibility as an anti-Nazi was destroyed. Apparently Furtwängler was not forewarned of the visitation, and he snubbed Hitler at the beginning of it by abruptly turning to the orchestra. This did not stop the dictator some months later from sending an inscribed silver-framed portrait of himself for the conductor's fiftieth birthday.

In any case, Furtwängler's relationship with Hitler is curious. On August 9, 1933, the conductor met with the Führer at Berchtesgaden. From the several drafts of the agenda that he had prepared for this occasion it is clear, Prieberg writes, that "the fight against racism was the central point of his program and that he really did hope to reverse Nazi policy toward Jews." He intended, more-over, to instruct the Führer concerning the

> conservative strand in Judaism—the long preservation of their identity is proof of it and signifies an unusual strength ... [which] must at all costs be preserved and put to good use.... [T]he fact that we are attacking innocent people puts foreign propaganda in a powerful position on the grounds of external relations. A man of such standing as the composer Arnold Schoen-berg should be given decent financial compensation. [The Prussian Acad-emy of Arts had not paid Schoenberg's salary and Furtwängler intervened several times on his behalf.]

Prieberg, whose source is a memoir by the conductor's Jewish secretary, Berta Geismar, says that the Führer infuriated his petitioner by giving him almost no opportunity to speak.

Shortly before the beginning of the war the idea that he "had to talk to Hitler was becoming an obsession" with Furtwängler, who seems to have felt that his aims could be achieved through a direct, personal appeal. He wrote to one of Hitler's myrmidons, threatening that "my continued productive work in Germany is firmly dependent on whether or not the Führer gives me an oppor-tunity to speak to him." But what he expected to obtain, as revealed in one of his private notes, suggests that he was temporarily out of touch with reality: "The task is to politicize the unpolitical. It cannot be accomplished through op-pression and force."

Hitler, preparing to invade Poland, did not see him. But he did attend some of his wartime performances, and mandated that he conduct the Bayreuth Fes-tival in 1943 and 1944. As a wartime Christmas present, Hitler sent a packet of coffee, explaining that he had received it from the Imam of Yemen. Later, when residences were impossible to find in bombed-out Berlin, Furtwängler received one in a neighborhood outside the city, equipped, on Hitler's orders, with a for-tified cellar.

Furtwängler's writings repeatedly distinguish between Nazis and "true Ger-mans," between the "community of compulsion" and the "community of love" that it has replaced, though exactly when this Agapemone is supposed to have existed is not divulged (sometime between the Thirty Years' War and Bismarck?). According to Professor Evans, Stauffenberg's early attempts (1942) to organize an anti-Hitler underground had little support among "true" Germans.

Furtwängler's own diaries[7] are by turns realistic and idealistic—with a propensity to philosophize in the spirit of Goethe—but the realism is limited to the musical scene. The war and the horrors of existence inside the prison that was Germany are scarcely noticed. To place the conductor's wilder claims in context—"Human beings are free wherever Beethoven and Wagner are played"—one should read Helmuth von Moltke's letters from the same years:

> Yesterday I said good-bye to a famous Jewish lawyer who has the Iron Cross First and Second Class, the order of the House of Hohenzollern ... and who will kill himself with his wife today because he is to be picked up tonight.... Every day brings new insight into the depths to which human beings can sink.... [T]he lunatic asylums are slowly filling with men who broke down during or after the executions they were told to carry out....[8]

One of Furtwängler's postwar statements claims, "I was able to do more for true Germany, and, as a result, for peace and the arts of the world here than anywhere else." But did the arts have any significant effect on political events between 1939 and 1945? Megalomania, or Keats's kindlier "the egotistical sublime," is an occupational affliction in Furtwängler's profession (see Canetti's *Crowds and Power*), and it seems a more precise diagnosis for him than political naiveté. Even after the war, in Switzerland, he could still write: "I myself was placed by fate in the situation of being able to be more honest than anyone else in Germany." Were Bonhoeffer, von Moltke, and Adam Von Trott Zu Solz, who died for their principles, less honest than Furtwängler?

Shirakawa writes indignantly about the injustice of the rapid denazification of Furtwängler's nemesis, Herbert von Karajan, a party member and ardent Nazi, while the exoneration process in Furtwängler's case dragged on for two years. Moreover, while the younger conductor's postwar American concerts were widely acclaimed, the proposed U.S. tour of the older one was blocked by pressure groups. The apparent reason for the unfairness is simply that Karajan and his past were as yet almost totally unknown outside Germany, whereas

---

[7] *Notebooks 1924–1954*, translated by Shaun Whiteside, edited with an introduction by Michael Tanner. London: Quartet, 1989.

[8] *Letters to Freya (1939–1945)*, by Helmuth James von Moltke, edited and translated from the German by Beate Ruhm von Oppen. New York: Knopf, 1990.

Furtwängler had been the conductor of the New York Philharmonic in the 1920s, and his 1930s performances in Paris and London were internationally celebrated events, prestigious ones for the Third Reich. The feelings of refugees in the United States who had seen the photographs of the Hitler handshake and had no way of knowing about Furtwängler's efforts on behalf of Jews, are readily understandable.

Shirakawa documents many cases in which the American press coverage of Furtwängler's denazification trial was "patently and willfully" biased against him.[9] The *New York Times*'s reporter, Delbert Clark, actually mistook a prosecution witness for a witness for the defense, with damaging consequences for the conductor. Even today, the brief film clip of Furtwängler conducting the Berlin Philharmonic shown in Public Television's documentary based on William Shirer's *The Rise and Fall of the Third Reich* seems unfairly to identify the musician with Nazi horror.

Some of Furtwängler's comments on music-making in America in the 1920s are still pertinent. American "luxury" orchestras, he writes, correspond to "the American self-image by being the most expensive.... [T]hey all have something of the beauty contest about them.... The question of whether or not a performance of a Beethoven symphony, say, is good, is entirely secondary compared with the question of whether the Philadelphia or the Boston Orchestra is better." To explain why the homogeneous tone quality of the Vienna Philharmonic cannot be found in America, and why the absence of a common cultural background precludes emotionally cohesive performances of the great classical composers, he resorts to an analogy: American orchestras have the best components—French woodwinds, German brass, etc.—but the result is like a statue or painting of Venus compounded of the most beautiful nose, arms, and legs borrowed from different models.

Furtwängler is scathing on period performances of Bach (sixty years before the "authenticity" movement) that "reduce the music to an historical affair," and high-minded about Beethoven, "the solitary man who creates an art of community as no one else does." But he is nearly always worth reading on music, and his own music making explains the current craze for his recordings, which have survived the inadequacies of the technology of his time and the wartime conditions of a half century ago to inspire a new generation. Compared to his intensely dramatic, soaring, passionately felt performances of Beethoven

---

[9] Ronald Harwood's highly successful play, *Taking Sides* (1995), directed by Harold Pinter, based on Furtwängler's trial, takes the view that the Americans were determined to "get" the conductor.

symphonies, quirky as they are, the efficient, strict-tempo "literal" readings of other conductors can seem intolerably shallow; Karajan's, in comparison, are overly polished, not to say mannered, and emotionally distanced. Furtwängler's studio recordings, particularly the 1952 *Tristan* and the Beethoven Fifth with the Vienna Philharmonic are no less powerful than his live performances, with their half-stifled coughs and, in the later war-years recordings, the sounds of bombs exploding in the background.

But Furtwängler can also exasperate, going into overdrive in a transition in the last movement of the Eighth, reducing the tempo to a trudge at the dotted-note figure in the first movement, changing tempos erratically in the first movement of of the Fourth, and smothering the articulation of the syncopations.

Furtwängler himself revealed the secret of his famous delayed beat: "The power to affect a note lies in the preparation of the beat, not the beat itself." Listening to his *Tristan* the reader might try to beat time along with the conductor during the latter part of the Prelude, until discovering that this is impossible: the music does not move in measured pulsations—the rhythmic element is epiphenomenal—but in nuances created by harmonic-melodic tensions and resolutions.

On Schoenberg

The following observations are concerned with five works from the last four periods of Schoenberg's creative life: the Five Pieces for Orchestra, from the apogean year, 1909; *Herzgewächse*, from 1911; the Serenade, from his final years in Vienna, 1921–1923; the Septet-Suite, from the early Berlin years (1924–1926); and *A Survivor From Warsaw*, from the latter part of his residence in America (1946–1947).

Five Pieces For Orchestra

More than any other music by Schoenberg, the Five Pieces and *Erwartung*, written immediately after, embody his artistic credo:

> Art belongs to the *unconscious!* One must express oneself *directly.* Not one's taste, or one's upbringing, or one's intelligence, knowledge, or skill. Not all these *acquired* characteristics, but that which is *inborn, instinctive.*

Composed in 1909, the Five Pieces, untitled originally, were performed for the first time by Sir Henry Wood and the Queen's Hall Orchestra, September 3, 1912, in Albert Hall, London. Schoenberg's diary for January 27, 1912, tells us that the publisher

> wants titles for the orchestral pieces, for publisher's reasons. Maybe I'll give in, since I've found titles that are at least possible. On the whole, unsympathetic to the idea. For the wonderful thing about music is that one can say everything in it, so that he who knows understands everything; and yet one hasn't given away one's secrets, the things one doesn't admit even to oneself. But titles give you away. Besides, whatever has to be said has been said by the music. Why, then, words as well? If words were necessary they would be there in the first place. But music says more than words. Now, the titles which I may provide give nothing away, because some of them are very obscure and others highly technical. To wit:

I. Premonitions (everyone has those)
II. The Past (everybody has that, too)

245

III. Chord-Colors (technical)
IV. Peripetia (general enough, I think)
V. The Obbligato (perhaps better the "fully-developed" or the "endless")
    Recitative.

There should be a note that these titles were added for technical reasons of publication and not to give a "poetic" content.

The titles first appeared in the 1922 edition of the score, which also revises articulations and dynamics, and adds tempo changes, numerous and significant enough in "Peripetia" to affect the whole character of the music.

"Premonitions"

The basic melodic-intervallic, harmonic, and rhythmic materials are exposed in the first three bars:

1.

The three-note motive of the upper line (cellos), with its repetition in sequence (cellos and oboe), describes an augmented triad on the longer, emphasized notes F, A, C-sharp. The pedal harmony that underlies the music from bar 23 to the end,

2.

is clearly derived from Ex. 1. The D is the referential pitch at the beginning of the second, fourth, and fifth pieces as well. The harmonic fifths in the middle staff of Ex. 1 are exploited in the body of the piece, and they recur in the second, third (as a principal motive in bar 9), and at the beginning of the fifth piece, thereby functioning as an interrelating link.

3.

The motive in bars 4–6 of Ex.3 and the octave in bar 7 return just before the end of the piece, treated as a separate motive. Bar 6, which apparently began as a simple extension of bar 5, begets the second part of another motive,

4.

and the first three of the 32nd-notes in the 2nd bar of Ex.3 repeat the intervals of the first three 16ths in the bass part of Ex.1.

All six notes of Ex.4 return in slower note-values near the end of the piece, octave-doubled in trombones, then in five octaves in the strings. Bar 6 in Ex.3, inverted, becomes a motive in its own right, exploiting the hemiola introduced in bars 2–3 of Ex.1:

5.

The last three notes here become a principal motive in the "Obbligato Recitative," and, as such, help to interconnect the Five Pieces. Still another motive,

6.

and in faster note-values

becomes a bridge from the start-and-stop introduction to the continuous main section of the piece. The three-note motive returns prominently near the end of "Premonitions." A steady tempo is established in the next passage, which exposes the principal motive at the climax of the piece:

7.

This settles into the *ostinato* figure

8.

recognized as the inverted order of the circled notes in the second part of Ex.6.

Beginning with the third repetition of the ostinato, Ex.8, the 3/8 motive of Ex.1, upper staff, is superimposed on the 4/8 meters, and from this point to the end the two meters continue simultaneously. If the most novel instrumental combination is that of contrabass clarinet and contra-bassoon doubling the bass line at the hairtrigger beginning, then the most novel instrumental effects are the rapid glissando-like chromatic figures—the parallel fifths in Ex.1—played by upper woodwinds and muted trombones in alternation, and the orchestral growl produced by the crescendo of fluttertonguing bassoons, muted tuba, and trombones that leads to the climax of the piece and returns at the end. The music of Ex.7 is heard at this climax in a two-voice canon at the octave in the upper strings, then in a four-voice canon in all the strings.

No one has written about "Premonitions" with as much insight as Larry Kart, book editor of the *Chicago Tribune:*

> The discontinuous continuity of "Premonitions" is the most extreme case in all Schoenberg. Even *Erwartung* is not comparable in this regard; though there is a near continuous avalanche of new material in that work, it is linked to a character, a drama, and a text, no matter how disordered all three may be. Nor does the emotional-musical texture of any Berg work seem as genuinely extreme as that of "Premonitions," while the eruptive-disruptive aspects of "Premonitions" have a quite different relationship to Schoenberg. It is as though this music that threatens to rend the fabric of music itself were being greeted by its maker with both delight (at the onset of an unparalleled fecundity of invention) and terror.

"The Past"

The second piece, like the first but in contrasting slow tempi to it, exposes the fundamental materials at the beginning and makes extensive use of *ostinati.* The sonata-type plan of exposition and recapitulation can be represented as abCa(bc), in which "a" is the introduction, "b" the exposition, "C" the body of the piece, and (bc) the telescoped returns. As in "Premonitions," "C," the core of the composition, combines rhythms in meters of 2s and 3s, 3s and 4s.

True to the title, the first melody is "old-fashioned" in sentiment, as well as in its surprisingly literal returns. The transfixingly beautiful final cadence begins with an upward d-minor arpeggio in the celesta that connects with the piccolo, which then repeats the first melodic interval of the piece above three final notes in the clarinets, recognized by every musical ear, consciously or otherwise (Brentano's distinction between sensory and noetic perception), as the first three notes of "Premonitions" in reverse order. The piccolo and clarinet parts are brought into relief by their placement in a four-meter bar within the three-meter of the rest of the orchestra, and, in the clarinets, by delayed harmonic resolution.

"Chord-Colors"

I cannot unreservedly agree with the distinction between color and pitch. I find that a note is perceived by its color, one of whose dimensions is pitch. Color, then, is the great realm, pitch one of its provinces.... If the ear could discriminate between differences of color, it might be feasible to invent melodies that are built of colors (*klangfarbenmelodien*). But who dares to develop such theories? (Schoenberg, *Harmonielehre*. 1911)

Rhythmic and motivic activity, dynamic and harmonic change, increase and quicken, until a boiling point two-thirds of the way through, then abruptly deconvect and return to the near stasis of the beginning. "Colors" is a crescendo-diminuendo of movement, as distinguished from the melodic-harmonic returns in "The Past," and the alternation of instrumental colors is the means by which the "changing chord" is kept in motion. The five-note chord is stationary at the beginning:

9.

This repeated, gradually-changing chord[1] overlaps and blends with itself in different orchestral combinations, thereby creating an antiphonal effect of canonic movement, at the distance of two beats in the upper parts and of one beat in the bass— the C played by sola viola on the strong beats and by bass on the weak.

Schoenberg's performance directions serve notice that "Colors" is "without motives to be brought out," or thematic development. All the same, the melodic structure shapes the piece. In the first section, which ends in a *fermata*, this reduces to

10.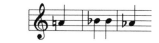

---

[1] "The color of a sustained chord keeps changing," Schoenberg's pupil Erwin Stein wrote (*The Elements of Musical Form*). But the pitches change, too, and the color does not "keep" changing at the outset but is limited to two regularly alternating and overlapping combinations.

The A-natural and A-flat, the before and after, are repeated several times, but the B-flat appears only twice, as in the example. A two-note motive is introduced in this section

11.  and later doubled by fifths above and below. The beginning of the second section, bars 12–19, in which the pitch range edges upward, is marked by harmonic relocation and a new application of the changing-colors principle: a different instrument, or combination of instruments, plays each different note of a chord, spreading the chord out, so to speak, and sustaining it. The third section, bars 20–30, joins more events in more movement, and at the zenith, with the beat subdivided into units of three and four, the flux of overlapping and dovetailing color particles challenges the analytical powers of even the keenest ear. The "leaping-fish"[2] motive, introduced in the second section, is heard eight times from there to the end, its six upward-directed forms at the same pitches, and its two downward-directed ones at their same pitches, an indication of Schoenberg's need at this stage to establish tonal identities. In the mounting movement, the Ex.10 motive becomes

12.

and finally the melodic content of the first section is compressed to:

13.

"Peripetia"

Peripetia, a sudden change of fortune, a sudden change of direction.
—Rudolf Kassner

The referential d-minor and the melodic form of the chord in Ex. 2 are

---

[2] In 1949, Schoenberg renamed the piece "Morning by a Lake," but he had always called it that privately (E. Wellesz: *Schoenberg*, Dent, 1925), and had even identified a "jumping-fish" motive:

exposed at the beginning:

14.

As in "Premonitions," the thematic materials are set forth in the first part of the piece, but their development here is successive rather than superimposed. The prominence of the augmented triad is another link with "Premonitions": the trumpet "smear" that follows the chord in bar 2 and returns at the end of the piece consists of seven parallel augmented triads. The following passage for horns, with the augmented triad as part of its frame,

15.

returns in the middle and conclusion of the piece at the same pitches, but in general the pitches of a motive or theme in "Peripetia" are the same on their returns. The Ex.15 phrase begins and ends on the same chord, which a Hegelian Determinist might think remarkable for a composer bent on abolishing tonal priorities. Another feature of "Peripetia" is the ingenious use of diminution and augmentation with respect to Ex.14: the motive is repeated in faster note-values, as well as in contrary motion, in treble (i.e., fast) instruments, and in slower note-values in bass (i.e., slow) instruments.

The ever-changing tempo, as the title allows, and the *rubato* character, are in extreme contrast to the quasi-motionless "Colors" and the even-keeled, one-tempo "Obbligato Recitative" that follows. The highlights of "Peripetia" are the rich thematic intrigue of as many as six voices toward the middle (bars 283–299); and the ending. The latter begins with three canonic pairs twirled in motion like a juggling act over three other polyphonic parts, followed by the swarming of the whole orchestra to a tremendous crash, which includes a whistling noise produced by drawing a cello bow along the rim of a cymbal (following the principle of rubbing the rim of a drinking glass with humected finger). The crash is followed by a gurgle in the clarinets, the *coup-de-grâce*, and a dust-settling tremolo in the lower strings.

"The Obbligato Recitative"

Unlike the other pieces, number five makes no use of *ostinati* and sustained chords, changes of tempo and meter. The rhythmic vocabulary, moreover, all but excludes triplets and is largely restricted to dotted and even-note figures: one of the latter, a rest at the beginning of a bar followed by five even notes, occurs 17 times. "The Obbligato Recitative" can be described as a composition in three- to six-voice atonal polyphony in which a leading line, indicated by Schoenberg, moves rapidly high and low through the orchestra, always speaking in a different voice. The form is dramatic and does not reflect any classical plan of exposition, development, recapitulation: two incomplete climaxes are followed by a third, fulfilled and extended, and a quiet ending in which the same chord is relayed through three overlapping combinations of instruments. The polyphonic texture is relieved by brief phrases for solo instruments—the bass clarinet before the start of the first climax, the trombone shortly after the principal one—and by homophonic orchestral passages in rhythmic unison. The referential tonal anchor is the bass D of the first chord. The first three melodic notes are the same and played by the same instrument (viola, doubled here by oboe), as those in the "b" segment of "The Past":

16.

Six bars later, the first melodic motive reappears, transposed, in the cellos and violas and, in the next bar, in the flute. The late distinguished musicologist Carl Dahlhaus remarked on the "rigorous avoidance of melodic restatement" in the piece, but restatements occur as early as bar 4, which repeats, untransposed, most of the principal-voice clarinet part of bar 2. Another high-profile instance of repetition is the falling minor-third in the same clarinet phrase: it reappears in the violas (octave-doubled by oboes) soon after, as well as in the section ending just before the start of the first aborted climax (trumpet, followed by bass clarinet), then in the top line at the breaking point of the next climax, and again in the final one. In fact, the coherence of the piece depends on these motives, on the continuity of the leading melodic voice as it passes through one combination of instruments to another, and on the contrast between close chromatic movement and wide intervals.

The instrumental voicing of the harmony is unprecedented. For one example, in the second phrase of the ultimate climax, the lowest line is assigned to trombones, tuba, bass clarinet, and bassoons, while the basses and cellos play middle voices. These chords, the densest in modern full-orchestra harmony, are perfectly balanced, perfectly transparent.

Herzgewächse

In *Herzgewächse*, completed December 9, 1911 but not performed until April 1928—in Vienna, conducted by Anton Webern with Marianne Rau-Hoeglauer as vocal soloist—the harmonium is the first instrument to sound, and it plays more continuously than the other two, having less than a single full beat of rest as against a total of six silent bars in the celesta and four in the harp. The instrument must have the following color stops: flute, oboe, English horn, clarinet, bass clarinet, bassoon, muted trombone, violin, viola, cello, and percussion. They change according to the musical phrasing but, mysteriously, no indications of timbral change are given in the nine next-to-last bars.

After a brief instrumental introduction and the first couplet of the vocal part, the music is harmonically dense: chords of nine, ten, and eleven different pitches are common. The instruments provide several pitch-cues for the singer, but actual doubling of the vocal part occurs on only a few notes. Schoenberg's setting of the text parallels the sense of the words in that, for example, the pitches for "sink to rest" descend to the lowest vocal note in the piece, quietly and without accompaniment, while those for "imperceptibly ascending" climb slowly, softly, and inconspicuously from a low note to high C. The vocal range is that of the Queen of Night (*The Magic Flute*) and Blonde (*Abduction from the Seraglio*).

Serenade

The most immediately striking aspects of the Serenade are its exuberant mood, melodiousness, and borrowing of classical form-models—Schoenberg's choice of a sonnet by the arch-classicist Petrarca as vocal text signals a major shift in twentieth-century musical aesthetics—and its unprecedented, for Schoenberg, repetition of entire segments of the form: 46 bars of the middle section of the first movement, or approximately one-third of the whole, are repeated exactly, and the movement itself returns as the last movement, albeit with differences near the beginning and end. Half of the Minuet is also repeated, and about a third of the Dance Scene. Uniquely in Schoenberg's music, as well, the March (first movement, not the last) is without tempo modification from beginning to end.

"Viennese strumming," Leos Janáček wrote after hearing the Serenade in Venice in September 1925, referring to the mandolin-guitar foundation of the sonority, the pizzicati and bouncing of the wood of the bows of the strings, as well as the fluttertonguing of the clarinets, all of which extend and complement the articulation of the strummed and plucked instruments. At the beginning of the repeated section of the first movement, these effects of bariolage occupy the center stage.

The Minuet, a quiet, mellow piece—the strings are muted throughout the first section and again in the Coda—is more song than dance in the main body of the movement, more dance than song in the Trio, which begins with an *ostinato* in the viola and guitar. The Variation movement, the most delectable of the seven for many, consists of a long theme in the clarinet, and six brief (the sixth is the Coda) variations, each with the same number of bars as the theme. The expressive intensities of the music are reflected in the frequent changes of tempo and the many tempo controls (*ritardando, più allegro*, etc.), as well as in the dynamic nuances. The Coda, with its dialogues between the clarinets and between guitar and mandolin, and its gradual slackening of pace towards the end, is the Serenade's most intricately carved jewel.

The Sonnet (No. 217 in Schoenberg's score but No. 256 in standard Italian editions of the poet) is the Serenade's centerpiece, at once the most highly organized movement of the seven and, on cursory acquaintance, the most chaotic-sounding. It marks the first appearance of a twelve-tone series in Schoenberg's music. At the beginning, the violin plays the first two notes of the series as a melodic fragment. Each note is followed by a mandolin / guitar chord containing five pitches which, together, make up the other ten pitches of the chromatic scale. The twelve pitches are exposed in melodic order in the vocal part, a separate note for every syllable, and repeated in the same order twelve times (the twelfth is incomplete), but with differences in octave registers, rhythm, and in the position of the series vis-à-vis the musical phrasing. Thus the first of the twelve notes becomes, successively, the second, third, fourth, and fifth note in the next four phrases, for the reason that Petrarca's hendecasyllabic lines leave one note of the series over each time it is used. Since the original first note becomes the last note *before the* longest (and most hectic) of the three instrumental interludes that separate the four stanzas of the poem, and notes 2–12 follow *after* this considerable break, Schoenberg cannot have intended the series to be heard integrally. In contrast to the jagged music of the instrumental introduction and interludes, the vocal part is consistently lyrical. The instrumental accompaniment imitates textual references, evoking the roar of a lion with loud glissandos and tremolos in the strings and clarinets, and, at the word "death" introducing a pulsation alien to the meter of the rest of the piece.

The melodies of the Dance Scene are the Serenade's most immediately memorable. The full *Ländler* tune, first exposed by the clarinet, and its countermelody, are repeated several times untransposed, rare instances of same-pitch repetition in Schoenberg's "atonal" period. Worth iterating, too, is the interruption of a four-meter ostinato in the mandolin and, later, violin, relieving the three-in-one rhythm.

The song in "Song Without Words" is sung by violin first, followed by cello, then by bass clarinet. The guitar accompaniment, with major-thirds doubled by viola and cello at the end of the first phrase, recalls "O Alter Duft," the nostalgic conclusion of *Pierrot Lunaire*. As aforesaid, the final March repeats the first movement, with alterations including the return of the *Ländler* as a countermelody, and, shortly before the end, a brief, slow-tempo inset in which the principal melodies of the two previous movements are combined.

Septet-Suite

The Suite for seven instruments, in its playfulness and sustained high spirits, resembles the Serenade. Five of the instruments, the strings and two of the clarinets, are employed in both pieces, moreover, and both employ neo-classic forms and *Ländler* styles. A typewritten note fastened to the sketchbook for the work indicates that, again like the Serenade, Schoenberg had a work of seven movements in mind originally, but from this description of them only the first two are recognizable in the finished, four-movement piece: "1. (Movement) 6/8, light, elegant, gay, bluff. 2. Jo-Jo. Fox-trot."

Schoenberg's biographer has classified the *Ouverture* as an example of sonata form, with two themes, development, reprise and coda, but the title should be thought of in Bach's sense, the opening movement of an early eighteenth-century dance-suite. True, the exposition of the first section is sonata-like, and its music returns three times as well as at the end. But the three-meter *Ländler* sections in between, both of them recapitulated (bars 30–49 returning in bars 145–162, and bars 68–127 returning in bars 202–220) account for more than half of the playing time.

The introduction is defined by four chords without piano, each one containing six pitches and each followed by six rapid piano notes. The four-chord pattern reappears in the cello (bars 14–17), viola with cello (bars 27–29), viola alone (bars 53–55), and in all three strings playing pizzicato at first (bars 125–127, 133–134, 135–136), then arco (bars 137–139), and finally in the coda (bars 228–229). After the opening chords, shorter motives lead to the two principal themes, exposed by violin and viola together.

The fast, jagged opening section gives way to a gentler, broader, melodically sustained one introduced by the violin alone. A return to the music of the first tempo follows, developing the second principal theme, then a still slower section with an extended melody in the muted viola in *Ländler* style, with waltz-rhythm piano accompaniment. The piccolo clarinet repeats the viola melody an octave higher, and a little later the violin plays it in the home "key" of E flat, in a section exploiting harmonics in all three strings. In the next episode, a reprise of the first-tempo music, the clarinets restate the first principal theme in the original and inverted forms, while the strings play triple-stop chords mounting to a climax marked by a pause. A return to the broader-tempo melody follows, this time in the cello, then again the music of the first tempo, and a final excerpt of the *Ländler*, ending with the piano playing what seems to be a reference to the bridge between *Parodie* and *Mondfleck* in *Pierrot Lunaire* in that the rhythm and directions of the intervals are the same. In the Coda, the strings play the first theme in unison and the movement ends, like the other three, on the offbeat.

The *Ouverture* is in 6/8, but 3/4 counter-rhythms, one of them identical to a figure in Liszt's C minor "Transcendental Etude," are common. (Some conductors actually beat the "3/4" measures in three, thereby destroying the against-the-beat rhythm Schoenberg so obviously intended.) The rhythmic vocabulary is remarkably simple: dotted figures in the first theme, then successions of 16ths and 8ths—the piano plays 16ths only in the first 24 bars—and "morse code"-style syncopations in the broader sections. Triplet figures occur in only one bar and not prominently there.

The piano, the principal solo instrument in the Suite as a whole, engages in dialogues with both the clarinet and string groups, which also alternate in playing each other's music. Twice in the movement the piano supplies transitional interludes from slower sections back to those in the first tempo.

E flat ("*Es,*" or *S,* in German) and G, the initials of the composer and his wife, Gertrud, are the first two notes of the twelve-tone series with which the piece is constructed as well as referential pitches throughout, providing a kind of tonal bracket for the whole Suite. The E-flat is sustained in unison toward the end of the first movement, and again near the beginning of the second in fortissimo in the bass clarinet alone, both instances doubtless being intended as private jokes. The E flat and G are the two top notes of the first chord of the second movement, *Tanzschritte* (Dance Steps), the foxtrot of Schoenberg's original title, and the first two notes of its main theme; they are also the first two harmonic notes of the third movement and the first two melodic notes (unaccompanied) of the last.

Like the *Ouverture*, *Tanzschritte* alternates sections of fast and slow music of contrasting character, and, another resemblance, the piano plays several solo interludes. In one passage (bars 56–58) the piano accompaniment recalls the effect, introduced in the slow movement of Haydn's A flat Sonata (No. 46), of making the rhythm appear twice as fast simply by steady syncopation between the left and right hands. Rapid repeated-note figures with wide leaps on accented offbeats are a feature of the movement, as well as string harmonics and strings playing with bouncing bow and *by* tapping the strings with the wood of the bow. The middle-register clarinet exposes the long, easy-to-follow main theme in both the original and, without break, reverse orders.

In the third movement, "Theme and Variations," Schoenberg demonstrates that a tonal-centered melody is not incompatible with atonal twelve-tone music. The melody, Friedrich Silcher's popular song, *"Ännchen von Tharau,"* is first heard in the bass clarinet in the key of E major. Since its third note is the same as the first, the remaining ten notes of the chromatic scale must be heard—a rule of twelve-tone composition at this time—before the repeated note; accordingly, the ten notes are sounded in the piano accompaniment to the first two clarinet notes. The same method is employed throughout the movement. At the beginning, the harmony consists entirely of sixths and thirds, the piano forming one of each of these by combining with the first two clarinet notes.

Each of the variations—Allegro Molto, Moderato, Slow, Moderato—is radically different in character, and the range of contrasts is greater than in the other movements. In Variation I, the piano interjects sprinklings of forte notes between groups of fast-tempo figures played quietly by alternating strings and clarinets. Variation II is a piano solo, Variation III a piccolo-clarinet solo, accompanied by rapid (128th) notes at the top of the piano register, together with still higher violin harmonics. Variation IV, a 6/8 dance evoking Bach, leads to a coda, the first part of which, in the same tempo as the beginning, repeats the *"Ännchen"* melody in the lower register of the piano. In the second, fast, part each clarinet plays a single explosive note in a rotation that sounds ♪♪ ⅞ ♪♩ in every bar.

The subject of the fugal "Gigue," played first by the middle clarinet, exposes the twelve pitches of the principal theme of the first movement, but here in equal-note rhythm. The bass clarinet responds, playing the inversion of the same notes in counterpoint to the continuing middle clarinet, followed by the piccolo clarinet restating the opening form of the subject an octave higher. The middle-register clarinet also introduces the second, *Ländler*, theme, which is broken into phrases with rests between. The four-beat pulsation gives way to six-beats and the polyphonic first part of the movement to block harmonies; from here to the end, the two rhythms and styles alternate and combine. The first half of the movement concludes, surprisingly, in a C-sharp major triad. The more densely contrapuntal second half begins with the inversion of the intervals of the first half. The slow section that precedes the ending consists of a long-line melody in the violin, a return, in the cello, to the theme of the third movement, and a stratospheric conversation between piano and piccolo clarinet, each speaking in six-note phrases.[3]

A Survivor From Warsaw

A Survivor From Warsaw is a fully-formed music drama of only seven minutes duration. Its effectiveness depends on dramatic contrasts: speaking (narration) *vs.* singing (the chorus); English (past-tense recollections for the descriptions) *vs.* German (present-tense reality for the impersonation of the Sergeant); the associating of bugle calls and rigid military drum rhythms with the Germans, and of ragged, limping, and irregular rhythms in the strings with their victims; the fragmentation of the first part of the piece *vs.* the unity and continuity of the choral ending (Auden: "Group singing in unison reduces the sense of diversity and strengthens the sense of unity"); the limitation to small groups of instruments in the first part *vs.* the full orchestra in the last; the fluctuating tempi and meters in the first part *vs.* the constant meter and scarcely inflected tempo in the last.

The horror of the scene is established in the first few seconds by distorted and dissonant bugle calls accompanied by violins and basses playing tremolo at extreme ranges, and by a piercing snare-drum roll. The picture is filled out and intensified by nerve-shattering instrumental effects: sudden,

---

[3] The Septet-Suite has now been vetted by Professor Claudio Spies of Princeton University, with the result that more than two hundred wrong notes (including numerous harmonic octaves, outlawed in 12-tone music), rhythms, phrasings, dynamics, and articulations have been corrected. One error has proved to be uncorrectable: the uppermost piano note in bar 116 of the last movement is above the range of the instrument. A recording made at the premiere of the piece, conducted by the composer in Paris, December 15, 1927, is the authority for performing bars 129–130 of the last movement in *accelerando* instead of, as printed, "*ritardando.*"

rhythmically disjunct outbursts of trills in the upper woodwinds and trombone; fluttertonguing in muted trumpets; rapidly repeated notes in bassoons, oboe, and high xylophone; high, needle-like attacks in violin harmonics; tapping on the strings with the wood of the bow; and loud detonations in low basses and high winds. Perhaps the most effective orchestral scene change is the use of percussion alone to accompany the sergeant's first command, and, to character-ize his emptiness and puppet-like rigidity, a repeated motive in the hollow sonority of the xylophone.

The return of the bugle calls after the word "sleep" is a structural de-vice, as well as a cruel irony. So, too, is the soft pre-echoing in muted horn near the beginning of the first six notes of *Sh'ma Yisroël*, the Hebrew prayer (Deuteronomy 6) recited at the immanence of a death, and, for protection, at-tached in mezuzahs to the doorposts of homes. People went to the gas cham-bers reciting, or singing, the *Sh'ma Yisroël*. (Another setting of the prayer is found in Massenet's *Hérodiade*.)

On the analogy of marble not outlasting immortal rhymes, *A Survivor From Warsaw* is the most powerful monument to the victims of the Holocaust because it is a living one, not a museum. It should have been heard at the end of *Schindler's List*, not because of its superiority to the commercial film score, but because of the feeling of triumph at the end that Schoenberg's music conveys. The entrance of the chorus is one of the most moving moments in twentieth-century music.

Rosen's Romantics

One can say with confidence that *The Romantic Generation*,[1] Charles Rosen's sequel to his *The Classical Style*, is the music book not only of 1995 but of many years to come. The author's ability to communicate his musical insights and immense learning has developed even beyond the capacities displayed in the earlier volume. No one else, certainly no other music historian, could have written any of the chapters in the new study, partly for the reason that its subject is the literature of the Golden Age of the keyboard, chiefly the 1830s, and Mr. Rosen is himself a world-class pianist. With incomparable lucidity and intelligence he analyzes the song cycles of Beethoven (*"An die ferne Geliebte"*), Schubert, and Schumann, the piano music of the latter and of Chopin and Liszt, in which he also instructs the performer in the subtlest particulars of playing it, and selected compositions of Mendelssohn (the *Wunderkind* years as well as the later "Invention of Religious Kitsch"), and Berlioz.

Fully to appreciate the book, the reader must be educated in the language of music theory and harmony (including a knowledge of figured bass), and in piano technique (variations of touch and fingering, pedal application, and the lighter action of an 1830s instrument as compared to a modern one). At the very least, he or she should be able to follow the hundreds of examples in music type illustrating the text. Although no pianist can afford to be without the book, musicians of every kind should partake of both its wisdom and its practical lessons. All of this may sound forbidding, but the rewards are worthy of every effort. Among non-musicians, anyone interested in the cultural and literary history of the period can feast on Rosen's introductory and incidental essays about the Romantic movement as a whole.

The discussion of Romantic imagery gives considerable space to the new awareness of Nature (landscape—mountains, ruins, forests, the sound of wind through leaves, distant horn calls), and the newly recognized world of emotions, of loneliness, idealized love, tragic early death (Schubert, Büchner, and Novalis, whose *Novices of Sais* and *Pollen and Fragments* should be read in conjunc-

---

[1] *The Romantic Generation* by Charles Rosen. Cambridge: Harvard University Press, 1995.

tion with *The Romantic Generation*), suicide, alienation, and insanity (Schumann, Hölderlin, Clemens Brentano, Gerard de Nerval, Cowper, Christopher Smart, John Clare). For Rosen, memory is "the central theme of early nineteenth-century lyric poetry," of which he offers a trove of *Lieder* poets including Goethe, Heine, Eichendorff, and Wilhelm Muller. An anthology of the book's German, French, Italian, and English prose would be much larger and include not only Schiller, Friedrich Schlegel (the creator of "the Fragment as Romantic form"); Kleist, and Novalis ("Romanticism makes the familiar strange and the strange familiar"); but also the eighteenth-century physicist, Johann Wilhelm Ritter ("Tones are beings who understand each other"); and the philosopher Hamman (Isaiah Berlin's "pioneer of anti-rationalism"). The early linguistic philosophers are encountered as well, from Vico, for whom language was aesthetic and expressive above all, to Fichte on its functional origins (he imagined "a primitive man frightened by a lion returning to his fellows and roaring at them to convey the presence of danger"), and on to Wilhelm von Humboldt, who perceived that language is not merely "the fundamental means of communication but an independent system … separate from the exterior world of reality and from the subjective world of consciousness." Rosen's most striking quotations from French, Italian, and English prose writers are by Louis Ramon de Carbonnières ("one of the greatest masters of landscape description"), Aurelia di Giorgio Bertòla, Locke, Roger Ascham, and Thomas Burnet.

Believing that Schumann's songs and short piano pieces are his most enduring achievement, Rosen does not discuss the composer's symphonies, chamber music, sonatas, and concertos. The music of the first two genres, however, is dissected on every level: phrase structure, the role of rhythm, the setting of the text, the relation of words and music, of one piece to another and to the cycle as a whole. The analysis of Schumann's harmony is consistently acute, as in the case of the "disruptive" chordal movement at the half-cadence ending the first stanza of *"Auf einer Burg,"* and the frequent use of out-of-phase effects between harmony and melody.

Rosen's advice to performers extends to such matters as the proper lengths of pauses between songs in *Dichterliebe*, showing how the tonal ambiguity and inconclusiveness of the first piece is resolved in the next one, and why two or three seconds of silence are required to make the point. Examining the connection between composition and performance, he explains that Schumann's direction to the player to cross thumbs in *"Des Abends"* blends the opposing rhythmic systems of the two hands and gives "a bell-like resonance" to a focal repeated note, in short, "the sound is conceived for the hands." Here one could add that George Balanchine's *Davidsbundlertänze* reveals that the choreographer understood on his own Rosen's observation that the first and last pieces of this "subtlest, most mysterious, and most complex" of Schumann's large works are "outside the principal structure." Turning to Schubert, the author notes that in one of the songs of the *Schöne Müllerin* cycle, "an exquisite display of three-and-four-part polyphonic writings," the accent on weak beats "requires an almost imperceptible rubato."

For many musicians and all pianists, the two hundred pages allotted to Chopin will prove to be the richest in discovery in the book. Rosen begins with a consideration of the misprinted repeat sign in the first movement of the B-flat minor Sonata, an error that Brahms perceived by himself but that countless performers before and after, as well as all twentieth-century publishers, have not. (Fending off controversy, perhaps, or provoking it, Rosen professes to be aghast at the inferiority of most Chopin criticism: "It is astonishing how even the finest writers lose their wits at moments when confronted with Chopin.") The author overturns countless accepted opinions and clichés about the composer, whom he calls "the greatest master of counterpoint since Mozart," whose technique of composition "was without equal in his generation," and who "carried the technique of suggestion further that any other composer." The crux of "the differences between Chopin's forms and those of his Classical predecessors" is that the latter combine contrast and the heightening of tension in their expositions, whereas Chopin delays build up until all the thematic material has been heard, and delays the resolution until the last moment. Rosen admits that Chopin's music is difficult to characterize "with a vocabulary invented largely for eighteenth-century forms." In a short review, it is difficult to characterize at all.

The chapter on Liszt is cogently argued, but arch-devotees of the Abbé are not likely to concur: "The early works are vulgar and great; the late works are admirable and minor," the author maintains, and, "Liszt was always a deeply and sincerely religious man, but the religion of the mid-nineteenth century was less that of the Gothic cathedral than that of the Gothic novel." He adds that "composition and paraphrase were not identical for [Liszt] but they were so closely interwoven that separation is impossible," and, in a memorable aperçu, "The invention of material was never [Liszt's] strong point; one suspects that as he developed new effects of realization, he created material to fit and show them off." Still, Rosen allows that Liszt's setting of Victor Hugo's *"S'il est un charmant gazon"* has a "lovely" ending, and that the shorter "characteristic pieces" and Etudes—in one of which only the composer's own fingering will produce the "snap" that a certain figure requires—mark "one of the greatest revolutions of keyboard style in history," whereas the Sonata, which earned him musical respectability, is overvalued and by no means free of "bombast" and "sentimental posturing."

The author deals with Berlioz more briefly, suspecting that his "Romantic madness" was only "skin-deep." Thus the most vaunted Berlioz work at present, the opera *The Trojans*, is "the most classical of all subjects and the most academic: Virgil's *Aeneid*." Rosen dismisses it as an "imperturbably earnest and pretentious historical costume drama in the high academic style." But the music he cites as evidence of Berlioz's greatness is limited to a few excerpts: the *idée fixe* in the *Symphonie Fantastique*, the love scene in the *Romeo and Juliet* Symphony, the openings of the *Requiem* and the *Enfance du Christ*, and *The Damnation of Faust*, this last mentioned only in passing. The damnation of Berlioz receives more space: "It is not the composer's eccentricities which made him great but rather his normality, his ordinariness." At "moments ... Berlioz has a genuinely original inspiration but does not know what to do with it." But Rosen's real trouble with the composer is that he was not a pianist and not brought up on *The Well-Tempered Clavier*, which he thought "a bore."

Rosen touches on—we wish he had expatiated on—the perplexing phenomenon that a solo tenor part sounds an octave lower than notated, but is heard as higher than the actually higher notes in the accompanying orchestra or piano. What is the explanation of the aural illusion that in the first act of *Tosca*, the tenor's high B-flat, following the soprano's high A-flat, seems to sound one note above the soprano rather than a seventh below, where in fact it does sound, and why does the interchange of bass and treble voices in a song not conflict with the counterpoint and harmony? Rosen's point in broaching the question is the suitability of a male *vs* a female singer in a song from Schubert's *Winterreise* (a work "unsurpassed in the art of musical representation"—i.e., in musical images of the text), in which the female voice falsifies the harmony for the reason that the song begins in a register below the bass of the piano accompaniment.

In a few instances the reader anticipates a different conclusion from the author's. Apropos Schubert's shifting major/minor stance, Rosen describes the sudden switch to the minor in the opening of the G Major Quartet as an "initial and fundamental shock," but he does not comment on the similar jolt, this time because of the weakness of the effect, of the all-too-foreseeable reverse from minor to major in the same figure later in the movement. A more important criticism of the book is that the chapter on opera, which includes a sympathetic discussion of Bellini and finds merits in Meyerbeer, does not mention Carl Maria von Weber. True, *Der Freischutz* is earlier (1820) than the prescribed period, but so is *An die ferne Geliebte*, and by any standard Weber's opera is full-blown Romanticism. The omission is the more odd in that, as Rosen observes,

Schubert's *Lindenbaum* imitates a quartet of horns, that feature of the Overture to Weber's opera. (This reader has never forgotten the thrill, at age 14, of walking into the Curtis Institute theater during a rehearsal of it by Fritz Reiner.) It should also be noted that Rosen overlooks the Orientalism of some of the early Romantics, the parallels to Sufism and Mahayana Buddhism in, for example, the anti-mechanical philosophy of Novalis.

Occasionally the tone becomes Olympian, as when the author assures us that the later transformation of the character of a phrase introduced near the beginning of Liszt's Sonata "does not, in fact, take much imagination," and that Berlioz could write correct counterpoint, which, however, "is not a very difficult craft." But this is offset by such disarming remarks as the one following a particularly involved description of harmonic events in a Beethoven song: "This kind of analysis in the style of a railway timetable ("We arrive at the tonic pedal at 119 and depart at 129") is generally neither interesting nor very enlightening." Moreover, Rosen writes brilliantly. His best aphorisms would grace a slender pocket-book spin-off: "Music does not communicate emotions or even express them. What it does is inspire and stimulate emotion"; "the test of a great contrapuntist is the ability to compose a single unaccompanied line that makes harmonic sense" (Bach).

William Empson distinguished two kinds of critic, the analytical and the appreciative. In Charles Rosen they are perfectly united.

"Les Grands Amants du Siècle"

M. Frédéric Mitterand, nephew of the late President of France, has launched a television series on great love affairs of the century with a survey of the fifty years together of Igor Stravinsky and Vera de Bosset, as the film's subtitle presents them. A number of film clips of whose existence I was unaware have been spliced together, as well as some I had known about but not succeeded in tracking down. Regrettably, two of the former are spurious. What purports to be footage of Nijinsky's scandalous antics in *The Afternoon of a Faun* (taking matters into his own hand) is actually a combination of stills and reenactment by Rudolf Nureyev. And the scene of the audience mêlée during the premiere of *The Rite of Spring* is an extract from Marcel L'Herbier's 1923 movie *l'Inhumaine*. No doubt the real fracas resembled the filmed one, the Théâtre des Champs-Elysées not having changed, and the earlier period, as evidenced in hairstyles, clothes, and the state of filming technology seems to have been faithfully reproduced; but in 1913 cameramen were not standing by for possible uprisings in theaters.

The footage that I had known about but not seen includes the episode of Stravinsky's May 1930 visit to Peter the Great's residence in Haarlem where he studied the science of shipbuilding. Bundled up but wearing knickerbockers, Stravinsky raises his cap and smiles ripplingly for the camera, to the music of the Larghetto from *Les cinq Doigts*. Hat doffing takes place again on Stravinsky's arrival in Moscow in September 1962, this time more sweepingly, as well as, perhaps, a trifle pointedly *for* the camera. Earlier in 1962, Stravinsky bares his head in U.S. television coverage showing him, his wife, and myself emerging from the Presidential limousine at the White House and being received on its porch by the Kennedys.

Many clips feature people and events with little or no connection to Stravinsky, but justifiable as providing period atmosphere. Stravinsky did not know Duke Ellington, or the young Yehudi Menuhin, or Isadora Duncan, or her friend the poet Esenin, or even Toscanini, seen here pacing up and down and spasmodically raising his eyebrows while the finale of the *Pathétique* Symphony wrings its withers in the background. Toscanini, like Bruno Walter a few frames before, is brought in to represent artistic opposition to Nazism, depicted aurally by the storm music at the beginning of *Die Walküre*, but neither conductor had any place in the composer's life. Nor did Anna Pavlova, in spite of which she has been allotted a solo scene and, together with Nijinsky, Balanchine, Cocteau, and Diaghilev, top billing. Serge Lifar, fencing with the Marquis de Cuevas—brandishing a rapier before, grandly removing a glove after—was never close to Stravinsky, and neither was Chaliapin, the giant with the flowing foulard (lavallière) who appears only moments before his funeral, which is overdubbed by a recording of his dolorous diapason.

George Gershwin, with whom Stravinsky had only one, though much quoted, verbal exchange, is seen playing the piano faster than the ghost in the machine—the pianola, that is—as well as playing tennis and swimming in a Hollywood pool. A glimpse of Marlene Dietrich—*"Marlène,"* M. Mitterand drawls—is always welcome, but though she and Stravinsky knew each other well, her cameo appearance misleadingly insinuates that a closer relationship obtained between them. In the snippet of Arthur Rubinstein at the Venice Film Festival in 1956, and Maria Callas, who was first introduced to Stravinsky by Leonard Bernstein in New York five months later, the picture editor has inexplicably, but perhaps merely inadvertently, cropped out Stravinsky in the front row; a still photo of the Rubinsteins seated behind the Stravinskys quickly follows. Footage is also shown of a scene two weeks later, "backstage," or "back-altar," in the Basilica of San Marco, of Stravinsky between Count Alessi and Alessandro Piovesan (white jacket), the two men responsible for commissioning and presenting the *Canticum Sacrum*. The few frames of Stravinsky looking at Picasso's portrait of him, and of the painter in old age daubing a ceramic, were dragged in apparently to substantiate M. Mitterand's introductory but long-worn-out parallel between the artists.

The focus of the film is confusingly divided between Stravinsky's "great love" and the wife he partly abandoned for her in 1921, but conjugally speaking had already done so in 1914, when her life in and out of tuberculosis sanatoria began, and his life in and out of the boudoirs of, among others, Coco Chanel. Referred to as *"sa propre femme,"* Catherine, spouse number one, is sympathized with at considerable length and long after her death, in 1939, which is at odds with the announced subject and presumed intent of the film. Footage of her pacing back and forth in front of her Ukrainian home is used as a visual *leitmotif* near the beginning, in the middle, and again, inappropriately in terms of the subject, toward the end of the film. (I do not know if any Stravinsky relative has been identified in the other period footage here, as in the scene of a canine adhering to a woman's skirt.) Further, M. Mitterand superimposes schoolgirl and movie-actress photos of Vera de Bosset (wrongly identified as

"Natasha" in the first Russian *War and Peace*: she was Helena Kouraguine) that cast her as a temptress lying in wait for Stravinsky a decade before she had heard of him. In fact, a competitiveness, not between the women themselves, who respected each other, but between the two families, is the film's subtext. Thus Vera Stravinsky's 1959 home movie of her husband strolling on their front porch and through the garden of their Hollywood *dacha* is balanced, or offset, by 1952 footage of Stravinsky's older son in his Swiss home, with his wife, father and step mother, adopted daughter, and, on the walls, designs for a Geneva production of *The Rake's Progress*.

Excerpts from Stravinsky's *Apollo*, *Orpheus*, String Concerto, and the 1940 Tango have been sensitively chosen as the film's theme music, but the association of the Greek ballets with both women is puzzling in that *Apollo* is known to have been dedicated to Vera, while *Orpheus* dates from long after Catherine's death. The String Concerto works well everywhere, the third movement surprisingly so in scenes of the Russian Revolution. The Tango, too, fits a variety of situations, undermining the Lifar-Cuevas duel—which Cuevas wins by inflicting a slight nick on his opponent's right arm—and bringing Biarritz into the jazz age, but it does not suit the image of Vera de Bosset as the Queen in *Sleeping Beauty*. The principal violin motive from the first scene of *Histoire du Soldat* establishes the move to Switzerland during World War One, and Parasha's aria the relocation of the Diaghilev ballet to Monte Carlo after it. So, too, the oboe melody near the end of the slow movement of the Piano Concerto is mood-perfect for Vera as an old lady painting in her New York studio, less fitting for the glimpse of her fifteen years earlier in Hollywood sharing a joke with Pierre Boulez. The *Ragtime for 11 instruments* is used for the still photo of Igor and Vera through the windshield of their 1920s Hotchkiss, which then takes off—a different auto, of course, with different driver, and in a different season. But the Serenata from Neapolitan *Pulcinella* is wrong for Venice, and the visual and aural conflicts are lethal in the late 1920s clip showing Stravinsky conducting irregular meters in a recording session, while we hear his 4/4 Andante, and, later, conducting we do not know what while we hear the *Dumbarton Oaks* Concerto.

Some musically misleading captions appear on the screen, as when we read *"Le Sacre du printemps"* but hear an excerpt from the third movement of the String Concerto, read *"Requiem"* but hear *Orpheus*, read "Concerto for Two Pianos" and *"Jeu de cartes,"* but in both cases listen to other music. *"Les [sic] Danses concertantes"* is the label for the burning of the S.S. *Normandie* in New York harbor, but the footage is accompanied by "Kastchei's Dance" in *Firebird*; and in any case this event had no bearing on Stravinsky, who was in California at the time. (I was there, having walked from the 123rd Street Juilliard School to the 57th Street pier, and I well remember the literally keeled-over, still-smoldering vessel.)

Partly to define departures and destinations, partly because the Stravinskys were so often en route, trains and transatlantic liners appear frequently in the film. Footage of the Stravinskys on the dock at Genoa in 1958 counting their baggage as it is unloaded from the S.S. *Cristoforo Colombo* conveys a sense of the arduousness of their almost continual travels. The film opens with footage of the Stravinskys in the rear seat of an automobile in Chicago in 1965, then, to the "Apotheosis" in *Apollo*, transported to the deck of the S.S. *Bremen* in the Spring of 1963, en route to Hamburg and the stage premiere of *The Flood*. Here, passing a potted sapling, Stravinsky stops to adjust one of its branches. This ultra-fastidious man was unable to ignore anything even slightly askew, un-aligned table utensils, it may be, or sloppily stacked piles of papers and books— or, indeed, untidiness of any kind. He would rewrite an entire page of full score because he had failed to center a few notes exactly, and his need to correct, fix, fold, straighten, smooth out, tamp, trim amounted to a mania.

Stravinsky's gallant, old-fashioned manners, and his histrionic talent are evident throughout the film, as when he imitates Nijinsky's sideline coaching during the *Rite of Spring* premiere for the *"petites demoiselles"* of the Paris Opéra Ballet; and when he illustrates his and Beethoven's dependence on musical concreteness by mouthing a pencil and pressing it like a stethoscope to the soundingboard of his piano to hear the vibrations. The same talent is at play in his response to a criticism by Shostakovich, read to him by David Oppenheim, director of the CBS Stravinsky documentary. As soon as Stravinsky understands that something negative is coming, a smile dawns, and, ignoring Shostakovich's opinion, he says: "You see ... they invited me ... to be polite ... and one year later ... BOOM!" The flourish of the left arm when he finishes conducting the *Symphony of Psalms* is still another *coup de théâtre*.

Stravinsky and Rolf Liebermann, director of the Hamburg Opera, are shown debarking from the *Bremen* in its home port in April 1963. On terra firma, the composer enters an automobile whose interior proves to be the same in which we saw him at the beginning of the film, in Chicago two years later. But the scene that follows could puzzle the viewer in that Stravinsky is conversing with, and looking beyond his wife in the direction of an excised, unseen and unheard, someone else, actually myself, on her other side. For the record, too, the same party is deleted from another automobile scene a little later, in Clarens, Switzerland, birthplace of most of *The Rite of Spring*. Also for the record, the composer is shown reading in his bunk aboard what the viewer chronologically assumes is the S.S. *Bremen*, but is actually the S.S. *Kungsholm*, bound from New York to Sweden at the beginning of May 1965.

Clips of other composers are incorporated, fascinatingly in the case of two glimpses of Arnold Schoenberg, the first in the mid-1920s and apparently in Salzburg, in view of the sign "Mozart's Geburtshaus" shown immediately before. Schoenberg is joking with members of the Kolisch Quartet, one of whom, Benar Heifetz, pretends to be playing a non-existent cello. The date of the second is 1938, and the place the Malibu home of Serge Hovey. The music here, from Stravinsky's Movements, may or may not be intended as homage, but the juxtaposition of the next photo, Stravinsky with hand cupped to ear, seems to suggest that he has been listening to Schoenberg. Serge Rachmaninov appears aboard a New York-bound steamship, looking dour but adjusting the brim of his fedora for the camera. His younger compatriots, Shostakovich and Prokofiev, are shown at their respective pianos in World War II newsreels. Prokofiev is with the director Sergei Eisentein, whose panorama of the Teutonic Knights advancing across frozen Lake Ladoga in *Alexander Nevsky* is shown accompanied by Prokofiev's sound track.

Rimsky-Korsakov and Debussy, the composers who most deeply influenced the young Stravinsky, are shown in, respectively, a still photo and the pastel portrait by Marcel Broschet, Rome 1884, more than thirty years before the composition of *The Martyrdom of St. Sébastian*, which we hear with it. M. Mitterand neglects to say, but perhaps is not aware, that Debussy and Stravinsky were closer than is generally known. In fact, Stravinsky's silver cigarette case and the cane he is seen leaning on in innumerable 1920s photos were gifts from Debussy.

Sleights of eye are performed, as when Stravinsky is shown at his piano in Hollywood drawing a staff with his stylus, but when the camera zooms in, manuscripts of *Les Noces* and *The Rite of Spring* have been substituted for the one currently in progress. The camera moves smoothly from a still of Stravinsky seated in a chair on his patio in 1946, through stills of W. H. Auden, C. Day Lewis, Spender, Isherwood, and Aldous Huxley, to footage of Thomas Mann ensconced in a similar piece of furniture and with a cigar ensconced in *him*. But since the Mann clip comes from the same Hovey home movie, and since it also includes Edwin Hubble, Bertrand Russell, Robinson Jeffers, and Aaron Copland, one regrets that M. Mitterand did not let us peek at them, both as comment on the intellectual distinction of Southern California at the time, and because these people had connections to Stravinsky, close ones in the cases of Copland and the astronomer.

Footage of contemporaneous historical events, including Tolstoy's funeral, scenes of the Russian army during World War One, and of the Russian Revolution—the smashing of a church bell fittingly matched to Mussorgsky's coronation music—provides a sense of the world of Stravinsky's origins, made the more remote in that, filmed at some 24 frames a second and screened at perhaps 30, the people in them move too rapidly. But chronology is seldom respected. One exception is the sequence showing the young Walt Disney inspecting drawings for *Fantasia*—to Dukas's, not Stravinsky's, music—then sitting with Stravinsky and, from him, switching to a spectacle of elephants performing a gymnastic feat as well as, presumably, Stravinsky's *Circus Polka*, which we hear. The woman is Vera Zorina, ballerina, movie star, and George Balanchine's wife at the time, who rode the front pachyderm. But the next recognizable music is by Prokofiev, mismatched to a vista of Hollywood Boulevard.

The film should be seen for the excerpts of Stravinsky conducting, and for Vera Stravinsky remarking on the question of whether Stravinsky was difficult to live with. "No," she says, "he was difficult with himself.... He does not want to show that he has emotions." This is an acute observation by the only person who knew Stravinsky in every way, in every situation, and for longer than anyone else. In another film he plays part of the first dance of *The Rite of Spring* on his piano, then lets us down by saying of this repertory classic long since beyond criticism: "The repeated chord is an invention, but I could have made the upper part more interesting." This is what Mrs. Stravinsky means by his demands on himself. Her remark also alludes to the distancing in his music, the irony that replaces the tragedy of Petrushka's captive spirit, the formality that conceals personal emotion and gives the *Symphony of Psalms* its dignity. Stravinsky often talked about the importance of "good manners" in music, incidentally, rarely about "style," and though he was aware that manners can mask hypocrisy, he also understood that they enforce restraint and control. Consider his "In memoriam" pieces, from the *Symphonies of Winds* for Debussy to the *Requiem Canticles* for, so I believe, himself. Personal feelings may break through in the lament for Dylan Thomas, but not in the *Ode*—part of which is heard—or the Elegies, the *Epitaphium*, the Dufy Canon, the setting of Thomas Dekker's "Prayer," the Variations, and the *Introitus*, of which some of the 1965 Hollywood recording session is shown; "*Robair dirige*," M. Mitterand acknowledges. These pieces are ritualistic observances, and for Stravinsky the ritual was all important, the priest/shaman a mere functionary.

Here I might add that Stravinsky, a communicant in Hollywood's two Russian Orthodox Churches during the 1940s, ceased his connection with them in the early 1950s because his confessor asked him for an autograph, thereby crossing the barrier of the impersonality of the office. (In one of his sketchbooks Stravinsky wrote that "Musical Art must be as indifferent to the element of motive as the church is to love or to any other reasons for which people marry. You do not tell a priest that you are in love. He does not need to know that.") It remains to be said that Stravinsky would have been horrified by the scene in the film in which, towelling his torso during a conversation in Russian with Nicolas Nabokov, in Hamburg, in 1963, the religious medals that he wore around his neck are in full public view, but he did not realize that he was on camera and, fortunately, never saw the picture.

Having said this, I will add that for me the note of personal emotion is distinct in the love music inspired by Vera de Bosset, beginning with the rarefied pas-de-deux in *Apollo* and continuing with the more earthbound one in *Orpheus*, the *Berceuse* in *Perséphone*, the love music in the final scene in *The Rake's Progress*, *The Owl and the Pussycat*, and the *Berceuse* that ends *Le Baiser de la fée*, very movingly heard in the film as the 93-year-old widow, having described her life as "full of new people ... and of deaths," rests on a Fifth Avenue sidewalk bench looking across the street and up to me standing in the window of her fourth-floor apartment.

Of the sequences of Stravinsky conducting, the most absorbing is the one of him in London listening to a recording of his Variations with Balanchine. To me, the cues he gives to instruments in the absent orchestra, are reflected in the music. He points abruptly, without preparatory beat, and grabs a chord with the swoop of a raptorial bird. He is also seen in Moscow in 1962, surrounded by musicians during a rehearsal of *The Rite of Spring* following the score and indicating the meters; this may perplex the viewer, since the stage, the orchestra, and the conductor with whom Stravinsky is keeping time, myself, are concealed. One other conducting scene is painful to watch because he is obviously tired: his beat lags behind the chorus and orchestra which, at the end, cut off before he gives the signal. But the music's angular articulation is reflected in his gestures. We cannot help noticing the total absence of the imploring, molding, hushing hands, and the facial intimations of agonies and ecstasies familiar from most of the profession's wand-wavers.

For me the most memorable moment occurs in an extract from NBC's "Wisdom" series filmed in Stravinsky's Hollywood home in May 1957, the only footage of the interior that survives from his time, a subsequent owner having rebuilt it. Stravinsky negotiates the two steps down from his dining room and sits next to me at a card table. We are conversing, supposedly, though the camera and the situation had paralyzed me and I could say nothing but only twitch nervously and look grim. "Ask me another," Stravinsky said again and again, but this footage is not used in the film. What does appear is Stravinsky, who knew exactly how I felt, reaching out his right hand and gently patting the back of my left.

Discoveries in
Stravinsky's Sketches

Patriotic Endings

Photos survive of Stravinsky hoisting the American flag above his home on Fourths of July during World War Two. After registering for war work at age sixty he was "called up," one might say, when the Office of War Information asked him to write an article about Rimsky-Korsakov for broadcast to the Soviet Union. He complied on the same day, March 15, 1944, and did so again on February 20, 1945, when asked to write an address for broadcast to Belgium and France. Throughout the war Stravinsky frequented newsreel theaters and saw such documentaries as *Stalingrad* and *Victory in Tunisia* repeatedly. He also followed the conflict on maps, adjusting the positions of the flagged pins he had planted along the Russian front in accordance with each day's news reports. Mrs. Stravinsky drew a map of the Naples combat zone, and on June 12, 1944, to keep track of the Normandy invasion, he purchased a Michelin map of the area and had it photostatically enlarged.

In August 1944, inspired by the liberation of Paris, Stravinsky wrote the words *"Paris n'est plus aux allemandes"* after the triumphal, but much-too-long, final chord of *Scènes de Ballet*. The ending of the Symphony in Three Movements, called "Victory Symphony" when commissioned by the New York Philharmonic, February 16, 1945, shows deeper involvement. The sketch-score stops at the conclusion of the second bar of rehearsal number [195], but the full draft-score adds the final two chords and the date "August 7, 1945," the day that Stravinsky heard the news of Hiroshima. Thus a historical event appears to have catalyzed a creative one. Whereas the E-flat that invests the August-7th chords with the feeling of finality is also present in the *preceding* bars in the sketch score, Stravinsky removed it in the draft score from the last three bars before the final two and saved it for the ending, the "Harry James chord" as the composer Paul Desmarais famously called it. On the same day Stravinsky also found the rhythm, the sustained note followed by the short, punctuating period.

On Not Beginning At The Beginning

Stravinsky's sketches reveal that in a significant number, perhaps a majority, of cases he pieced his compositions together backwards from the end, an unusual practice that he attributed to the difficulty of composing the introduction to an as-yet-unwritten work. Consider the Octet. The first installment composed, twelve bars intended for the *Symphonies of Winds* but used at the beginning of the waltz variation in the second movement of the later piece, dates from the spring of 1919. The second installment, eventually the last variation, dated January 1921, was originally a fugato for two-pianos. Its subject employs the same intervals as the waltz entry, which Stravinsky seems not to have recognized at first as the theme of the variations. The first Allegro was composed next, followed by the second and third movements, and, last of all, the Introduction to the first movement.

The first notation for the Capriccio is found at the very end, starting one bar before [95]. The two sketches that follow were used at [86] and at [70–71], respectively. Stravinsky turned to the second movement next, sketching the music at [41] and at the end of the movement through the cadenza. The initial notation for the first movement, before [18], repeats the same four notes as the beginning of the first sketch for the third movement. The music at [10] came next, followed by three bars of the piano part at [6], the music at [14] and, in that order, at [11]. Suddenly he conceived the opening and composed the first movement straight through, the previous sketches for middle-section episodes falling into place.

Pasted to the flyleaf of the lined notebook containing the sketches for the *Symphony of Psalms* is a newspaper cut-out picture of Christ on the Cross with spokes of light emanating from His head and a board above it inscribed in Latin letters, "IMRI," which means "Judahite" in the Hebrew Bible; the base of the Cross bears the caption *"Adveniat Regnum Tuum."* The picture disturbs us, or at least me, partly because it is devoid of artistic merit, an example of *"Bondieuserie,"* and partly because the Hebrew Psalms do not seem to be the most appropriate place for it.

The first notation for the Symphony, the triplet upbeat figure followed by the dotted half-note and quarter-note (bar 4 of [5]), is found near the beginning of the orchestral allegro in the *last* movement; the sketch is harmonized and scored for trumpets and horns, as in the final score. The first dated entries, "24-XII-1929, 6-I-1930" (in the Julian calendar, which Stravinsky used until his American period), were intended for the first movement, the 39th Psalm. Among the ten notations subsumed under these dates are the ostinato figure of minor thirds connected by a major third, used in the final score a minor-third higher, and the octave leap upward followed by a whole-step down used in the choral chant at [10], but here assigned to horns. Three more pages of sketches for the same Psalm follow, dated March 4, none of them resembling the completed music. During January and February Stravinsky had been concertizing in Berlin, Leipzig, Vienna, Bucharest, Budapest, and Prague.

On March 10, he composed the opening three bars of the last movement, first in abbreviated form and without the G in the bass against the A flat for the third syllable of "Alleluia," then on seven staves, *with* the G and as we know the setting today. He wrote the Vulgate text on the facing page, adding a French translation in small letters under the words *"secundum multitudinem magnitudinis"*— *"selon la grandeur de son magnificence"*—for no reason that I can discover except to confound future scholars, since it is impossible that he did not know the meaning of the Latin. The handwriting here, exuberantly larger than that for the text of the 39th Psalm, suggests that composing the "Alleluia" had been an epiphanic experience for him. He drafted the music from here to the end of the movement in the order we know, with a minimum of correcting and rewriting and none at all in the section for full chorus before and through the second "Alleluia." After completing the movement, April 27, he wrote it out in condensed score form.

Resuming the first movement, May 10, Stravinsky wrote the first choral entrance over the minor-thirds accompaniment figure, but he soon interrupted himself for concerts in Amsterdam. In June he abandoned the first movement once again and began the second, writing out the fugue subject a half-step lower than we know it (starting on B rather than C), an infrequent instance of this in his sketches, in which the pitch is most often the same as in the final score. On June 21 he discovered the subject of the choral fugue, combined it with the instrumental subject in the bass, and composed from there in sequence to the end, which is dated July 17. After writing the condensed score, he accompanied Mme Sudeikina on a holiday to Avignon, Vaucluse, and Marseilles.

The composition of the 39th Psalm was begun in earnest on July 29 with the writing of a Russian translation under every word of the text, conceivably in this instance because he was seeking further perspectives of meaning in his mother tongue. On completing the movement, he drew a Russian-style cross in the manuscript as an envoi and dated it, in French, "August 15, The Feast of the Assumption in the Roman Church." Having composed the piece in Nice and under the same roof as his wife, Catherine, he invited her to attend the premiere, in Brussels, December 13, 1930. On December 14, after her departure, Mme Sudeikina arrived and Stravinsky, resuming the other side of his bigamous life, went with *her* to Amsterdam for more concerts.

* * *

The first nine pages of the sketchbook for the Two-Piano Concerto are remarkable in that the music is without meters, and that every entry is meticu-
lously dated. Stravinsky began the first movement on November 14, 1932, and
composed daily thereafter through the twenty-seventh. The sketches, however,
are pieces in a frameless jigsaw puzzle. What would ultimately become bars
16–19 were written on the sixteenth; bars *137* and *140*, and *147–148* on the
twentieth; bars 134–136 and 138–139 on the 21st; and bars 32–33 on November 26: we can only assume that he had a coherent, integrated conception of
the movement before beginning to compose it. On the twenty-seventh, at the
end of a number of other entries, he wrote what became the first bar, but compared to the preceding sketches the notes are hurriedly drawn and as if in an afterthought. The next dates, "Paris 15 May [to] 4 June," can only refer to 1934;
Perséphone was composed and performed in the interim. The three bars worked
out between May 15 and June 4 belong to the latter part of the first movement.
The final eleven bars were written on June 9 and 10, but *before* the last entry,
signed "Voreppe, 10 August, 1934," which covers the connection from the
12/16 middle section to the 4/4 of the closing section.

The "Notturno" was written in June and July 1935, after the longest hiatus
from original composition in Stravinsky's artistic maturity, not fully accounted
for by the violin and piano versions of excerpts from his theater pieces, by an
American concert tour of four months, by European concerts and recordings,
by the publication of an autobiography he did not write, by an appendectomy,
and by the bureaucratic business of becoming a French citizen and of canvass-
ing for election to the French Academy. The fourth movement, the Prelude and
Fugue, was composed next and completed on August 31, 1935. The third movement, the Variations, was not finished until November 9, after a concert tour in
Scandinavia in October. The completed manuscript retains the order of the
Prelude and Fugue followed by the Variations, but Stravinsky's word *"attacca"* at
the end of the Variations confirms that he was never in doubt about the sequence of the movements. In view of the sixteen-month interruption for *Perséphone* and the ten months from August 1934 to June 1935, the most astonishing
attribute of the Concerto is its unity of style, but no less remarkable is the absence of any apparent relationship between the mellifluous, homophonic, lan-
guorously paced *Perséphone* and the dissonant, polyphonic, and fiercely
propulsive Concerto.

* * *

The first idea for *Danses concertantes*, the melody in bars 3 and 4 of the A-
major/F-sharp-minor variation, is preserved in the message space of a partly

torn Western Union form, "Holiday Telegram Of Your Own Composition, 35 cents," stapled to a same-size sheet of white paper dated by Stravinsky "Oct. 1940"; Stravinsky was a fanatic believer in Occam's Razor, in so far as it concerns the principle of parsimony. For the composer, economy of means was a moral virtue. The notation, later scored for clarinet and oboe and preceded by two bars under the title *"Une des 8 variations"*—he composed only four—appears at the head of the first page of the complete sketchbook for the opus. The locution "O.K." appears in this same book for the first time in Stravinsky's hand. He often autographed scores for queued-up admirers after concerts by writing "O.K." under his printed name.

* * *

The music of the first sketch for *Scènes de Ballet*, dated June 22, 1944, is found in the Variation at [89]. On July 3, Stravinsky wrote the first "Pantomime" [54]–[58], and by July 23 he had composed the music between [40] and [43] as well as the whole of the first dance of the Corps de Ballet, [5] to [41]. Exactly a month later, on August 23, the *Apotheosis* was completed in full score, but the Introduction was not finished until August 29.

* * *

Stravinsky's first sketches for the 1945 Symphony are of the music used at rehearsal number [71] through the second bar of [80]. The first part of the third movement, as far as the leapfrogging canon for bassoons, was drafted next, then the music of preceding episodes of the first movement, [59] to [70], followed by [34] to [56]. As he continued backwards toward the beginning, he was invited to write the score for a film about Nazi-occupied Norway eventually published as *Four Norwegian Moods*. He copied the originals of two tunes used in its first piece, "Intrada," on a page facing Symphony sketches, and over one of them wrote dotted rhythms in the only place where the Norwegian original does *not* use them, and straight eighths where the original rhythms are all dotted.

* * *

The sketches for the *Trois Mouvements de Pétrouchka* reveal that the bar before [119] in the original orchestra score is missing in all editions of the piano piece including the first. It is present and accounted for in the two-piano arrangement by Victor Babin, made under Stravinsky's supervision and with an extended passage rewritten by him. Glaring though the omission is, it mars every recording of the work that I have heard, thereby convicting its performers, after 74 years, of ignorance of the orchestral original. The missing bar in the printed music comes between the end of one score-system and the beginning of the next, which suggests that the mistake is a printing error. That Stravinsky himself did not discover it can be explained by the circumstances that he never attempted to play the arrangement, did not examine the proofs of the original, and did not look at the Boosey and Hawkes reprint. He did not discover that the published piano score of *Apollo* lacks bar 17 of the Coda until playing it for Balanchine in 1928.

A Special Case

Most commentaries on *Le Baiser de la fée* attempt to establish parallels between Pergolesi-Stravinsky and Tchaikovsky-Stravinsky, but the only exact one is that both collaborators were composers of the past. The unique entirely original Stravinsky music in *Pulcinella* is a short bridge section and the introduction to the Tarantella. *Le Baiser de la fée*, at another extreme, is largely original composition. Stravinsky altered, developed, and elaborated his borrowed bits and scraps of Tchaikovsky, expanding them into sizable ballet numbers forming a continuous dance symphony. He was so familiar with his collaborator's stylistic features, melodic, harmonic, and instrumental, that he could compose more Tchaikovsky himself.

The sketches for *Le Baiser de la fée* do not contain a single reference to sources in Tchaikovsky, but perhaps more than those for any other Stravinsky work the sketches bear out T. S. Eliot's dictum that "the mark of the master is to be able to make small changes that will be highly significant." In some instances Stravinsky simply changes Tchaikovsky's tempo. Thus the *Scherzo Humoresque* becomes the slow-tempo song at the beginning of Scene III of *Le Baiser de la fée*, and Tchaikovsky's *Allegretto grazioso* is wholly transformed by being played at half tempo: Stravinsky retains the melody, rhythm, and even the harmony of the original. Stravinsky had a genius for perceiving the slow-tempo lyrical piece in the fast-tempo one, the attractive melody obscured by the dull rhythm. Thus the male dancer's Variation later in Scene III changes Tchaikovsky's 3/4 Nocturne to 6/8 and his monotonously repeated 8th-notes to quarters followed by eighths. Eliot again: "Appreciation is akin to creation." I should add that the ballet also transposes the piece from A down to G, but that, clearly, was to accommodate the high notes of the horn.

The most remarkable transformation in *Le Baiser de la fée* is that of the early song "Both Painful and Sweet" into the Ballad that concludes Scene II. In the first five notes of the theme, Stravinsky reverses the melodic sequence E, C-sharp, D-natural, to E, C-natural, D-sharp, thereby changing A major to A minor, but preserving the ambitus. He also rewrites Tchaikovsky's rhythmic pattern of quarter-note beats and eighth-note offbeats to on-the-beat triplets, with a rest replacing the third note, as in the piano and string ostinato in the first movement of the 1945 Symphony; this transforms the mood from one of resolution to one of agitation. What amazes us, however, is the mileage that Stravinsky gets out of this fragment in its development, repeating it in different octaves, progressively slower tempos, and longer note-values, until, at the end of the scene, the bass clarinet plays it slowly beneath six ascending octave scales in the flute, the first four notes of which are in Stravinsky's A-minor, the last four in Tchaikovsky's A-major, a subtle collaboration indeed. I should mention that a scale in the lower strings earlier in the dance is octatonic.

Agon

The dance critic Arlene Croce followed her excoriation of the New York City Ballet's Balanchine centenary celebration—the performances were shabby on every level, she averred—with an important essay on what may well be the last jointly composed, dance and music, ballet masterpiece; her article "The Spelling of Agon" was published in the *New Yorker*, July 12, 1993. For lack of sources, Ms. Croce imagined her way into the mind of "Balanchinsky," as she conflates the phenomena, and reconstructs what may have transpired there concerning the germination of the ballet. Her inductions are ingenious, but before they become incontrovertible facts, some of them require amplification, as well as several peeks at Stravinsky's sketches.

As it pertains to music, Ms. Croce's thesis mentions certain "brainstorming" Dutch musicologists. This can only mean the writer Elmer Schoenberger, the composer Louis Andriessen, whose number-symbolism theory[1] in relation to Stravinsky's *Requiem Canticles* has clearly influenced her, and Pieter van den Toorn, who has described *Agon* as "well-nigh miraculous" in its synthesis of tonal and serial procedures, as well as in its "vast, pluralistic reach in historical reference."[2]

Ms. Croce states that the only surviving document from the conference in the summer of 1954, when work on the ballet began, "is a chart that Stravinsky made afterward listing the order of dances, their timings, and the number of dancers, with stick figures for males and females." In truth, the chart, which is

[1] See their book, *The Apollonian Clockwork: On Stravinsky*, translated by Jeff Hamburg. Oxford: Clarendon, 1989.

[2] See *The Music of Stravinsky*, by Pieter van den Toorn. New Haven: Yale University Press, 1983.

part of the sketches, dates *from* those conferences, not "afterward." In it the first and last pieces are called "Sinfonia" and "Epylogue [*sic*]," titles that cannot have been written later than August 1954 when the first piece was composed and named "pas-de-quatre." The chart reveals that not all of the dances were included in the original scenario, and that titles had not yet been chosen for some of them. The rubrics "Sarabande" and "Gaillarde" were entered after these pieces were completed, three months later.

Ms. Croce tells us that the second part of the pas-de-deux is identified in the chart as, "6/16, 7/16. 5/16, etc.," as are other sections by tempo markings, but whereas the timings of the pas-de-deux were appended to the chart after the movement was completed, some are projections of approximate lengths of dances not yet begun. From watching Balanchine and Stravinsky working together on *The Flood*, I picture the choreographer proposing the order of the dances and the composer taking them down, drawing the stick figures—triangular tutus for females—as he went along. They are hastily, less carefully, written than they would have been at any time "afterward."

"On August 12, [1954]," Ms. Croce recounts, "Stravinsky chose his Greek title. He was thinking in Greek." In London, in 1950, she goes on, T. S. Eliot told Lincoln Kirstein that the Balanchinsky *Orpheus* was "the most wonderful stage experience he has had since he could not remember when," but he was "unable to provide an idea for a sequel to *Apollo/Orpheus*. He did say that he would be delighted to work with Stravinsky on a ballet of 'Sweeney Agonistes'.... Craft thinks it was 'Sweeney Agonistes' that put the title *Agon* into Stravinsky's mind." Well, Craft still does. In 1950, Stravinsky's language was macaronic, a mix of Russian, English, German, French, and Italian, but not Greek, which he did not know and in which, therefore, he could not cogitate. After reading Eliot's *two* "Agon" poems and the great *agon* between Aeschylus and Euripides in Aristophanes' *Frogs*, he became interested in the "contest" concept, and it stuck.

Ms. Croce reveals that: "Stravinsky had been studying a seventeenth-century dance manual sent him by Kirstein, but the actual style or content of the dances cannot be traced to anything that passed between him and Balanchine in 1954—unless, of course, we assume that Balanchine's statement 'We constructed every possibility of dividing twelve' means *every* division and every application of that division." But surely "6/16, 7/16, 5/16" indicates something of the sort, not to mention the *preconception*, as the chart and the sketches show, of a ballet for twelve dancers, with solos, duos, trios, quartets, and an octet. The manual, F. de Lauze's *Apologie de la danse* (1637), was the probable source for the three bransles—the engraving of two trumpets reproduced in the book clearly suggested the two trumpets of the Bransle Simple—but it must be borne in mind that Stravinsky had already composed a bransle, the passepied in the third movement of the Symphony in C. As the chart testifies, the rhythmic scheme of the Gaillarde follows the definition of the dance in Littré's *Dictionnaire de la langue française*, cited in Stravinsky's sketches.

Ms. Croce tells us that "Stravinsky met Balanchine in September 1956 [in Venice] and played for him as much of the score of *Agon* as he had composed, which was up to the end of the second pas-de-trois," the Bransle Simple. But the sketches strongly suggest that he had also composed, and hence would have played, much or most of the pas-de-deux. The Bransle Gai, which follows the Bransle Simple, was finished in Hollywood, June 8. He began the pas-de-deux, the next movement, in New York between the nineteenth and the twenty-seventh, and worked on it continuously upon his arrival in Venice at the end of July, seven weeks before the audition for Balanchine on September 17. Another meeting with Balanchine about the ballet followed in Berlin on September 27, as Stravinsky's diary tells us. Whether or not the shakier bar lines toward the end of the piece are attributable to the stroke he suffered in Berlin on October 2, I cannot say, but they do not correspond to any alterity in creative imagination.

Ms. Croce argues that the Bransle Gai contains the "skeleton" of the ballet, partly because it is the first of the 6/16, 7/16, 5/16, etc. pieces. But she forces the parallel between "Terpsichore's famous pauses or poses [in *Apollo*], the music stopping as the sense of flow continues," and the "four measures of silence during which the castanets keep time" in the Bransle. Unlike the pauses in Terpsichore, which occur close together at the beginning of the second half of the dance, the castanet solos in the Bransle frame the beginning, the end, and all three internal divisions. And whereas the pauses are silent, the castanet clacks.

Ms. Croce says that "in Stravinsky's mind," the twelve dancers in *Agon* signified "the 12-tones of the dodecaphonic scale, just as the dancers in the cast of *Apollo* ... had signified the seven tones of the diatonic scale." But "dodecaphonic" implies an ordering, a series or a row, *not* a scale. So-called diatonic *Apollo* employs the same twelve tones of the chromatic scale as partly dodecaphonic *Agon*, but relates them differently, hierarchically. Ms. Croce has been misled by a remark from a Stravinsky interview published in *Preuves*, Paris, May 25, 1952: "Personally, I find quite enough to do with the seven tones of the scale." But the statement makes no sense without an involved explanation of the difference between what Stravinsky said and what he meant to say. He had always composed with the twelve tones of the chromatic scale, of course, not with seven tones.

After crediting Couperin with having united the Italian and French styles, Ms. Croce announces that "Stravinsky and Schoenberg ... were the Lully and Corelli of their era." She asks, "who first proposed that Stravinsky become his own Couperin and attempt a similar union with the Vienna school? Robert Craft, who guided both Stravinsky and Balanchine in their initial investigations of serial and twelve-tone form, nowhere names Couperin as a role model, or Couperin's *Les Apothéoses* as a factor in Stravinsky's preparations for *Agon.*" She is referring, of course, to Couperin's trio-sonata for Corelli and the instrumental concert for Lully. She goes on: "It's impossible that so wise and conscious an artist as Stravinsky would have been oblivious to the parallel...." Here Ms. Croce is forgetting that Stravinsky did not set out to fuse two different "styles" and that this came about only gradually, two years after he had begun the composition and when the score was half complete, by which time Couperin, except for his Tenebrae, was remote from Stravinsky's musical spheres.

"In Stravinsky's stylistic imitation of Italian Baroque music, heard most clearly in the second half of the Prelude ... the sound is more Monteverdian than Corellian," Ms. Croce announces. More Renaissance than Baroque, certainly, and in the Landini cadences centuries earlier than Monteverdi. The flutes together with flute-like bass harmonics, a feature of the Gaillarde as well, are the most striking sonorities in the score. Stravinsky loved string-bass harmonics, and had famously exploited them in the Introduction to *The Rite of Spring*. I have often heard him imitate the *"strascicante"* (strangulated) effect himself by opening his mouth, tightening his neck muscles to form a sound box, and flicking his middle finger from the thumb against his throat, which emitted a hollow, piping note.

"To Stravinsky and Balanchine, as to Dante, Goethe, Schiller, Bach, and Mozart numbers were charismatic," Ms. Croce writes. Yes. What one doubts is her claim that Corelli's "obsession with twelve could easily have provided a reason to settle on twelve without waking the dragon dodecaphonism." The rationale for this is that Corelli published his works in clutches of a dozen—as, indeed, did other composers of the period. Music apart, the reason would be in Stravinsky's belief that the Biblical number was sacred, the dodecasyllabic Alexandrine virtually a Law of Nature.

Balanchine "launched his own investigation of 12-tone theory," Ms. Croce tells us. What this amounts to is that on July 29, 1953, Balanchine, in Los Angeles with his dancers for performances at the Greek Theater, dined at the Schoenberg home with the composer's widow, daughter, pupil Richard Hoffmann, and myself, seeking permission to base a ballet on a Schoenberg twelve-tone work. Balanchine did not know which one, however, whereupon I suggested the *Accompaniment to a Cinematographic Scene*, Opus 34, because its ensemble is comparatively small and because the only other purely orchestral twelve-tone pieces, the concertos and the Variations, Opus 31 did not seem suitable. The next day, in the Stravinsky home, I played a tape recording of the work for Balanchine several times. (Stravinsky was in Mount Sinai Hospital July 22 to August 4 recovering from surgery and the effects of a clumsily injected epidural anesthetic.) Balanchine quickly understood the musico-dramatic form, of course, classical protasis, epitasis, catastrophe, but not the pitch organization. The notion of repeating the seven-minute work and choreographing it differently the second time occurred to him almost immediately. It became his ballet *Opus 34*.

On Apollo *and* Orpheus

Apollo

If Apollo's mother was Leto then certainly his father was Fyodor.

—George Balanchine, in a birthday telegram to Igor
Fyodorovitch Stravinsky, June 18, 1945.

Orpheus

Quis et me inquit miseram et te perdidit, Orpheu?

—Virgil, *Georgics*, IV

Stravinsky chose the subject of *Apollo*. The following text, adapted into French from the "Homeric Hymn to the Delian Apollo" and pasted at the head of the first page of his sketchbook, was clearly inspirative:

Ilithya arrives at Delos. Leto was with child and, feeling the moment of birth at hand, threw her arms about a palm tree and knelt on the soft grass. The earth smiled beneath her and the child sprang forth to the light.... Two goddesses, Leto's handmaidens, washed the child with pure, limpid water. For swaddling clothes they gave him a white veil of fine linen tissue, binding it with a golden girdle. Themis brought nectar and ambrosia.

Apollo was the son of Zeus, the god, and of Leto, a mortal. Leto was in labor for nine days and nights before Eileithyia ("Eleuthis," on a tablet found at Knossos), the deity of childbirth, came to her. Themis was the goddess of Justice.

Apollo, the sun god and god of music, is associated with the Oriental sacred number seven, which corresponds to the diatonic mode that the composer seems to have had in mind from the beginning. As Francis Poulenc testified, Boileau's *L'Art Poétique* had excited Stravinsky's imagination at the time and was an important contributing factor: the music's rhythmic language would be based on the French Alexandrine. Apollo was the preferred persona of *Le Roi Soleil*, who actually danced the part in one of his court ballets. Stravinsky's *Apollo* renders homage to the Greek concept of the unity of music, dance, and poetry, but by way of seventeenth-century French Classicism—Racine, Arbeau (not yet known to the composer), Poussin, Lully.

It is also probable that Stravinsky viewed the subject as an allegory of his own religion, Apollo as man-god, with a human nativity and divine ascension.

283

Arlene Croce observes that, like Apollo, "The Christ child was wrapped in swaddling clothes," and Stravinsky may have been struck by such other parallels as the "threes" of the Muses, the Magi, and triadic harmony, as well as by the imagery of the darkness before Apollo's entrance and the light that accompanies it.

The composer is also the author of the scenario. On January 4, 1928 he informed his Paris publisher that the music was ready to be copied but not the *argument*, which, "as I envision it, requires mature reflection." The manuscript score of the first scene includes Stravinsky's curtain, lighting, exit and entrance cues, as well as some indications for the coordination of music and stage action.

The music for the Prologue, The Birth of Apollo, Apollo's first Variation, and the Pas d'action was composed in Nice between mid-July and mid-September 1927. On September 28, Stravinsky played his piano arrangement of these pieces for Diaghilev who described the occasion in a letter to Serge Lifar two days later:

> I spent the whole day with him, and at five saw him off at the station. It was an eminently satisfactory meeting…. After lunch he played the first half of the new ballet for me. It is, of course, an amazing work, extraordinarily calm and with greater clarity than anything he has done: filigree counterpoint around transparent, clear-cut themes, all in a major key, music not of this world, but from somewhere above…. The tempo of all this part is slow, yet at the same time perfectly adapted to dancing. A short, fast movement forms part of your first variation. You will have two variations as well as the opening danced to an unaccompanied violin solo. Very remarkable! He played it to me three times, so I have the clearest idea of it now. The *Pas d'Action* has a broad theme that runs concurrently in four different tempos. The harmony is most satisfactory. I embraced him and he said: "It is for you to produce it properly for me…." When his train had already begun to move he shouted to me: "Find a good title!"

The title, *Apollon Musagète*, was not established until two months after the completion of the score.

In an interview in *Excelsior* (Paris, October 27), Diaghilev is quoted as saying that "in the Adagio the first musical part plays at a speed twice as fast as the second, three times as fast as the third, and four times as fast as the fourth. Thus the same melody has four different aspects." (Apparently nothing was said about the relationship between this *stretto* and the four dancers.) Two remarks in the Lifar letter require clarification: the "fast movement" is danced by Leto's two handmaidens ("*déesses*"), hence is not part of Apollo's first variation; and only the first part of the violin solo is unaccompanied. The interview is more seri-

ously misleading in that the episode of the four speeds, which are not propor-
tionalized as described, occurs in a "Moderato," not in an "Adagio" movement.
This momentarily tripped even our keen Ms. Croce into confounding the
"dance adagio"—in which, she writes, "the first musical part plays twice as fast,"
etc.—with the *Pas de deux*.

The destination of Stravinsky's train was Paris. He arrived on the twenty-
ninth, celebrated Vera Sudeikina's Name Day with her on the thirtieth, and on
October 2 escorted her to London, where he had concerts. On the eighteenth,
back in Paris, he and Maurice Ravel co-conducted the inaugural concert in the
new Salle Pleyel. On October 29, Stravinsky and Mme Sudeikina drove to Va-
lence, spent the night there, and the next day continued to Nice, reaching the
city at 1:00 a.m. on October 31. In the following three weeks Stravinsky composed the Calliope, Polymnia, and Terpsichore variations. He drew a Russian-
style cross under the final bar of Polymnia (to commemorate I do not know
what) and to the left of the page added the note, *"Durée*—1'20'"; the commission
for the ballet stipulated a half-hour of music, and he was becoming concerned
about the length of his score and the remaining time for composing. But not too
concerned: he was in Paris again on November 24, and did not resume work in
Nice until December 2. The full score was completed on January 20, and on
January 22 he played it for Diaghilev and Balanchine.

With one exception each movement begins with the most prominent note
or notes in the last chord of the piece before; the exception, Apollo's second
variation, is clearly intended to give him greater distinction. Thus each dance,
however different from its neighbors, is closely linked to them. The harmonic
transparency of the music is another of its most striking features. Though a degree of density might have been expected from the six-part structure of the orchestra, almost a third of the score is in only three parts. Stravinsky wrote that:

> Contrast is an element of variety, but it divides our attention. Similarity is
> born of a striving for unity.... Contrast is everywhere.... Similarity is hid-
> den, it must be sought out, and it is found only after the most exhaustive
> efforts. When variety tempts me, I am uneasy about the facile solutions it
> offers me.

Apollo is both tightly cohesive and rich in variety of dance forms, tempo,
rhythm, harmony, instrumental combination and color.

On July 16, 1927, Stravinsky entered his bars of music in his sketchbook
in which the "Apollo chord" (bar 4, final score) occurs twice. The next entry is
a version of the melody at bars 3-5 of the *Pas de deux*, the next-to-last movement
composed. The remaining sketches are for the opening phrase of the piece
(which Robert Garis, in *Following Balanchine*, singularly recognized as a "ques-

tion") up to and including the accompaniment figure at rehearsal no. [4]; the majestic march melody itself appears on the next page. The following two pages contain more sketches for the same dotted-rhythm music, so similar to the Largo introduction in Stravinsky's Piano Concerto of 1924, even melodically (compare bar 4 in each piece), that we must accept the composer's claim to have been blessed with a memory that erases connections of this kind. On July 20 he wrote the music from the opening through bar 8, in which the bass parts are scored for harp and piano, a holdover combination from his *Oedipus Rex* of the previous year. The *Pas de deux* melody reappears on the 21st, this time in the remote key of D-flat but otherwise closely resembling its final form. Stravinsky attaches it to a Prologue sketch, sees that it does not fit, then shelves it until composing the dance-duo five months later. On the 22nd, he discovers the precise moment of Apollo's birth, the 3rd quarter-beat of [6], marks it as such (in Russian), and repeats the simple syncopated figure in *accelerando*, the quickening of life.

On the same day he notates the theme of the cut-time dance for Leto's handmaidens (that Diaghilev mistook for Lifar's dance). They run in widening circles unwinding Apollo's swaddling clothes, the musical image for which is the increasingly wide upward-interval loops in the violins. The fast movement concludes with the bumpy birth motive repeated above a rapid downward figure based on the intervals of Apollo's chord. With the return of the Largo—the musical form of the Prologue is the slow-fast-slow of the Baroque French Overture—the stresses are on the short notes of the dotted figures as they are in the beginning of the Piano Concerto. The handmaidens carry the godling toward Mount Olympus. Shortly before the musical halfway point, a blackout occurs. In the final bar, the grown-up Apollo, educed from the larval, embryonic stage to maturity in 30 seconds, stands alone in dazzling light.

Ms. Croce has remarked that a lute is one of the props in Balanchine's ballet, but "its sound is not in Stravinsky's orchestra, unlike the lyre in *Orpheus*." This is true with respect to timbre, but not articulation. Plucked accompaniments are conspicuous in every movement except the last, and in the Prologue Allegro and Apollo's first Variation they are employed throughout. The *Pas d'Action*, the Polymnia and Calliope variations, and the *Coda* conclude with lute- or guitar-like effects, the *Coda* with a visual-musical duplication, the Muses clapping their hands with the pizzicato and Apollo resting his head on their extended palms in time with the sustained chord that follows.

The violin-solo prelude to Apollo's first Variation is a cadenza in the sense of virtuosity—trills, double-stopping, appoggiaturas, and the feeling that the music is being invented on the spot—but not in its strict tempo and strict, albeit not-written-out, meters. Its relation to the accompanied part of the piece becomes clear only with the recapitulation of the beginning of the cadenza near the end of the variation, as befits both the godlike bearing of Apollo and his inexperience as a dancer, the accompanied part of the piece is slow. Dotted rhythms, virtually absent in the cadenza, are heard throughout the body of the variation, but set off by passages of even note-values.

The diminished chord spread out melodically at the beginning of the *Pas d'Action* functions as a modulation and inevitably as a portent, though the music thereafter could hardly be more radiant. The idea of the *stretto* seems to have occurred to Stravinsky soon after writing the first theme, to judge by his exploration of its possibilities in the earliest sketches. The return of the first theme in the bass in emphatically masculine form, with a feminine response, in repeated three-note treble triads on the unstressed part of the bar, is an instance of Stravinsky's kinetic imagination: the music places Apollo in a choreographic dialogue with the Muses. The second theme, which, like the first, appears among the sketches for the Prologue, is more a continuation of the first than a contrast; both are developed in the home key and in closely related ones. In the *stretto*, the second theme is exposed simultaneously in the second cellos in 8th-notes; in violas and first cellos (and in second violins in canon at the octave with them) in half- and quarter-notes; and in first violins in quarters, half-notes, and double-whole-notes (but not in the speeds as described in the Diaghilev interview). The first theme returns in a violin solo of ineffable tenderness accompanied by a single line of counterpoint in the cellos and long bass notes. The piece concludes with a repeat of the diminished progression, the sustained dominant of the key (representing Apollo), and two quiet pizzicato chords (representing the Muses) spaced to indicate the ending, which is not punctuated.

"Calliope, receiving the stylus and tablets from Apollo, personifies poetry and its rhythms," Stravinsky wrote. His subtitle ("The Alexandrine") and his inclusion of the anapaestic motto from Boileau in the published score[1] prepare the listener for the twelve- and six-note musical phrases that correspond to French alexandrines. The novelty of the accompaniment to the twelve-bar cello solo at the midpoint of this short piece merits mention: two solo violins and a viola play the same music pizzicato an octave below the *ripieni* violins and violas who play it (softly) with bows, a delectable effect. The final phrase, a full twelve-note musical alexandrine, is gentler than the rest of the piece, and the perfect cadence is not noticed until it is over. As Ms. Croce *did* notice, Cal-

---

[1] "Let meaning in your verse that shapes each word. / Always halve the line so that a rest is heard." (Translated by Richard Howard).

liope's dance is marked by starts, falters, and stops, like the writing of poetry.

"Polymnia, finger on lips, represents mime," Stravinsky wrote, and the Muse holds her finger to her lips throughout the dance. In contrast to Calliope's music, Polymnia's scampers from beginning to end in rapid 16th-notes. The second theme, two notes with quick crescendo followed by two in sudden *piano*, is derived from the accompaniment figure after the repeated statement of the first theme. A transformed pizzicato version of the first theme, a musical image of mimicry, leads to the final cadence.

According to Stravinsky, "Terpsichore, combining in herself both the rhythm of poetry and the eloquence of gesture, reveals dancing to the world, and thus takes the place of honor beside Apollo." The "rhythm of poetry" refers to the iambics on which the piece is based, and the "eloquence of gesture" to the five fermatas during which the dancer briefly holds a pose (or poses)— "huge sustained attitudes," Lincoln Kirstein calls them, but each caesura lasts for only a tiny fraction of a beat. (Since these fermatas appear in Stravinsky's first sketch, one wonders what *he* meant by them.) The first of the five occurs on the last note of the introduction, before the upbeat to the melodic arc, which is re-peated four times. The remaining fermatas occur close together at the begin-ning of the second half of the movement, the only one in the ballet with no change of meter. Most of the music is in three harmonic parts, the arc-shaped melody is in only two, and the introduction is an unaccompanied but punctua-ted line.

The music of Apollo's second Variation is the most original in the ballet, as well as, in a piece that replaces dramatic conflict with musical contrasts, its mu-sico-dramatic climax. Uniquely in this variation, Stravinsky eschews the pattern accompaniments of the Delibes tradition. As a saraband, moreover, it is the one dance that directly recalls the century of Lully and the Sun King. Its "thew and sinew" masculinity is evoked by the resonant full-orchestra chords at the be-ginning, middle, and the end, so remote from the feminine dances of the Muses.

During a quiet passage, Apollo performs hand flexions in strict-rhythm, like a pull-cord doll, that may have been intended as a spoof on athletic exer-cises. The dance contains the ballet's most purely diatonic music and its sim-plest key relationships, and it is the only piece that exploits the solo-*ripieni* style of the Pre-Classical period. Stravinsky's biographer E. W. White mentions a "brief episode for solo quintet," but in fact solo groups play more than half of the piece: a string quintet (seven bars), a string quartet (fourteen bars), and a solo bass (three bars). Other features are a rising scale harmonized in thirds and a descending scale harmonized in parallel fourths. That Stravinsky trademark, the simultaneous legato and pizzicato articulation, makes an appearance in solo and *ripieni* cellos.

The same double articulation pinpoints the first note of the *Pas de deux*. Bowed by violas and plucked by cellos, it is the musical image of the almost-touching fingertips of God and Adam in the Sistine ceiling, borrowed by Balanchine for Apollo and Terpsichore. The second note, on the same pitch an octave higher and harmonized by the major-third lower, retroactively endows the first with still greater singularity and mystery. The next notes complete the triad and begin an ethereal melody, embellished but not prettified by trills, turns, appoggiaturas, harmonics, and pizzicato arpeggios, in the velvet tones of the muted strings.

The music of the *Coda* is the least Apollonian in *Apollo,* *the* sudden forte beginning, the harsh juxtaposition of key, the turbulent introduction, and the increasingly fast tempos. The *Coda* is also the only dance that exploits triplet rhythms and, in a middle section, disjunct ones. The 2/2 final episode restores the character of the ballet as a whole, partly by recalling melodic fragments from the violin cadenza in the upper strings. The piece is a traditional nineteenth-century Gallop, in which the Muses prance behind Apollo, harnessed to an imaginary chariot. The basic rhythm, a quarter-note followed by an eighth, is another variant of the alexandrine. The tempos relate proportionally: the quarter-note of the introduction equals a metronomic 76; the dotted-quarter of the exposition equals 112, which is half again as fast as the preceding; the quarter in the 3/4 section equals 168, which is half again as fast as that. The 6/8 *Agitato* that follows, also at 168 for the dotted-quarter, is another notch faster in that three notes are played in the time of two; and the final 2/2 section is faster still in that four notes are played in the time of the preceding three. At [73], bar 3, the theme (violas) is a variation of Apollo's birth-music. It returns at [83] in uneven rhythms.

"The ending of *Apollo* is tragic. When Apollo and the Muses leave, they leave us behind in our mortality...." Robert Garis's insightful remark (in *Following Balanchine,* p. 362) explains Stravinsky's "tragic note of eternal loss" in this most moving piece in the ballet, the only one in a minor key. In the poignant final bars, five ostinato figures are simultaneously elongated by means of rhythmic augmentation. One of them, the four-note violin figure (doubled two octaves lower by first cellos) is repeated four times, each one extending the 4th note by one beat, from three to four to five to six to seven—Apollo's sacred number and the number symbolizing the diatonic language of the music.

The sketchbook lacks these last bars and the four before them, but under the one before that Stravinsky wrote (in Russian): "Finished the third day of Christmas 1927 (9 Jan, 1928)," and, beneath this, "*le 9 Janv /28 IStr*"; the French version is in ink, and the handwriting dates from his Hollywood years, as does that of the words added in English to the book's title page: "rough sketch pencil manuscript."

* * *

On April 6, 1927, Stravinsky received a cable conveying an invitation from the Library of Congress in Washington to compose a ballet employing four dancers and a small orchestra for performance at the Library's auditorium one year later. The premiere, with Adolph Bolm as Apollo and choreographer, took place on April 27, 1928. The birth scene was cut—this was the America of the Eighteenth Amendment—but no matter: the production was immediately forgotten. The first European performance, June 12, 1928, at the Théâtre Sarah Bernhardt, Paris, presented by Serge Diaghilev, choreographed by the 24-year-old George Balanchine, and with Serge Lifar in the role of Apollo, launched what would soon be recognized as one of the greatest of all ballets.

Shortly before the Paris premiere, Diaghilev demanded that Alice Nikitina replace Alexandra Danilova as Terpsichore, though Balanchine had already tailored the choreography to Danilova's technique and bodily movement. A compromise was reached after some dickering, and the two prima ballerinas alternated in the role, each executing slightly different movements. Suddenly, inexplicably, Diaghilev began to fulminate against the music of the Terpsichore variation, insisting that it was "too long"—it is one of the ballet's shortest dances—and that Stravinsky must cut it. (Lifar recalled that Diaghilev had "advised Stravinsky to make a number of cuts in it," though even one would be inconceivable.) Music apart, the Terpsichore Variation is the axis of the ballet's "thread of story," as Balanchine described the plot. Apollo's beguilement with Terpsichore's dance is the reason that he chooses her rather than Calliope or Polymnia as his partner in the *Pas de deux;* to omit it is to destroy the meaning of the ballet. Yet, and despite Stravinsky's protests, it was dropped in the second and third Paris performances and on tour. Not until 1970 was the truth behind Diaghilev's erratic behavior revealed (in Lincoln Kirstein's *Movement and Metaphore*). Nikitina, it seems, was the mistress of Lord Rothermere, the press baron who had financed two of Diaghilev's London seasons. On learning from her that the role was being shared, Rothermere withdrew his support.

In 1978 a much larger and infinitely unkinder cut was temporarily instituted by, of all people, George Balanchine himself. For a new production with Baryshnikov, he excised the entire Prologue, Apollo's birth, and most of his first variation. Robert Garis attributes this "violent" turn against *Apollo* to Balanchine's dislike of the "narrative elements" in his early work. (At the first New

York performance of this mutilation, I thought Balanchine had come unglued, but during an intermission conversation with him realized that he was seeking approbation.) Less surprising, since the ending without the beginning relates to nothing at all and deprives the form of its symmetry, the mountain (staircase) at the conclusion was also missing, and instead of the most beautiful recapitulation in twentieth-century music, the ballet's signature tune was heard for the first time.

Performance notes: Musically intelligent performances of *Apollo* have been exceedingly rare. Stravinsky's own recording on the Sony label has more intensity, even more vitality, than those by conductors less than half his age, but it provides a misleading model. Steeped in Baroque music, he decided to double-dot the rhythms in the Prologue and Apollo's first Variation. The shortened second note short-changes the rhythm, however, and destroys the stylistic consistency of the whole. Most other recorded performances are marred by uncertainty of tempo, the metronomic 84 in the *Pas de deux* being misread as the time-value of the 8th-note instead of the 16th, and accordingly twice too fast. (The metronome in the sketches is even slower, 80 instead of 84 for the 16th; under one sketch for a 4/8 bar, Stravinsky has written out the eight 16th-note beats.) Further, some conductors halve the value of the upbeat to the main part of the Terpsichore Variation, which deprives the body of the piece of a real beginning, and some allow their solo violinist to play G instead of E as the 7th-note in the 2nd score-system of the cadenza, and to hold the fermatas in Terpsichore too long.

Orpheus

The movements of *Orpheus* follow each other without pause and in some cases (1–2, 7–8, 11–12) overlap. Since the tempo, or pulsation, remains constant in numbers 2, 3, and 4, the action in these movements must be followed through the music's changes of character.

Scene I

1. *Lento sostenuto*. Orpheus, alone, grieves for his wife, Eurydice, who has died from the bite of a serpent.
2. Air De Danse. Orpheus. *Andante con moto*. The piece is in three parts. A short measured pause separates the first two, and a change of key marks the beginning of the second. The third part recapitulates the first.
3. Dance of the Angel of Death.
4. Interlude. Taking pity on Orpheus, the Angel leads him to seek his wife in Tartarus, the abode of the dead.

Scene II

5. Dance of the Furies (Erinyes). *Agitato*. The piece is in two parts. The second is marked by a change of key and slightly slower pulsation.

6. Air De Danse. Orpheus. *Grave*. Recitative (harp, solo string quintet) and Aria (oboes and harp).

7. Interlude. The Tortured Souls of Tartarus implore Orpheus to continue his song.

8. Air De Danse (conclusion). Orpheus grants their wish.

9. Pas D'Action. *Andantino leggiadro*. Tantalus, ruler of Tartarus, frees Eurydice. She dances. The Furies surround Orpheus, blindfold him, join Eurydice's hand to his, and guide them to the path to Earth.

10. Pas De Deux. Orpheus and Eurydice. *Andante sostenuto*.

11. Interlude. Orpheus alone. *Moderato assai*.

12. Pas D'Action. Vivace. The Thracian women (Bacchantes) tear Orpheus to pieces.

Scene III

13. Apotheosis. Apollo appears and Orpheus's lyre is borne heavenward. *Lento sostenuto*.

The choice of subject was George Balanchine's. He had produced Gluck's *Orfeo* at the Metropolitan Opera in 1936, but the story continued to attract him. He and Stravinsky worked out the scenario in the composer's home between April 4 and 31, June 8 and 24, 1946, and in the intervening month Lincoln Kirstein commissioned the ballet. In September 1947, after the completion of the score, composer and choreographer spent a further week together in Hollywood to discuss the staging. Stravinsky had wanted his friend Pavel Tchelichev to create the decors, but on October 6 Kirstein wrote to say that the painter was not available and would be wrong for it anyway. Isamu Noguchi was Kirstein's inspired choice, though the Orpheus dancer objected that the headgear designed for him, two round lateral bars across the face like a baseball-catcher's mask, impeded his view of the floor.

Stravinsky identified his and Balanchine's source as Book Ten of Ovid's *Metamorphoses*, but the discrepancies between the Latin poet's version of the myth and the ballet scenario are substantial. Ovid's Hades is a man, not a place, as the ballet scenario inconsistently has it, and his Pluto is a woman, Tantalus's mother by Zeus. Whereas an angel guides the Orpheus of the ballet from Earth to Tartarus, Ovid does not mention any intermediary. Unlike the hero of the ballet, Ovid's Orpheus is not blindfolded for his return to Earth, nor does Apollo appear at the end, as he does in the ballet, to elevate the lyre heavenward.

The beginning is the same in poem and ballet: Orpheus mourns Eurydice, who "Took in her heel the serpent's tooth and died." The ballet does not mention the Styx, but Ovid's Taenarus allows the wandering-minstrel father-of-music to reach the river's "phantom shore," and, beyond,

> Proserpin and the gloomy king
> Of grisly realms [to] tune his voice and string.

(The oldest sculptural representation of Orpheus, on a metope found at Delphi, portrays him with a lyre.) Ovid's Orpheus pleads with Tantalus to

> Revoke, I pray, my wife's untimely doom
> Until her lawful term will end, and she, like all,
> Will then beneath your jurisdiction fall....

Ovid's Furies, unlike those of the ballet, do not threaten Orpheus as he arrives in Tartarus, where, instead, his "blend of lyre and word / Made bloodless ghosts fall weeping as they heard." "Tantalus clutched no more" and "Ixion's wheel was tranced ... / Sisyphus upon his boulder lay / Then first the Furies wept / Neither the Queen of Hell nor he who ruled the depths / Could set aside Orpheus's plea." They called Eurydice,

> who from the throng
> Of new-made ghosts came with slow step along
> Lame from her wound; and Orpheus with his wife
> Was told the terms on which they gave her life.
> He must not, till he left the Avernian Vale
> Turn back his eyes, or else the gift would fail.

Ovid describes the path back to earth as "dark and steep, thick with fog and hushed with silence." Almost within reach of Earth's boundary, his Orpheus looks around at Eurydice, who is then "swept backward to rejoin the dead." Orpheus goes back to the Styx, but is not permitted to recross it. After seven days stranded on the shore, he returns to Earth, where he "shunned the love of womankind," even though

> Many a maid for him with passion burned
> And many grieved to find their passion spurned.

Whether the quatrain that follows contains a clue to Ovid's own long exile from Rome, it suggests an angle—see Robert Graves's *The Greek Myths* in this connection—that choreographers wishing to update the ballet could exploit:

'Twas he that first in Thrace the example showed
Of love perverse on budding youths bestowed;
And this side manhood, in the transient hour
Of boyhood's spring, to pluck the short-lived flower.

The *Orpheus* music marks a radical turn away from the explosive Symphony of 1945. Unlike Classical *Apollo*, of which it is both the Romantic sequel and counterpart, it celebrates in music of personal, passionate feeling a human love story . Its strongest dramatic affinities are with *Perséphone* (1934), in that both are quests involving journeys to and from the Underworld, the one ending joyfully, the other tragically. Further, both protagonists are earthlings, though Perséphone is the daughter of the goddess Demeter, and Orpheus the son of the god Apollo and the Muse Calliope.

The musical associations between the two works are found in their respective qualities of tenderness, and in their different evocations of the bleakness of the Underworld. The harp is the most prominent instrument in both scores, and the principal instrumental aria in both is sung by the oboe. Both share an obsession with the interval of a minor-second and a type of rhythmic figure, the first example of which, below, is from the third *Orpheus* Interlude, the second from the Saraband Interlude in *Perséphone*:

1. (*Orpheus*)

2. (*Perséphone*)

The exceptionality of *Orpheus* among Stravinsky's creations is in the contradictions between the nature of its musical emotion and his aesthetics and practice in the preceding twenty-five years. *Orpheus* is his only score after *Firebird* in which the term *"espressivo"* occurs frequently, in the music of the *Furies* (*"sempre p ma espressivo"*) as well as in the Pas de deux, along with such markings as *"cantabile," "poco animando," "maestoso ma sempre in mezza voce"*; beginning softly with a melody of same-length single notes in the harp over a sustained note in violas, and ending *"diminuendo"* in a quiet string chord, the music is virtually all *"mezza voce."* No less surprisingly, the score is descriptive, pictorial, rich in musical symbols and in the matching of musical imagery with stage action. For only one example, when Orpheus's lyre ascends to the firmament after his death, the harp plays two solo strophes in a *perpetuum mobile* rhythm that suggests the continuation of the music without the player.

Orpheus is also the most pantomimic, the least danced, of Stravinsky's ballets after *Firebird*, and the only one after *Petrushka* in which the scenic element—sets, costumes, curtains, lighting, props—is an integral part of the musico-choreographic performance. The billowings and shimmerings of the white, diaphanous china-silk curtain lowered during the first and third Interludes are part of the action, and when the prop forms a shroud for the dead Eurydice, it becomes a living force. For this alone, Isamu Noguchi's name should appear together with Stravinsky's and Balanchine's as one of the ballet's creators.

Stravinsky began the composition (October 20, 1946) with the three-note trumpet motive—embedded in chords played by seven other winds—signifying the entry, at [2], of Orpheus's forest friends, fauns, dryads, satyrs, bringing gifts and expressing sympathy. The actual beginning of the score, the downward-scale harp-lyre figure accompanied by strings softly intoning a chorale, was composed next, followed by the minor-key but livelier *Air de danse*, a violin solo intermittently joined by flute, featuring the minor-second interval. The second section, in the major key a third above, introduces a melody (Ex. 4) that recalls the finale of the Symphony in C (Ex. 3):

3. (*Orpheus*)

4. (Symphony in C)

Horn in F

The music of The Angel of Death, which begins and ends with the same three-note motive that concludes the previous piece, is a dialogue between strings and winds (with harp). The harmony is harsh at first, as befits the subject, and the triplet and dotted rhythms evoke a grotesque personage with bizarre body movements. To begin the descent to Tartarus, the Angel of Death, a black rope wound around his arms, legs, and torso, ties himself to Orpheus, and links hands with him after suspending the lyre on his extended arm. They look like "two mountain climbers yoked together," as Arlene Croce remarked. The *misterioso* music combines the trombone in a low register with upper strings playing tremolo, a musical image of the distance between Earth and Underworld.

The appropriately slow Interlude is fugal, the traditional musical form for journeys; its subject, wide downward intervals—more musical imagery— sounds as if Stravinsky might be ready to experiment with twelve-tone-rows. Trumpet and trombone take up the fugue subject, with octave displacements, followed by oboe and English horn.

The Furies, costumes sprouting floppy, tail-like appendages from every part of the body, threaten Orpheus, poking and kicking at him as he enters Tartarus, and menacing the Tormented Souls as well, shoving and vaulting over them. The first of their two dances is distinguished by high-kicking in both music and dance movement. Thematically it develops the minor-second figure of the *Air de danse* in a new way, but its ascending main motive is octatonic in construction. The musical novelty of the second dance, a can-can, is that the key-signature of the violas is C-major, those of the other strings C-sharp minor, which, of course, results in numerous minor-second harmonic clashes.

The Tormented Souls beseech Orpheus to play to them. Granting their wish (aria for harp, oboes, and strings, later with English horn in canon), he lulls them to sleep and calms the Furies. Tantalus, also seduced by the music, emerges from the back of the stage with a door attached to his back. As he turns slowly around, Eurydice is discovered fastened to its reverse side. He releases her and she dances to debonair, quasi-boogie-woogie music. Meanwhile, the Furies have blindfolded Orpheus. Joining his hand to hers, they lead the pair to the Earthward path, where they walk slowly, in arabesques, Eurydice repeating each of her spouse's steps after him.

Trying to make him look at her, and failing to understand why he does not, she caresses him, coiling herself around his body, half climbing on his back. Recalling their past life, they pause to play, and the music becomes playful as well, a flute suggesting the flute of ancient Arcadia. A transitional passage in clarinet and harp leads to the return of the string music of the beginning, and the musico-erotic tension quickly mounts. Finally Orpheus tears off his blindfold and

Eurydice falls dead at his feet. Her death is observed by silence, in the tradition of classic Chinese theater, but the piece concludes with the same lush string music with which it began, now agonizingly sorrowful. The fugal Interlude that follows is based on the same pitches as the subject of the first Interlude, but in reversed intervallic directions. The mists clear and the sky reddens, foretelling Orpheus's death.

The scene of the vulturine Thracian women is the only one for full orchestra, though it plays together in only a dozen bars. Stravinsky's biographer E. W. White wrote that the "dissonance and violent syncopations" here "evoke parts of *The Rite of Spring*." In truth, the exceptionality of the piece is in its quiet nervousness, the sudden, jerky, starts-and-stops created by innumerable short, uneven rests, a fragmentation at an opposite extreme from the continuity of the Pas de Deux. Metrically the dance is four-square (with two scarcely noticeable exceptions), and the dissonance is not especially remarkable.

A different combination of instruments is employed in each piece. Thus the first is scored for harp and strings, with two brief interjections for eight winds and one bar of three trombone notes. The second adds clarinets and bassoons to the same combination, and the third adds three horns, oboe, and English horn. A characteristic of the orchestration is that strings and winds are more often heard in alternation than in combination. Another is the prominence given to chamber-size groups, as in Orpheus's aria, a trio for harp and oboes with patches of string cushioning, and in the Apotheosis which, until the last string chord employs only five instruments.

Stravinsky imitates archaic sonorities. The harp, which appears in every movement except that of the Thracian women, is generally articulated near the table of the instrument in order to produce a dry, less-than-normally resonating, lyre-like sound. The cellos play *"flautando"* near the beginning, and a solo violin, at the end plays *"ponticello,"* which, doubled by muted trumpet, suggests the sonority of a Renaissance *"vielle."* So, too, Orpheus's aria is sung by dolorous oboes in the style of the cantatas and Passions of J. S. Bach.

But the Greek modes are the main archaizing element. The opening, in the Phrygian, haunts the whole piece, and it returns at the beginning of the Apotheosis, switching to Dorian at the start of the fugue for two horns, where the bass line (harp) switches its direction upward, symbolizing the ascent of the lyre and the eternal life of music. This, of course, is the composer's "message": music redeems. Why, then, does Bosch, hardly a Neo-Platonist, punish music and musicians so harshly in his Hell, crucifying the harpist on his instrument? In both vase and wall painting in Roman catacombs, Orpheus is portrayed as a harbinger of peace and joy.

On Stravinsky's
Symphony of Winds

The Symphony was designed as an objective cry of wind instruments.

—Stravinsky: *New York Times*, January 6, 1925

I am wondering how these incredible patterns of form and tone appear to any soul, how can the wonder and beauty of what you say come to anyone like that [...] all the miracles of the ancient, barbaric, passionate world are there, and all the human heart is there....

—Letter from Stark Young to Stravinsky, April 1948, after hearing the *Symphonies of Wind Instruments.*

J & W. Chester, Ltd., as Stravinsky's first representative for the *Symphonies of Wind Instruments*, prepared the orchestra parts for the premiere, conducted by Koussevitzky, Queen's Hall, London, June 10, 1921; or at any rate the blue-penciled directive to the copyist on the first page of Stravinsky's manuscript is in English: "18 parts." On January 19, 1922, the Société des Auteurs, Compositeurs & Editeurs de Musique, 10 Rue Chantal, Paris, became the proprietor of the work, followed on September 23, 1923 by the Edition Russe de Musique; Stravinsky's contract of the latter date mentions a copy of the score, undoubtedly his manuscript, and a set of parts. No orchestra score was published, however, but only a faulty piano reduction (1926) prepared by Arthur Lourié. After the hostile reception of the *Symphonies* at the premiere and the second London performance, conducted by Eugene Goossens, December 12, 1921, as well as at subsequent perfomances—Geneva (Ansermet, December 26, 1921), Paris (Ansermet, December 26, 1922), Philadelphia (Stokowski, November 23 and 24, 1923), Brussels (Germain Prévost, January 5, 1924), New York (Stokowski, February 5, 1924)—Stravinsky withdrew the piece from performance by all conductors except Ansermet, who performed it in Leningrad in March 1928, and himself, though *he* did not conduct it publicly until April 11, 1948, in New York, in his new, 1947 version.

The score was apparently being prepared for publication in the summer of

1933, but only three generations of proofs appeared, none of them dated and none wholly correct. For some reason, the score of the error-filled second proofs—the pirated Kalmus edition of it eliminates mistakes but adds many more new ones—was used after WW II for performances and recordings rather that the far more correct third proofs. On December 11, 1945, Stravinsky orchestrated the so-called Chorale, the last section of the piece, for an ensemble of wind instruments (without clarinets) as a companion work for a half-hour broadcast of the *Symphony of Psalms*.[1] He worked from a photostat of the piece in the original album dedicated to the memory of Debussy, without the aid of either the second or third proofs or his manuscript, which were not received from London until 1949. In the autumn of 1947, he rewrote the entire *Symphonies* based on the disastrously incorrect first proofs, sent from the Editions Russe de Musique in Paris a few months earlier. By the time he received the later sets, he was immersed in the composition of *The Rake's Progress* and had neither the time nor the inclination to compare them with his new version. Erwin Stein, his editor at Boosey & Hawkes, *had* compared them, however, and he urged Stravinsky to do so, delaying the engraving of the 1947 score until 1952 in the hope that he would rewrite, or at least revise it. Stein had undoubtedly discovered such lapses as the writing of the English horn part a major third too low in the second and third bars of [73] (1947 score), and the exact doubling of tuba and contrabassoon in the third, fourth, and fifth bars of [73], which destroys the alternating style and varying note-values of the instrumentation established in the preceding and following bars.

The germination of the *Symphonies* cannot be traced without the twenty-seven sketchbook pages and the twenty-three additional loose sketch pages now in the Paul Sacher Stiftung, Basel. Unfortunately, the facsimile volume of the short and full scores (Amadeus Verlag, Winterthur, 1991) reproduces only parts of two pages from the sketch-books (one of them miscaptioned), and one loose sketch page. Further, the commentaries on the facsimiles state that the closing section of the piece "represents the actual beginning of the compositional process," a claim irrefragably contradicted by the sketches. In actuality the "compositional process," which had probably been underway from March 1918 and certainly was from 1919, began at the beginning of the work. The first entry, in what the commentaries have designated as Notebook V, is for the keening motive with which the *Symphonies* begins. The second entry, found in Notebook VII, is for the music at [4], as the melody, the confinement to the tre-

---

[1] After hearing this performance, the present writer wrote to Stravinsky asking to borrow the score of the Symphonies, a request that he fulfilled two years later.

ble register, and the accompaniment of major-sevenths and a minor-ninth confirm. The fifth entry—two in-between notations were not used—is a more developed version of the first, conjoined at the end to the motive used at [5] (and
[21]). The top entry on the next page, with different bass and different harmony, was used in the final hymn (bars 7–10 of [42]); here, in the sketch, it
connects at the end to the notation found at two bars before [26]. At the bottom of the same sketch page is an extension of the same music (two bars before
[26], as well as at [34], three bars before [27], four bars before [35], and at [38]).

The entry that follows is found in the same place in the final hymn with
identical bass and harmony. Next to it, however, is a revision in syncopated
form that makes it more dance- than hymn-like. At the foot of the next page,
after three entries remote from the *Symphonies*, is a sketch for the oboe motive
three bars before [3] and, as the subject of all of the fast music, throughout the
latter part of the piece before the hymn. The next entries, written across two
pages, include two more notations for the keening motive, and one for the motive at three before [2] (as well as at three before [7]; two, three, four, five, and
six after [7]; at [16]; three before [17]; four before [26]; three before [40]; six
before [41]).

The next page contains a sketch, the first with meters, for the music at bars
3, 4, and 5 of [32]. Further along are sketches for the music between [7] and [9]
and at [14] (oboes), as well as three sketches for the music incorporated at [4],
[15], and [20]. On the following page is a sketch for the music that became the
alto flute and alto clarinet duet, together with an entry, first used at three bars
before [8] (trumpets), and many places thereafter (three before [13], [14], and
in the corresponding places in the repeat of the section).

The point of all this is that with the exception of the two-note threnody
figure that follows the keening motive, the materials of the work had been established *before* the composition of the final hymn, and frequently in the same
order as in the final opus. The manuscript of the hymn itself, also in Notebook
VII, supports the conclusion that it was not the starting line of the "compositional process." At the foot of the hymn page is Stravinsky's copy of the seven-
chord progression taken from a later sketch of the first part of the piece and
used at bar 3 of [3]. The hymn draft reveals that he wished to repeat the motive, first heard at three bars before [2] and used in the hymn, in sequence and
at a higher pitch, as at the beginning of the piece, where the *second* component
of the sequence *is* the seven-chord progression. The hymn draft lacks the *first*
component of the sequence, not the second. To repair the omission, Stravinsky
transposed the last six melodic notes of the seven chords to the tonality of the
hymn, simplified the harmony to correspond to the *second* component, and

placed the six rewritten chords above the staff at the point where he would in-sert them as the *first* component. One should also mention that Stravinsky's lines and arrows in the hymn draft indicate a rearrangement of the succession of its phrases and a repeat of three bars interpolated from the first to the mid-dle part of the piece; moreover, his fast metronome for the hymn, a quarter equals one hundred, and his crescendo to triple *forte* in the last bar suggest that his initial concept was different in character from the piece we know.

Apart from this major gaffe, the commentaries to the facsimiles are richly confusing. They quote a 1947 letter from Stravinsky to the present writer say-ing that "I have only a very dirty proof of the orchestra score in the last revi-sion made before the war." The commentaries deduce that "probably" this refers to "the third of the proofs." But Stravinsky's memory was at fault. The proofs he used, 39 unbound sheets printed on only one side and with the publisher's cata-log number merely penciled-in, are obviously the first. Not only do they con-tain hundreds of editors' inked, penciled, and red- and green-penciled corrections—some of them of engraving mistakes: in one place the first oboe part is printed in the second flute part—but they also preserve many of Stravin-sky's revisions for the 1947 version.

The commentaries further assert that Stravinsky's addition to his manu-script score of "an accidental 'F sharp' [actually two F sharps] on p. 26 ... is taken into account in the first proof." The reference is to the quarter beat in the second horn part on page 18 (not 26) at rehearsal no. 27 [and to the eighth-note in the same part in the next bar]. But this is not the composer's only emen-dation here: he also reassigns the two notes from the third to the second horn and rewrites them an octave lower. The change is not "taken into account" in *any* of the proofs.

"In general Stravinsky follows the notation of the short score exactly in working out the full score," the commentaries announce. This is true. Never-theless, every page of the full score revises the short score in several particulars, mistakenly in the case of the sharps added to seven notes in the alto clarinet part between [36] and [38], though Stravinsky corrected his corrections at a later date. With the exception of the A for B in the melodic line at [21], the short score is more reliable than the full score in questions of pitch. Moreover, "Claude Debussy," in the dedication on the first page of the short score, be-comes "Claude-Achilles [*sic*] Debussy" on the cover of the full score.

Any reconstruction of the original version (1920) of the *Symphonies* must rely on the third proofs, which implement all but one of Stravinsky's red-inked corrections in his manuscript full score, including his major substansive revi-sions at [16] and between [24] and [25], and at the same time improve the manuscript in numerous other ways, as in the subtle and beautiful division of the single ligature in the first flute part at [4] into four units of unequal length. The one red-inked correction overlooked in the third proofs, the parenthetical natural sign before the third note of the second oboe in the bar before [9], is not strictly necessary.

A copy of the *Symphonies* that follows the manuscript before Stravinsky revised it surfaced at the University Library, Cambridge, in 1994, a bequest of the late Norman del Mar. It abounds in errors of omission and commission on every page, and most of its indications for phrasing, as well as a great many for articulation and dynamics, are either missing or incorrect. It is valuable, nevertheless, for two notations in Stravinsky's hand, the added natural sign to the second E (written) in the English horn part two bars before [9], missing in both the short and full-score manuscripts, and the inserted half-note G-sharp in the contrabassoon part in the bar before [40]. But while many pitches in the Cambridge copy are wrong, it also corrects mistakes found in the second proofs, and even one mistake in the manuscript full-score: the second note in the second oboe in the second bar of [19] should be G-sharp, as in the piano reduction.

When did Stravinsky revise his manuscript? Most likely after hearing rehearsals and performances of it (the 1921 premiere in London and the 1924 concert in Brussels; he did not hear Ansermet's Paris performance), but if so why were his changes not incorporated in the first and second proofs which had apparently been engraved by the Russisches Musikverlag in Berlin in 1932? Ansermet's queries in his 1933 correspondence with Stravinsky concerning the work are directed to the second proofs. And when did the third proof appear? One likes to think that Stravinsky had been reviewing the *Symphonies* in 1937 or 1938, since one of the phrases in the final hymn and the first motive of the Symphony in C are the same in matters of pitch.

A comparison of the first page of each of the proof scores will suggest the extent of the changes on the subsequent 38 pages. Page one of the first proofs is darkened with 50 or more inked-in corrections of notes, errors in rhythm, articulation, and dynamics, many of which are corrected a second time in the margins. The first page of the second proofs corrects all but three of these errors. It also adds the date, "1920"; the catalog number, "RMV 459"; respaces the words and letters of the title; and confines the use of upper-case to the first letter of each word of the dedication and to the composer's first name.

In the first proofs, the publisher's identification, at the foot of the page, is given as :

PROPRIÉTÉ DE L'EDITEUR POUR TOUS PAYS

EDITION RUSSE DE MUSIQUE
Russischer Musikverlag G. M. B. H. Berlin

The second proofs revise this as follows:

EDITION RUSSE DE MUSIQUE
Russischer Musikverlag G. m. b. H. Berlin, S.W. Dessauerstr. 17.
Tous droits d'exécution publique, d'adaptation, d'arrangement de reproduction reservés.

In the third proofs, the publisher's identification is the same as in the second, except that the notice *"Imprimé en France"* is printed after the catalog number. The following stamped notice is found in the lower right corner:

SOCIÉTÉ ANONYME DES GRANDES ÉDITIONS MUSICALES
22, Rue d'Anjou-Paris (8e)
R.M.V. 459 Imprimé en France

and the line, missing in the first proofs and italicized and abbreviated in the second:

Tous droits d'exécution, de reproduction et d'arrangements reservés pour tous pays

Stravinsky's copy of the second proofs has not been corrected. It contains only a few penciled markings, none of them in his hand.

Tempos in the second and third proofs are the same but differently indicated. The three relate proportionately to a single pulsation:

Tempo primo: quarter equals 72
Tempo secondo: quarter equals 108
Tempo terza: quarter equals 144.

The tempo changes with each new or repeated segment of the form for a total of 18 times.

The third proofs implement all of Stravinsky's red-inked corrections in his manuscript, except the aforementioned parenthetical natural sign. The most important of these revisions corrects the bassoon and horn notes in bars 6, 7, and 8, and the scoring between [24] and [25]. The composer's corrections in black ink, the sharp added to the second note of the English horn, bar 3 of [36], and the deleted sharps in the 5th, 6th, 8th, 9th, 10th, 11th, and 12th bars of [36], are also incorporated in the third proofs, as are some of his penciled-in phrasings. Hardly less important in the third proofs are the many improvements on the manuscript.

The first page of the third proofs correct the first page of the second proofs as follows:

>1. In bars 1, 2, and 3, the horn parts have been transferred to the first and second bassoons, following Stravinsky's red-inked directive on his manuscript full score, *"aux bassons!"* (He neglected to add *"ainsi à* [2] *et* [6]," but the transferals at these repeats have been carried out by an editor.
>2. In bar 1, "M. M. quarter equals 144" has been inserted at the head of the score, a (written) A-sharp eighth-note, marked "sf," has been inserted on the first beat of the A-trumpet part, and the second A-sharp, in the same bar of the same trumpet part, is marked "sfp," replacing the "mf" of the second proof. Further, a "p" follows the "ff" at the beginning of the alto clarinet part in the third proofs, and the second clarinet plays eighth-notes followed by eighth-rests, instead of doubling the first clarinet, as in the second proofs. The trombone dynamic is changed from "p" to "poco sf."
>3. In the second bar, the ligature in the alto clarinet has been removed, the re-attack on the third eighth is accented, and the word *"simile"* (referring to the first bar) has been added.
>4. In the third bar, second quarter-beat, the ligature between the two eighth-notes in the clarinets has been deleted.
>5. The fourth bar is unchanged except that "M.M. quarter equals 72" is added in parenthesis at the top of the score.

In the third proofs, the spacing of the letters of the title is improved, as is the spacing of the score systems on page 17. Double bars have been added at [7], [15], [20], [24], and the mistakenly added sharps in the alto clarinet part between [36] and [38] have disappeared. The last bassoon note in bar 4 of [37] and the first bassoon note in the next bar have been corrected in conformity with the manuscript. The wrong-way-around rhythm of the clarinets at [7] has been corrected, and the frilly flute upbeat to [24] has been sobered to an eighth-note. The major changes in instrumentation at [16] have been effected, as aforementioned, and a full quarter-rest with a fermata rightly replaces the eighth-rest (and eighth-note) in the bar before [25].

The third-proof corrections are mistaken in two instances, the deletion of the over-the-bar ligature in the trumpets in the fourth and fifth bars of [7], and the deletion of the ligature in the tuba part one bar before [45]. The third proofs also fail to correct the missing sharp in the fourth horn in the second bar of [3], the B natural, for A, in the second flute at the beginning of [14], the clef in the second horn part at three and two bars before [35], and the wrong notes in the alto flute and alto clarinet upbeats to [24] (both should sound F, the alto flute an octave above the alto clarinet and an octave below the first flute). The fourth eighth-note in the second bassoon at [31] is correct only in the sketches and manuscripts; and the sharp before the second note of the second oboe in the second bar of [19] is correct only in the short score. The first note in the third trumpet in the third bar of [40] is incorrectly sharped in the proofs, a mistake by Ansermet, who thought the phrase, transposed a full step higher than the previous one, should exactly parallel it. Stravinsky crossed out the bar in his copy of the second proofs of the Debussy album piece because of this mistake and another one in the last bass note. In Stravinsky's original draft of the final hymn, the G-sharp in the first of the two "parallel" phrases is a G-natural. The out-of-character "F pesante" marking for the "parallel" phrase that follows appears, writ large, in the Cambridge copy. Since this is only two bars after Stravinsky's added contrabassoon C-sharp, he may have seen it, but it is not found in his hand in any score.

Mysteries remain. How could conductors and proofreaders have failed to add a sharp to the last note of the alto clarinet in the fifth bar of [19] when the note is correct in exactly the same music in the fourth bar of [14]? In the third bar of [40], the last note of the third trumpet should be F-natural, as corrected by Stravinsky both in his copy of the Debussy album and in his 1965 version of the "Final Chorale"?

Ernest Ansermet rehearsed the "old" version of the *Symphonies* with the NBC Symphony in New York in 1948, until Stravinsky obliged him to play the new one. Did he use a score of the second or of the third proofs? (The Cambridge copy, marked by a conductor on every page, is too blighted with errors to have been acceptable to him.) One suspects that Stravinsky wanted Ansermet to perform the 1947 version chiefly in order to have a recording for his own study.

Stravinsky's copy of the third proofs, like his copy of the second, does not contain any marking in his hand, but markings by an editor and a conductor are found in the third proofs, one of them a comment *in English* on a discrepancy between the score and parts. Perhaps the *Symphonies* in third-proof form were played in England shortly before, during, or soon after WW II. The piece definitely was played in Paris, whether or not in that form, at the end of WW II, conducted by Roger Désormière.

Interview

AM: Welcome back from the shelf, R. C.

RC: I climb down intermittently, you know, and in recent years have had to be dusted off fairly frequently.

AM: For a starter, do you see any resemblances between the present decade and the "Gay Nineties" of a century ago?

RC: Our *fin-de-siècle*, unlike the one when Brahms, Mahler, Strauss, and Debussy were in the firmament, and the Finn-*de-siècle*—Sibelius—was on the way, has no composer within light-years of these, no "gay genius" in Wordworth's phrase, if that is what you mean. Even the possibility that one might be waiting in the wings, ready to take off, is all but unimaginable both as to his or her musical heredity and the particular, inevitably divergent, path he or she might pursue. In the 1920s, Jacques Rivière spoke of the young artists' "radical powerlessness to produce something in which they have faith"; the spectre of that powerlessness has grown more fearful today. Nobody has a *Weltanschauung*.

AM: Has confusion increased in the nineties?

RC: It is both deeper and more widespread. The most popular musical instrument in the seventies was the turntable, the loss of which I regret because it made specific passages easy to find. The CD, when finally adjusted to, seemed to offer a respite of stability in the midst of ever-accelerating obsolescence. But now, as the digital-audio tape-recorder comes on the market, we are being told that the world will soon become laser-optical.

If the early nineties can be characterized, it would be as a time of "the return to"—to period instruments, tonality, Romanticism, the American symphonists. These last, Hanson, Harris, Piston, Sessions, Schuman, Cowell, Copland, Diamond deserve a new hearing, whether or not they stay revived. But then, not much new music survives its "world premiere," as the ads say, the first performance also being the last.

For better or worse the phenomenon of the eighties, with roots back to Hindemith's Bach in the fifties, is the movement toward so-called period-faithful performance; at one point, momentum and clamor increased to the extent that our philharmonic orchestras might have been obliged to play one set of instruments in the opening Haydn symphony and another in the closing Shostakovich symphony. Granted that period instruments can influence performance style, as in curved-bow articulation, but even at the technical level, in, for example, the interpolation of ornaments, performance practices of the Baroque and early Classical are far from generally understood.

Consider the case of Nikolaus Harnoncourt, to whom we are indebted for letting us hear the Bach cantatas with authentic instruments and all-male—prepubertal trebles—choruses and soloists. (One wonders how the authenticity movement will cope with coloratura castrato parts.) Yet Harnoncourt's recordings indicate that he has never heard of *Messa di voce*, and, more importantly, of rhythmic alteration, the quasi-triplet short-long and long-short execution of dotted figures; his writings on performance discuss the question of fluctuating tempo, but not of rhythm. Still more surprisingly, his own performances are virtually bare of embellishments, and sometimes even the harmonically necessary appoggiaturas are missing. Not that he is alone in this. Even so highly esteemed a pianist as Pollini, apparently unaware that Mozart always wrote out fast appoggiaturas, plays the "leaning note" appoggiatura in the middle episode of the last movement of the A-Major Concerto, K. 488, as a sixteenth instead of an eighth, thereby vitiating a beautiful melody.

AM: How do you see the main developments since 1945?

RC: No differently than most people of my generation. The first postwar decade was marked by the mass conversion of composers to the twelve-tone school, and, equally, by their failure to convert the musical public to the same cause, or even to win a degree of tolerance for it. Today, half a century later, the situation vis-à-vis the audience is unchanged and dodecaphonists are an extinct species. The period otherwise was distinguished by technical and technological innovations that communicated very little. The late-1940s experiment in total serialism, extending the pitch parameter to rhythm, as Webern had already begun to do, and on to timbre, intensity, and register, ended in total stasis. So, too, the new dawn of electronic music was quickly overtaken by an early-gathering dusk; but electronic music still splutters in campus laboratories, and tape mixed with and extended from live is very much around. Next came aleatory, multiple ensembles, and the performer as collaborating composer.

Turning to the present, I do not have to say that the most clearly recognizable voice is that of the American folk hero Philip Glass—the sound of sharpening chisels near Mount Rushmore is quite distinct—severer of the Gordian Knot of serial complexities and the first composer of any kind of contemporary music to attract sellout audiences. While modern-music concerts are always heavily papered, Glass soirées—at the Met, Carnegie Hall, the Brooklyn Academy of Music—are hot tickets.

AM: What is the New Romanticism?

RC: A label that does not help to identify the product. As Schoenberg said, "If making music is not romantic, what else can it be?" In other words, music, a language of the emotions, is romantic by nature; Schoenberg's own twelve-tone Violin Concerto is as "romantic," for me anyway, as his *Verklärte Nacht*. For the New Romanticists, the *via negativa* is serialism, notoriously described by George Rochberg as "the cultural pathology of my own time." On the positive side, they propose to link up with the traditions of the great music of the past by means of, first of all, tonality; but Rochberg has fully set forth the program in his essay "Reflections on the Renewal of Music." In practice, the incorporation of historical styles inevitably sounds like collage, even in the music of Berio (*not* a New Romanticist), whose comments about his intentions in his *Sinfonia* attempt to defend it from that classification. The quotations from Mahler's Second, *Sacre*, and *Agon* in the piece are so much more attractive than Berio's context, that it cannot contain them: the listener wants to go along with the excerpts rather than with their frame. The most skillful Neo-Romantic score that I have heard, even though it made me ill, is John Williams's music for *Indiana Jones and the Last Crusade*. The Grail scene in the movie is accompanied by a purée of *Parsifal*, a *Parsifal* slickly reprocessed and updated.

AM: Is the New Romanticism comparable to Stravinsky's 1920s New Classicism?

RC: Not in quality; it has produced nothing that could stand within miles of *Oedipus Rex*. But the musico-political parallel is undeniable: the Viennese atonalists—Romantics all, in or out of tonality—regarded Stravinsky's neoclassicism as a reactionary movement, much as, today, IRCAM must regard Corigliano and Druckman. At any rate, I *assume* that Berg, from the perspective of his *Kammerkonzert*, must have thought Stravinsky's contemporaneous Octet, with its transparent harmony, ostinato bassoon-bass, and C-chord finish, an arrant regression. For myself, I love both the Octet and the *Kammerkonzert*; but then, I am a pluralist.

Having mentioned Berg, let me remind you that his 1929 lecture on *Wozzeck* says, in effect, that the return to tonality in the orchestral interlude between the opera's two final scenes is his own, first-person "appeal to humanity." He does not say why this appeal had to be made in the language of the musical past rather than in the atonal language of the remainder of the opera, why atonal music cannot appeal universally. Nowadays, many of us think of the appeal as more effectively built-in everywhere else in the opera, and think of the D-minor interlude as a major flaw. But Berg, reluctant to sacrifice such tonal properties as the major and minor modes, was always backsliding. I do not have to say that the harmonically lush *Wozzeck* interlude scarcely resembles the tonal-harmonic palettes of the New Romantics.

AM: Is tonality anachronistic? Is it here to stay?

RC: "Notions of evolution" that become "a means of disowning the past" do not apply in music, where the *Prima Prattica* and the *Seconda Prattica* alternate. The tonality door can be opened more than once, and tonality and atonality can exist side by side and in the same work. But the new triadists opened a very different door from the one Schoenberg closed in 1909.

AM: What 1950s and 1960s music do you most esteem today?

RC: All of Stravinsky, from the *Rake* to the *Canticles*.

AM: Stravinsky apart, which composers of the period interest you most?

RC: Carter above all. Clearly no composer has attained anything like the stature of Stravinsky, Schoenberg, and Berg in the first half of the century. In the second half Messiaen has had the widest influence—on Glass (the repetition, the music of the subcontinent) as well as on Boulez (tropical percussion)— and his originality is beyond dispute. But the Messiaen world is very much smaller and more circumscribed than are the worlds of the three earlier masters. I liked *Couleurs de la cité céleste* when I conducted the U.S. premiere in 1968, but I like it less now. And a visit to any record store will show you that CDs of Shostakovich outnumber CDs of Schoenberg a hundred to one.

AM: Your 1958 recordings of the *Marteau sans maître* and *Zeitmasse*, together with your Stravinsky books rigged in favor of these pieces, made household names of their composers. Then what happened?

RC: I could not follow either of them much beyond their early works, and, by criticizing their later ones, and challenging their stranglehold—or was it only a half-Nelson?—I committed musical suicide; I am still taking heat for that. One consequence was that Sony plowed my recordings, not always replacing them with superior performances—mine of Schoenberg's First Chamber Symphony and *Die glückliche Hand* still seem to me superior to any others—and in many cases not replacing them at all. Why my recording of *Von Heute auf Morgen* was suppressed, while my ancient Varèse records were promoted, I do not know.

AM: And your stable of twentieth-century classics?

RC: It is radically catholic, ranging from Partch (if I can find the instruments) to Prokofiev (First Violin Concerto), from the *Glagolitic Mass* to *Glass Pieces*.

AM: Did you say *Glass Pieces*?

RC: If not that, then the *Mikrokosmos*-like (Book VI) meter-shifting of the

"Train" and "Trail" pieces from *Einstein on the Beach*. I am aware that "serious" composers and the Ayatollahs of the avant-garde look down on this music as puerile doodling, the musical equivalent of junk food. But Glass is an original, and a purist, the Webern of "repetitive music"; one comes to scoff and stays to, well, respect his chutzpah. Further, he must be approached as an individual, not as one of a group. John Adams, for comparison, with his less restricted harmonic and rhythmic language, is also, and correspondingly, a less distinctive personality, though the transformation of the foxtrot theme in the *Chairman Dances* from the fast middle section to the slow, sentimental final one, when Mr. and Mrs. Mao are transported back to Yunan "dancing to the gramophone," is effective.

Glass Pieces is something else, the work of a single, unmistakable voice. So far from my presuppositions, "Rubic," the *perpetuum mobile* first piece, is subtly constructed, formed by the repetition, two, three, four, six, and eight times, of discrete units (identified by pitch content and rhythmic figuration), as well as the repetition of combinations of these units, and one non-repetition; by a melody confined to five different pitches but varied in articulation, changing harmonization, duration, rhythm, and accent; by rhythmic figuration—only two figures, three if articulation is counted—variously combined and minutely modified in pitch content; by an unchanging sonority (flutes, saxophones, horns, organ); and by a harmonic journey from the mediant minor through the dominant major, the subdominant, and so on to the home key ending in the first inversion. This deconstuctionist description conveys no idea of what the piece actually sounds like, of course, but it should suggest that the elements of music have been put together in a new way.

The baleful, blues-like saxophone in the second piece, "Façades," shows, if nothing else, that Glass can write a melody. The last piece, "Funeral," from the opera *Akhnaten*, the most interesting of the three but too intricate to be picked apart here, ends suddenly and as if arbitrarily—a Glass trademark—thereby incorporating the ensuing silence in the preceding whole.

AM: How do you reconcile *Glass Pieces* with Carter's *Double Concerto*, a true modern classic and a prime example of "cerebral music"?

RC: The plan of the Concerto may be "cerebral," meaning theoretical, but not the result—the sudden explosions, the funny wallops on the drums in the slow movement, the fortissimo *tutti* after the general pause. Certainly the Concerto is at a polar remove from *Glass Pieces*: Glass's beat is relentlessly regular, and his tempos are unchanging, while Carter's, for the most part and in both instances, are in constant flux, speeding up or slowing down by means of metrical and note-value proportionalism, the tempo-modulation concept first exploited by Berg in the *Lulu* Monoritmica. Carter's pace is rapid, while Glass inches along; the Carter topography is undulating, the Glass topography is flat; Carter's vocabulary is extensive while Glass sticks to Basic English; and so on through all the terms of antithesis. But inimical and symmetrically converse as the two works may be, either/or makes little sense when both are legitimate. Composers must take sides but performers cannot afford to. The two works might even be programmed together—the horns of the dilemma, so to speak, the whirlpool and the rock, present-day musical Manicheism.

AM: How, in retrospect, do you view your association with Stravinsky?

RC: The early gift of his friendship, the greatest compliment of my life and the most crushing, has always and continues to puzzle me. From about 1957, when I began to deputize for him as a conductor and had become the instrument of his wish to speak his mind, perhaps he could with some reason feel confidence in me. But in 1948? True, I pointed him in new ways from the first, introduced him to contemporary music that he knew nothing about, and provided a bridge to the America in which he had chosen to live; but this was natural, simply my part of an exchange. No less true, he could find sources of nourishment almost anywhere—what I most marveled at in his genius was its renewing and redemptive powers—but if he found any in me, it had to have been planted by him. In so far as I can reconstruct myself as I was then, and wary of betraying my earlier self, I am certain that I did not possess all of the abilities he seemed to think he perceived in me—which is not to impute any impercipience to him.

AM: Oops! We are at the end of the tape.

RC: Good. When you print it out please follow Henry James's request: "Supply a query after every assertion and enclose the whole in a great parenthesis and interrogation point." Voila! The *fin de millénaire*.

Index

ROBERT CRAFT

A widely respected critic and commentator on music and culture, and the author of more than a dozen books, Robert Craft has conducted and recorded with orchestras around the world. In addition to his special command of Stravinsky's and Schoenberg's music, Craft is well known for his recordings of works by Monteverdi, Gesualdo, Schütz, Bach, Mozart, Berg, and Varèse. In recent years, Craft has devoted much of his energy to writing about the arts, in the process becoming one of the most urbane and entertaining critical voices in our language. He is also the author of *Stravinsky: Chronicle of a Friendship* (revised and expanded edition, 1994), which has been called "the most important body of words about music since the war."

THE MOMENT OF EXISTENCE

was composed electronically using
Weiss types, with
Minion display embellishments.
The book was printed on acid-free, recycled
Glatfelter Natural paper, with Rainbow antique endsheets,
Smyth sewn, and bound over 88-point binder's boards in
Arrestox cloth, by Braun-Brumfield, Inc. The dust jackets
were printed in four colors by Vanderbilt University Printing Services.
Book and jacket designs are the work of Gary Gore.
Published by Vanderbilt University Press
Nashville, Tennessee 37235